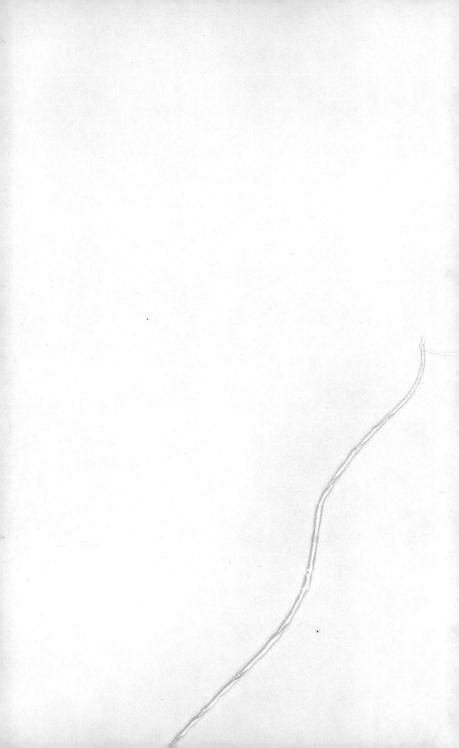

THE JEW IN THE LITERATURE OF ENGLAND

THE JEW IN THE LITERATURE OF ENGLAND

To the end of the 19th century

Montagu Frank Modder

MERIDIAN BOOKS, INC. *New York*
THE JEWISH PUBLICATION SOCIETY OF AMERICA *Philadelphia*

MONTAGU FRANK MODDER

Montagu Frank Modder was born in Ceylon on November 24, 1891. He was educated in England and at the University of Michigan, where he received his Ph.D. in 1935. Mr. Modder was a journalist and illustrator as well as a teacher. He died in 1959.

TO MARY, ANNE, LUCY

Published by Meridian Books, Inc. and
The Jewish Publication Society of America March 1960
First printing February 1960

PREFACE

The object of this introductory study is to tell the story of the Jew as a character in the literature of England, and to make available to the general reader a selection of the considerable amount of material not easily accessible in the average library. The scope of previous books on the same subject has been extended by attaching due significance to the economic conditions which signally affected the social status of the Jews in England during the eighteenth and nineteenth centuries; and by paying attention to the diffusion of liberal principles in government, leading to the removal of political disabilities in 1832, and to the "emancipation" bill of 1858. It will be seen, as the story unfolds itself, that invariably the poet, the novelist, and the dramatist reflect the attitude of contemporary society in their presentation of the Jewish character, and that the portrayal changes with the economic and social changes of each decade.

As a chapter in Jewish history this book inspires optimism. One must note the relation which it establishes between social prejudice and social change, between diminishing ignorance and diminishing hostility, between the growth of humanitarianism and the growth of human freedom. Anti-Jewish feeling is here proved to be a symptom of existing social ills.

Georg Brandes described anti-Semitism as a mixture of

hypocrisy and nonsense. This book proves that its roots sometimes go deeper than that; it may also rise out of fear of the unknown, light-hearted pandering to popular prejudice, and mere unwillingness to accept the processes of social progress.

In the preparation of this study, books of criticism, articles in magazines and reviews, and monographs of special writers have been laid under contribution, and it is hoped that a certain breadth and freshness have been gained by the re-study of the works of several of the great English writers.

To various authorities and scholars I wish to express my indebtedness. My thanks are due, first of all, to Dr. David Philipson and Dr. E. N. Calisch, early laborers in this field, who have helped me with letters of personal encouragement when I first took up this study; and to the late Dr. Oscar L. Joseph, for a discriminating examination of the manuscript in its early stages. I wish to express my gratitude to Professor Howard Mumford Jones, under whom I had the privilege of studying, for his sympathetic criticism of the manuscript in thesis form, and for his guidance in the revision of the present text. My indebtedness to Mr. Edward D. Coleman, librarian of the American Jewish Historical Society, who helped me with his rich store of information and scholarship in the preparation of the bibliography; to the late Dr. Isaac Husik, Editor of the Jewish Publication Society of America, and to his successor, Dr. Solomon Grayzel, who have shown a personal interest in the work, and have given wise advice in matters pertaining to technical and literary detail, cannot be stated in adequate terms.

M. F. M.

CONTENTS

CONTENTS

INTRODUCTION

I do not know whether to admire more the range and variety of Mr. Modder's reading or the patience and objectivity of his study. Anyone who has had to pursue a single theme relentlessly through the centuries knows how wearisome his task becomes. One starts out as a runner in a race, but by and by one sinks to a jog-trot. Eventually it appears that there is no originality in the human race and none in the imaginative mind. The same stereotypes occur from age to age, the same characters are invented by author after author. One begins to feel that everything has been said already, and that error is the only eternal and recurrent truth.

Weariness of this sort in literary study is an occupational disease. If Mr. Modder suffered a spell of intellectual grippe, he has not transferred its symptoms to these pages. The twentieth recurrence of the same caricature finds him gentle and eager in correcting falsehood. The fiftieth rehearsal of man's inhumanity to man leaves him hopeful, objective, and kind. The charity of his judgments and the breadth of his view are sufficient justification for literary study, which, by the unenlightened, is supposed to assume that all the good authors are dead authors.

The amazing collection of cartoons which Mr. Modder has here hung in a single gallery for the edification of mankind suggests certain interesting speculations about the conventional judgments upon literature as a mirror of particular times and places. Does the hostility towards the

Jew, evident in much of the material he has surveyed,
originate in experience or in literary convention? Does art
imitate nature, or does nature, as Oscar Wilde hinted, imitate art? Confronted by the practical problem of the Jew
in a hostile world, we discover to our amazement that what
we thought were idle questions of aesthetic paradox have
become practical problems influencing the conduct of men.

It has been remarked that the villain in English (and
American) literature is seldom or never a blond. Custom-
arily he has the dark complexion, the exotic moustache, the
cruel smile, and the dapper manner which the Anglo-
Saxons have conventionally associated with the Latin, or
at any rate the Mediterranean, peoples. Blond villains do
occur, as in the memorable case of Uriah Heap or the horrid
red-head whom Mr. Hugh Walpole invented not long ago,
but perhaps the very creepiness of these fictions is due to
the fact that we are trained to regard blond villainy as
almost impossible, so that, when it appears, it seems the
more sinister. Our normal villains are swarthy, foreign-
looking men.

Does the expectancy that a villainous character shall be
dark reflect a Northern terror of the South? Is it simply a
literary convention established so long ago that the memory
of man runneth not to the contrary? Shall we suppose that
the Italians who lurk in the novels of Mrs. Radcliffe are
wholly false, and that the Italians who live in the novels of
F. Marion Crawford are not artificial? If the picture of
the Jew or of the Italian or of the Spaniard which one gets
in English literature is no truer to fact than the picture of
the American that one gets in English literature, what
happens to the supposed usefulness of literature in breaking down the barriers of race and nation? Shall we refuse

the villains because they are "bad" and accept the heroes because they are "good"? Shall we suppose that Shylock is mostly a literary figment, and accept Siegfried as a deeply idealized portrait of a continuing racial reality? If, to take a different example, Natty Bumppo is an idealized portrait, half romance and half reality, are Cooper's heroines also idealized portraits, half reality and half romance; and having the reality part in mind, can we truly believe that American women were ever so tiresome and sappy as most readers find the Cooper heroine to be? When does literature mirror life, and when does it impose wholly fictitious judgments upon us?

Mr. Modder's study not only suggests questions like these, but it suggests even more important questions about the sociology of literature. According to one theory of literary history, books reflect life so immediately that one can argue from literary decadence to social decadence, so that, from the novels of Faulkner and Hemingway and others, one infers the death of contemporary American society in its present form. What, however, shall we do with the attitude of authors towards the Jew? Why is the tradition, as Mr. Modder traces it, generally inimical to the male Jew and generally tender to his wife or daughter? Is this a mark of gallantry, or does it infer, as ridiculous anti-Semitic propaganda might assert, that horrid capitalists, long ago instinctively recognizing incipient Communism, have strongly influenced writers to be hostile towards the generations of Israel? This logic is not more wildly absurd than the logic of those who naively insist that literature mirrors social change directly, nor more idiotic than those who talk about the international Jew and international Communism.

Whatever the true answer may be to the complex question how far literature is a true and faithful duplicate of society, Mr. Modder, by isolating the treatment of a particular group and faithfully recording the variants in that treatment, has contributed importantly not merely to an understanding of the emergence of literary types but also to a comprehension of the ways by which literature nourishes prejudice and sympathy, ignorance and comprehension.

HOWARD MUMFORD JONES

Harvard University.

CHAPTER I

IN MEDIEVAL ENGLAND

It is difficult to say when the Jews first came to England. If, as some historians maintain, there were Jews in England in Saxon times, their numbers could not have been great. But, with the advent of the Normans, the situation changed. According to Holinshed, William the Conqueror (1066–1087) himself "brought the Jews into the land from Rouen" in 1070, and "appointed them a place to inhabit and occupy in London, and in Oxford." The words "appointed them a place to inhabit and occupy" are significant. Their religion set the Jews apart from the rest of the inhabitants of the country, all of whom were members of one organized Christian church which not only exercised spiritual control throughout the realm, but also concerned itself with the most ordinary aspects of a churchman's life. Birth, marriage, death, the inheritance of property, and the organization of industry and government, all came within the sphere of church influence. Under the circumstances, the Jews could not be fitted into the framework of the body politic. They lived in separate quarters, or "Jewries," in the larger English towns, sharply separated from the rest of the population, Norman as well as Anglo-Saxon, by race, religion, peculiarities of custom and speech; strangers in a strange land. They were held to be living in the country, not by common right, but by the special consent of the king, under his protection, and subject only to his regulations. However, it must not be supposed that the royal protection was dictated by any spirit of toleration or mercy. To the monarch the Jews were a "mere engine of finance." It was in the coffers of the Jews that the rulers found strength to hold their realm and keep their enemies at bay.

These "engines of finance" were beneficial to the nation at large. They brought with them the capital necessary for the building of industry and the advancement of the government of the conqueror. In the first six years of his rule (1066–1072), needing money for the tremendous task of hammering the country into an organic national state, William I naturally encouraged the immigration of Jewish capitalists who became his chief source of revenue. It was the gold of the Jewish financiers that strengthened the position of the new regime, and made the Conqueror's program a certainty.

Medieval economic life suffered from the lack of a system of credit. The attitude of the church, developed during a purely agricultural age, considered as usury and a grievous sin any premium or increase upon a loan of money or goods. It severely punished clerks and laymen for practicing money-lending on the sly. The extending of credit thus became a monopoly of the Jewish traders who followed William from Normandy. Their keen abilities found expression in England, as on the continent, in finance. Through the exercise of financial acumen, many of them acquired considerable capital in a few years; and thus, by a natural development, they became the bankers of the realm, usurers in the terms of that day, and glad to pay freely for the royal protection which enabled them to prosper without competition. That some took advantage of the situation to charge high rates may well be true. Moreover, that so-called usurers in general filled a crying economic need is proved both by the high rates permitted by law and by the rapid development of Christian money-lending associations that succeeded in circumventing ecclesiastical legislation. In the meantime the need for their economic activity was an even more important reason for the success of the Jewish money-lender than his financial ability, and this success on the part of a religiously different group was a potent cause for the hostile attitude toward it on the part of the Christian population.

The Conqueror's son and successor, William Rufus (1087–1100), gave further encouragement to the Jewish capitalists. Finding himself involved in a succession of disputes with the Norman barons and with the Church, the Red King stood in constant need of loans. The extent of the protection which the Jews received from this profligate and extravagant prince depended both upon the urgency of the monarch's need of capital at the moment, and upon his power to enforce his royal will upon a jealous, turbulent and treacherous nobility. The king is reported to have forbidden the conversion of a Jew to the Christian faith; it was a poor exchange, he said, that would "rid him of a valuable property and give him only a subject!"

In the reign of the next monarch, Henry I (1100–1135), a royal charter was granted to Joseph, rabbi and chief Jew of London, and his followers, under which the Jews were permitted to move freely in the country, together with their chattels, without pay of tolls or customs. It is probable that the royal policy of protection, and the exemption from the common taxation and common justice, sometimes had an ill effect on individual Jewish usurers and money-lenders. Certain cases of insolence are reported to have grown out of this royal protection. Here and there, a Jewish financier or tax-gatherer, assuming an attitude of proud and insolent defiance, aroused the bitter animosity of the inhabitants who were powerless to deal with him under common law.

But the prosperity that attended the Jewish traders and usurers during the first Henry's memorable reign was followed by grievous disorders and civil strife under Stephen (1135–1154). In the complete breakdown of royal power, the Jews were the most oppressed of all the wretched inhabitants of the country. At the same time, it was generally rumored that the Jews were in the habit of killing a Christian every year, as a sacrifice for the Passover. Such tales aroused the fanatical fury of the ignorant and the superstitious country folk, who were ready to believe almost anything about the strange people in their midst. Within a short time, the Jews of Norwich in particular were attacked by the populace; some were killed, some brutally treated, and all Jewry was placed under suspicion.

It was not until the reëstablishment of order under Henry II (1154–1189), the first of the Angevin kings, that the English Jews were again free to travel without let or hindrance, and allowed to establish burial grounds for synagogue worshipers in the provincial towns. By special royal order, they were permitted to lend money on their own terms, usually about sixty per cent, to litigants, ambitious prelates, or impoverished monasteries. Again several Jewish financiers rose to great opulence.

Perhaps the most famous of the Jewish financiers of Henry II's reign was Aaron of Lincoln. At one time it was rumored that the king himself was in the debt of this veritable Croesus. It was Aaron who raised and advanced the money for the building of the Abbey of St. Albans and the Cathedral at Peterborough. As early as 1166, he did business under royal protection in nine shires, and when he died in 1187, his fortune was "escheated to the Crown." So great was Aaron's wealth that a special department of the Exchequer (*Scaccarium Aaronis*) was organized for the purpose of winding up his affairs.

The growing prosperity of the Jews in England served only to increase the suspicion and ill-will of the people against them, and to arouse the avarice of succeeding monarchs. At the coronation of Richard I (1189–1199), when a Jewish deputation, bearing congratulations and costly gifts for the king, presumed to approach the hall in which the Lion Heart dined, a cry was raised, "Destroy the enemies of Christ!" The Jews took to flight and were pursued by the mob. Like wildfire the rumor was spread that the king himself had issued orders for their massacre. The homes of the richest Jews were forthwith fired, and many of the community killed. The news spread through Lynn, Colchester, Thetford, Ospringe, Lincoln, Stamford, and Bury St. Edmunds, in which centers the Jews were brutally persecuted. The climax was reached at York, where over 500 of the unfortunate people, having sought refuge in the castle, found it impossible to keep back the infuriated mob. In desperation, the Jews murdered their own wives and children, and then, setting fire to the buildings, perished in the flames.

Later, when Richard I needed heavy levies for his wars,

and for the ransom following his capture after his with-drawal from the Third Crusade, the Jewish communities were compelled to contribute as much as the whole city of London. Upon his return to his realm, the king appointed a board of officials to report on every transaction to which Jews were a party, thus making it easier for the royal treasurer to check up on the wealth of all Jewish subjects, in order that he might more conveniently ascertain just where ready money would be available. This was the beginning of the famous "Exchequer of the Jews," a court which registered all effects belonging to the Jews and required that all contracts be made in the presence of two Jewish and two Christian witnesses and two public nota-ries. These contracts, still preserved in the Record Office, were called in Hebrew *shtar*; and the room at the Exchequer where the chests containing these *shtars* were kept was, in all probability, called the Star Chamber.

The establishment of the Court of Exchequer precisely suited Richard's brother and successor, John (1199–1216), who, when the time seemed propitious, imposed a tax or 66,000 marks upon the entire Jewish community, in addi-tion to forcing individual Jews to disgorge large sums at frequent intervals. A recalcitrant Jew who failed to comply with the royal demand for money was sentenced to lose a tooth daily until all the money had been collected. Ac-cording to Matthew Paris (*Chronica Majora*, III, 528), in the days of John Lackland "Jews and Jewesses were re-duced to such poverty that they begged from door to door and prowled about the city like dogs."

The "tallaging" of the Jewish community in the long and ignoble reign of Henry III (1216–1272), began in 1230, when taxes on one-third of the property of the Jews were levied indiscriminately. The king felt himself complete master of the Jews of the realm. Having borrowed 5,000 marks from the Earl of Cornwall, his majesty handed over to that noble the right to collect from all Jews in England. Between the years 1255 and 1273, upwards of four hundred thousand pounds were reported "escheated to the Crown" from the legacies of deceased Jews. The average annual contribution made by the Jews to the royal treasury during the latter part of the twelfth century was probably about a twelfth of the whole royal revenue. The kings, not the Jews, profited from the money-lending operations.

As the avarice of the kings made heavier and more frequent demands on the purse of the Jews, their liberties and privileges became increasingly curtailed. In conformity with the decision of the Fourth Lateran Council, decrees were issued in 1222, and again in 1275, compelling Jews to wear badges on their breasts, thus making their isolation certain and complete. The order of 1253 provided that Jewish worship in the synagogues should be carried on in a low voice, inaudible to Christians; that Jews should not employ Christian women to suckle or nurse the children of Jews; and that Jews should not eat or buy meat during Lent.

It might be supposed that the Jews would have voluntarily left a country in which they received such harsh treatment. As a matter of fact, they sued for permission to leave England. But, in the opinion of the royal treasurer, they were far too valuable a source of income to the realm, and their expatriation was forbidden. The royal hold on the Jewish communities was tightened by an edict, passed in the third year of Henry III's rule (1219), ordering the closing of the Cinque Ports to the Jews.

The coming of the friars into England, during the reign of Henry III, stirred up a fresh interest in the children of Israel, whose conversion to the Christian faith became a matter of concern among the new orders. The first work of the friars, says Green, was to settle in the Jewish quarters and attempt their conversion, but the popular fury rose too fast for these gentler means of reconciliation. In 1232, a house (*Domus Conversorum*) was opened in London by the king's orders, for the reception of Jewish converts. Each convert was offered the legal possession of at least one-half of his property which had formerly been at the uncontrolled disposal of the crown. All efforts, however, to convert and to protect these people proved futile and even dangerous. To the old economic cry against the usurer was added the fanatical outburst against the infidel.

In the reign of Henry's successor, Edward I (1272–1307), popular feeling against the Jews reached a high point. The people beheld with fear this group which continued to live apart, keeping its own counsel, attending its own places of worship, and enjoying the privilege of exemption from the common law and the usual burdens of the realm. Poor and miserable themselves, the masses, understanding nothing of economic trends, and forgetting the profit derived from Jewish money-lending by King and noble, saw these strangers financially prosperous, and knew that the Jews had become rich through what was known as usury, and — so the rumor ran — through "coin-clipping." Restrictive legislation reached its complete measure in 1275, when the Statute of Judaism was passed, forbidding Jews to hold real property, to employ Christian servants, to move through the streets without badges which distinguished them. With the advent of the Italian bankers in the field of commercial finance, Edward I found that his Jewish money-lender was no longer indispensable to the royal treasury. Now that there were Christian financiers with whom the Christian state would rather do business, it seemed feasible to serve Mammon without upsetting God! Therefore, in 1290, the historic order of expulsion was issued, ordering all Jews to quit the kingdom before a certain day, under the pain of death. It is said that 16,511 Jewish emigrants left England before the Feast of All Souls, in the autumn of the year. The king allowed them to take their goods and money with them, and sent royal officers to the ports from which the Jews were to embark, to protect them from any popular demonstration of ill-will. However, in spite of this precaution, the expulsion resulted in dire tragedy. Of the number that left the shores of Britain, the majority reached France. Many were wrecked, others robbed and flung overboard.

During the two and one quarter centuries of their settlement in England, it is to be expected that the Jews should leave a lasting impression on the English mind. On the whole, however, the impression was by no means favorable to the Jews. Religion, economics, and a sense of strangeness combined to produce this result. From the start, the Church inevitably showed bitter hostility towards these people of mystifying and unyielding religion. As time wore on, in the stress of economic adjustment, the clergy were not slow in rousing public fanaticism against the "Christ Killers," whenever opportunity presented itself. During the era of the Crusades (1095 ff.), it was a simple matter to turn against the Jew the religious fervor which fanatical churchmen had engendered against the Mohammedan. Religious prejudice alone would have been sufficient to make the

Jews hated by the ignorant and superstitious masses who held the whole people responsible for the crucifixion of Jesus. Also, since ignorance always regards with distrust that which is strange to a community, it seemed natural that the ignorant English peasants should regard with fear and suspicion this group whom they called a "race of usurers" that lived apart from other groups, followed its own laws and customs, and enjoyed the special protection of royalty. In the towns of wealthy East Anglia, the peasants saw the stone houses of the Jews, not easily broken open, standing as rivals to the stone churches and cathedrals, among the mud and timber hovels of the poorer Christians.

It is clear that from 1066 to 1290, as money-lenders, the Jews seemed to play the part of the devil in the piece. The economics of the situation was inevitably against them. It must be remembered, too, that money was not loaned in that era for use in productive enterprises. Medieval business and industry were organized on a small scale and conducted with such small capital as the business men possessed. Therefore, when a knight-at-arms or noble borrowed money, it was to pay some pressing debt, to meet some sudden demand, or to equip some marauding or crusading expedition. Money so invested was unavoidably a cause of bitter feeling between debtor and creditor. The fact that the great barons and the personal advisers of the king were frequently in debt to the Jewish money-lenders made the gentiles and the Jews implacable enemies. The monarch's practice of getting money from the Jews to wage wars against refractory nobles no doubt added fuel to the flames.

These factors provided the almost perfect setting in a period of national confusion and religious fanaticism for the persecution and ultimate expulsion of the Jews from

England. The accusation that the Jews seized and sacrificed Christian boys in religious services, a story which originated in Syria in the fifth century, was revived during the Crusades and spread throughout Europe from the twelfth century on; and, when religious fanaticism reached a high point among the masses, the story of William of Norwich, the lad of twelve who was said to have been lured into a Jew's house and crucified during Passion Week, was retold in order to increase the popular sentiment against the so-called enemies of Christ. In 1181, 1192, and in 1234, similar ritual murders were reported. The most famous of the boy-martyrs was Hugh of Lincoln, the story of whose murder in 1255 was described by Matthew Paris (c. 1200–1259), the great monastic historian, in his *Historia Major*:

> About the feast of Peter and Paul, the Jews of Lincoln stole a child called Hugo, being eight years old; and when they had nourished him, in the most secret chamber, with milk and other childish aliments, they sent to almost all the cities of England wherein the Jews lived, that, in contempt and reproach of Jesus Christ, they should be present at their sacrifice at Lincoln; for they had, they said, a certain child hid to be crucified. Whereupon many assembled at Lincoln. And coming together, they appointed one Lincoln Jew for the Judge, as it were for Pilate. By whose judgment, by the consent of all, the child is afflicted with sundry torments. He is whipped even unto blood and lividness, crowned with thorns, wearied with spittings and strikings . . . and after they had derided him in diverse manners, they crucified him . . .

The popularity of this tale is attested by the fact that twenty-seven versions of it have been assembled by literary historians, ten of these versions having been found in manuscripts of the thirteenth century. Some of these are in prose, some in poetry, but all alike breathe the popular hatred of the Jews. The annals of Waverley are full of the death of Hugh of Lincoln, for whose murder eighteen of the richest and most eminent Jews of Lincoln are reported to have been "hanged on a new gallows," and twenty others imprisoned in the Tower.

After 1290, no unconverted Jew was permitted legally to enter England. Royal permission was occasionally given to eminent Jewish physicians to attend on the royal household, as in the case of Master Elias, a Jewish doctor, who, in 1390, was sent to England by the Duke of Brabant, husband of the Princess Margaret, to attend on the king, Richard II. Royal permission was also granted certain Jewish doctors to attend on the Lady Alice, wife of Sir Richard Wittington, Lord Mayor of London. It is also reported that in the reign of Henry VIII, an eminent Jew, Mark Raphael, was invited to advise the king in matters concerning his divorce; and that another Jew, Joachim Gaunce, helped to introduce German methods of mining into England. It is probable that from time to time so-called "Lombard" money-lenders, who were Jews in disguise, drifted to England in small groups, and carried on their business in secret. However, the records of the five reigns — from Henry V to Richard III (1413–1485) — are silent with regard to the presence of Jews within the realm, although this silence does not indicate that the English had ceased to think of the Jewish problem.

Whether or not there were Jews in Chaucer's England, we are not certain. However, their memory was kept green in ballad and story. The incident of the martyrdom of little Hugh of Lincoln, which had been given wide currency by

Matthew Paris, was circulated among the country folk for
many generations in crude ballad form, under the titles of
"Sir Hugh," "The Jew's Daughter," and "Sir Hugh or the
Jew's Daughter." In these stories the superstition persisted that the Jews were allies of the Devil, and that they
worked harm on Christian homes. Evidence of this is clearly
seen in Chaucer's Prioress, who, in her sad tale of the "litel
clergeoun," repeats what may have been a widely accepted
belief in fourteenth century England:

> Oure firste foo, the serpent Sathanas,
> That hath in Jewes herte his waspes nest.

The fact that the prioress' Jews lived in Asia would lead us
to believe that in the latter half of the fourteenth century
the Jews had already become utter strangers to the English
people. But the memory of their evil reputation is present
in the lines:

> . . . . a Jewerye,
> Sustened by a lord of that contree,
> For foule usure, and lucre of vileynye,
> Hateful to Crist and to his compaignye . . .

> O cursed folk of Herodes al newe!
> What may youre yvel entente yow availle?
> Mordre wol out certeyn, it wol nat faille,
> And namely, ther thonour of God shal sprede
> The blood out-crieth on youre cursed dede.

The prejudice against the character of the Jews finds expression also in the works of Chaucer's contemporaries, in *Piers
the Plowman* (c. 1362), in John Gower's *Confessio Amantis*
(c. 1392), and in the legend of the Jewish shoemaker, Joseph
Cartaphilus, who, according to the legends, was doomed
by the Saviour himself, to "tarry till I come."

The story of the Wandering Jew, first told in Roger of Wendover's *Flores Historiarum* (1228), was later copied into Matthew Paris' *Chronica Majora*, and circulated in several popular ballads. The following stanzas give the details of the medieval narrative:

> When as in faire Jerusalem
>   Our Saviour Christ did live,
> And for the sins of all the worlde
>   His own dear life did give;
>
> The wicked Jews with scoffs and scornes
>   Did dailye him molest,
> That never till he left his life
>   Our Saviour could not rest;
>
> .   .   .   .
>
> Our owne deare crosse he bore himselfe
>   A burthen far too great;
> Which made him in the street to fainte,
>   With blood and water sweat;
>
> Being wearye thus, he sought to rest,
>   To ease his burthened soule
> Upon a stone; the which a wretch
>   Did churlishly controule.
>
> And sayd, "Awaye, thou king of Jews,
>   Thou shalt not rest thee here;
> Pass on; thy execution place
>   Thou seest, now draweth neare."
>
> And thereupon, he thrust him thence;
>   At which our Saviour sayd:
> "I sure will rest, but thou shalt walk
>   And have no journey stayed . . ."

In medieval drama, too, the character of the Jew was elaborated with an evident prejudice against the money-lender of the years before their expulsion in 1290. The memory of the massacre of Jews in 1190 may have added vigor, and perhaps a subconscious need for self-justification, to the histrionic efforts of the actors in the York cycle of plays; for the scenes of the buffeting and the scourging, with all the brutality emphasized, made the crucifixion pageant at York almost intolerable. In every manner possible, the players vilified the Jewish characters, turning them into comic types to be derided, hissed at, and generally ridiculed. To the imagination of the average English audience, the Jews continued to be represented as nothing but malicious usurers who flourished in Norman and Angevin England, and who, having been found guilty of clipping coins in Edward I's time, were ultimately driven out of the realm by a special statute. This is about all the early Tudor period remembered, or cared to remember, about the Jewish character. What the average playgoer expected to see, and did see, in the stage-Jew was the incarnation of all the evil and unsocial traits of the medieval money-lender and tax-gatherer. Wherever the Corpus Christi pageants were presented by the various guilds of hosiers, plumbers, pattenmakers, pinners, latoners, and the like, the people, who saw no Jews in actual life, accepted the diabolical and grotesque stage-Jew as the real thing. In the pageant entitled *The Betraying of Christ*, Judas appeared before them in a fiery red wig — which was the orthodox wig worn by the Devil in other plays — and a long nose of the same flaming color. In another play, entitled *The Judgment Day*, they could plainly judge the evil deeds of the Jews, when the Saviour paused in the midst of the pageant to say:

> The Jewes spitte on me spitously;
> Thei spared me nomore than a theffe.
> When theirme strake, I stode stilly;
> Agaynste tham did I no-thyng greve.

And, in the final scene, it was declared in clear terms that the Jews, with the rest of the bad souls, were condemned

> In helle to dwelle with-outen ende;
> Ther ye schall neuere butt sorowe see
> And sitte be Satanas the fende.

CHAPTER II

THE TUDOR RENAISSANCE

Although, after 1290, no Jews were permitted by law to settle in England, it is not unlikely that, with the great changes in trade and commerce stimulated by the Renaissance in Italy, English and Jewish merchants and traders did business with each other in France and Italy, and that the English people were kept in fairly close touch with the vicissitudes of the Jews in other lands. English travelers, no doubt, brought back stories of the treatment of the Jews in the neighboring countries. In 1306, there were reports of the expulsion of a hundred thousand Jews from France, where they had resided for nearly a thousand years. During the period of the Black Death, when more than one-third of the population of Europe was carried off by the terrible epidemic, stories were circulated, particularly in Germany, about the Jews to whom the ignorance and wild fantasy of the age attributed the origin of the plague and its spread by poisoning the wells and rivers which supplied drinking-water for the Christian communities. Also, during the Hussite Wars (1419–1436), popular excitement was fed by stories about a rich Jew, Israel of Enns, who — so the rumor ran — purchased from a sexton's wife a consecrated

17

wafer in order to profane it. In consequence, the Jews were set upon, along with other heretics. In Spain, the friction between the Jewish and Christian communities grew apace, until in 1483, matters reached a woeful climax in the horrible "engine of the Inquisition," committed to the care of Torquemada, who, within a year, instituted several autos-da-fé, in which hundreds of crypto-Jews were burned alive at the stake. At Avila and elsewhere, the old stories were revived that the Jews had killed Christian children for ritual purposes, and Torquemada, making capital of these rumors, forced the hand of authority to issue the dreadful edict of expulsion in 1492. Thus, in the same year that Columbus set out to discover the New World, the Jews were driven out of Spain, to seek refuge in Germany, Italy, Holland, and Turkey. In time, the news of all these happenings drifted to England, where, no doubt, the Jews were the subject of discussion and conversation, although there is scant reference to them in early Tudor publications.

To those rumors and reports, perhaps, may be attributed a part of what passed for knowledge of the Jewish character displayed by the Elizabethan dramatists. In the spacious days of the English Renaissance, Jews were not unknown to the English citizens. From a reference to them in *The Wandering Jew Telling Fortunes to Englishmen* (1640), we learn that "Store of Jewes we have in England; a few in Court, many in the Citty, more in the Countrey." Also from a passage quoted by Sir Sidney Lee from *Every Woman in her Humor* (1609), we learn that the Jews in the larger cities commonly followed the trade of old-clothes dealers. Cardozo, however, believes that there were no Jews in England between the accession of Elizabeth and the closing of the theaters in 1640. He writes: "English merchants and adventurers came in contact with Jews in Mediterranean regions, Italy, Barbary, and Turkey; after 1600, also in the Netherlands. But to the home-keeping majority, including the playwrights, the Jew was an exotic, or an abstraction, known through the Bible, ancient history (Josephus), sermons, and rumor. There is no relation between the familiarity with the term 'Jew' in the literature of the time, and the supposed presence of overt Jews in England."

As early as 1578, John Lyly in his *Euphues* — that well-spring from which Elizabethan writers drank so freely — made the following statement about Jews:

> Consider with thyself that thou art a gentleman, yea, and a Gentile, and if thou neglect thy calling thou art worse than a Jew.

Lyly in turn may have been influenced by North's *Diall of Princes*, which in the 1568 edition contained this phrase:

> Let him take heed also, that he do not call his servants drunkards, thieves, villains, Jews, nor other such names of reproach.

Such, then, was the soil in which literary ideas concerning the Jews grew and multiplied, and from which Christopher Marlowe (1564-1593) and William Shakespeare (1564-1616) gathered their notions for the portrayal of the Jew, as money-lender, villain, and hook-nosed hankerer after Christian blood.

In the delineation of his Jewish character, Barabas, Marlowe is believed to have had a particular Jew in mind — a certain Joseph Nasi, Duke of Naxos (d. 1579), who was reported to have played an important part in Turkish history during the second half of the sixteenth century. Another theory points to a certain David Passi, a Jew involved in the Turkish designs on Malta, and closely connected with English diplomacy in the Mediterranean from 1585 to 1591, as the original of Barabas. Whoever may have been the actual original of the Jew of Malta, the fact remains that Marlowe's creation is the embodiment of the most terrifying of Elizabethan bogeys. Barabas was, as G. B. Harrison points out, "the incarnate spirit of Machieval, and a Jew."

From the start, *The Jew of Malta*, first produced on Saturday the 26th of February, 1592, drew a good house. The popularity of the play, which on the evidence of Henslowe's *Diary* exceeded that of any contemporary play, was no doubt due in the first instance to the dramatist's portrayal of the Jew, and to the masterful impersonation of Barabas by the favorite actor of the day, Edward Alleyn. The prologue is spoken by Machieval, who introduces the Jew as one

> Who smiles to see how full his bags are cramm'd,
> Which money was not got without my means.

In the opening scene the Jew himself is discovered brooding over his wealth:

> So that of thus much that return was made;
> And of the third part of the Persian ships,
> There was the venture summ'd and satisfied.
> As for those Samnites and the men of Uz,
> That bought my Spanish oils and wines of Greece,
> Here have I purs'd their paltry silverlings.
> Fie, what a trouble 'tis to count this trash!

Besides his wealth, the Jew of Malta has two master passions, a daughter and a revengeful hate for Christians. When the Christian rulers of Malta confiscate his property, turn him out, and convert his house into a nunnery, Barabas instructs his daughter, Abigail, to ask admission into the nunnery, feigning herself a Christian convert, so that she may secure for him a secret hoard concealed in his old home. In the night he waits under the balcony, and, when the bags are thrown down to him, hugs them passionately as he cries out:

> O my girl,
> My gold, my fortune, my felicity!
> Strength to my soul, death to mine enemy!
> Welcome the first beginner of my bliss!

Thus armed with the means of power, Barabas proceeds to rebuild his fortunes, with the added zest of an intensified hatred for all Christians and a passion for vengeance:

> I am not of the tribe of Levi, I,
> That can so soon forget an injury.
> We Jews can fawn like spaniels when we please:
> And when we grin we bite; yet are our looks
> As innocent and harmless as a lamb's.

Having again become rich, he is about to realize his dreams of revenge, but is checked by the intervention of a rascally Turkish slave, an accomplice of his misdeeds, who betrays the Jew to a courtesan, who in turn reveals all the villainies to the governor. But although the wicked Jew is thrown over the walls as a dead man, his career is not yet at an end for he has merely feigned death. Later he joins the Turks in the siege of Malta. The citadel is taken; the governor and people are in the Jew's hands. Once more he is master of the situation. But his politic cunning now suggests to him the necessity of making friends with his former foes. He proposes to entertain the departing Turks at a farewell banquet, in the course of which he will contrive to put them all to death. In this way he hopes to win the gratitude of the Christians, remain governor, and be master of the future as well as of the present. The Christians pretend to fall in with this Macchiavellian scheme, but only in order to catch the Jew in his own trap, of which he has revealed the secret. Thus, instead of the Turkish leaders being crushed by the fall of the banqueting-room, Barabas alone is precipitated into a cauldron of fire held in readiness beneath; and, foiled at last, expires with a curse on his lips.

The success of the Jew of Malta was in no small measure the reason for Shakespeare's production of the *Merchant of Venice* (1597–1598). In an interesting comparison of the two plays, Sir A. W. Ward has pointed out the close parallels in the two portrayals, Barabas and Shylock. Both Marlowe and Shakespeare present the money-lender as a swarthy-complexioned, gesticulating Jew, to whom the accumulation of money is the chief purpose of life. Marlowe's Barabas declares that he has

> . . . . learned in Florence how to kiss my hand,
> Heave up my shoulders when they call me dog,
> And duck as low as any barefoot friar;

and Shakespeare's Shylock makes a similar speech:

> Still have I borne it with a patient shrug,
> For sufferance is the badge of all my tribe . . .

> Shall I bend low, and in a bondman's key,
> With bated breath and whispering humbleness,
> Say . . . . . ?

Barabas is persistent in his cruelty, especially when he has a Christian in his power. He tells his daughter that "it is no sin to deceive a Christian," and runs about the stage, vexed and tormented, "with fatal curses towards these Christians." In the same spirit, Shylock refers to Antonio:

> I hate him for he is a Christian . . . . .
> Cursed be my tribe if I forgive him . . . . .
>
> If I can catch him once upon the hip,
> I will feed fat the ancient grudge I bear him.

Hated and hating, reviled and reviling, the two usurers are enemies of Christian society. Says Barabas:

> I walk abroad o' nights
> And kill sick people groaning under the walls;
> Sometimes I go about and poison wells . . .
>
> Then after that was I an usurer,
> And with extorting, cozening, forfeiting,
> And tricks belonging unto brokery,
> I fill'd the jails with bankrupts in a year,
> And with young orphans planted hospitals,
> And every moon made some or other mad,
> And now and then one hang himself for grief,
> Pinning upon his breast a long great scroll
> How I with interest tormented him.

If we are to judge by the terms of opprobrium with which Shylock is accosted by the Christians in Shakespeare's tragi-comedy, the Jew of Venice was regarded as capable of as much evil-doing as the Jew of Malta.

On the other hand, there are some who regard Shylock as a creation intended by Shakespeare to serve as a protest against Marlowe's "mere monster" of a Jew. Dr. Philipson points out that between the two characters there is all the difference between a frightful and hideous caricature and a heroic, intensely tragic figure. He sees in Barabas a representation calculated to stir only the worst passions of a listening multitude; but he detects in Shylock a characterization presented with the purpose of doing some degree of justice to the despised race. In certain passages, Shakespeare may be given credit for revealing the indignities thrust upon the Jewish people. He makes an indirect protest against the injustice of Christian intolerance, and seems to manifest a sympathy for the Jews in the speech by Shylock:

> He hath disgraced me, and hindered me half a million: laughed at my losses, mocked at my gains, scorned my nation, thwarted my bargains, cooled my friends, heated mine enemies; and what's his reason? I am a Jew . . . .

> If you prick us, do we not bleed? If you tickle us, do we not laugh? If you poison us, do we not die? and if you wrong us, do we not revenge?

There is, however, no mistaking the fact that Shylock is a Jewish money-lender. Because he has suffered insult and inhuman treatment as a Jew, he exults in the thought that he has the whip-hand and can now feed fat an ancient grudge:

> If a Jew wrong a Christian, what is his humility? Revenge. If a Christian wrong a Jew, what should his sufferance be by Christian example? Why, revenge. The villainy you teach me, I will execute; and it shall go hard, but I will better the instruction.

If the portrayal of the Jew in Elizabethan literature is prejudiced and false, the reason may perhaps be attributed to a lack of firsthand information concerning the Jewish character. It is open to question whether Marlowe and Shakespeare knew anything about the contemporary Jew, although in 1594, shortly before the *Merchant of Venice* was written, something of a stir was being made in London over the trial and execution of a Jew, Dr. Lopez, the Queen's physician, about whose private life much was said in public. The crimes of the "perjured and murderous Jewish doctor" were the subject of court and tavern talk. The bitterness of feeling provoked by the unfortunate incident clearly revealed the fact that, even as late as the end of the sixteenth century, three hundred years after their expulsion from England, the Jews were discriminated against with the same race-hatred that prevailed in Angevin times. And, as Professor Stoll points out, race-hatred, indeed, or the desire to profit by it, may have prompted the writing of the *Merchant of Venice*, in order that Shakespeare's company might in the present excitement compete with Henslowe's in their *Jew of Malta*. The judges who tried Dr. Lopez referred to him as "that vile Jew," "wily and covetous," "mercenary" and "corrupt;" and it is evident that Shakespeare puts into Gratiano's mouth a speech which clearly associates Shylock with Lopez:

> O, be thou damn'd, inexecrable dog!
> And for thy life let justice be accus'd.
> Thou almost mak'st me waver in my faith
> To hold opinion with Pythagoras,
> That souls of animals infuse themselves
> Into the trunks of men; thy currish spirit
> Govern'd a wolf, who, hang'd for human slaughter,
> Even from the gallows did his fell soul fleet,
> And whilst thou lay'st in thy unhallow'd dam,
> Infus'd itself in thee; for thy desires
> Are wolfish, bloody, starv'd and ravenous.

Also, it is interesting to note that Shakespeare names Shylock's foe Antonio, the identical name of Dr. Lopez's chief enemy, Don Antonio.

Some critics, William Hazlitt among them, feel disposed to believe that Shakespeare sympathized with Shylock as a man "no less sinned against than sinning," and that the impression of sympathy which the figure of the Jew evokes is the effect that the dramatist intends to produce on the audience. However, if Shakespeare had the figure of Dr. Lopez in mind while creating the character of Shylock, is it not possible that the dramatist shared the contemporary sentiments against the Queen's physician, to whom even his judges referred as "that vile Jew"? Solomon Hurwitz points out that Shylock appeared on the Elizabethan stage as a purely comic character, and that the tragic element of racial suffering, his prominent feature to-day, is the outgrowth of modern thought and modern criticism. Judging from the earliest stage directions for the play, Shylock was first presented as the Hebrew usurer with a hooked nose of high dimensions, and of generally slovenly appearance; a character not calculated to attract, but rather to repel. Also, it is evident that the plot contains several features of pure comedy. Professor Stoll, in his scholarly analysis of the character of Shylock, calls our attention to the principle that often, in comedy, the comic character is *unsocial* and out of harmony with his environment; and that the prejudice brought to bear for comic effect in the presentation of Shylock is the prejudice against Jew, miser, usurer. In each of these roles singly Shylock could not but be a purely repellant or comic figure on the Elizabethan stage because he was an object of derision on the street; and in these roles combined and united, not in a tragedy, but in a comedy, how could he possibly be thought pathetic at all? Says Professor Stoll, "Wrenched from the context, there are phrases, even sentences, that may, indeed, seem pathetic. But Shakespeare, as soon as Tubal enters, lets Shylock strike up the tune of 'my daughter — my ducats,' and, adhering to the method of comic alternation throughout the scene, plays the familiar dramatic trick of taking the audience in for a moment and of then clapping upon the seemingly pathetic sentiment a cynical, selfish, or simply incongruous one." Says Shylock:

> Two thousand ducats in that; and other precious jewels. I would my daughter were dead at my foot — and the jewels in her ear! Would she were hears'd at my foot — and the ducats in her coffin . . ."

In the trial scene, Shylock's triumph is turned into defeat; an apparent tragedy into a comedy. What had been offered to him and refused by him, he is now, when he demands it again, refused. The outcries against the Jew give place to the jeers of Gratiano. At every turn that the course of justice takes (welcomed by Shylock with gloating), while it was in his favor, in the early part of the trial, there are now peals and shouts of laughter.

In the case of the literary portrayals of feminine characters, another curious development is evident. Although the Jew is represented as a villain, the Jewess, on the other hand, is idealized. She is seldom portrayed as other than a creature of great attractiveness and physical charm. However, the introduction of the beautiful young Jewesses, Abigail and Jessica, as motherless heroines, alone at home with non-Jewish servants, seems to reveal a lack of knowledge of Jewish households on the part of the Elizabethan dramatists. Calisch maintains that Abigail, the faithful, obedient daughter of the Jew of Malta, "fully compliant to the wishes of her father even to her sorrow and against her will," is a more faithful portrait of a daughter of Israel than

Jessica, the rebellious, thieving, deceitful, and apostate daughter of the Jew of Venice. Be this as it may, the tradition once established has persisted in literature from the Elizabethan days down to the time of Scott and beyond that the Jewess is beautiful, very attractive to Christian men, and possessed of ability and rare intelligence.

In the fifty years, from the creation of Shylock to the temporary suppression of the theaters by the Puritans (1642–1656), the attention devoted to the Jew is significant of the popularity of the Shylock type as a medium of entertainment. There are at least nine plays with prominent Jewish roles. The Jew invariably makes his appearance on the boards with an extraordinary nose, as a money-lender scheming to get the Christian into his clutches, and shouting aloud for his "pound of flesh." For example, in the *Tragicall Raigne of Selimus, Emperor of the Turks* (1594) by Robert Greene and Thomas Lodge, a Jewish prisoner, Abraham, is presented as

> Withal a man so stout and resolute
> That he will venture anything for gold;

in *Woman Pleased* (1620), by Fletcher, the table of the sordid usurer, Lopez, is heaped with gold and jewels; and in *A Challenge for Beauty* (1636), one of the characters exclaims:

> Your English Jews, they'll buy and sell their fathers, prostrate their wives, and make money of their own children.

Likewise, in *Jack Drum's Entertainment* (1601), by John Marston, there is Mammon, the usurer, who, "with a big nose," is modeled after Shylock; and in *The Travels of Three English Brothers* (1607), by John Day, George Wilkins

and William Rowley, the Jewish character, who is a mere
repetition of Shylock, openly brags that he is

> .... a Jew,
> A crucifying hangman trained in sin,
> One that would hang his brother for his skin!

and indulges in a soliloquy after the style of the Jew of
Venice:

> A hundred thousand ducats! .... Who owes it?
>   A Christian,
> Canaan's brood; honey to my joyful soul —
> If this sum fail (my bond unsatisfied),
> He's in the Jew's mercy; mercy! ha! ha!

In the portrayal of the Jew at the end of the sixteenth
century, there is still all of the prejudice and bitterness
of the Middle Ages against the usurer and "killer of
Christian boys." The Elizabethan dramatists were not willing to run counter to the feelings of their time, which was
still unsympathetic toward the Jew, and doubly hostile to
the Jew-usurer. But at least the "Monster Jew" may now
be humanized. The Shylock type is extravagant in the
fierce love of money and wolfish in the thirst for revenge;
yet the audience is shown the sad and sordid conditions
which give rise to these perversions of humanity:

> For sufferance is the badge of all our tribe.
> You call me misbeliever, cut-throat dog,
> And spit upon my Jewish gaberdine ....

The audience is made to see that, in a great measure, the
Jew's behavior is due to his treatment at the hands of an
intolerant Christian community. The Jew is cut off from
the full feeling of citizenship; he is driven back into the

sentiment of a tribe, and of a tribe that is alien and out-raged. An advance is perceptible in the Elizabethan portrayal, over the portrayal of the Middle Ages, in the delineation of the Jew; he is now a creature of flesh and blood, of feelings and sentiments; yea, even a comic character capable of providing entertainment, rather than a bogey-monster, an unreal thing, an ally of the devil. Gradually the Jew in literature is emerging into an everyday world of common experiences. It is the undertaking of the poet and the dramatist to make readers realize that the Jew has, in the words of Shylock, eyes, hands, organs, dimensions, senses, affections, passions; that he is fed with the same food, hurt with the same weapons, subject to the same diseases, healed by the same means, warmed and cooled by the same winter and summer, as a Christian is.

CHAPTER III

THE RETURN OF THE JEWS TO ENGLAND

The early years of the seventeenth century seem to have witnessed the first return of the Jews to England in any considerable numbers. A Marrano colony is reported to have established itself in London in the first quarter of the century — at first accepting baptism and going to the Christian services to escape detection and persecution, but still remaining Jews in their hearts; and later, openly professing their own religion and acknowledging their real identity as Jewish merchants. It is probable that when Robert Burton (1577–1640), in his *Anatomy of Melancholy* (1621), commented on the Jewish character, he had these Marranos, meaning "accursed ones," in mind. Burton observes that the Jews have "goggle eyes," and are "most severe in their examination of time," that is, that they are "very industrious, while amongst Englishmen the badge of gentry is idleness, to be of no calling, not to labor . . . to be a mere spectator, a drone, *fruges consumere natus*;" that "as a company of vagabonds, they are scattered over all parts of the globe;" that they are "so ignorant and self-willed withal, that amongst their most understanding Rabbis, you will find naught but gross dotage, horrible hardness of heart, and *stupend* obstinacy in all their actions, opinions, conversations, and yet so zealous withal, that no man living can be more, and vindicate themselves for the elect people of God;" that they are "strict in the observance of the Sabbath;" and that they "are tolerated in most provinces of Europe."

It is a matter of conjecture whether the Government of Charles I (1625–1649) knew these Marranos were "secret Jews." They were of a pronounced Caballero type, living outwardly as Roman Catholics, and attending synagogue services in private. Except for occasional references to complaints made by the Levant Company to injuries suffered owing to the illicit practices of Jewish traders in Asia Minor, the Jew is rarely mentioned in contemporary State or other publications. In 1641, when the fate of the Earl of Stafford hung in the balance, a long list of members of Parliament hostile to him was posted in sundry places in London with the title, "Anabaptists, *Jews* and Brownists;" but these names were given in abuse and the list may prove nothing. In 1648, the year before the King was executed, the matter of repealing the statute of banishment of the Jews was taken up for discussion before the General Council of Officers sitting at Whitehall. A petition in favor of removing the ban was presented to Lord Fairfax by the Cartwrights of Amsterdam, and it duly reached Parliament. Also, in 1648, a tractate entitled *An Apology for the honorable nation of the Jews and all the sons of Israel* was published by Edward Nicholas, who pleaded that

> for the glory of God, the comfort of those afflicted people, the love of my own sweet native country of England, and the freeing of my own conscience in the day of account, we show ourselves compassionate and helpers of the afflicted Jews.

There is scant reference to the Jews in contemporary poetry, and it is indeed remarkable that even the observant and critical character-writers, who were always on the look out for unusual and strange figures about town, should have missed describing the Marranos in London. Sir Thomas Overbury, whose *Characters* was published in 1614, describes "A Devilish Usurer," but there is no hint of the evil creature being of the race of Shylock. Sir Francis Bacon, however, in his essay *Of Usury*, published two years earlier, recommended that all usurers "should have orange-tawny bonnets, because they do *Judaize*." A caustic description of the usurer is included in Nicholas Breton's *Characters upon Essays*, published in 1615; but, here too, there is no hint that "this figure of misery," "the hate of a Christian," is a Jew. In 1649 King Charles was executed, and England became republican. Oliver Cromwell, as Lord Protector of the Commonwealth (1653–1658), seemed aware of the usefulness of the Jews in building up British colonial and commercial expansion. The Marranos who were already engaged in business on the continent, had dealings with other Jews in other parts of the world. Thus they were in a position to secure information that was beyond the reach of Cromwell's government, and in this way are said to have kept Cromwell and his state department in touch with the activities of the Spaniards in America, and with the plans of Charles Stuart in Holland. The Lord Protector was aware of the value of the Marranos as traders and financiers, and, in connection with the commercial policy which led to the Navigation Act of 1641, was desirous of attracting to London, through them, the rich Jews of Amsterdam, so that there might be a transfer of Jewish trade interests with the Spanish Main from Holland to England. Overtures to the Jews in Holland were made through Manasseh ben Israel, an eminent rabbi of Spanish or Portuguese birth then settled in Amsterdam, and who had already corresponded with Englishmen on the subject of the readmission of the Jews to England. In 1650, Manasseh felt encouraged to address a petition to the Long Parliament, begging that Jews be readmitted with the right to trade and build synagogues. It must be noted, however, that not all the Jews in Amsterdam were in sympathy with Cromwell's policies. There were many among them who were Royalists and staunch supporters of the House of Stuart. In a letter dated June 29, 1654, to the exiled Charles II, that gallant royalist soldier, Sir Marmaduke Langdale, reported that "the Jews are numerous and rich, and offer great matters for their privileges in England;" and in another despatch, three months later, Charles II's secretary, Sir Edward Nicholas, observed, "Cromwell has agreed with the Jews; and some of their rabbis (i. e., in Holland) are learning English and will go from several parts to settle Judaism in England." Cromwell's attitude was plainly indicated by the message with which he passed Manasseh ben Israel's petition to the Council of State: "His Highness is pleased in an especial manner to recommend these papers to the speedy consideration of the Council." It is a matter of singular interest that, being a Puritan and talking in the spirit of the Old Testament, the Lord Protector shared the view that found frequent expression in his day, namely, that the Messianic Age would not dawn until the Jews were to be found in every land under the sun. In 1654, Thomas Barlow, in a tract entitled *Case of the Lawfulness of the Toleration of the Jews*, expressed this strong Puritan conviction in the statement that "there lies a heavy and sacred obligation upon Christians . . . to endeavor the conversion of the Jews, which certainly cannot be by banishing them from all Christian commonwealths."

In October, 1655, Manasseh arrived in London to plead in person for the readmission of the Jews into England. He was received very graciously by Cromwell, and the famous Whitehall Conference was summoned to consider the question of Jewish naturalization. On a dark day in December, 1655, the Conference assembled in the long gallery of Whitehall. The Lord Protector sat in the chair of state and presided over the deliberations of this august body. In the words of Thomas Carlyle,

> Highest official persons have met here to advise, by reason, law-learning, scripture prophecy, and every source of light for the human mind, concerning the proposal of admitting Jews ... They were banished near four-hundred years ago; shall they now be allowed to reside and trade again? The proposer is Manasseh ben Israel ... and so they debate and solemnly consider; and his Highness (Cromwell) spake; and says one witness (Sir Paul Rycaut) "I never heard a man speak so well."

Several reports of the Whitehall Conference exist, the most detailed being that attributed to Henry Jessey, and published at the time as a sixteen-page pamphlet with the title, *A Narrative of the Late Proceedings at Whitehall concerning the Jews who had desired by Rabbi Manasseh, an Agent for them, that they might return into England, and worship the God of their Fathers here in Synagogues*, etc. . . . (1656). It was the opinion of the lawyers at the Conference that there was no law by which the Jews could be kept out of the country. With this matter settled, the Conference proceeded to discuss the question, "If it be lawful, then upon what terms is it meet to receive them (the Jews) into the country?" It is reported that merchants argued that the admission of the Jews would "enrich foreigners and impoverish the natives of the land;" that the divines "assailed each other furiously with texts of Scripture, and spent so much time in turning over their Bibles for proof, that they passed four days in discussion;" and that Cromwell "grew tired and told them with some warmth that they did not answer his expectation." Ultimately, it was voted that the Jews had no place in a Christian commonwealth, and that they could not settle in England "except by private sufferance of His Highness."

Amongst those who wrote against the readmission of the Jews into England, and whose opinions were most influential in turning the vote against Manasseh ben Israel's cause, was William Prynne, the famous author of *Histriomastix* (1632) and sometime Keeper of the Records in the Tower of London, who stated that

> .... it was now a very ill time to bring in the Jewes, when the people were so dangerously and generously bent to Apostacy and all sorts of novelties and errors in religion, and would sooner turn Jewes than Jewes Christians .... The Jewes had been formerly great clippers and forgers of money, and had crucified three or four children in England at least, which were the principal causes of their banishment ....

In a pamphlet entitled *Short Demurrer to the Jews Long Discontinued Remitter into England*, the first part of which was printed in 1655, the second in 1656, and both parts reprinted in 1656, Prynne bitterly attacked any attempt on the part of the government to force the readmission of the Jews into England. He was willing, he wrote, to pray for their conversion. but he was opposed on religious grounds to the granting of their petition.

While the conference was still in session, the shrewd Secretary Thurloe wrote to Henry Cromwell, then Lord Deputy in Ireland:

> We have had very many disputations concerning the admittance of the Jews to dwell in this Commonwealth, they having made an earnest desire of His Highness to be admitted .... What the issue thereof will be I am not able to tell you, but am apt to think that nothing will be done therein.

He judged accurately. A multitude of counselors failed to give unity, and, to the Lord Protector's disappointment, no decision was arrived at. The deputation of Jews that had come to London from Amsterdam and other cities, when they heard of the failure of the petition, "removed hence again to beyond the seas with much grief of heart that they were thus disappointed of their hopes." Their leader, Manasseh ben Israel, however, encouraged by the courtesy paid to him by some scholars, preferred to remain in London. In 1656, he addressed a petition to Cromwell, in which he thanked the Lord Protector for allowing a small group of Jews resident in London to meet in their private houses for devotion, but now begged to have that protection set down in writing, so that they might have no fear of molestation. The last years of the rabbi's life are described by John Sadler, for a time Cromwell's secretary, in a letter dated January 4, 1659, addressed to Richard Cromwell, as follows:

> He (Manasseh ben Israel) stayed here so long he was ashamed to return to those that sent him with so little success. Your father granted him 100 pounds a year,

which he resigned for 200 pounds, but though he procured several seals he never got a penny. At length, broken-hearted with losing his only son, his time and his hopes, he got away with so much breath as lasted him in Middleburgh, where he died — November 20, 1657 — leaving a widow who had no money to bury him.

Although the decision of the Whitehall Conference was disappointing to Cromwell, Manasseh ben Israel, and their Jewish friends, the opinion of the lawyers marked a change in the status of the House of Israel in England, for it was now clearly established that there was no legal obstacle to the return of the Jews into the realm. However, although no general permission to enter the country was granted, but only freedom to individual applicants, the result was clear that the Jews regained their old influence, and much more, by a gradual, and for a long time an imperceptible, process of peaceful penetration.

The public recognition of the return of the Jews to England is casually referred to in a sentence in Evelyn's *Diary*, under date of December 14, 1656: "Now were the Jews admitted." But there is not even a passing reference in the papers of Cromwell's Latin Secretary, John Milton, who, no doubt, shared the Protector's sympathies with the Jews, and who, on his own account, owed so much to the inspiration and culture of the Hebrew people.

At the time of the Restoration (1660), the Jewish community in England, though still small in numbers, totaling 150 persons, impressed the newly-returned prince by the wealth that they had brought into the country and the fruitful colonial trade in which they engaged. Charles II (1660–1685) appreciated the value of Jewish capital and enterprise in British trade and remembered the considerable financial support given to the Stuart cause during his exile by the Mendes da Costas, the Augustine Coronel-Chacon, and other loyal Jewish families. At the very outset of his rule, the Merry Monarch assured the English Jewry of his protection and a continuation of the tolerant policy of his predecessor. The new king characteristically ignored the numerous petitions presented by London merchants, praying for the banishment of these same Jewish subjects. He may have weighed these petitions against his commercial ambitions for the kingdom as a whole. In any event, he proceeded to grant letters of denization and other concessions to individual members of the Jewish community.

In 1663, the synagogue in London was enlarged, public services were instituted, and Jacob Sasportas of Amsterdam was appointed Haham or Chief Rabbi. In the same year, under date of October 14, Samuel Pepys (1633-1703) records his visit to this synagogue, in the company of his wife and a friend. The entry in the famous *Diary* affords us an interesting comment by a contemporary man-about-town, to whom a Jewish service was indeed a novel show. Pepys writes:

> After dinner my wife and I, by Mr. Rawlinson's conduct, to the Jewish synagogue; where the men and boys in their veils, and the women behind a lattice out of sight; and some things stand up, which I believe is their law, in a press, to which all coming in do bow; and in the putting on their veils do say something, to which others that hear him do cry, Amen, and the party do kiss his veil. Their service all in a singing way, and in Hebrew. And anon their Laws that they take out of the press are carried by several men, four or five several burdens in all, and they do relieve one another; and whether it is that every one desires to have the

carrying of it, thus they carried it round about the room while such a service is singing. And in the end they had a prayer for the King, which they pronounced his name in Portuguese; but the prayer, like the rest, in Hebrew. But Lord! to see the disorder, the laughing, sporting, and no attention, but confusion in all their service, more like brutes than people knowing the true God, would make a man forswear ever seeing them more; and indeed I never did see so much, or could have imagined there had been any religion in the whole world so absurdly performed as this.

Judging by the description and the date, this visit took place on *Simhat Torah*, the "Rejoicing with the Torah," a holiday during which an exceptional ceremonial is followed. The scrolls are taken from the Ark and are carried through the synagogue while the entire congregation joins in the singing. The usual restraints are not enforced on this day, and children are encouraged to participate in the procession, with the result that decorum frequently is wanting. It is most unfortunate that the diarist visited the synagogue on that particular occasion.*

Three years later (1666), under date of February 19, Pepys reports another matter concerning the Jews of London, that they were betting on the advent of their Messiah. This report is interesting, because in the days of the Protectorate there were some among the Jews who identified Cromwell with the Messiah who had been foretold, but who, on the failure of the Whitehall Conference, abandoned the notion. The expectation of a coming champion long continued to fire the imagination and agitate

· * For this valuable bit of inside information, which I have not found in the notes on Pepys' account, I am indebted to Dr. Solomon Grayzel.

the minds of the Levantine Hebrews. Here we have Pepys' account of the revival of the expectation in his day:

> I am told for certain, what I have heard once or twice already, of a Jew in town, that in the name of the rest do offer to give any man 10 pounds to be paid 100 pounds, if a certain person now at Smyrna be within these two years owned by all the Princes of the East, and particularly the grand Signor, as the King of the World, in the same manner we do the King of England here, and that this man is the true Messiah. One named a friend of his that had received ten pieces in gold upon this score, and says that the Jew hath disposed of 1100 pounds in this manner, which is very strange; and certainly this year of 1666 will be a year of great action; but what the consequences of it will be, God knows!*

It was indeed a year of great action — the year of the plague, described in later years by Defoe, and the year of the Great Fire of London, so graphically described by Pepys and John Evelyn in their respective diaries, and by John Dryden in his poem, *Annus Mirabilis* (1666). It may indeed seem strange that no mention is made of the activities of the Jews during the plague and the fire. The assumption is that their numbers being so small, they did not attract attention in the confusion and horror of the tragic happenings. With the rebuilding of London, however, and the consequent assertion of the power of the wealthy landowners during the rest of the century, the Jewish immigration grew apace, adding substantially to the influence of the Jewish settlement in England. To John Dryden (1631-

---

* The reference is to the false messiah, Sabbatai Zevi.

1700), the greatest poet of his day, the city of London in 1682 was the "great Emporium of our Isle", in which "of Israel's tribe there is a numerous band."

Perhaps the presence of the Jews in their midst made Englishmen relish the analogy and satire of Dryden's famous poem, *Absalom and Achitophel* (1681). It will be remembered that in this attack on the political situation stirred up by the crafty Earl of Shaftesbury, the satirist describes London as Jerusalem and the inhabitants of the city as Jews.

> The Jews, a headstrong, moody, murm'ring race
> As ever tried th' extent and stretch of grace;
> God's pampered people, whom, debauch'd with ease,
> No King could govern nor no God could please . . .

The conflicting persons and interests are represented as characters in the Old Testament narrative. Monmouth becomes Absalom, noble, but wayward and misguided; Charles is King David, sorrowing for his son; and Shaftesbury is Achitophel, the giver of crafty and evil counsel. The "Second Part" of the poem (1682) was mainly the work of Nahum Tate, but Dryden is known to have contributed lines 310–509, in which the satirical application of the Hebrew narrative to the modern situation is as pointed as in the earlier part. For example, in the portrayal of Ben Jochanan one can see the parallel effectively described:

> A Jew of humble parentage was he,
> By trade a Levite, though of low degree;
> His pride no higher than the desk aspir'd,
> But for the drudgery of Priests was hir'd
> To read and pray in Linen Ephod brave,
> And pick up single Sheckles from the Grave.

More serious perhaps in purpose is Dryden's *Hind and the Panther*, written the year after he became a convert to Romanism (1684), in which poem there is a reference to "captive Israel .... multiply'd in chains, a numerous Exile;" a sentence which aptly describes the scattered people during the last years of the seventeenth century.

When William III (1689–1702) came to the throne, a closer connection was established between the London Jews and their coreligionists in Amsterdam. The new king, desiring to extend the trade interests of his English realm, engaged in a series of continental adventures which plunged England into the full current of European affairs, thus starting the nation on its career as a greater trading power. The Jewish merchants and bankers of London did such a flourishing business with the Dutch financiers, that before long the success of the Jewish men of business provoked a feeling of resentment among English merchants, who, through their representatives in Parliament, prevailed on the legislature to pass an order making the Jews liable to Alien Duty (1690). The success of this anti-Jewish legislation was followed in the spring by the attempt to amend an act "for the more effectual suppressing of Blasphemy and Profaneness," so as to make all persons professing the Jewish religion liable to severe penalties. Fortunately for the Jewish community, the amendment was rejected. In all this there is sufficient evidence that the English merchants, resenting the intrusion of the Israelite merchant on the Exchange and in the profitable trade with the Indies and the New World, sought every opportunity to fill the word "Jew" with the evil meanings attached to it in the Middle Ages. The opposition zealots made capital of the fact that the Jew was still legally classed as an "alien" and an "infidel" and, as such, was to the mind of his envious business rivals a source of danger in a Christian commonwealth.

The "alien" charge was neither satisfactory nor convincing, especially at a time in English history when the king himself was a foreigner, and when, as Daniel Defoe (1660?–1731) pointed out, it was embarrassing to protest against the alien composition of the "True Born Englishman." Defoe wrote:

> These are the heroes who despise the Dutch,
> And rail at *new-come Foreigners* so much;
> Forgetting that themselves are all deriv'd
> From the most Scoundrel Race that ever liv'd,
> A horrid Crowd of Rambling Thieves and Drones,
> Who ransack'd Kingdoms and dispeopled Towns . . .
> A True-Born Englishman's a Contradiction,
> In Speech an Irony, in Fact a Fiction . . .
> A Metaphor invented to express
> A Man *a-kin* to all the Universe!

But the outcry against the "infidel" and "alien" was carried into the next century, especially during the periods of greatest commercial activity, when English citizens bought and sold, not only stocks and bonds, but electoral votes and political influence as well. To what extent the wealthier members of the Jewish community were accused of contributing toward the corruption in elections and appointments may be surmised perhaps from the rumors circulated at the time, to the effect that certain Israelites had offered "My Lord Godolphin five-hundred thousand pounds — and that they would have made it a million — for the town of Brentford, with leave of settling there entirely, with full privileges of trade." The offer, it is reported, was refused on the ground that it would provoke two of the most powerful bodies of the nation to opposition against the government; namely, the clergy and the merchants. What truth there was in these rumors cannot be discovered.

At the end of the century, there was still the strong feeling — stimulated, no doubt, by the Puritan element, who, though in the minority in political affairs, still retained some influence in matters of theology,— that the conversion of the Jews to Christianity was desirable, if the Jews were to be a part of the body politic of a Christian commonwealth. On this question, Sir Thomas Browne (1605–1682) wrote with some emotion in his famous *Religio Medici*, as follows:

> I am ashamed at the Rabbinical interpretation of the Jews upon the Old Testament, as much as their defection from the New; and truly it is beyond wonder, how that contemptible and degenerate issue of Jacob, once so devoted to ethnic superstition, and so easily seduced to the idolatry of their neighbors, should now in such an obstinate and peremptory belief adhere unto their own doctrine, expect impossibilities, and, in the face and eye of the Church, persist without the least hope of Conversion. This is a vice in *them*, that were a virtue in *us*; for obstinacy in a bad cause is but constancy in a good.

The fact that they continued in their obstinate resistance of all efforts to convert them to the Christian faith, made the Jews, in the eyes of patriotic English citizens especially, the objects of pity, distrust and suspicion. In the next chapter we shall see how this circumstance influenced the literary portrayal of the Jew in the eighteenth century.

CHAPTER IV

THE EIGHTEENTH CENTURY

The London of Queen Anne's reign (1702–1714) saw the establishment of the Bank of England (founded in 1694) and the creation of the National Debt. These developments indicated a shift in the center of influence from the landed gentry to the moneyed classes of the metropolis. "Trade," says the *Spectator* (May 19, 1711), "has given us a sort of additional empire," and multiplied the number of the rich. Joseph Addison (1672–1719) amuses himself in several essays with "speculations on the race of people called the Jews," many of whom he has met with in most of the considerable towns, and who are, in some measure, responsible for the present stimulation of trade. In the *Spectator* of September 27, 1712, he writes:

They (the Jews) are, indeed, so disseminated through all the trading parts of the world, that they are become the instrument by which the most distant nations converse with one another, and by which mankind are knit together in a general correspondence . . . They are like pegs and nails in a great building, which, though they are but little valued in themselves, are absolutely necessary to keep the whole frame together.

Commenting on the "remarkable particulars" of the dispersion of the Jews throughout the world, the essayist attributes their numbers to "nothing but their constant employment, their abstinence, their exemption from wars, and above all, their frequent marriages."

According to contemporary reports, "the most notorious Jew" of Queen Anne's reign was Sir Solomon de Medina, chief among the Hebrew financiers, who came over to England with William III, and was long associated with public affairs. For his services to the Crown, he was the first Jew to receive the honor of knighthood. As army contractor during the war with France, Medina's name was "less honorably linked with certain accusations of bribery in connection with the Duke of Marlborough." The feelings of the Duke's opponents were revealed by Jonathan Swift in the pages of the *Examiner* (June 12, 1712, and November 13, 1712), in which Medina is attacked by name. In the *Examiner* of April 14, 1712, there is a scurrilous epigram:

A Jew and a G-n-l both join'd a Trade,
The Jew was a Baker, the G-n-l- sold Bread . . .

Another Jewish financier, but more worthily prominent in the public affairs of the eighteenth century, was Sampson Gideon, one of the Governors of the Bank of England. It was Gideon's ambition to buy a large estate and found a family. To this end he obtained, through Sir Robert Walpole, a special act of Parliament, legalizing a purchase of land; and he brought up his children in the Christian faith. His only son was created a baron, with the title of Lord Eardley.

Although Gideon was generally regarded as an industrious and persevering financier, and was respected as the oracle of Jonathan's Coffee House in Exchange Alley, his success in amassing gold stirred up considerable hostility and prejudice against him personally, and revived the ancient antagonisms and prejudices against Jews.

From the dangerous speculation carried on by the "crowd of companies" which sprang into existence in the first twenty years of the century, the London Jews, as a class, are reported to have held aloof. No doubt some of them participated in the scramble for South Sea stocks that began in 1711, and were shrewd enough to save themselves from the final panic when the bubble burst. In the opinion of Stokes, however, Sampson Gideon was a "steadying influence" during this period, and "the conduct of the Jews was helpful to the Government."

With the general extension of prosperity and trade during the first quarter of the century, observes Green, the town was coming into greater prominence as an element of national life. It was natural that this tendency should be reflected in literature. Indeed, it was the proud boast of the Augustans that literature was becoming more and more an expression of the life of the towns; and it was town life which was now giving to literature its character and form.

It is natural, therefore, to expect that the Jew, who was becoming a familiar figure in English town life, and, as Addison assures us, was playing an important part in the commerce and trade of the nation, be included in the descriptions and records of contemporary life. But were the portrayals of the Jew of that day drawn from life? The practical unanimity of the authors and playwrites in giving the Jew a bad character is in itself a cause for suspicion. Add to that the difference in point of view between national leaders who saw in the Jew a national asset, and the city tradesmen who saw in him a source of danger, and one begins to see in the Jewish villain of the literature of that day a figment of popular imagination having little or no relation to the Jew who lived and labored in eighteenth century England. We shall see that not only the lesser writers, but the literary masters of the age — Addison, Defoe, Pope, Swift, Richardson, Fielding and Smollett — have mentioned the Jew as an inevitable figure in the passing show of the age.

In the *obiter dicta* of the journalists of the period, it is possible to sense the popular feeling toward the Jews as a community of traders and agents on the metropolitan rialto. For instance, in the writings of Ned Ward, "The London Spy" (1698–1703), and Thomas Brown, the "Witty Journalist" of the day (1720), one may find passages with uncomplimentary references to the Jews. The prejudices of the market place put the Jew in a class with the rogues and vagabonds of the town.

> O search this sinful town with care;
> What numbers, duly mine, are there!
> The full-fed herd of money-jobbers,
> Jews, Christians, rogues alike and robbers,
> Who sit on the poor man's toils
> And fatten by the nation's spoils!

In that part of Thread and Needle Street and 'Change Alley, where the desks and counters of stock-jobbers and brokers blocked the thoroughfare in the days of the South Sea speculations, the Jew, according to contemporary versifiers, was notorious for driving his bargains. The follow-

ing lines by Arthur Murphy (1791), refer to the Jew as a
conspicuous element in the world of business:

> In London stands a famous pile,
> And near that pile an Alley,
> Where merry crowds for riches toil,
> And wisdom stoops to folly.
>
> Here stars and garters too appear
> Among our herds, the rabble;
> To buy and sell, to see and hear
> The Jews and Gentiles squabble!

In the *Spectator*, Addison's frequent references to the
Jews in business reveal rather a tolerant attitude. Describing himself as the "Spectator," the essayist says:

> I have been taken for a merchant upon the Exchange
> for above ten years, and sometimes pass for a Jew in
> the assembly of stock jobbers at Jonathan's.

This spirit of tolerance does not appear in the writings of
Daniel Defoe, whose animosity toward the Jews is expressed
in the words, "the execrable Jews, crucifying the Lord of
Life," and similar phrases. In the *Mercurius Politicus* of
January 1717, there is the report of the trial of one Francis
Francia, a Jew who had taken part in the Jacobite rebellion
of 1715, and had consequently been accused of high treason;
and in *Mist's Journal* of April 1, 1721, a brutal reference to
certain Jews, "late South Sea Directors," who "have left
off boiling their Westphalia hams in Champagne and bur-
gundy." In the picaresque novel, *Roxana; or the Unfortunate
Mistress* (1724), the novelist portrays a Jew, to whom the
beautiful heroine takes her jewels. Says Defoe:

As soon as the Jew saw the Jewels, he falls a jabbering, in Dutch or Portuguese, to the merchant; and I could presently perceive that they were in some great surprise, both of them; the Jew held up his hands, looked at me with some horror, then talked Dutch again, and put himself into a thousand shapes, twisting his body, and wringing up his face this way and that way in his discourse; stamping with his feet, and throwing abroad his hands, as if he was not in a rage only, but in a mere fury. Then he would turn and give a look at me like the devil. I thought I never saw anything so frightful in my life.

Eventually it transpires that this nameless Jew, who is referred to as "that cursed Jew," "the malicious Jew," "that dog of a Jew," "that traitor of a Jew," is a perjurer, extortioner and murderer.

What actuated Defoe to label such a figure, without any mitigating element, a Jew, is difficult to explain. Dr. H. R. S. Van der Veen is of the opinion that Defoe, who was in monetary difficulties — in 1692 he became a bankrupt — with a deficit of about seventeen thousand pounds, may have had some unfortunate dealings with Jewish money-lenders.

Other references to Jews are made by Defoe in *Robinson Crusoe* (1719), *The Memoirs of Captain George Carleton* (1726), and *The Life and Adventures of Mrs. Charles Davies, commonly called Mother Ross* (1740), wherein Jews are reported to follow the army to purchase pillage.

Among the works of Alexander Pope (1688–1744), there is a satire with the title: *A Strange but True Relation how Mr. Edmund Curll, of Fleet Street, Stationer, out of an Extraordinary Desire of Lucre, went into 'Change Alley, and was converted from the Christian Religion by Certain Eminent Jews;*

and how he was Circumcised and initiated into their Mys-
teries — in which there is a shameless libel on the Jews. The
satirist comments on the avarice of the ancient people in
general, and the greed of certain London Jews in particular.
The disgusting details of the treatment of Curll, the book-
seller, at the hands of six Jews, ends with the following
prayer:

> Keep us, we beseech thee, from the hands of such bar-
> barous and cruel Jews, who albeit they abhor the blood
> of black-puddings, yet thirst they vehemently after the
> blood of the white ones. And that we may avoid such
> like calamities, may all good and well-disposed Chris-
> tians be warned by this unhappy wretches woeful ex-
> ample, to abominate the heinous sin of avarice.

Perhaps the two significant references to Jews in Pope's
poetry are to be found in the description of Belinda's jewels:

> On her white breast a sparkling cross she wore,
> Which Jews might kiss, and infidels adore;

and in Satire II of the *Satires of Dr. John Donne Versified*,
in which the poet uses the phrase "out-usure Jews".

We come now to Pope's friend and most celebrated contemporary, Jonathan Swift (1667–1731), who was seldom
pleasant on the subject of the Jews. In the *Examiner* of
April 12, 1711, the satirist complains that the dissenters
have entered into a league with Papists and a Papist prince
to destroy the Church of England, and asks:

> What if the Jews should multiply and become a formid-
> able party among us? Would the dissenters join in
> alliance with them likewise, because they agree already
> in some general principles, and because the Jews are
> allowed to be a stiff-necked and rebellious people?

In a pamphlet entitled *A Complete Refutation of the False-hoods against Erasmus Lewis, Esq.* (1713), Swift attacks Henry Levi, a German Jew, who had calumniated Lewis, the Dean's intimate friend; and speaks of Levi's associates as "low intellectuals." In *Reasons for Repealing the Sacramental Test in Favor of the Catholics* (1733), the Jews are placed in the same category with Turks, Infidels and Heretics, a practice perhaps learned from the *Book of Common Prayer* (1548), and from contemporary writers. In his poetic satire *On Dr. Rundle, Bishop of Ferry* (1734), Swift says:

> Make Rundle bishop! fie for shame!
> An Arian to usurp the name!
> A bishop in the isle of saints!
> How will his brethren make complaints!
> Yet, were he Heathen, Turk or Jew,
> What is there in it strange or new?

The satirist repeatedly employs phrases like "as rich as a Jew," "richer than a Jew," "rich as Jews," and "as rich as fifty Jews" — echoes, perhaps, of the popular reports concerning the growing prosperity of the Jewish communities in the modern world. In a poem entitled *On the Words Brother Protestants and Fellow Christians* (1733), Swift makes the disparaging comment:

> And thus fanatic saints, though neither in
> Doctrine nor discipline our brethren,
> Are brother Protestants and Christians,
> As much as *Hebrews* and Philistines;

and in a satire on one Mr. Whiston, who had prophesied that the world would come to an end in a few days, offers the following ironical observation on 'Change Alley:

There was little or nothing transacted; there were multitudes of sellers, but so few buyers, that one cannot affirm the stocks bore any certain price except among the Jews, who this day reaped great profit by their infidelity.

In 1711 was published *The Antiquities of the Exchequer of the Kings of England*, by Thomas Maddox (1666–1727), in which a chapter (VII) was devoted to the history of the Exchequer of the Jews. This work is still regarded as a model of accuracy and industry, and has served to throw considerable light on the value of the Jewish community to the trading interests of the nation. In 1714, another work, entitled *Reasons for Naturalizing the Jews of Great Britain and Ireland on the Same Foot with All Other Nations*, revived the discussion on the subject of Jewish political rights. It was answered in the following year by a pamphlet entitled *Confutation of the Reasons*, with a list of the "crimes, frauds, insolences, etc." committed by Israelites in England. The controversy which kept up through the succeeding years called forth in 1736 a piece of writing entitled *The Complaints of the Children of Israel Concerning the Penal Laws*, presenting a picture of the sufferings and grievances of the English Jews, and praying for the repeal of the Test Act. In refutation of the accusation generally made that the Jews were despicable in the pursuit of riches, the defenders of Israel contended that,

We find the most sanctified Christians, in respect of worldly lucres, as little scrupulous of taking the profits to themselves as they are of throwing the scandal upon us. We get what we can, and keep what we get, not by any principle of religion, but of convenience, which principle reigns in as full perfection amongst the saints at Hackney, as amongst the Children of Israel in Bury Street or Duke's Place.

In 1740, a measure of relief was extended to English Jewry by the passing of the Act permitting any Israelite who had resided in the British colonies for a period of seven years to become naturalized. Thirteen years later, in 1753, the Prime Minister, Henry Pelham, gave his sanction to the introduction of a bill granting naturalization to all British Jews on application to Parliament. The measure was presented and passed without a division, but when the bill came before the Commons for discussion, a cry of protest was suddenly heard over the country. A veritable stream of pamphlets, petitions and sermons against the Jews produced considerable bitterness and confusion. Although the Jew Bill was passed by a vote of 96 to 55, it was soon repealed (1754), "as a point of political policy." The consequences were most unfortunate for English Jewry. Several leading families of the Sephardic section, representing the Spanish and Portuguese families of wealth and culture, realizing the hopelessness of their situation as Jews, either gave up Judaism and joined the English Church, or withdrew from active participation in Jewish affairs.

During the second half of the century, when so much that was controversial appeared in essays and pamphlets, it seemed inevitable that the Jew, his activities and his manners, should provide a source of exotic interest to literary speculators.

Among the writers in the Johnson Circle, Doctor Johnson (1709–1784) himself was the most outspoken on the Jews. In the *Rambler* of February 11, 1752, he ridicules Abram Ben Hannase, a rabbi who recommended the "Calamita" as a means of discovering the fidelity of a woman to her husband. Later, in the *Idler* of June 17, 1758, Johnson introduces an anti-Popist character who rejoices over the admission of the Jews to the privileges of English Society, because he thinks that a Jew would never become a Papist. There is, however, no important essay in the *Rambler* or the *Idler* of which the Israelite is the principal subject. Also, we look in vain through the works of the other members of the Johnson Circle for any report or comment on the Jewish question in England.

Oliver Goldsmith (1728–1774), in his tale of *The Haunch of Venison*, presents a Jew "with his chocolate cheek," in the company of a "d——d Scottish rogue," to provide some slight entertainment for his circle. In his Essays (1758–1765) there are references to a Jewish peddler with whom "Mr. Dibbins was disputing on the old subject of religion," and to "a long story of Moravia the Jew" (Essay No. 1); to "Nathan Ben Funk, the Dutch Jew" (No. 2); to "that venerable, unshaken, and neglected patriot, Mr. Jacob Henriquez, who, though of the Hebrew nation, hath exhibited a shining example of Christian fortitude and perseverance." Other kindly references to the Jews are found in *The Bee* (1759), where the essayist observes that the Jews of Alexandria are "its most industrious inhabitants;" and in the seventy-second letter of *The Citizen of the World* (1760–1762), where it is clear that the author's generous disposition prevents him from concurring with and imitating the novelists, who appeared unwilling to write favorably of the contemporary Jew.

Unquestionably the most public-spirited and philosophic member of the Johnson club was Edmund Burke (1729–1797), to whom we refer next because, in his *Abridgment of*

English History, he takes cognizance of the historical fact
that in the early Norman times, the Jews were —

> Slaves to the King in the strictest sense; insomuch that,
> besides the various tollages and fines extorted from
> them, none succeeded to the inheritance of his father
> without the King's license and an heavy composition . . .
> They were almost the only persons who exercised usury,
> and thus drew to themselves the odium and wealth of
> the kingdom; but they were only a canal, through which
> it passed to the royal treasury . . . Through them al-
> most the whole body of the nobility were in debt to the
> King; and when he thought proper to confiscate the
> effects of the Jews, the securities passed into his
> hands . . .

As a member of the Johnson social circle, Frances (Fanny)
Burney (1752–1840) may be mentioned here. It is interesting to note that in her *Early Diary*, first published in
1842–46, several letters appear in which intolerant opinions
of the Jews are expressed by a Mr. Crisp. A letter dated
April, 1774, begins as follows:

> I tell you what — you are a Jew — an Ebrew Jew —
> one of the line of Shylock . . .

Later, in her *Cecilia; or Memoirs of an Heiress* (1782), Miss
Burney introduces the heroine's trustee, Mr. Harrel, who
is in want of money, to a Jew, "of whose honesty he had
made undoubted trial." Another money-lender, Mr. Zackery,
appears in a subsequent scene. Of these Jews, Mr. Harrel
says:

> I dread the whole race. I have a sort of superstitious
> notion that if once I get into their clutches, I shall never
> be my own man again.

Throughout the novel, Mr. Zackery is represented as a sordid usurer who stands for the whole Jewish people; and "Honest Old Aaron" is the exception which proves the rule. All other Jews are rascals and extortioners. As Dr. Van der Veen in his analysis of Fanny Burney's work points out, these extraordinary views of the novelist are due more or less to literary influences of the day — in particular, to dramatists who caricatured money-lenders and impressed these stage characters during the greater part of the century on the minds of the writers of novels.

It was in 1753, the year of the passing of the Naturalization Bill, that the foremost novelist of the age, Samuel Richardson (1689–1761) produced *Sir Charles Grandison*, a novel in which Solomon Merceda, a profligate Jew, appears in Letter XXXV. The description of Merceda is not lacking in the details of horror usually supplied by the stage. He is a mysterious creature, of whom little is known, and very rich, or else he could not move in aristocratic circles. Being a Portuguese, he speaks English with a foreign accent, and is diabolically wicked. It is probable that Richardson remembered the despicable Jewish character that appeared five years before in Smollett's *Roderick Random*. In his first two novels, Richardson had no Jewish characters, and it is likely that he received a hint or two from Smollett's vigorous presentation of profligate Jews, for the creation of Mr. Merceda.

In the novels of Tobias Smollett (1721–1771), there is much attention paid to the Jews. Starting with *The Adventures of Roderick Random* (1748), the novelist creates a money-broker, Isaac Rapine, and a nameless Jew who is associated with a gaming-house. In the company of Isaac is a girl about town, who addresses the following words to him:

> Let us be sociable and merry — what do you say, Isaac? Is not this a good notion, you doting rogue? Speak, you old cent-per-cent fornicator. What desperate debt are you thinking of? What mortgage are you planning? Well, Isaac, positively, you shall never gain my favor till you turn over a new leaf, grow honest and live like a gentleman. In the meantime, give me a kiss, you old fumbler.

In his next novel, *Peregrine Pickle* (1751), Smollett portrays another Jew, a Rotterdam merchant, who, says the novelist, "unbended his aspect into a grin that was truly Israelitish." In this work, too, we notice the first appearance of the Jewess in the eighteenth century novel. We learn that Peregrine, thinking that he was courting Emilia, a Christian girl of charm and character, was, in reality, pursuing the only daughter of a rich Jew, who, later in the story, like Shakespeare's Jessica, elopes with a Christian apprentice.

Smollett seems to have relented his brutal treatment of Jewish characters, and, in *The Adventures of Count Fathom* (1753) made bold to produce what is definitely a benevolent and munificent Israelite. Dr. Van der Veen calls our attention to the fact that it is a strange coincidence that the year which witnessed the introduction of the so-called Jew Bill, was also the one in which the first pleasant words were expressed in literature for the Jews in England. In the story, Count Fathom's friend, Melvil, who has applied in vain to his Christian friends for financial aid, says in despair:

Since we have nothing to expect from the favor of Christians, let us have recourse to the descendants of Judah.
Though they lay under the general reproach of nations,
as a people dead to virtue and benevolence, and wholly
devoted to avarice, fraud and extortion, the most savage
of the tribe cannot treat me with more barbarity than
I have experienced among those who are the authors
of their reproach.

Melvil and Fathom go to the home of a rich Spanish Jew,
whose voice and face are repulsive, at first, but whose kind
heart is soon moved by Melvil's situation. Without much
hesitation, Joshua Manasseh, as the Jew is called, advances
the necessary money, refusing to take one farthing of interest.
Later, it is discovered that the "honest Hebrew," as he is
often styled, has been generous to a wide circle of men —
Jews and Gentiles alike. It is evident that in creating Manasseh, Smollett has exaggerated the Jew's munificence to
a ludicrous extreme. Manasseh is just as impossible as a
sentimentally good Jew, as Isaac Rapine is impossible as
an avaricious villain of a Jew.

The question is naturally asked, why did Smollett have
a change of heart with respect to the portrayal of the Jewish
character? Was it due to the influence of such Jews as
Sampson Gideon, who voluntarily served the country
during the financial and political panic of 1754, by raising
loans for the support of the government and by averting
a run on the Bank of England? For these generous services,
the Whig government, it will be remembered, introduced the
Jewish Naturalization Bill, which raised a storm of protest
stimulated by the Tories, against the Jews. It is probable
that Smollett, who was a Whig himself, favored the Whig
bill and became convinced that he had wronged the Jews

in his earlier novels. In order to make amends, therefore, he set before his readers a new character, named after Manasseh ben Israel, the famous Portuguese Jew of Amsterdam, whose noble qualities of mind and character had won for him the respect of Cromwell and his court. Just as Manasseh, a century before, had pleaded for the admission of the Jews into the Commonwealth of England at the Whitehall Conference (Vide Chapter III), even so Joshua Manasseh makes an effort to plead for the admission of the Jews into the hearts of Smollett's contemporaries.

Another possible reason for Smollett's new attitude may be found in the *History of the Swedish Countess of Guildenstern* by C. F. Gellert, professor at the University of Leipzig, published in 1752, the year before the appearance of *Count Fathom*. In this epistolary novel, Gellert narrates the adventures of Count G, who, in the course of a military campaign, is taken prisoner by the Russians and sent to Siberia. Here he saves the life of a Polish Jew, who, out of gratitude, befriends the count for the rest of his life. The Jew is described as a pious old man of venerable appearance and of a kind, honest, unselfish and true-hearted character. The similarity of portrayal by Gellert and Smollett is clearly seen in the close resemblance, item by item, between the Polish Jew and Joshua Manasseh. Both Jews are sentimental, they deliver letters for the persons whom they befriend, and in both stories the figure 10,000 is recorded in connection with a wedding-gift.

Other references to Jews by Smollett are to be found in the adventures of *Sir Launcelot Greaves* (1762), in which Mr. Isaac Vanderpelft, "a stock-jobber of foreign extract, not without a mixture of Hebrew blood, immensely rich," is a sort of boastful stump-orator; in *Travels Through France and Italy* (1765), in which the author observes that "the Jews are the least of any people that I know addicted to a military life;" and in *Humphrey Clinker* (1770), a novel in which Mr. Wilson, a strolling player, disguised as a Jewish peddler, gains admission to his sweetheart, and is referred to by the lady's brother as "that rascally Jew." In these harsh descriptions we notice Smollett's return to the prejudices of his earlier works. It is reported that between the years 1753 and 1756 the novelist experienced severe financial distress which may have brought him into contact with Jewish brokers and money-lenders. These experiences, in addition to the disappointment over the failure of the Jewish Naturalization Act in 1754, may have had something to do with his reactionary attitude.

Two other novelists of this period provide us with a variety of references to the Jew in eighteenth century England: Henry Fielding (1707–1754), and Laurence Sterne (1713–1768). Both writers are as uncomplimentary as Defoe and Swift.

In Fielding's *History of Joseph Andrews* (1742), Parson Adams, after an adventure in an alehouse, observes that he "almost began to suspect that he was sojourning in a country inhabited only by Jews and Turks." Since there are neither Jews nor Turks among the characters in the novel, the expression must be taken as a term of abuse in the sense of "villains and scoundrels." Jews are mentioned in *An Enquiry into the Causes of the Late Increase of Robbers*, as receivers of stolen goods; and in *A Journey from this World to the Next* (1743), in the person of Julian the Apostate who returns to this earth as an avaricious Jew named Balthazar; and in the posthumous *Journal of a Voyage to Lisbon* (1755), in the character of a celebrated Jew who —

when filled with Calipash and Calipee, goes contentedly home to tell his money, and expects no more pleasure from his throat during the next twenty-four hours.

One might be pardoned for expecting Henry Fielding, at least, to say something more about contemporary Jews. As magistrate and man about town, he had the opportunity of meeting with a greater variety of London characters than either Richardson or Sterne. However, he includes no full-length portraits of Jews in his panoramic surveys of English life, and is as silent on the subject of the Jewish problem as are the other major novelists of the period.

Sterne, in one of his sermons, entitled *The Ingratitude of Israel*, smugly uses the arrogance and disobedience of the ancient race as a case in history, to point a moral and adorn his pulpit discourse. He says:

A people with so many testimonies of God's favor, who had not profited thereby so as to become a virtuous people, must have been utterly corrupt; and so they were ... Doubtless there is no nation which ever had so many extraordinary reasons and supernatural motives to become thankful and virtuous as the Jews had ...

In *The Life and Opinions of Tristram Shandy* (1759–1765), the novelist says, with reference to Tristram,

Never was the son of a Jew, Christian, Turk or Infidel initiated into the religious rites in so oblique and slovenly a manner,

and repeats the idea in a couplet in chapter CCLXX,

A devil 'tis — and mischief such doth work
As never yet did Pagan, Jew or Turk.

In a later chapter, there is the story of Corporal Trim's brother and the Jew's widow at Lisbon. The fact that Sterne makes a Jew's widow the heroine of a disgraceful episode, does not leave the reader in doubt as to the novelist's opinion of the Jewish people — an opinion borne out by an observation in the same author's *Sentimental Journey through France and Italy* (1768):

> I looked at Monsieur Desslin through and through — eyed him as he walked along in profile — then his face — thought he looked like a Jew — then a Turk — disliked his wig — cursed him by the gods — wished him at the Devil!

We have already noticed the oft-repeated association of Jew and Turk in the writings of Swift, and now it appears in a paragraph by Sterne. The phrase "Jews, Turks, Infidels and Heretics" was familiar to most churchmen since it appeared in the Book of Common Prayer, and in the Collects for Good Friday. As early as 1601, in *Jacke Drum's Entertainment*, a character in the drama calls out "Villains, Rogues, Jews, Turks, Infidels!", and a century later, in George Granville's *Jew of Venice* (1701), Gratiano says:

> Jew, Turk and Christian differ but in creed;
> In ways of wickedness, they're all agreed.

At the very beginning of the century, the Jew filled a conspicuous place as a character in drama, making his debut in Granville's comedy of *The Jew of Venice*, at Lincoln's Inn Fields, May, 1701. The theme is a re-working of Shakespeare's tragi-comedy. Shylock the Jew lends money to Antonio, a merchant, and, when the money is not returned in due time, the Jew demands his bond —

a pound of flesh from the Christian merchant's body, nearest the heart. Ultimately, the Jew is defeated. Granville, in making changes in the *dramatis personae*, omits the character of Tubal, "another of the tribe" and friend of Shylock, thus cutting out the possibility of the humorous scene between the two Jews, wherein Tubal's double news about Antonio's lost argosy and Shylock's lost jewels produce a laughable conflict between grief and joy in Shylock's conversation. In an effort to be original, Granville devises an innovation: in a banquet scene, Bassanio and Antonio are placed at one table, and Shylock by himself at a separate table. Both boards are covered with food and drink. After Antonio toasts his dear friend Bassanio, who in turn drinks to the health of his charming Portia, Shylock rises to propose the following toast:

> I have a mistress that outshines 'em all —
> Commanding yours — and yours tho' the whole sex;
> O may her charms encrease and multiply;
> My money is my mistress! Here's to
> Interest upon interest!

Granville's Jew is beyond all question a caricature of Shylock. It is probable that, taking a hint from Dryden's *Love Triumphant*, in which play a Jew appears as the laughing stock of the audience, Granville turned Shakespeare's tragic Jew into an object of general derision. Granville's own feeling towards the Jews is expressed in the Prologue:

> To-day we punish a stock-jobbing Jew.
> A piece of Justice, terrible and strange;
> Which, if pursued, would make a thin Exchange.
> The law's defect the juster Muse supplies,
> 'Tis only we can make you good and wise,
> Whom Heaven spares, the Poet will chastise.

In this play, even the Jew's daughter ridicules the Jew. She says:

> Shut doors after you; fast bind, fast find,
> These were his last words; Thus I avoid the
> Curse of disobedience! Be thou shut till I
> Open thee —

and, later, holding up a bag of gold, says to Lorenzo with whom she elopes:

> So whilst old Laban snored in Bed,
> Jack with sprightly Rachel fled.
> His gold and gems and price they took,
> And eke the flower of every flock.

Among other early dramas in which slight attention is paid to the Jew may be mentioned Theophilus Cibber's *The Harlot's Progress* (1733), Fielding's *Miss Lucy in Town* (1742), and two anonymous works, *The Jew Decoyed* (1735) and *The Jerusalem Infirmary* (1749).

Cibber's *Harlot's Progress*, in which the vicissitudes of a country girl are described, was a play inspired by the famous series of engravings by William Hogarth, entitled "A Harlot's Progress" (1733). Kitty, the country girl, arrives in town and becomes the mistress of a rich Jew, Beau Mordecai. Throughout the play, the dramatist vilifies the Jew, whose character is more objectionably treated by Cibber than by Hogarth.

Hogarth's description of the Jew also inspired the anonymous author of the ballad opera, *The Jew Decoyed*, who acknowledges his source in the Prologue:

> From the keen satyr in sly Hogarth's prints
> We own we took for most that follows — hints.

The Jew in the play goes by the name of Manasseh ben Israel, which is a slander on the character of the beloved Rabbi Manasseh who pleaded the cause of the English Jews before Cromwell. After Moll, the girl in the play, has been debauched by Colonel Goatish and Squire Spruce, she becomes the mistress of the Jew, who is introduced to the audience in the following words:

> At last, of Israel's scattered race there came
> A wealthy lover, welcome to the dame.
> Gold soon prevailed — vain was old Lurewell's weeping,
> The Jew she hated, but was fond of keeping;
> Manasseh had her — at a price how dear!
> Will quickly from the following scene appear.

A new development is noticed in the fact that this stage-Jew cannot speak English very well. A so-called Jewish dialect is used as a new means to ridicule the character. When Manasseh says "Dis is my watch; I vil swear dat, Mr. Justice," he is introducing a style of "gibberish" that is to have a long run on the English stage.

Another play influenced by Hogarth's engravings is Fielding's *Miss Lucy in Town*, a farce with songs. The Jew in the play, Zorababel, is a highly offensive creature who patronizes Mrs. Midnight's house of ill fame. Strangely enough, this same character appears also in Joseph Reed's two-act farce, *The Register Office* (1761) with the name Zorobabel Habakuk, and is engaged in the same business of patronizing brothels.

During the agitation caused by the debates in Parliament on the Jewish Naturalization Bill, the Jews were the subject of considerable ridicule and satire on the stage. The name of Charles Macklin (1697?–1797), actor and playright, is associated with a series of plays in which Jewish characters

were presented. In 1738, he played the part of Beau Mordecai in the *Harlot's Progress* and three years later gave a
masterly treatment of Shylock in the *Merchant of Venice*.
In 1742, he personated Zorobabel in *Miss Lucy in Town*.
As a dramatist, he is of interest to us as the author of *Love
à la Mode* (1759), a farce in two acts, in which a foppish
Jew, Beau Mordecai, is reviled and teased by the rest of
the characters. The Jew is taunted by such expressions as:
"my chield o' circumcision," and "my bonny Eesraelite."
Sir Archy MacSarcasm, the haughty and avaricious Scotch
Knight, is frequently exploding with uncomplimentary
sentiments. He complains to Charlotte, the beautiful ward
of Sir Theodore Goodchild:

> What a fantastical baboon this Eesraelite makes o' him-
> sel'! The fallow is the mockery o' the hale nation . . .
> O! yes, he is ridiculous, therefore very usefu' in society;
> for wherever he comes, there maun be laughter . . . the
> fallow's walthy, 'tis true; yes, yes, he is walthy, but he
> is a reptile — a mere reptile! . . .

Nor is the Jew spared by the Irishman, Sir Callaghan, who
regards Mordecai as "a very impertinent coxcomb."

Contemptuous nicknames show the attitude of this
particular cross-section of British society for the Jew.
The drunken squire calls Mordecai "little Shadrach," and
Sir Archy speaks of him as "the Moabite," and the like.
These ungracious epithets are more or less justified by the
sort of Jew Mordecai turns out to be. He is an insufferable
dandy, and certainly a disgrace to his people. No doubt
the presentation of such a ridiculous character indicates the
dramatist's own feeling toward the contemporary Jew. It
is reported by *The Connoisseur* of January 31, 1754, that

Macklin, in order to be better equipped for the presentation of Shylock, "made daily visits to the center of business, the 'Change and the adjacent coffee-houses, in order that, by a frequent intercourse and conversation with the unfore-skinned race, he might habituate himself to their air and deportment." Macklin produced another play, *Man of the World* (1781), in which the Jew again appears in an un-favorable light; and one is led to believe that to the very end of his days, the old actor-dramatist allowed himself to be carried away by his hatred of the Jews and also tried to prejudice his audience against them.

Like Macklin, in his animosity towards the Jew, was Macklin's friend, Samuel Foote (1720–1777), who intro-duces into his plays a satirical treatment of the contem-porary scene and includes the Jew as a ridiculous figure in the passing show. In one of his earliest plays, *Taste* (1752), Foote presents a Jew broker, named Mordecai Lazarus, in connection with an auction scene; in *The Mirror* (1760) there is casual reference to a money-lender, Nebuched-nezzar Zebulon; and in *The Commissary* (1765), there is a Jewish broker, Mr. Abednego Potiphar, and frequent use of the expression "as rich as a Jew." The appearance of Jewish physicians in English society is noted in *The Devil upon Two Sticks* (1768), in which Dr. Habakkuk, who abhors hogs' pudding and observes the Sabbath, loves money and shares dishonor and ill-favor with a Quaker doctor, Melchisedech Broadbrim. Two Jewish brokers, Moses Mendoza and Nathan, are included in *The Nabob* (1772), a comedy in which Foote satirizes Englishmen who return from India with fabulous wealth which they squander in riotous living. The Nabob in the play is Sir Matthew

Mite whose arrogant, blustering and profligate behavior attracts all sorts of fawning and cringing parasites, among whom are the two gibberish-speaking Jewish brokers.

Another Hebrew broker, Moses Manasses, is introduced in Foote's *The Cozeners*, giving one the preposterous idea that in the second half of the century London teemed with Jewish brokers of questionable reputation. Moses Manasses engages in business with two cozeners: an unscrupulous woman named Mrs. Fleece'em and her unprincipled lawyer, Mr. Flaw, with a view to entering society, or "to get into de Boodles, de Almacks, or von of de clubs."

The outstanding playwright of the latter part of the century is without question the Irishman, Richard Brinsley Sheridan (1751–1816), who is chiefly remembered for *The Rivals*, *The Critic*, *The Duenna*, and *The School for Scandal*. In the last two plays, Jewish characters are introduced. The rich Jew, Isaac Mendoza, in *The Duenna* (1775), is a well-drawn character portrayed with all the prejudice current in that day. Don Jerome, a Spanish nobleman living at Seville, desires his daughter, the beautiful Donna Louisa, to marry the Jew. When the girl refuses, the irate father swears never to speak to his daughter again till she obeys him, and puts her under lock and key. Disguised in the dress of her guardian, the Duenna, Donna Louisa makes her escape. When Isaac calls, he is received by the ugly and aged Duenna, who in the dress of Donna Louisa, takes the heroine's place and woos the Jew. " 'Tis well my affections are fixed on her fortune, and not her person," says the deceived Israelite. The more she flatters him the less ugly she becomes in his eyes. He even thinks that there is something pleasing in the tone of her voice when she flatters him. Shortly, the Jew is so overcome by her flattery that he carries the Duenna off. After the marriage, however, the unhappy Jew discovers that the Duenna has no dowry. She who had flattered him, now calls him, "a little insignificant reptile!" The frequent references to "little Isaac," and "little Hebrew scoundrel," denote that Sheridan's Jew was of small stature — one of the stock characteristics of the eighteenth century Jew.

In *The School for Scandal* (1777), Sheridan presents his second Jewish character, Moses, a broker, who is described as a friendly Jew. After an absence of fifteen years, Sir Oliver Surface, the rich and childless uncle of two dissipated and extravagant young men, returns from India; and, hearing many things about his nephews, who do not know him, he resolves "to make a trial of their hearts." To this end, he secures the assistance of Moses, who instructs the Knight in the practice of usury. All in all, the dramatist deals kindly with the Jew's character in this play, and such expressions as "a friendly Jew" and "the honest Israelite" may indicate a change of opinion on Sheridan's part toward Jewish brokers.

Another great name in the English theater of the times should be mentioned in this connection. David Garrick (1716–1779), evidently inspired by the success of contemporary plays with Jewish characters, produced a farce, *Lettre* (1740), to which he added, in 1777, the figure of an ungrateful Jew, for the entertainment of a distinguished audience. The Jew in this play was received as "an excellent new character," although, in proving to be a miscreant who ill-treats a benefactor, he behaves in the conventional manner of the unlovable stage-Jew of the Elizabethan period.

During the last decades of the eighteenth century, to

which Dr. Van der Veen refers as "the heyday of the Jew drama," several such plays were produced but not published. Among them were the following: *The Contrast, or The Jew and the Courtesan* (1775); *Moses and Shadrac, or A Specimen of Jewish Education* (1780); *The Israelites* (1785); *The Fair Refuge, or, The Rival Jews* (1785); *A Specimen of Jewish Courtship* (1787); *The Diamond Ring, or The Jew Outwitted* (1788); *Mordecai's Beard* (1790); and *The Jew and the Gentile* (1795).

From the old Jewish calendars of the coaching days, periodical publications which provided Jewish communities with lists of fares, the distances between provincial towns, prognostications of the weather, and the like, we judge that contemporary society had little or no toleration for the itinerant Jews. The poor Jew was treated no more sympathetically than the rich one. These calendars provide us with some idea of the operations of the increasing number of Jewish peddlers. Thus we are told that these traders had connections wherever dockyards were situated, and had a monopoly of the itinerant jewelry business.

In the latter part of the seventeenth century, there was a steady increase in the ranks of English Jewry, brought about by the immigration of German and Polish Jews who were driven from their homes by the Thirty Years War. A horde of peddlers and petty traders from the Rhine countries, about 20,000 of them, mostly very poor, flocked into London, and composed the bulk of that section of English Jewry commonly known as the Ashkenazim. Apart from a few wealthy merchant-families, like the Goldsmids, the Ashkenazic element consisted of a large number of hawkers and petty traders and old-clothes men.

To a great many people in the latter part of the eighteenth century, the old-clothes man, in his long gaberdine and grizzly beard, was a familiar figure. His trade was a branch of business much more important then than in the nineteenth century, because, according to Sir Walter Besant, "women did not wear calicoes and things that could be washed, but thick quilted petticoats and gowns of stuff; men wore wigs which lasted a long time, and costly coats and small clothes of velvet, silk and finely-embroidered stuff. At death, these things, unless they were left by special bequest, were generally sold to the itinerant old-clo' man, and taken off to Monmouth Street; there to be got up again almost as good as new." As the foreign-looking, quaintly-attired old-clo' man passed through the villages, he seemed to invite attention to himself and proclaim the fact that he was there to be made fun of. It was considered good sport among schoolboys to pelt "the old Jew" with over-ripe fruit, and even barbarously maltreat him in the principal streets.

In the 'eighties, the Jewish community came in for considerable publicity through the "eccentric behaviour" of Lord George Gordon, younger son of the Duke of Gordon. In 1780, the young lord led the so-called Gordon Riots, as a result of which twenty-five offenders were executed, among them being a certain Jew named Samuel Solomons. Lord George Gordon himself was arrested on high treason, committed to the Tower, tried for his life, and ultimately acquitted. Shortly after, however, he once again became the center of popular attention by openly confessing a love for the Jews, and by becoming a member of the Jewish faith in 1787. His lordship's conversion became the occasion for all kinds of humorous thrusts, not only at "the Christian turned Jew," but at the entire Jewish brotherhood in London.

At this point, the story of Daniel Mendoza should be told, a Spanish Jew, who became the champion prize-fighter of the day. For, strangely enough, it was through the exploits of this "Light of Israel," as he was called by his admirers, that the Jewish community were able to "redeem themselves" in the eyes of the British public and win favorable notice. Those were the days when men boxed with bare knuckles and under Broughton rules. Among those who cheered for the Jew was the Prince of Wales, later George IV. At a memorable match, arranged by the heir to the throne, Mendoza met and defeated Martin, the "Bath Butcher". Over five thousand people from all parts of the country witnessed the champion bruiser of the Israelites "pitch into Martin" and "finish him off in quick time", much to the delight of the Prince, who shook Mendoza's hand and gave him 500 pounds in addition to the money the victor realized by betting on himself. Mendoza's sudden rise to wealth, royal patronage, and championship, brought great credit to English Jewry. His greatest achievement followed, when, in 1789, he defeated Humphries, the Champion of England.

It is believed that the example set by Mendoza stimulated an interest in boxing among the boys and young men of English Jewry. Sir Walter Besant has the following interesting story to tell about this innovation in Jewish life:

One day, I know not where or when, at the accustomed yell of hooting, and at the familiar whizzing of the rotten eggs about his ears, the Old Clo' man turned upon his adversaries, selected the Christian who was the strongest and the most energetic, invited him to take off his coat and have it out; and proceeded to show that Christian a little of the dexterity of his compatriot, Mendoza.

Throughout the centuries before the French Revolution, the underlying principle of Judaism emphasized the temporary character of the dispersion of God's Chosen People. The restoration of the national Jewish polity was a fond dream that might be expected to materialize at any moment. Moreover, the Jews were not made to feel that they were an integral part of the state or country in which they happened to live. On the contrary, they were considered a distinct and compact unit, separated not merely by religion, but also by social and national character. But, after their admission to French citizenship in 1791, the Jews began to see themselves in a new light. No longer were they temporary sojourners; now they were permanent citizens with a permanent abode, and with permanent interests in the home of their adoption.

This was true not only in France, but in England as well. The Jews of the younger generation, although their fathers and grandfathers had come from abroad, felt themselves as much entitled to be called true-born Englishmen as were the grandchildren of George I. England was their home, the only home they knew. The new philosophy of the French Revolution, with its emphasis on the rights of man, was gradually paving the way for change of public opinion; and it is possible to note the beginnings of a new life manifesting itself in the spirit and temper of the younger generation of English Jews.

From the sermons preached by the *Rav* or Chief Rabbi, Hart Lyon, at the Great Synagogue, Duke's Place (1756–

1763), one catches glimpses of the changes affecting the economic and social life of at least one section of English Jewry. The preacher seems much disturbed by the fact that Jews of the Ashkenazic community are rapidly adopting the manners of the gentiles. The synagogue worshipers shave their beards, visit the theaters and operas, waste time at cards in the coffee-houses, and even keep the Christian feasts to the neglect of their own. Lifting his voice in warning against mixed marriages, the Rabbi declares:

> The children of a non-Jewish wife are sure to become Christian, and although the non-Jews of our own day cannot be regarded as heathen, still they are in the category of *ger toshab* (literally, a settled stranger), one outside the Covenant of Abraham; and they have not taken upon themselves the observation of the Torah and its precepts (*mizwot*). To marry a non-Jewess is, therefore, tantamount to abandoning the faith, even if she should become a Jewess.

In the matter of Sabbath observance, the Rabbi says that not only do Jews cook meals on the holy day, but they are even in the habit of gathering together before the post-office on Sabbath mornings and having their letters opened for them by non-Jews. Of the Jewish women, the preacher complains that they wear wigs and décolleté dresses, open two spans low in front and back, and that "their sole aim is not to appear like daughters of Israel."

In the following chapters, we shall follow the changes after 1800, in social relationships and political adjustments as they affected the Jews in England, and show the reflection of these changes in the fiction produced in England from 1800 to 1900.

CHAPTER V

THE DAWN OF A NEW ERA: 1800–1833

At the opening of the nineteenth century there were in England about eight thousand men, women and children of Jewish origin. Their status was that of aliens, because, although according to the common law every person born within the dominion of the Crown is a British subject, the Jews were precluded by special laws from exercising most of the privileges of citizenship. The Corporation and Test Acts, which obliged all persons desiring to hold corporate office to take the sacrament in accordance with the rites of the Established Church of England, and the form of the required oath, "On the true faith of a Christian," effectually excluded the Jews from public office. They were barred from the House of Commons, restricted in the professions, and politically ostracized.

Yet, in spite of their civil and political disabilities, the English Jews, as a whole, seemed to regard themselves as better off under the British flag than they would have been elsewhere. They were permitted to live after their own style, to worship in their own synagogues, and to think their own thoughts in peace and security. No particular dress was enjoined on them by law, nor, indeed, was any such mark of distinction necessary. They were sufficiently distinguished from the rest of the population by manners and habits peculiar to the community to which they belonged.

It may be well at this point to observe that, although to the average Englishman in the first quarter of the century all Jews were alike, there were two distinct communities in English Jewry: the *Sephardim*, made up of Jews whose ancestors had come to England in the middle of the seventeenth century from Spain and Portugal; and the *Ashkenazim*, made up of Jews who, driven from their homes in Germany and Poland in the latter part of the seventeenth century, had found a refuge in this comparatively tolerant country. The members of these communities were unlike each other, not only in language and culture, but also in stature, features and complexion. The two groups kept apart from each other, praying in separate synagogues, and using somewhat different rituals. The Sephardic congregation, representing class-conscious families of wealth and culture, maintained a dignity suitable to the position of merchants and bankers in good standing in London and the larger industrial centers, and worshiped in the Bevis Marks Synagogue. They considered themselves superior to the Ashkenazim, who had but recently arrived from the foul ghettos of central Europe, and whose place of worship was the Duke Place, or Great Synagogue, opened in 1722.

The Jewish population was considerably increased within the first decade of the century by an extensive immigration of merchants and their dependents from Holland and the Rhine region, many of whom, no doubt, came on the recommendation of the Jews who were already doing fairly well in England. Gradually the numbers grew from 8,000 to 12,000; and at the end of the period under review, it was estimated that the number of Jews reached the total of 27,000.

In popular conception, the Jewish quarter in London — the region bounded to the north by High Street, Spitalfields; to the east by Middlesex Street, commonly called Petticoat Lane; to the south by Leadenhall Street, Aldgate, and the end of Whitechapel; and to the west by Bishopsgate — must have seemed to be the new Jerusalem. Here nothing was to be seen, above, below, and around, but Jewish physiognomies, Jewish homes, and Jewish occupations. Within this modern ghetto there were of course all classes and conditions of men: some perhaps were more Jewish than others, showing no tendency toward the assimilation of English manners; while others were rapidly taking on the coloring of their English environment. The rabbis constituted a sort of nobility in both communities, moving among the various classes as keepers of the group conscience and acting as shepherds of a peculiarly mixed flock.

Apart from a comparatively small group of cultured representatives of the Sephardim, and an even smaller number of bankers and brokers of the Ashkenazim, the bulk of the Jewish population in the chief industrial centers was composed of hundreds of small traders, petty money-lenders, stock-jobbers, peddlers and old-clothes-men. The more enterprising individuals of this class soon set themselves up as merchants, jewelers, and shop-keepers outside the city of London, and sent out their poorer coreligionists with various wares every Monday morning to the neighboring villages, to make what little they could by buying and selling in places somewhat removed from the traffic of the cities. The following statement in Robert Southey's

Don Manuel Alvarez Esperiella's Letters from England (1808), is of interest here:

> There are Jew peddlers everywhere traveling with boxes of haberdashery at their backs, cuckoo clocks, sealing-wax, quills, weather-glasses, green spectacles, clumsy figures in plaster of paris, which you see over the chimney of an alehouse parlor in the country, or miserable prints of the King and Queen, the Four Seasons, the Cardinal Virtues, the last Naval Victory, the Prodigal Son, and such like subjects; even the Nativity and the Crucifixion . . .

Every village and hamlet in the British Isles was thus penetrated by the wandering peddler and hawker, who carried in their packs the heavy watches the old squire would desire, the ring that would please his lady, the ribbons and laces that would delight the heart of the maid. They supplied the needs of the cottage and the farm, and so played their part in the general scheme of economy during the days of the Napoleonic wars, endeavoring with all energy and resourcefulness to improve their position in the land of their choice. So much for the status of the English Jews at the turn of the century.

If the population of the "ghetto" was gradually becoming Anglicized, the change was naturally much more rapid among the more favored families, the Goldsmids, the Cohens, the Levy Solomons, and the Rothschilds, who moved in the company of the social and financial aristocracy of the land. With the establishment of the powerful house of Rothschild in England in the early years of the century, the financial prestige of the Jews was greatly enhanced. The head of this great house in England was

Nathan Mayer Rothschild, who staked all his wealth and the wealth of his family on the ultimate defeat of Napoleon (1815), and won. The battle of Waterloo was indeed a brilliant triumph for the Rothschilds, a triumph earned by loyalty to the English cause through the darkest hours of a very uncertain war. After the death of Nathan Mayer, the succession of the house passed to the eldest son, Lionel, whose interest in both English and Jewish institutions was manifested by his philanthropies. Lionel Rothschild was limited by no petty prejudices; he gave liberally to all, irrespective of class or creed. His London mansion and famous country home at Gunnersbury Park, which had formerly been the country place of Princess Amelie, the aunt of George III, became centers for the society of the mid-Victorian era. Everyone of consequence — princes, ambassadors, bishops, statesmen, men of letters — came to the great Jew's home. Disraeli owned Lionel Rothschild as one of the friendliest men he ever knew, and used him as the model for the Adrian of his *Endymion*, the brilliant character who combines financial genius with culture and ambition. Lionel Rothschild's social position was further strengthened by the skill with which his brothers, Mayer and Anthony, made themselves popular in English society through their love of art and sports, the latter being a truly English predilection.

It was a matter of general observation that the relationship between the English aristocracy and the wealthier members of the Jewish community was mutually cordial and profitable. Wealthy Jews mingled freely in the higher circles and were warmly received in the homes of the leaders in politics, letters, art and music of the day. The Duke of

Sussex, who had studied Hebrew under the Rev. Salomon Lyon of Cambridge, was hailed by his friend, Rabbi Hirschell, as "the friend of Israel and the zealous patron of justice, humanity and liberality." The diaries of both Sir Moses and Lady Montefiore reveal an intimate and friendly relationship with the leading English families. Friendly dinners and entertainments were frequently exchanged between Jew and gentile for the purpose of affording friends of religious and civil liberty an opportunity to set forth their views.

We have already had occasion to note (Ch. IV.) the beginning of a secession movement from Judaism to Christianity on the part of some of the leading Jewish families after the failure of the Jewish Emancipation Bill of 1753. When Sampson Gideon, the head of the Jewish community in the latter part of the 18th century, determined to bring up his children as Christians, he set an example which was followed by many of the chief Jewish families during the remainder of the 18th century and the early years of the 19th. The wealthy classes found that as Jews they could not satisfy their social and political aspirations. They saw, too, that conversion to Christianity would remove the obstructions which made their position intolerable. So a number of prominent families, the Bernals, the Lopezes, the Riccardos, the D'Israelis, the Aguilars, the Besavis, and the Samudas, for instance, severed their connection with the Synagogue, and allowed their children to grow up without any religion, or in the Established Church. In the main, these secessions arose not from religious conviction, but from social and personal causes. It is significant to note that the approximation of the manners and habits of many of these households to the English character and habits had already been so complete that many individuals found no difficulty in putting society before religion.

There were, of course, causes other than ambition that led to secession from Judaism. Marriage into Christian families was more common among the Sephardim than among the Ashkenazim; the way for such unions being easily opened by the wealth which the Jews were known to possess. The children of Christian mothers and Jewish fathers invariably adopted the maternal surname and religion, and became part of the Christian population. Through this process many an ancient Jewish family was absorbed by the English order.

Another cause for the secession of influential families was the strictness of synagogue discipline, especially among the Sephardim. This was a contributing cause to the withdrawal of Isaac D'Israeli, whose son, Benjamin, was baptized into the Anglican fold, and remained a conforming Christian all his life. Furthermore, the practice of sending Jewish children to mission and public schools, where the influence of Christian thought and manners was sure to impress the young mind, led ultimately to a change in many a Jewish household. There is no doubt that the part played by the Christian Jews of the better class, as they moved among Jews and Christians alike, helped gradually to modify the extreme opinions that had prevailed in both circles.

A different type of religious conversion was brought about through the efforts of the Evangelicals. The mania for conversion and baptism that spread over Europe in the first quarter of the nineteenth century was one of the manifestations of the emotional revival that followed the wars and revolutions of the century before. A new puritanism took possession of certain Christian communities, first among the newly-organized Methodists of the Nonconformist group, and then among the Anglicans. Earnest leaders of the movement held to the doctrine that all professions of Christianity were worthless unless accompanied by a new zeal for the extension of God's kingdom on earth through the conversion of non-Christians. Thus the winning of souls to the Christian faith became the dominating purpose of religious work. What might be regarded as a clarion call in behalf of the Jews in England was sounded in 1802 by the Rev. Dr. John Mackenzie, minister of Portpatrick, who in the eighth of his published sermons, made a vigorous appeal (*British Critic*, XX, 600):

> Let us remember that once favored people, who were the means of enlightening us. Let us study their important history and give due merit to their policy. Let us also remember them in our prayers. As they were the means of our improvement, may we be the means of theirs . . . . They are the Israelites. To them pertained the adoption and the glory and the Covenant. Theirs was the giving of the Law, the Service and the Promises. Theirs were the Fathers, and of them sprang the Messiah. Ah! once happy people! Ah! favored nation! What vicissitudes have been yours!

In the summer of 1806, evangelical work among the Jews was further stimulated by the announcement that the rapid succession of events brought about by the changes of industry at home and by the Napoleonic wars on the continent, had

> authorized the expectation of the near accomplishment of prophecy; and the time has come for the Christian world to consider the present state of the Jews . . .

The spiritual welfare of the Jews became the special concern of the London Society for Promoting Christianity among Jews, founded in 1807, and, whatever the success of these zealous missionaries in winning converts from Judaism may have been, their work expedited the infiltration of sympathy for the Jews into the Christian community.

Obviously, the increased social contact between the two groups which we have observed in the higher circles through the intermingling of eminent Jewish families with the British aristocracy, and in the "ghetto" through the religious and educational work done by Jews and some non-Jews, tended to break down English as well as Jewish prejudice, and to awaken among the English people an interest in, and sympathy for, the hitherto misunderstood group. For the concrete expression of such interest and sympathy, the times were propitious. Humanitarianism was, so to speak, in the air. The economic forces that were released by the rapid changes from agricultural to industrial occupations, and the far-reaching social changes wrought by these transformations had made social and political reform an imperative necessity. The public conscience was deeply stirred by the clamor for recognition of thousands of hitherto unrecognized and neglected human beings.

The Humanitarian movement, founded on the instinct of compassion, and chiefly interested in the prevention of cruelty and wrong-doing, attempted to educate and organize public opinion in favor of social justice. Increasing attention was given to the claims of the masses as against those of the privileged few. The abolition of slavery under the British flag (1807) was but "another manifestation of the growing belief in the value and dignity of the individual human soul," and other abuses as degrading as black slavery called for drastic treatment. There was a spreading interest in factory reform, led by Lord Ashley; in prison improvement, under the inspiration of John Howard and Elizabeth Fry; and in reform of the criminal code, led by Romilly and Mackintosh. The humanitarian interest in legislative reform was closely allied with the political movements for the extension of the franchise to the masses; and both were bound up in the religious revival referred to in preceding paragraphs. Several humanitarian projects which under less favorable conditions had failed, or only partially succeeded, were now to be revived, and among them that of Jewish emancipation. For an eventually favorable consideration of this project, humanitarianism was helping to prepare the way.

There were economic causes, too, for the development of a more just attitude towards the Jews. The necessity of earning a living in the only way left open to them, had, as we have seen, put the English Jews in the exchange business and behind the bargain counter. The bulk of the Jewish population were engaged in petty trading, in peddling and hawking from village to village. A smaller number earned whatever they could in stock-jobbing and money-lending. A very small proportion of the remainder, representing the wealthy and cultured families, prospered as bankers and financiers. However, the general impression was that all Jews were clever in the handling of money and capable of driving a hard bargain.

At the time when Napoleon attempted to exclude English merchandise from the European markets, the Jewish traders and merchants in England are reported to have availed themselves of the opportunity offered by the quick changes in commerce and finance, and even to have carried on an extensive contraband traffic, alike profitable to themselves and to the English manufacturers. During the brief period of wild speculation and industrial prosperity (1812–1815), there was considerable competition between English bankers and the Jewish stock-jobbers who came into the open market. At one time the Quakers were numerous in both stock-jobbing and stock-broking; but their numbers soon diminished and they were replaced on the Exchange by a number of more enterprising Jews.

The rise of the House of Rothschild in England is inextricably intertwined with the history of the Jewish banking of the 19th century. The London firm was reported to have undertaken loans amounting to 21,800,000 pounds between 1815 and 1818, of which the loans to Great Britain alone amounted to 12,000,000 pounds in 1819. It is little wonder that the members of this and other Jewish families of great wealth were able to mingle freely in the higher literary, artistic and political circles of the realm.

However, a dark side to Jewish intimacy with the English aristocracy was rumored. It seems that the Jews were doing a thriving business to the disadvantage of the improvident aristocracy, nearly three-fourths of whose estates were reputed to be mortgaged to money-lenders. Similar reports came from army circles, where sons of the aristocracy were the shining examples of extravagance and reckless living. Charges that "our aristocracy" was "entirely at the mercy of a posse of Jew money-lenders," that the noble lords were obliged to "cringe before the Jew and fawn on him, like the veriest slaves to their tyrannical masters," were frequent. Shakespeare's Shylock did not come in for a greater share of vituperation than, at times, did the Jewish money-lender in the fashionable clubs and mess-rooms of the Regency period. Yet, though frequently denounced, the English Jew was beginning to be socially accepted.

What of the status of the Jew in English politics? Since the middle of the eighteenth century, the aristocracy of England had been the absolute rulers of the country. As far back as 1770, Burke had complained that the House of Commons, dominated by these aristocrats, was exercising control upon the people, whereas, said he, "it was designed as a control *of* the people." Lifting his voice in protest against the insidious influence of a secret cabal, the great statesman called upon the people to defeat the aims of corrupt leadership by compelling public men to pay attention to popular opinion, so that the House of Commons might again become what it ought to be, "the express image of the feelings of the nation."

Among those who had legitimate grievances against the injustice of the English parliamentary system, and clamored for urgent reform in the first quarter of the century, were the Irish Catholics. In 1800, Pitt had promised that they should have the same rights as their Protestant fellow-subjects. But, owing to the obstinacy of the king (George III) and the indecision of leaders, Pitt was unable to redeem his pledge. The matter was temporarily shelved. However, when in 1829 the Test and Corporation Acts were repealed, permitting Dissenters to hold corporate office without the necessity of taking the sacrament, the Catholics, who were still excluded from Parliament by the act of 1678 — which obliged members of both Houses to take a Protestant oath against Catholicism — resumed their old fight for political rights. After a strenuous and exciting session, the Catholic Emancipation Bill of 1829 was passed, permitting Catholics henceforth to enter all offices and participate in the Parliament of the realm.

The removal of Catholic disabilities filled the English Jews with hope in regard to their own emancipation. Naturally, they felt that if Parliament was willing to admit that the Catholic religion — so long connected with traditions of disloyalty in England, and with the rebellion in Ireland — was no longer a bar to office or a seat in Parliament, surely an extension of the franchise to the Jew would not seem so terrible a risk. But the Duke of Wellington, having made himself sufficiently unpopular by emancipating seven million Catholics, was not disposed to repeat the experiment in favor of thirty thousand Jews. Nevertheless, in 1829, soon after the passing of the Catholic Bill, a group of Liberals and certain leaders in English Jewry took steps to have the question of Jewish emancipation brought up for reconsideration before the Commons.

The first move was made by a group of liberal leaders, among whom was William Huskisson, famous as the revolutionizer of England's commercial policy, who presented a petition signed by 2,000 merchants and others of Liverpool. There were other petitions from members of the bar and from citizens of Bristol and Southwark. The movement made an auspicious start, with no signs of protest anywhere, and its success appeared to be more or less assured, especially when Sir Isaac Lyon Goldsmid secured the aid of Lord Holland, the Marquis of Lansdowne and the Duke of Sussex, in behalf of the Jewish cause.

In a short time, the Jewish emancipation question was before the House of Commons for discussion. Mr. (afterwards Sir) Robert Grant introduced a motion for permission to bring in a bill for the repeal of civil disabilities affecting British-born subjects professing the Jewish religion. The debate that followed Grant's speech was made memorable by the fact that Thomas Babington Macaulay, in supporting the motion, delivered his maiden speech in the Commons.

There was a majority of 18 in favor of the introduction of the Bill, but it was thrown out on the second reading by a majority of 228 over 165. This defeat was probably due to the political insignificance of the Jews and the lack of sufficient enthusiasm on the part of the liberal sponsors, many of whom perhaps looked upon the bill as a piece of casual legislation, even as a joke. In his famous "Noctes Ambrosianae" papers (*Blackwood's Magazine*, XXVII, 807), John Wilson ("Christopher North") hits off the situation in the following humorous dialogue:

Tickler: "What say ye, James, to the vote t'other day in Parliament about the Jews?"

Shepherd: "I hae nae objections to see a couple o' Jews in Parliament. Wull the members be made to shave, think ye, Sir? Ould cloes! Ould cloes! A' that the Hoose 'll want then, for picturesque as weel as political effeck, will be a few Blacks — here and there a negro!"

North: "Gentlemen, no politics!"

In 1832, however, the victory of the Reform Act took the control of Parliament out of the hands of the aristocracy which had dominated it so long, and put it into the hands of the middle classes; and such a victory could not but encourage the friends of Jewish emancipation. The hope was entertained that the Reformed Parliament, rising above the prejudices of the defeated aristocracy, would proceed to extend further the enfranchisement of the middle classes to include the English Jews.

Banking on the support of the Whig majority in the new Parliament, advocates of the Jewish cause again submitted the Grant Bill for parliamentary action. The Commons received it favorably. Sir Robert Peel raised his eloquent voice in its support on April 17, 1833. Said Peel:

If, as a legislature, we had authority to determine religious error, and a commission to punish religious error, it might be our painful duty to punish the Jews. But we have no such commission. If the Jews did commit an inexplicable crime nearly two thousand years ago, we have no authority given us, even if we could determine who were the descendants of the persons guilty of the crime, to visit the sins of the father upon the children, not unto the third or fourth, but unto the three-hundredth or four-hundredth generation. That awful right is not ours. I cannot, therefore, admit the right of the legislature to inflict a penalty for mere religious error.

But it was plain that there was not enough popular enthusiasm and sympathy as yet to offset the opposition of
the diehards in the Upper House. The Lords rejected the
measure by a majority of 92.

Yet many things had been accomplished by 1833, although
the Emancipation Bill had failed. In 1831, certain trade
restrictions, which had prevented any one professing the
Jewish faith from opening a shop within the limits of the
City, were removed. In 1833, Francis Henry Goldsmid, a
professing Jew, applied to the benchers of Lincoln's Inn to
be called to the Bar, and to be permitted to omit the final
words from the oath. After some discussion, Lord Campbell proposed that the application be granted, but the leader
of the Midland Circuit, representing the Tory Evangelical
view, said, "Let him become a Christian, and be d—d to
him!" Fortunately, this was not taken as a serious argument. The application was granted. The Jew was permitted
to omit the words "on the true faith of a Christian" from
the formal oath, and was unanimously called to the English
Bar. The precedent was followed by the other Inns of
Court.

Thus two tangible victories had been won by the Jews
during this period. If their other gains were more intan-
gible, they were none the less real. Their leaders had become an economic power in the kingdom; even the political
situation was far from unpromising. The growth of the
new reform spirit in politics and the swinging of the commercial interests of the rising towns into political action,
had prepared the way for the eventual enfranchisement of
the Jews. The barriers of prejudice and misunderstanding
that had separated the races for so many years were gradu-

ally crumbling. The triumph of tolerance seemed nearer than ever before.

Perhaps no type of literature reflects more clearly and directly the changes in English thought and sentiment with reference to the Jews than does that written for publication in journals, pamphlets and periodicals. The journalist, having for his immediate material the political, religious and social controversies of his day, depicts them with almost the sharpness of a photographic negative. So the changes effected in the status of the English Jews during the first thirty years of the nineteenth century by evangelicalism, by political reform, by humanitarianism, and by the commercial prosperity of the upper class Jews, did not escape the notice of the contemporary English press. Each of these movements was discussed pro and con, not once but many times.

If we are to judge by the number and the variety of essays, articles, and letters published in the early years of the century on the subject of the Jews, we may assume that the Children of Israel were regarded by most editors as a subject of growing popular interest. "In a single number of a monthly magazine published in 1810," says James Picciotto, "we find no fewer than seven papers on the subject of the Jews."

The popular attitude toward the Jew at the turn of the century is well expressed by a letter signed "Abraham Abrahams," published by Richard Cumberland in *The Observer* (1798):

> I remember to have read an account in a foreign Gazette of a dreadful fire, which broke out suddenly in a house where a great many people were assembled,

that five hundred persons perished miserably in the flames; the compiler of this account subjoins at the foot of the above melancholy article, that it is with satisfaction he can assure his readers, *all the above persons were Jews.*

These poor people seem the butt, at which all sects and persuasions level their contempt. They are sojourners and aliens in every kingdom on earth, and yet few have the hospitality to give them a welcome. I do not know any good reason why these unhappy wanderers are so treated, for they do not intrude upon the laborer or manufacturer; they do not burden the state with their poor . . .

It is to the honor of our nation, that we tolerate them in the exercise of their religion, for which the inquisition would tie them to the stake and commit them to the flames . . . .

Beside this may be set the comment of the editor of the *New Monthly Magazine,* at a time when Jew and Christian joined together in a mass meeting held in London (1828), to protest against the brutality of the persecution of the Jews by the Russian government:

We think with them (the Jews) that persecution for religion is most unworthy and dishonorable. We do not think very highly of Jews as loan-jobbers; but we do think the right of conscience of the Jew as sacred a thing as that of the professors of our own faith, and that even the absolute Nicholas has no right but power, to mark it with penal decrees.

The fact that such a joint mass meeting of Christians and Jews could be held in London was in itself a significant commentary on the change which the new age of toleration was bringing about. In the *Gentleman's Magazine* for 1828, we find a sympathetic reference to the plight of the Jews in Russia. The editor takes the liberty of reminding the English public that the frightful series of atrocities in Russia, like the massacres and persecutions to which the Jews were subjected in England from the Conquest down, has been brought about by the caprice or avarice of the sovereign, and by the ignorance or bigotry of the people. The same view of the situation is taken by the scholarly dean of St. Paul's, in his *History of the Jews*, published in 1829:

> Christianity, to work any change on the hereditary religious pride of the Jew, on his inflexible confidence in his inalienable privileges, must put off the hostile and repulsive aspect which it has long worn; it must show itself as the faith of reason, of universal peace and goodwill to men, and thus, unanswerably, prove its descent from the All-wise and All-merciful ... The religious obligations of mankind to the Jews it is impossible to appreciate in all their fulness. The Jews are the religious parents, in a certain sense, both of Christianity and Mohammedanism. To the Christian the Jews are the appointed conservators, not only of their sublime monotheism, but guardians of the oracles of that one God.

A similar tolerance is shown in the writings of the Rev. Charles Foster, whose *Mahometanism Unveiled*, appearing in the same year (1829), contains a lengthy tribute to the important services rendered by the Jews towards the advancement of European learning.

The Evangelical movement was inevitably productive of a great quantity of controversial literature. As long as religion remained an incentive to philanthropic effort, it met with little opposition. Occasionally, however, the enthusiasm of individual workers who sought the conversion of their Jewish brethren at any cost brought forth warnings and even protests from Jews and Christians alike. When, as sometimes happened, the old brand of theology, which held Jews to be the object of divine wrath, and, therefore, suffering for their transgressions, animated the missionaries, bitter protests were certain to follow.

In 1800, Rabbi Tobias Goodman issued a pamphlet protesting against the London Society's activities, and resenting the proselytizing of his people by methods that were open to question. In the same year, from another source, came a warning to missionaries among the Jews, to be "cautious how we intrude our doctrines upon a quiet people who are only irritated when the religion of their fathers is invaded." In 1810, Thomas Witherby, a retired bookseller, made a vigorous plea for the Jewish communities, defending them against "the intolerant fanaticism and wiles of certain conversionists." Witherby declared that he could not "bring himself to think but that the Jews are now actually under the favor of God, and that the blood of Christ has been their atonement."

The increase in general interest in the Jews, for which the Evangelical movement was partly responsible, led to the publication of a number of histories designed to give the public a clearer and more circumstantial knowledge of both the past and the present of the race. We have already mentioned the liberal views expressed by Dean Milman, in his *History of the Jews*. Another contribution to this end was made by William Brown, whose *Antiquities of the Jews* (1820) was described, on publication, as "a sensible, useful and sound compilation, well calculated to please the grave and inform the general reader." Extracts from this interesting work were from time to time reprinted in magazines and newspapers, throwing light on the customs and manners of the Israelites in all lands.

The old diehard spirit, however, still continued in some quarters. In the *Concise History of the Jews* (1813), specially prepared for the schools by the Rev. John Hewlett, Chaplain in Ordinary to the Prince Regent, the medieval view is reiterated that, throughout the ages, "the Jews have been marked out as objects of divine judgments" for their numerous transgressions. This view is emphasized in an extract printed (1813) in the *Gentleman's Magazine* (LXXXIII, 146):

So far as being considered the Chosen People of God by their fellow creatures, they are viewed as outcasts, and appear to be the decided subjects of severe and long-continued discipline. The world at large contemplates them with a mixture of pity and contempt; and they have no other relief than that they are not persecuted with the unrelenting hatred of former ages.

We have already noted that the establishment of mission schools for Jewish children was part of the Evangelical program. Jewish education was of course a moot problem in this period. The *London Chronicle* (April 18, 1805) was perhaps making a tacit suggestion in its comment on the situation when it suggested "the children of Jews should be received at all the public schools, and there instructed like other children." In the same year, the *Monthly Magazine* (XIX, 234), commented on the situation at Cambridge University:

The Jews had no dealings with Samaritans, and the *Alma Mater* has no dealings with the Jews. At least in her character of an academia, distributing *lucem et pocula sacra*, Christ would have blamed them both; and they manage these matters better in some foreign universities, on the broad foundation of Mr. Locke's Treatise on Toleration. But ever proud of bearing testimony to the very semblance of liberality, we must acknowledge, though our venerable mother does not admit Jews into her bosom, that she indulges them occasionally with her smiles, and has condescended to receive favorably a Hebrew Grammar or a Book of Fluxions, from the hands of the late Mr. Israel Lyons, a Jew, formerly of Cambridge. This gentleman taught, at the time, Hebrew to the gownsmen, though not of the gown himself. There is, at present, also, in the town an academy for the Jews, and we should be happy to see the time when they might be permitted not only to view the beef, but to sup the broth.

This time was not yet, however.

It was to be expected that the balance of opinion on the economic and social progress of the Jews during this period should be unfavorable to the Jews. But when the question of the removal of trade restrictions against Jews in the City was raised (1831), the following statement in the *Westminster Review* (X, 435) shows that favorable comments were not lacking:

Every restriction inflicted on a Jew, on pretence of his being what Dr. Southey calls a "misbeliever," is a request to take something out of the public purse, for the benefit of the pious people who ask for it. If the Jew is to be put out, it is because it would be to the advantage of the public that he should stay in ... A Jew that should keep a retail shop could only hold his ground by being pleasing to his customers; and why are we, the good Christians, to be deprived of the retail shop that pleases us? If a Jew sold naughty figs, or made his bread with the leaven of the scribes and the Pharisees, there is no need to call in the Thirty-Nine Articles for the regulation of groceries and the protection of penny-rolls. Men had both, without the Thirty-Nine Articles; and might have them still.

Another liberal critic, in *Fraser's Magazine* (I, 541), also assails the position of the opposition:

Christianity is no doubt much advanced by an old clothes man being prevented from selling his wares in Fleet Street, when he can vend them with impunity in the Strand; and the liberties and security of England are much secured by the guardian-barrier of Temple Bar, which keeps out the circumcised dealer in sealing-wax and oranges ... The truth is, that ... the Christian dealer in smuggled muslin is afraid of the superior talents of his Jewish brother in the same trade.

On the increasing wealth and resultant social advancement of the upper class Jews, William Cobbett (1762–1835) spoke in season and out, with the characteristic prejudice of an English yeoman. In one of his weekly tirades (*Political Register*, September 6, 1806), he says:

Till lately, the richest Jews amongst us affected poverty for fear of envy, and ate their unleavened cakes and counted their usuries in secret. And now, they are the companions of our feasts, the pride of our assemblies, the arbiters of our amusements. This speculation becomes important when it is considered that the remarkable changes we have spoken of are chiefly connected with the growth of the commercial among us. Indeed the treatment of the Jews from the beginning has always been milder in proportion to the commercial advancement of the states in which they lived ...

Cobbett's attitude towards all Jews is violently intolerant. He classes the Jewish stock-broker and stock-jobber with "the horrible tribe of borough-mongers, placemen, and others" who are "exploiting the interests of honest labor." "They (the Jews) have pelted me," says the editor of the *Political Register*, in a great rage, "many times with snow-balls, or rotten apples, or clods of dirt." This must be a mistake, observes the *Westminster Review* (XIII, 188); "the youthful patriot pelted *them*. They invaded not his bacon, nor trampled upon his turnips; but the juvenile philosopher knew by their beards that they deserved punishment at his hands, and the spirit that fell on him told him that he was to be the avenger of his country."

Charles Lamb (1775–1834) admitted a dislike for the Jews, but, with gentle irony, stated his reasons for finding them less objectionable on the 'Change than elsewhere. In an essay entitled "Jews, Quakers, Scotchmen and other Imperfect Sympathies," published in the newly founded *London Magazine* (IV, 152), he says:

> I should not care to be in habits of familiar intercourse with any of that (the Jewish) nation . . . Old prejudices cling about me. I cannot shake off the story of Hugh of Lincoln . . . A Hebrew is nowhere congenial to me. He is least distasteful on the 'Change,— for the mercantile spirit levels all distinctions, for all are beauties in the dark . . .

We have already had occasion to quote press comments on the small traders, peddlers, fruit vendors and old-clothes men who hawked their wares in city streets and country districts. As we shall see later, these came in for even more frequent reference in the drama, the music hall songs and skits of the period. To the writers of the first third of the century they afforded comic relief, but the humor with which they were treated usually carried a sting.

The controversial literature produced in the course of the political struggle for emancipation was of course violent on both sides. The wonder is, not that so much was argued against the Jews, but that so many and such eloquent voices were raised in their defence. The growth of a more liberal public sentiment is here clearly indicated. The arguments offered against emancipation during this period were for the most part the old stock arguments with which we are already familiar. An anonymous writer, in an *Essay on the Commercial Habits of the Jews*, published in London in 1809, states the case from an "economic" point of view:

> Many forcible objections present themselves against the naturalization of the Jews, the principal of which are: First, the pecuniary power of that people; Secondly, the pernicious effect which might be produced by such an open encouragement of immorality and religious infidelity . . .

The religious argument of the Tory wing of the Evangelicals is already familiar to us. It was the fashion among certain pious church workers to refer to the Jews as "despised," "peculiar," and "obstinate." To them the thought of emancipation without previous conversion to Christianity was abhorrent. If the Cloth dared to be as profane as the Bar, they would doubtless have echoed the sentiments of the leader of the Midland Circuit already cited, "Let 'em become Christian, and be d—d to 'em!" In their view, to grant privileges to the Jews would destroy the Christian character of the state and subvert England's most cherished institutions.

In the literary world of 1830, no man of the period made a more vigorous and reasoned attack on Tory bigotry than did William Hazlitt (1778–1830) in his famous essay on the Emancipation of the Jews, published in the *Tatler* (II, 701 ff.). In the course of his discussion, Hazlitt says:

The emancipation of the Jews is but a natural step in the progress of civilization . . . It is true we no longer burn them at the stake, or plunder them of their goods; why then continue to insult or fix an idle stigma on them? At Rome, a few years ago, they made the Jews run races (naked) in the Corso on Good Friday. At present they only oblige them to provide asses to run races on the same day for the amusement of the populace, and to keep up the spirit of the good old custom — though altering it they confess that the custom is wrong, and that they are ashamed of it. They also shut up the Jews in a particular quarter of the city, and at the same time will not suffer the English as heretics to be buried within the walls of Rome. An Englishman smiles or is scandalized at both these instances of bigotry; but if he is asked, "Why, then, do you not yourselves emancipate the Catholics and the Jews?" he may answer, "We have emancipated the one." "And why not the others?" "Because we are intolerant." This and this alone is the reason.

We throw in the teeth of the Jews that they are prone to certain sordid vices. If they are vicious, it is we who have made them so. Shut out any class of people from the path to fair fame, and you reduce them to grovel in the pursuit of riches and the means to live. A man has long been in dread of insult for no just cause; and you complain that he grows reserved and suspicious. You treat him with obloquy and contempt, and wonder that he does not walk by you with an erect and open brow.

We also object to their trades and modes of life; that is, we shut people up in close confinement and complain that they do not live in the open air. The Jews barter and sell commodities, instead of raising and manufacturing them. But this is the necessary traditional consequence of their former persecution and pillage by all nations. They could not set up a trade when they were hunted every moment from place to place, and while they could count nothing their own but what they could carry with them. They could not devote themselves to the pursuit of agriculture when they were not allowed to possess a foot of land. You tear people up by the roots and trample on them like noxious weeds, and then make an outcry that they do not take root in the soil like wholesome plants. You drive them like a pest from city to city, from kingdom to kingdom, and then call them vagabonds and aliens....

As to the assertion that Christianity is part of the law of the land, as Popery is part of the law of Rome, and a good reason for hunting Jews and refusing Christian burial to Protestants, by whom is it made? Not by our Divines. They do not distrust the power of our religion; and they will tell you that if Christianity, as sanctioning these cruelties or any miserable remnant of them, is part of the law of the land, then the law of the land is no part of Christianity. They do not forget the original character of the Jewish people, and will not say anything against it. We and modern Europe derived from them the whole germ of our civilization, our ideas on the unity of the Deity, or marriage, or morals.

The great founder of the Christian religion was himself born among that people, and if the Jewish nation are still to be branded with His death, it might be asked on what principle of justice ought we to punish men for the crimes committed by their co-religionists near two thousand years ago....

While it was supposed that the Jews eat little children, it was proper to take precaution against them. But why keep up ill-names and the ill-odour of a prejudice when the prejudice has ceased to exist? It has long ceased among the reflecting part of the community; and although the oldest prejudices are, it is to be lamented, preserved longest in the highest places, and Governments have been slow to learn good manners, we cannot but be conscious that these errors are passing away. We begin to see, if we do not fully see, that we have no superiority to boast, but reason and philosophy, and that it is well to get rid of vulgar prejudices and nominal distinctions as fast as possible.

Hazlitt's essay was published two months after, although written some time before, an essay on "Jewish Disabilities" by Thomas Babington Macaulay (1800–1859). There is a similarity of argument in the two essays which might suggest a common source of information. Landa is of the opinion that both Macaulay and Hazlitt were influenced by a pamphlet written by Francis Henry Goldsmid and published in 1829. For, as we may suppose, the Jews did not lag behind in their own defence. In the 'thirties a coterie of Jewish writers was contributing letters and papers to the English press. Prominent among these writers were Dr. Bernard Van Oven, Francis Henry Goldsmid, and David Salomons.

Van Oven's *Appeal to the British Nation in Behalf of the Jews* appeared in 1829; Goldsmid's spirited pamphlet, *Remarks on the Civil Disabilities of the Jews*, in 1830; and Salomons' pamphlets on *Parliamentary Oaths* and *The*

Altering of Oaths shortly after. In addition to these, there were articles on "The Emancipation of the Jews," contributed to the *London Times* (1830–1831) by Arthur Lumley Davids; "A Brief Sketch of the State and Expectations of the Jews" from the pen of Ridley H. Herschell (1833); and various papers on the modern Jews in *Chambers' Edinburgh Journal*; all of which no doubt helped to spread information about the aspirations of the English Jews, and to bring about a change in public feeling on the Jewish question. Evidence of this change is suggested in two essays written by Basil Montagu, son of the Earl of Sandwich, in advocacy of Jewish emancipation; one addressed to the Right Reverend, the Bishop of Chichester, and the other to Henry Warburton, M. P. (1833). To the Bishop, Montagu puts the question:

> Do we really imagine that our cathedrals and churches will be converted into synagogues, and that our clergy in a few years will assist in the restoration of Jerusalem? . . . Why are we in alarm as if Christianity were a cunningly devised fable?

And in the letter to Warburton, he expresses the conviction that:

> The time is not far distant when all our fellow countrymen will be permitted to go to Heaven their own way, and we shall trouble ourselves in considering only whether they virtuously discharge their duties on earth. The time is not far distant when our oppression of the Jews will be no more. We may attempt, but shall attempt in vain, to continue to oppress them. Errors cannot resist the progress of knowledge. The Philistine may go forth with his helmet of brass on his head, and his coat of mail weighing 500 shekels of brass, and his

staff like a weaver's beam; but he will be met by a youth from the mountain side in the name of the Lord of Hosts, the God of the Armies of Israel.

In these various expressions of opinion in the public press and in privately circulated pamphlets and letters, it is possible to trace the development of a feeling of sympathy and tolerance for the Jewish people and their problems. The liberal tendency is to point out the injustice and the unreasonableness of the old theological view of the Jews as being the objects of divine judgments and to point out the necessity for a recognition of the worthiness of English Jews to share in the affairs of state and society. Not much progress is indicated in the direction of liberal thought by the bulk of letters and pamphlets on the subject of Jewish emancipation. But, in the essay by Hazlitt, the speeches and essay by Macaulay, in the scholarly investigations of Milman and William Brown, together with the combined efforts of the *Westminster Review, Fraser's Magazine*, the *Edinburgh Review*, and other liberal journals, a start is made toward a freer and more courageous examination of the status of the Jews in England. The pens of several English writers and journalists of recognized ability are enlisted on the side of the Jews. At the conclusion of his essay on the "Civil Disabilities of the Jews," Macaulay voiced the sentiments of a section of English society as follows:

Last year, we remember, it was represented by a pious writer in the John Bull newspaper, and by some other equally fervid Christians, as a monstrous indecency, that the measure for the relief of the Jews should be brought forward in Passion Week. One of these humorists ironically recommended that it should be read a second time on Good Friday. We should have had no objection; nor do we believe that the day could be commemorated in a more worthy manner. We know of no day fitter for terminating long hostilities, and repairing cruel wrongs, than the day on which the religion of mercy was founded. We know of no day fitter for blotting out from the statute book the last traces of intolerance, than the day on which the spirit of intolerance produced the foulest of all judicious murders ...

CHAPTER VI

THE ROMANTIC REVIVAL

The literature of a nation must inevitably bear the imprint of its political, religious and social life, reflecting the trivial as well as the serious ideas, the fashions, sentiments and fancies of a day. So we may expect to find in English literary works of the first third of the nineteenth century some reflection of that more tolerant attitude toward the Jew, the development of which we have been studying. Obviously this will be more noticeable in some types of literature than in others. Then, too, in every age there are writers who are obsessed by images and ideas of the past, while others cry out as voices in the wilderness, preparing the way for the future. It is not our purpose to force the issue by binding social, religious and political movements with literary shackles never meant to hold them, for literature presents no such orderly development. Yet it is possible to show, by a careful study of the Jew as he is portrayed in the literature of the Romantic revival, that the writers have, on the whole—although certainly not without some exception—treated him with a sympathy and understanding quite alien to an earlier age.

The poet attempts no such photographic portraiture of an age as does the journalist and pamphleteer. Yet, unquestionably, the Romantic poets of the early nineteenth century were profoundly influenced by the ferment of the new ideas of the day. Stimulated as they were by the transformation of English industrial life, by the Evangelical Movement, and the French Revolution, they manifested an interest in the past, in the remote or exotic, and in humanity. It is a commonplace that the sensitive genius of poets such as Wordsworth, Coleridge, Southey, Scott, Shelley, and Byron, was inspired by ideals of faith, and loyalty to humanity, by pity for the unfortunate and by a desire for universal justice. These sentiments are admittedly implicit in their works, and, one must suppose, would tend to predispose them to sympathy and tolerance for the Jews as for all humanity laboring under oppression. The questions we have to consider then are, to what extent does the figure of the Jew appear in the works of these poets, and of what significance is their treatment of the Jew in relation to the status of the Jew in the England of their day?

The Jew figures in only two poems of William Wordsworth (1770–1850), and these are separated in time by at least twenty-eight years. In 1800, he wrote *Song for the Wandering Jew*, which, as Calisch points out, indicates a breaking away from the conventional sectarian abhorrence. The poet recognizes his universal humanity in a way that would perhaps have been impossible to a writer of an earlier and less tolerant age.

> Day and night my toils redouble,
> Never nearer to the goal;
> Night and day I feel the trouble
> Of the Wanderer in my soul.

The second poem, *A Jewish Family*, was written as a reminiscence of a trip which the poet and his sister took with

Coleridge in 1828. While the party were traveling along the banks of the Rhine, they met a Jewish family, exceedingly poor and in rags, yet self-respecting and proud in their poverty. In a prefatory note, the poet said:

> We had taken a little dinner with us in a basket, and invited them to partake of it, which the mother refused to do, both for herself and children, saying it was with them a fast day; adding diffidently, that whether such observances were right or wrong, she felt it her duty to keep them strictly.

The poem is a tribute not only to this little family, but to the people from which it sprang.

> I see the dark-brown curls, the brow,
>   The smooth transparent skin,
> Refined, as with intent to show
>   The holiness within;
> The grace of parting Infancy
>   By blushes yet untamed;
> Age faithful to the mother's knee,
>   Nor of her arms ashamed.
>
> Two lovely sisters, still and sweet
>   As flowers, stand side by side;
> Their soul-subduing looks might cheat
>   The Christian of his pride;
> Such beauty hath the Eternal poured
>   Upon them not forlorn,
> Though of a lineage once abhorred,
>   Nor yet redeemed from scorn.
>
> Mysterious safeguard, that, in spite
>   Of poverty and wrong,
> Doth here preserve a living light,
>   From Hebrew fountains sprung;

That gives this ragged group to cast
    Around the dell a gleam
Of Palestine, of glory past,
    And proud Jerusalem!

Samuel Taylor Coleridge (1772–1834), like his friend
Wordsworth, displayed an early and ardent enthusiasm
for the liberal tendencies of the period, an enthusiasm which
later disillusion never entirely quenched. Few writers have
influenced English thought more than he. In his *Table Talk*
we have the poet's *obiter dicta*, casual remarks, stray jot-
tings, on a variety of subjects. Here too we have his observations on the Jews and Judaism. "I have had,"
he says, "a good deal to do with Jews in the course
of my life, although I never borrowed any money from
them." He records several conversations with Jews, and
does not hesitate to admit that he mostly got the worst of
the argument. He argued with one about conversion and
he cites the Jew's answer: "Let us convert Jews to Judaism
first." On another occasion, he had an interesting en-
counter with an Old Clothes Man, and was "floored" by
the Jew:

He passed me several times crying out for old clothes
in the most nasal and extraordinary tone I ever heard.
At last, I was so provoked that I said to him, "Pray,
why can't you say *old clothes* in a plain way as I do
now?" The Jew stopped, and looking very gravely at
me, said in a clear and even fine accent, "Sir, I can say
old clothes as well as you can; but if you had to say so
ten times a minute, for an hour together, you would
say *Ogh Clo*, as I do now;" and so he marched off. I was
so confounded with the justice of this retort that I followed and gave him a shilling, the only one I had.

Among Coleridge's intimate friends was his neighbor at Highgate, Hyman Hurwitz, professor of Hebrew at University College, London. Through the Hebraist Coleridge became interested in a volume of Rabbinical Tales, which both men were to prepare for Murray, the publisher. But Coleridge was rich in plans which he failed to accomplish, and this turned out to be one of them.

On the whole, Coleridge was not unkind to the Jews. He noted the fact that the Jews were destined to "remain a quiet light among the nations for the purpose of pointing out the doctrine of the unity of God;" but revealed a tendency to mix his original judgments with conventional uncomplimentary views, by adding that "the religion of the Jew is indeed a light; but it is the light of a glow-worm, which gives no heat, and illumines nothing but itself." Jacob, he declared, was a "regular Jew, because of his trickiness;" and then hastened to take the sting out of the remark by adding, "No man could be a bad man who loved as he loved Rachel."

Of the interest of Robert Southey (1774–1843) in Jewish matters there is some evidence, in that he shared the views of Wordsworth and Coleridge with reference to Hebrew poetry. In a letter dated October 16, 1808, the poet laureate says:

> All Oriental poetry that I have seen is bad, and the superiority of the Hebrews is truly marvelous; it almost requires a belief in inspiration to account for it.

Like Coleridge, Southey read a great deal about Judaism, and from a letter written by him in 1830, we learn that at one time he meant to write a paper concerning that religion, "but there was some notion of D'Israeli doing it;"

and so he gave way willingly to one better acquainted with the subject. However, the poet's opinion of Judaism was not flattering to the Jews. He believed that "the corruptions of Judaism have found a most curious parallel with those of Popery, and in both, tradition has been set up above the written word." In the same letter he refers to the Jews as being "found everywhere," and declares that, as long as they are Jews, they will continue to be, however corrupted, a peculiar people, all whose observances are intended to keep them so." Further on in the same epistle, Southey speaks contemptuously of the futile endeavor to make Christian proselytes of the Jews. "The society for converting the Jews," says he, "has wasted more money than any other society in this country, which is saying a great deal."

In Southey's Common Place Book we find several scraps of information and opinion relating to the Jews. There are quotations from the *Vindiciae Judaeorum* by Rabbi Manasseh ben Israel, which work, says Southey, constitutes "a satisfactory refutation of the calumnies against the Jews, made by a liberal and learned man in an age when such a refutation was necessary." Also, there are citations from Henderson's *Biblical Researches and Travels among the Jews in Russia*, R. Barrow's "memorable remarks concerning the Jews," and extracts from the *English Anecdotes and Fragments from Espriella*. In his poetical works, however, Southey gives no evidence of any interest in the Jews. He does not seem to have been particularly impressed by the Jew as a character in romantic literature or as a figure in contemporary life.

Chief among the younger Romantic poets was George Gordon, Lord Byron (1788–1824), whose lifelong sympathy with nations struggling for their liberty was sealed by his premature death in Greece. To what extent he was sympathetic with the Jews in their struggle for emancipation cannot be easily ascertained, but his interest in Jewish subjects is revealed in his volume of early lyrics, published in 1815, under the name of *Hebrew Melodies*. These poems, we learn, were written at the request of a friend, Byron supplying the words to the music composed by a Jewish singer, Isaac Nathan. There are several poems dealing with biblical and Palestinian themes and stimulating a sympathetic interest in the *Weltschmerz* of ancient Israel. In "Jephtha's Daughter," the spirit of self-sacrifice is illustrated in the maiden's willingness to die "since our country, our God, Oh, my sire, demand it!" The "Song of Saul Before His Last Battle" is chanted like the swan song of a hero leading the Hosts of the Lord. "The Destruction of Sennacherib" offers a magnificent portrayal of the Assyrian attack on Palestine, "where the blue wave rolls nightly on deep Galilee." "A Spirit Passed Before Me" is a noble paraphrase of a passage from Job, and "The Vision of Belshazzar" tells the story of the last ruler of Babylon. The "Songs of Zion" convey a strong feeling for Israel oppressed; they breathe the spirit of Judah Halevi's *Zionides*. Isaac Nathan himself felt that the poem, "O! weep for those that slept by Babel's Stream," reached the acme of emotional sympathy for persecuted Israel.

> O weep for those that slept by Babel's stream,
> Whose shrines are desolate, whose land a dream;
> Weep for the harp of Judah's broken shell;
> Mourn—where their God hath dwelt the god-
>   less dwell.

And where shall Israel lave her bleeding feet?
And where shall Zion's songs again seem sweet?
And Judah's melody once again rejoice
The hearts that leap'd before its heavenly voice?

Tribes of the wandering foot and weary breast,
How shall ye flee away and be at rest!
The wild dove hath her rest, the fox his cave,
Mankind their country—Israel but the grave.

"The Wild Gazelle" carries out the same motif; the happy creature skips around on Judah's hills, and the cedars wave on Lebanon,

But we must wander witheringly
In other lands to die;
And where our fathers' ashes be
Our own may never lie.

It would seem natural that the power and sympathy with which the poet portrays the sorrows of the outcast people can only be the expression of a man free from racial and religious prejudice. However, to this extent only does Byron's poetry reflect the spirit of toleration for the Jews which was characteristic of the liberal minds of his day. In his letters and satires there are some extremely uncomplimentary remarks with reference to the contemporary Jewish bankers and financiers.

In *Don Juan*, there is a passing reference to Israelites in general:

Believe the Jews, those unbelievers, who
Must be believed, though they believe not you;

and in *The Age of Bronze*, composed at Genoa as a "derisory farewell to 1822," there is a very decided thrust at the machinations of the Jewish bankers at the Congress of Verona.

Percy Bysshe Shelley (1792–1822), like Byron, was interested in the Jew as a romantic figure, but, unlike Byron, he makes no reference to the Jew in contemporary life. During the winter of 1809–1810, Shelley and Tom Medwin were inseparable companions. In their long walks through the leafless glades of St. Leonard's Forest, these two young men conceived the idea of producing a "wild story"—with a hideous witch for its principal character. Soon they found themselves engaged in the much higher and more arduous enterprise of a grand metrical romance on the subject of *The Wandering Jew;* an enterprise which was further encouraged by one of those accidents which so often influence, and sometimes determine, the course of human genius. On his way through Lincoln's Inn Fields, Tom Medwin picked up at a bookstall a passage from a free English rendering of Christian Schubart's rhapsodical poem, *Der ewige Jude.* The scrap of paper was carried to Shelley; Shelley carried it to Byron; and both poets were powerfully affected by it. The passage described Ahasuerus, the Wandering Jew, creeping forth from the dark cave of Mount Carmel:

> Near two thousand years have elapsed since he was first goaded by never-ending restlessness to rove the globe from pole to pole. When our Lord was wearied with the burden of his ponderous cross, and wanted to rest before the door of Ahasuerus, the unfeeling wretch drove him away with brutality. The Saviour of mankind staggered, sinking under the heavy load, but uttered no complaint. An angel of death appeared before Ahasuerus, and exclaimed indignantly: "Barbarian! thou hast denied rest to the Son of Man; be it denied thee also, until he comes to judge the world!"

A black demon, let loose from Hell, goads Ahasuerus now from country to country; he is denied the consolation which death affords, and precluded from the rest of the peaceful grave. He creeps forth from the dark cave of Mount Carmel; he shakes the dust from his beard and, taking up one of the skulls heaped there, hurls it down the eminence. It rebounds from the earth in shivered atoms. "This was my father!" roars Ahasuerus. Seven more skulls roll down from rock to rock; while the infuriate Jew, follows them with ghastly looks, exclaims: "And these were my wives!" He still continues to hurl down skull after skull, roaring in dreadful accents, "And these, and these, and these are my children! They *could die*; but I! reprobate wretch, alas! I cannot die.... Rome, the giantess, fell—I placed myself before the falling statue—she fell, and did not crush me...From cloud-encircled cliffs did I precipitate myself into the ocean; but the foaming billows cast me upon the shore ... I leaped into Etna's flaming abyss ... The volcano fermented and in a fiery stream of lava cast me up ... I roared defiance to the infuriate Gaul, defiance to the victorious German; but arrows and spears rebounded in shivers from my body. The Saracen's flaming sword broke upon my skull, balls in vain hissed upon me ... in vain did the elephant trample on me, in vain the iron hoof of the wrathful steed ...

Byron was so impressed by this passage that he used some of the thoughts contained in it, in *Manfred* (Act II, Sc 2, ll. 229 ff.). On Shelley, the vision of the undying Jew had an even greater effect—it led to deep and frequent ponderings on the hideous doom of deathlessness, and Ahasuerus figures in *Queen Mab* (I, 55), written in 1812–1813; in *Hellas* (IV, 43), 1821; and was in the poet's mind when he composed the following lines of *Alastor*, in 1815:

O, that God,
Profuse of poisons, would concede the chalice
Which but one living man has drained, who now,
Vessel of deathless wrath, a slave that feels
No proud exemption in the blighting curse
He bears, over the world wanders for ever,
Lone as incarnate death!

Shelley's metrical romance of *The Wandering Jew*, written in collaboration with Medwin, in 1810, was sent to Ballantyne, the publisher; but "in view of the bigoted spirit which yet pervades many cultivated minds," it was thought inadvisable to publish it. Not until 1829 was *The Wandering Jew*, considerably altered in form, given to the world. The motto on the title-page was from the twenty-second chapter of St. John's gospel: "If I will that he tarry till I come, what is that to thee?—follow thou me."

Another poem by Shelley, entitled *The Wandering Jew's Soliloquy*, is a passionate restatement of the ideas contained in the German fragment already referred to:

Is it the Eternal Triune, is it He
Who dares arrest the wheels of destiny
And plunge me in the lowest Hell of Hells?
Will not the lightning's blast destroy my frame?
Will not the steel drink the blood-life where
    it swells?

No—let me hie where dark Destruction dwells,
To rouse her from her deeply caverned lair,
And taunting her cursed sluggishness to ire
Light long Oblivion's death torch at its flame
And calmly mount Annihilation's pyre.

Tyrant of Earth! pale misery's jackal thou!
Are there no stores of vengeful violent fate
Within the magazines of thy fierce hate?
No poison in the clouds to bathe a brow

That lowers on thee with desperate contempt?
Where is the noonday pestilence that slew
The myriad sons of Israel's favored nation?
Where the destroying minister that flew
Pouring the fiery tide of desolation
Upon the leagued Assyrian's attempt?
Where the dark Earthquake demon who ingorged
At the dread word Korah's unconscious crew?
Or the Angel's two-edged sword of fire that urged
Our primal parents from their bower of bliss
(Reared by thine hand) for errors not their own
By Thine omniscient mind foredoomed, foreknown?
Yes! I would court a ruin such as this,
Almighty tyrant, and give thanks to Thee—
Drink deeply—drain the cup of hate—remit this
    I may die . . .

It is obvious, then, from this study of the Jew as he is
portrayed in the works of the romantic poets of the period,
that he had little interest for them as a contemporary problem; and this is of course what, from the very nature of romantic poetry, we might expect. But it seems just as evident that, in the poems in which the Jew appears as a
figure of romantic and historical significance, his universal
humanity is recognized. The poet enters into his sorrows,
and feels "the trouble of the wanderer in his soul."

While it is true that under the influence of the Romantic spirit, all literary types showed a renewed vigor, it is
also a significant fact that in the drama of this period there
was a dearth of productions of any high quality. However,
in the drama which had reached a very low ebb as a literary
type, we may expect to find some fairly definite portrayal
of the life and thought of the period. Some of the plays
afford an illuminating commentary on public sentiment,
not less so in their specific delineation of the Jew, than in

their general portrayal of fustian tragedy and sentimental comedy.

One of the most interesting developments of this period is the emergence of the Jew as a comic character. The omnipresent Jewish peddler, with his lisp and gesticulations and uncouth garb, attracted public notice wherever he went. His peculiarities of manner and talk became the signs by which the whole group was to be distinguished. His was a figure which lent itself to cartoon and comedy, and comic playwrights and music hall artists were not slow in recognizing his value as a figure of fun. In many of the songs circulated through the music halls in the early years of the century, the Jewish peddler, the Old Clo' Man, the slop-seller and petty trader, are used as laugh-provokers.

> A peddling Jew, often jeer'd,
> Vat d'ye vant, Moses? Get along, Moses!
> Never mind dat, for who's afeared?
>   So let 'em cook up dere noses.
> In spite of all dey do and tink,
>   Ve buys and sells and gets de chink.

In a popular song of the time, entitled *Mr. Abraham*, the Jewish peddler tells his hearers:

> In mai business I knows every trick,
>   Vat's belongs to all sorts of Jew pedlercals,
> Makes and sells vat make people rich,
>   Mock rhubarb and other such medicals . . .

In another song, *The Old Clothes Man*, Smouchy Abrahams, discloses the secrets of his business:

> I cries my old clothes about the streets to gain
>   an honest penny,
> And then on Sabbath, I can dress much better,
>   sirs, than any!

Jewish peddlers and brokers supplied the comic relief in various popular plays of the period. *The Invisible Girl* by Theodore Hook (Drury Lane, 1806), presents a character disguised as a Jewish broker, Moses Melchiseck; *The False Friend* by J. C. Cross (The Circus, 1806), has Zaluch, a Jew who is set upon by bandits and rescued by sailors; and *The Vindictive Man* by Thomas Holcroft (Drury Lane, 1806), includes in its cast the comedy figure of Abrahams, a Jewish dealer.

To the informed reader of these skits and comedies, it is evident that the authors have based their portrayals, however modified or exaggerated, on casual observation of the Jew of the poorer class as he appeared in the English scene. Such delineations are suggested no doubt by the large number of Jewish traders and refugees seeking refuge in England in the early part of the century. The portrayal of the Jew, not in his conventional character as an object of fear and abhorrence, but as a comic figure, indicates a real gain in public favor, in spite of the fact that such a portrayal was deplored by the Jews themselves and by those who upheld the dignity of their cause.

In Richard Cumberland's play, *The Jew* (1794), a work which had considerable influence over the more serious drama of the period, we find evidence of a more sympathetic attitude. Cumberland's principal Jewish character, Sheva, is a kind-hearted Jewish philanthropist and money lender. In the first scene, voicing the tragedy of his people, he appeals to the English public in a significant speech:

> We have no abiding place on earth—no country, no home. Everybody rails at us, everybody points us out for their may-game and their mockery. If your playwrights want a butt, or a buffoon or a knave to make

sport of, out comes a Jew to be baited and buffetted through five long acts, for the amusement of all good Christians. Cruel sport! merciless amusement! Hard dealings for a poor stray sheep of the scattered flock of Abraham! How can you expect us to show kindness, when we receive none?

Sheva's words immediately elicited apologies from the Christians in the play. Other dramatists copied Cumberland's Sheva. Songs about Sheva became popular, and for a number of years the character of Sheva helped in promoting the spread of a more generous feeling towards the Jews among the theater-going public. In a play entitled *The Jew and the Doctor* (Covent Garden, 1798), Thomas Dibdin presents a Jewish character, Abednego, after the Sheva type. Abednego is a kind and generous Jew who brings up a Christian girl, Emily, from her infancy, and in the end, renders possible her marriage with her lover by giving her a dowry of five thousand pounds. According to contemporary reports, the play drew abundant tears from both the Jews and the gentiles in the audience.

Among the earliest plays of the century, another play by Dibdin, *The School for Prejudice* (Covent Garden, 1801), did much to win sympathy for the Jewish community by the presentation of honest Ephraim, who, finding bills to the value of ten thousand pounds in the lining of an old coat, restores the money to the owner. Renamed *The Lawyer, The Jew and the Yorkshireman*, the play was revived in 1825, and kept its place in public favor for some time.

Alongside these more liberal interpretations of old Jewish character, there still remained a tendency to present the Jew in the role he had been made to play in former years. An interesting type of play, from our standpoint, is that in which actual Jewish characters do not appear, but in which other characters resort to Jewish disguise to supply comic relief, or to further some villainous scheme. It is illustrated by *Ella Rosenberg* (Drury Lane, 1807), a two-act melodrama adopted from the French, in which the villain, desiring to gain access to the heroine, assumes the garb of a Jewish picture-dealer in order to carry out his plans. In another play *Rochester, or King Charles Second's Merry Days*, by W. T. Moncrieff (Olympic Theater, 1818), both Rochester and Buckingham don Jewish old-clo' disguises, and each accuses the other of fraud, demanding that his rival shall speak in Hebrew to vindicate himself. Thereupon one jabbers in Latin and the other in Greek, to the great amusement of the audience. Similarly, in the *Jew of Lubeck* (Drury Lane, 1819), the chief character is not a Jew, but an Austrian nobleman, who, denounced as a traitor, escapes to Lubeck, and there saves himself by living as a Jew.

Many of the plays of the period in which the Jew appears are historical in character. Four dramatic versions of Sir Walter Scott's *Ivanhoe* were staged in London in the 'twenties; the first by Dibdin (Surrey Theater, 1820), in three acts, two others by G. Sloane, under the title of *The Hebrew* (Drury Lane Theater, and Covent Garden, 1820); and another by Moncrieff, which does not seem to have been produced before. A play entitled *The Hebrew Family, or a Traveler's Adventure* (Covent Garden, 1825), has some Jewish interest because it deals with the story of an Englishman who, condemned by the Inquisition and escaping from the scaffold, finds refuge in the home of a kind and hospitable Jewish household.

In the year 1830, when the struggle for Jewish political recognition was attracting attention, Douglas Jerrold produced *The Painter of Ghent* (Strand Theater, 1830), in which Ichabod, a Jewish picture-dealer, tells a monk, "Ye treat us as we were a lot of loathsome worms and then marvel if we sometimes crawl." An effort to deal more fairly than before with Jewish characters in dramatic literature is seen in *The Jew of Aragon, or the Hebrew Queen*, by Thomas Wade (1805–1875). The play is dedicated to "the Jews of England," and contains a dignified plea for toleration. Wade was sincerely interested in the emancipation of the English Jews. With Robert Grant, Macaulay and others, he advocated the removal of Jewish disabilities. Addressing the Jews as "countrymen," he writes:

> The same great progress of reason, and therefore of justice and liberality, which has already delivered you from those manifold persecutions under which you, and your brethren of other countries, writhed for so many centuries of bigotry and darkness, in its swift and eternal advance, will ultimately disenthral you from those unworthy bonds with which you still remain encumbered.

In the final scene of the play, Xavier, one of the chief characters, exclaims:

> At the portals of eternity
> Darkly we stand sublime.
> . . . I've learned a truth:
>
> Our sun hath shone! The weight of the
>   world's scorn
> Is heavy on us that we cannot rise,
> Or rising for an instant, cannot stand;
> And 'tis a truth that makes me wish to die.

But a feeling of hope is expressed in the concluding sentences:

> Yet will her full hour come—hear it!
> 'Twill come . . .

This play proved to be too strong a diet for the English theater-going public, who, still in the process of being weaned from past prejudices, could not as yet stand so powerful a dose of toleration. Charles Kemble, who took the part of Xavier the Jew, and Fanny Kemble, who appeared as Rachel, the Jew's daughter, were severely criticized for identifying themselves with such a production. Much success, however, attended the milder presentation, in 1831, of a play by C. Z. Barnett, entitled *The Rise of the Rothschilds, or the Honest Jew of Frankfort.*

This brief summary of the treatment of the Jews in early nineteenth century drama will show that they were decidedly better known to both dramatist and audience between 1800 and 1833 than in any earlier period. By 1825, the Jew had become a part of the English scene. He was a public figure. Even such as did not wish to associate with Jews could not help hearing about them and seeing them; and if they wished, they could meet hundreds of Israelites in business, in the streets, and even in their own homes, and approximate the truth about individual money-lenders, scholars, traders and bankers. This increased knowledge had its effect on the dramatic delineation of the Jew even in this negligible period of the drama, when tragedy was almost comic in its extreme sentimentality, and comedy was all but tragic in its bad taste. The portrayal of the Jew as a comic character, rather than as a malicious villain, marked a deviation from older methods, and a distinct gain in the direction of fraternization. What the public could laugh at, it had come to tolerate. The prophecy with which the *Jew of Aragon* closes is not to be long in fulfillment; the hour for full equality is almost within reach.

CHAPTER VII

THE REGENCY NOVELISTS AND
SIR WALTER SCOTT

The changes in social and economic conditions which marked the progress of the latter part of the eighteenth century and the first quarter of the nineteenth, produced corresponding changes in the experience and outlook, as well as in the numbers, of the reading public in England. The novel provided the ideal vehicle for the speculations of the time, supplying as it did a frame-work in which the reading public could study both the general organization of society and the individual differences of birth and temperament which prevent a person from fitting himself into the accepted pattern. Novelists were not slow to recognize their opportunity. In 1785, Clara Reeve observed that the press groaned under the weight of novels, which sprang up like mushrooms. Succeeding years witnessed no slackening. "Every work of any merit," said Miss Reeve, "produced a swarm of imitators, till they became a public evil, and the institution of the circulating libraries conveyed them in the cheapest manner to everybody's hand." New themes, new characters, new situations were eagerly sought for by publishers. All sorts of bastard products, whose home would now be the columns of the

126

sensational press, appeared on the library shelves. Contemporary scandals and *causes célèbres*, lightly dished up, appeared under the title of *The Unhappy Wife*, *The Innocent Adulteress*, or the *Memoirs of an Unfortunate Lady of Quality*. Novelists were recruited from every rank of society, for the novel was held to be an unexacting form of literature, easy to produce and possibly remunerative. Accepted themes were repeated, and, as the taste for strong scenes grew more insistent, were overlaid with all the romantic incidents of disguise, lost heirs, abduction, mistaken identity, and all the horrors with which the Gothic school had long familiarized the reading public. The popularity of the "Gothic" novel continued well into the nineteenth century, and so obviously well suited to its atmosphere was the old conventional portrait of the Jew as a figure of mystery and terror, that it is not surprising to find that many of the Jewish characters of the early nineteenth century fiction were of this type. The authors of these "thrillers" were, like the romantic poets, interested in the Jew as a historical figure, and not as a contemporary problem, and their work does not reflect his changing status. Moreover, the legends and prejudices of the past were the materials used by these authors as historical facts.

Prominent among these novelists was Ann Radcliffe (1764–1823). As a thorough-going romancer whose main endeavor was to fabricate an exciting plot, with scenery in proper keeping and characters suited to the mysterious, sinister atmosphere, it seems strange that she did not make greater use of Jewish characters. Only one, Aaron of Lincoln, appears in her work. A money-lender in the court of Henry III, he plays a small part in the novel *Gaston de Blondeville*, published in 1823. The Jew enters the court at Kenilworth "to pay the Queen that surplus of the King's fine, called *Aurum Reginae*." When he offers to give evidence against a merchant, there is a protest, "He is a Jew! His oath may not be taken." But, as everybody knows, many at the court are in the Jew's debt; therefore, his testimony is accepted.

Among the many who followed in the fashion set by Mrs. Radcliffe and her school, was Matthew Gregory Lewis (1775–1818), who is best remembered for his "Gothic" story, *Ambrosio, or The Monk* (1795). In this work, "Monk" Lewis succeeds in shaking the nerves of his readers with the most gruesome charnel-house horrors—repulsive diseases, loathsome crimes and the cries and escapades of diabolical characters. In order, however, to add special piquancy to his horrors of the crudest description, the romancer drags in the ancient legend of the Wandering Jew. After centuries of ceaseless wandering, the despised creature makes a dramatic appearance in the sensational episode of the Bleeding Nun:

> He seemed to have no acquaintance in the town, spoke very seldom, and never was seen to smile. He had neither servants nor baggage, but his purse seemed well furnished . . . Some supposed him to be an Arabian astrologer, others to be a traveling mountebank, and many declared that he was Dr. Faustus, whom the Devil had sent back to Germany . . . His countenance was strangely marked; his eyes were large, black and sparkling; yet there was something in his look which, the moment that I saw him, inspired me with a secret awe, not to say horror . . . He talked of various matters. He named people who had ceased to exist for many centuries, and yet with whom he appeared to have been personally acquainted. I could not mention a country,

however distant, which he had not visited, nor could I sufficiently admire the extent and variety of his information.

In the eyes of this Jew there is an expression of fury, despair and malevolence, as he says: "God has set His seal upon me . . . I am doomed to inspire all who look upon me with terror and detestation." Fate obliges the wanderer to be constantly in movement. He is not permitted to pass more than a fortnight in the same place. He has no friend in the world and, from the restlessness of his destiny, he can acquire none. In despair he cries:

> Fain would I lay down my miserable life for I envy those who enjoy the quiet of the grave; but death eludes me, and flies from my embrace. In vain do I throw myself in the way of danger. I plunge into the ocean; the waves throw me back with abhorrence upon the shore. I rush into the fire; the flames recoil at my approach. I oppose myself to the fury of banditti; their swords become blunted and break against my breast. The hungry tiger shudders at my approach and the alligator flies from a monster more horrible than itself . . .

This weird legend of the unfortunate Jew is again given "new treatment with the addition of much historical material" by John Galt (1779–1839) in *The Wandering Jew, or the Travels and Observations of Harreach the Prolonged* (1820). Also, in 1828, the story is further expanded in a new version entitled *Salathiel*, by George Croly (1780–1860), and dedicated "to his grace the Duke of Newcastle." In the preface to the first edition, Croly observes:

> There has appeared from time to time in Europe, during the last thousand years, a mysterious individual, a sojourner in all lands, yet a citizen of none . . . a wan-

derer and unhappy, the most afflicted of the people of affliction . . .

The novel reiterates the ancient tradition of the famous Jew, forever suffering and yet undying, forever doomed to wander and without any fixed abode, forever persecuted and yet strangely flourishing in spite of it all. Under different titles, as *Salathiel, the Immortal, or the Wandering Jew; Salathiel, or Tarry Till I Come*, Croly's book had wide popularity for many years.

While the popularity of the Gothic and historical novels continued unabated in the early years of the nineteenth century, there was developing side by side with them the novel of manners, in which extravagant fancy gave way to realism. The writers of this new school attempted to draw the novel nearer to life and to direct attention to circumstances of contemporary interest. In their works, too, the Jew appeared, not always in a favorable light, and rarely showing signs of the authors' acquaintance with the subject.

The author who came to be regarded as a pioneer in the new realistic school of novelists was Maria Edgeworth (1767–1849), who, in *Castle Rackrent* (1800), a story of Irish life, showed the compelling interest of local color. From the reported statement of Thady Quirk, the faithful and admiring servitor of the Rackrent family, the reader learns the inner history of the deterioration and ruin of a family of spendthrift baronets. Jews were evidently as unpopular in Ireland as in England. It may be noted that Ireland, too, had its wealthy Jewish families, descendants of Portuguese Jews who had settled there in Cromwell's time. In Miss Edgeworth's novel, the one character with whom honest Thady does not seem to be in complete sympathy is the Jewish wife of Sir Kit, new master of the Castle. According to Thady,

> She was a Jewish by all accounts, who are famous for their great riches . . . She spoke a strange kind of English of her own . . . objected to sausages . . . went neither to Church or to Mass . . .

> Mercy upon his honor's poor soul, thought I; what will become of him and his, and all of us, with this *heretic* at the head of the Castle Rackrent estate!

> . . . Sir Kit used to swear at her behind her back, and refer to her as his *stiff-necked Israelite;* though before he married her, he called her *My pretty Jessica.*

> . . . She was fond of money; would not part with any of her jewels . . . and outlived Sir Kit.

Maria Edgeworth's masterpiece in the art of fiction was *The Absentee*, published as a novel in 1811. In this rich comedy of Irish manners there is a character, Mr. Mordecai, a wealthy coach-maker, who may be Jewish. He is described as having a "dark wooden face," and is, in the opinion of Lord Clonbrony, a "damned rascal." The criticism may be due to the fact that Mordecai demands the payment of debts, and offers to "compromise and split the difference" with Sir Terence O'Fay.

In Miss Edgeworth's *Moral Tales*, published in 1801, there are three Jewish villains. The first of these, Solomon the Jew, appears in "The Prussian Vase;" he is an old rascal who is ultimately found guilty of fraud by the Court and sentenced—not to a year's imprisonment, according to the laws of Potsdam, but to sweep the streets of the city for a twelvemonth. The object of the sentence, so we are led to understand, is not so much to punish the offender, as to humiliate and disgrace the Jew. The second Jewish character appears in another tale, "The Good Aunt;" he is Mr. Carat, a jeweler, who, extremely cunning and untrustworthy, conducts a fraudulent lottery and cheats English school boys. The cheat is discovered in time, just before he succeeds in robbing a widow of her possessions. In the third tale, "Murad the Unlucky," a Jewish money-lender, Rachub of El Arish, is a heartless villain who attempts to kill his enemies by spreading plague germs in old clothes which he manages to sell to the victims of his wrath. The Jew escapes before he is found out. In Miss Edgeworth's full-length novel, *Belinda*, published in 1801, there is a Jewish money-lender named Solomon — the name Solomon seems to be a favorite with early writers of fiction!—who turns out to be the typical hard-hearted creature who takes advantage of a Christian in need by driving a hard bargain.

In these stories, Miss Edgeworth has not presented one honest Jew to redeem the race. However, it is obvious that the author has simply taken over the old stock figure of the wicked Jew, placed him in a modern setting, and there left him to do his worst. In fact, later in her literary career, the novelist makes a statement to this effect. Through one of her favorite characters, she explains that

> . . . not only in the old story books, where the Jews are as sure to be wicked as the bad fairies, or bad genii, or allegorical personifications of the devil, and the vices in the old emblems, mysteries, moralities, etc., but in almost every work of fiction, I found them — invariably represented as beings of a mean, avaricious, unprincipled, treacherous character . . .

And thus in her earlier novels she portrayed them. However, in a later novel, *Harrington*, published in 1816, she does much to repair this wrong.

In a preface to *Harrington*, the novelist's father, Richard Lovell Edgeworth, informs the reader that Maria Edgeworth received a letter from a Jewish lady in America, Miss Rachel Mordecai of Richmond, Virginia, reproaching the novelist for her unpleasant representations of Jewish character, and begging her to write a romance with a good Jew in it. In response to this request, and as an "apology" to the Jews, *Harrington* was written.

The story commences at about the middle of the eighteenth century, in the period when the English Jews were exposed to popular persecution. In the opening chapter, the hero, Harrington, age six years, is introduced while he is playing in the balcony of his father's home in London. It is dusk, and the lamp-lighter is making his rounds. The boy is interested in watching the faithful fellow fix and mount his ladder, with red smoking torch in hand.

> Just when he reached the ground . . . his torch flared in the face and figure of an old man with a long white beard and a dark visage, who, holding a great bag slung over one shoulder, walked slowly on, repeating in a low, abrupt, mysterious tone, the cry of "Old Clothes! Old Clothes! Old Clothes!"

The old man's appearance is as mysterious as that of the Wandering Jew in the terror-tales. Soon he is to serve the purpose of a bogey-man, to scare little Harrington.

> The maid nodded to him; he stood still, and at the same instant, she seized upon me, exclaiming: "Time for you to come off to bed, Master Harrington." I resisted

and, clinging to the rails, began kicking and roaring.
"If you don't come quietly this minute, Master
Harrington," said she, "I'll call to Simon the Jew
there" — pointing to him, "and he shall come and carry
you away in his great bag."

The threat has the desired effect. The boy obeys instantly.
But the fright does not subside with the occasion for it.

To sleep I could not go, but full of fear and curiosity
I lay, pondering on the thoughts of Simon the Jew and
his bag . . . His face with the light of the torch upon it
appeared and vanished, and flittered before my eyes.

In the days that follow, the maid, having discovered the
little boy's apprehensions, does not hesitate to augment
them with stories about Jews who have been known to steal
children away for the purpose of crucifying them at their
secret feasts and "midnight abominations."

The less I understood, the more I believed. Above all
others, there was one story — horrible! most horrible! —
which she used to tell at midnight, about a Jew who
lived in Paris in a dark alley, and who professed to sell
pork-pies; but it was found at last that the pies were
not pork — they were made of the flesh of little children. His wife used to stand at the door of her den to
watch for little children, and, as they were passing,
would tempt them with cakes and sweet-meats. There
was a trap-door in the cellar, and the children were
dragged down; and — Oh! how my blood ran cold when
we came to the terrible trap-door. Were there, I asked,
such things in London now? "Oh, yes; in dark narrow
lanes where there are Jews now living and watching
always for such little children as you . . ."

These horrible tales become, in time, so ingrafted in little
Harrington's imagination that, every night, the moment

the maid leaves the room, taking the candle with her, the boy lies in indescribable agony of terror. He sees faces of Jews around him, grinning, glaring, receding, advancing, and finally turning into the face of Simon with a long beard and terrible eyes. And then he sees the bag in which the Jew carries the mangled limbs of children.

The purpose of the opening chapters is to show how, once Harrington's fears and prejudices are awakened, they grow into a general antipathy towards all Jews. This antipathy is encouraged and stimulated by Harrington's father who has a decided aversion to "dealing with the Jews."

> I asked what this meant, and was answered "'Tis something very like dealing with the devil, my dear." My father added, "It is certain that when a man once goes to the Jews, he soon goes to the devil. So Harrington, my boy, I charge you at your peril, whatever else you do, keep out of the hands of the Jews — never go near the Jews; if once they catch hold of you, there's an end of you, my boy."

When Harrington goes to school, he discovers that there are other boys who entertain the same prejudices against the Jews. In the course of the term, however, he comes in contact with a poor Jewish peddler, Jacob, who is persecuted and tormented to such an extent that the injustice and the inhumanity of the whole thing stirs Harrington to a realization of the unfairness of the situation. Harrington is attracted by the Jew's helplessness, humility and sufferings. As the story progresses, Harrington's feeling towards Jews is considerably changed. In the final scenes, he goes so far as to permit himself to be captivated by the beauty and charm of a young lady of the Hebrew stock. Still, the lovely, sensitive, interesting Miss Montenero's religion is an insurmountable bar to marriage. Harrington's parents are sure to set up opposition of the most violent nature to any such union. What is the hero to do?

It would be far more to the purpose if Harrington really, and not apparently, overcame his prejudices. The truth of the matter is that Maria Edgeworth has not herself conquered her own prejudices. At the eleventh hour, the novelist probably finds that she cannot reconcile herself to letting her hero, an Englishman of good social position, marry a Spanish Jewess. And, since Harrington has shown himself willing to do so, and has openly expressed a deep and sincere feeling of friendship for the Jewish people, the novelist doubtless holds that she has done enough for Jewish emancipation. Harrington, however, must be spared from the undesirable union. How can this be done? It is suddenly discovered, to the great relief of Harrington and his proud family, that Bernice Montenero, whom we have been led to regard throughout as a daughter of Israel, is not a Jewess at all. The whole fabric which the novelist has raised falls suddenly before the single fact that Bernice is the child of a Christian mother, and that she was christened in her infancy. Harrington is, therefore, able to marry the girl he loves, without any sacrifice to his social and racial prejudices, and the day is saved — for conventionality!

In all this it is clear that there is little to show that the novelist knows anything of Jewish life and character. It seems to us that the novelist has created her Jewish characters out of her moral consciousness, and that her delineations are superficial. If it was Maria Edgeworth's aim to give a faborable impression of the Jews to the Lady Brantfords of English society, who cannot abide Jews; to all the Harringtons of the world, who swear they will have none of the ancient race in their circle; and to all the prejudiced readers of her generation, who desire to overcome their resentment against Jewish peddlers and old clothes men with a new story of injustice and suffering — if this is the novelist's generous motive in writing *Harrington*, then, it must be confessed that the novel, regarded as an exposition and a defence of the English Jews, is a feeble performance. The Jewish characters, through whom the "amnesty" is to be effected, are not convincing as Jews, and surely cannot have satisfied the American Jewess, at whose request the story was written.

Yet, with all its palpable defects, and although it cannot take rank with the best of Maria Edgeworth's studies of society, *Harrington* is significant as the first work to advertise the fact that a Jew may be a gentleman merchant, like Mr. Montenero; a gentleman professor of Hebrew like Israel Lyons; a gentleman old-clothes-man, like Simon the Jew; and an honest peddler, like Jacob the Jew. The obvious hope of the novelist is to drive out the ancient and intolerant conceptions of the Jew as a repulsive and horror-provoking creature, and to substitute a new and more flattering portrait. The novel thus deserves notice because it marks a departure in the interpretation of Jews in the everyday life of modern England.

The most famous of the sympathetic portrayals of Jewish character in Regency literature are of course those of Isaac of York and his daughter, Rebecca, in Sir Walter Scott's *Ivanhoe*, published in 1819. Hundreds of readers in England who had never read a line of Jewish history were introduced, in *Ivanhoe*, to the romantic aspects of the sufferings of this ancient and oppressed people in England, by the touching story of Isaac and Rebecca. That Scott's picture of the

Jewish money-lender, though painted after a medieval model, is colored by the broad human sympathies of the nineteenth century, is evident. Says Dr. Philipson· "There can be no doubt that sympathy with an oppressed people who, in his own land in that late year wherein he lived, still suffered under civil disabilities, had much to do with the production of the work; for his was a peculiarly generous nature, and throughout his writings, the sympathies of the reader are always enlisted on the side of the weaker side."

The question naturally arises, how far are Scott's interpretations of Jewish life and character based on a study of the Jews of his time, and what is the source of his interests? He is reported to have been much impressed by a description of the Jews in Germany given him by a friend, Mr. Skene, who, incidentally, suggested that a group of Jews would be an interesting feature in a romantic novel. The suggestion seemed to appeal to the novelist's mood at the time. Though he began to work under the handicap of poor health, Scott endeavored to make a thorough job of it, by turning over the pages of dusty tomes, and investigating with care the conditions of Jewish life in the medieval period. It does not seem to have occurred to him, as he proceeded to write on a medieval theme, that a study of a modern Jew might help him to a better understanding of medieval Jewry. He confined himself mainly to the chronicles of Matthew Paris, and chose, as his model for the character of Isaac, the famous Aaron of York.

We cannot fail to see in *Ivanhoe* that Scott, probably as a result of his study of medieval times, finds it difficult to break away entirely from the old, traditional pictures of the Jewish money-lender. Isaac has much of the stage Jew in him. He is the rich miser, trembling for his hoard, and scarcely resenting the indignities placed upon him because he is a Jew. At the head of the chapter in which the novelist introduces Isaac, there stands the famous quotation from Shylock's speech:

> Hath not a Jew eyes? Hath not a Jew hands, organs, dimensions, senses, affections, passions . . . ?

and, at the head of Chapter X, a passage from the *Jew of Malta*. These quotations suggest that the two famous Elizabethan portraits of Shylock and Barabas were before the novelist as he wrote. Yet, in Scott's work, the character of the money-lender seems softened and humanized. If we study the pictures of Shylock and of Isaac, side by side, we see clearly that in the delineation of Isaac, the religious prejudices of the sixteenth century have been somewhat modified by the broader toleration of the nineteenth.

From the very outset, the appearance of the Jew and his daughter in Ivanhoe kindles in the reader's heart a sympathy for them, and, as the story progresses, the author does not hesitate to show the intolerance and cruelty of medieval Christian society in its unkind and even brutal treatment of these so-called infidels.

> Oswald, returning, whispered into the ear of his master, "It is a Jew, who calls himself Isaac of York; is it fit I should marshal him into the hall?"

> "Let Gurth do thine office, Oswald," said Wamba with his usual effrontery; "The swineherd will be a fit usher of the Jew."

> "St. Mary," said the Abbot, crossing himself, "an unbelieving Jew, and admitted into this presence."

> "A dog Jew," echoed the Templar, "to approach a defender of the Holy Sepulchre."

"By my faith," said Wamba, "it would seem the Templars love the Jew's inheritance better than they do their company."

"Peace, my worthy guests," said Cedric; "my hospitality must not be bounded by your dislikes. If heaven bore with the whole nation of stiff-necked unbelievers for more years than a layman can number, we may endure the presence of the one Jew for a few hours. But I constrain no man to converse or to feed with him."

*   *   *   *   *

"Unbelieving dog," said the Templar to Isaac the Jew, as he passed him in the throng, "dost thou bend thy course to the tournament?"

"I do so propose," replied Isaac, bowing in all humility, "if it please your reverend valor."

"Ay," said the knight, "to gnaw the bowels of our nobles with usury, and to gull women and boys with gauds and toys — I warrant thee store of shekels in thy Jewish scrip."

"Not a shekel, not a silver penny, not a halfling — so help me the God of Abraham!.. I go but to seek the assistance of some brethren of my tribe to aid me to pay the fine which the Exchequer of the Jews have imposed upon me — Father Jacob be my speed! I am an impoverished wretch — the very gaberdine I wear I borrowed from Reuben of Tadcaster."

The novelist gives the reader no cause for doubting the honesty of the Jewish money-lender's offer to be of service to the Christian knight, Ivanhoe.

"As I say," cried the Jew; "O! believe it, I say but the truth; I am a plundered, indebted, distressed man . . .

Yet I can tell thee what thou lackest, and, it may be, supply it too. Thy wish even now is for a horse and armor."

The Palmer started . ."What fiend prompted that guess?" said he hastily.

"No matter," said the Jew smiling, "so that it be a true one — and, as I can guess thy want, so can I supply it" . . . and drawing forth his writing materials in haste, he began to write on a piece of paper . . ."In the town of Leicester, all men know the rich Jew, Kirjath Jairam of Lombardy; give him this scroll — he hath on sale six Milan harnesses . . . ten goodly steeds . . . of these he will give thee thy choice, with every thing else that can furnish thee forth for thy tournament . . . The blessing of Our Father will be upon thee. Thy lance will be powerful as the rod of Moses."

Sometimes the Jewish money-lender rises to conduct of unselfish devotion. He stipulates that the ransom paid Front-de-Boeuf shall release not only himself and his daughter, but all his fellow captives.

"Grant me," he said, "at least with my own liberty, that of the companions with whom I travel. They scorned me as a Jew, yet they pitied my desolation, and because they tarried to aid me by the way, a share of my evil hath come upon them . . ."

Isaac's impassioned offer to deliver himself up to torture and ruin in order to save his daughter's honor, serves further to emphasize the sympathetic viewpoint of the nineteenth century novelist.

"Take all that you have asked," said Isaac; "Sir Knight — take ten times more — reduce me to ruin and beggary, if thou wilt — nay, pierce me with thy poniard, boil me in that furnace, but spare my daughter, deliver her in safety and honor. As thou art born of a woman, spare the honor of a helpless maiden — she is the image of my deceased Rachel. Will you deprive a widowed husband of his sole remaining comfort... Think not so vilely of us, Jews though we be . . . the hunted fox, the tortured wildcat loves its young — the despised and persecuted race of Abraham love their children . . ."

In the final scenes, Scott further reveals the Jew's magnanimity in his treatment of Ivanhoe, wounded and apparently abandoned by all the world.

"Holy Abraham!" Isaac the Jew exclaimed, "he is a good youth and my heart bleeds to see the gore trickle down his rich embroidered hacqueton and his corslet of goodly price — but to carry him to our house — he is a Christian, and by our law we may not deal with the stranger and Gentile, save for the advantage of our commerce ... nevertheless, the good youth must not bleed to death. Let Seth and Reuben bear him to Ashby."

So much for Isaac, whom, despite his faults, the author has led us to pity and admire. In much greater measure does the portrait of Rebecca awaken our sympathies. As she moves through the story, we admire her dark beauty of raven hair and flashing eye, her modesty, dignity and courage. Although she feels keenly the degradation and humiliation of her position as one of the outcast people, there is not the slightest evidence of bitterness or despair in her attitude towards life. She endures the hardships of her lot with calm resignation and extraordinary religious faith. Set beside the frivolous daughter of Shylock, Rebecca shines forth as "an ideal figure of true Jewish womanhood, faithful in the defence of her people, her religion and her honor."

In his treatment of Rebecca, Scott has shown a marked partiality, a sympathy and tenderness of understanding which no writer of an earlier age would have attempted in portraying Jewish character. Yet, for all his partiality, he would not permit a union between Rebecca and Ivanhoe, although he might easily have arranged for a romance to spring up between them, whereas Shakespeare allowed Jessica to elope with a Christian. As to the reasons for the inconsistency in the *Merchant of Venice*, we can only speculate. But Scott, in the Introduction to *Ivanhoe*, dated Abbotsford, 1830, explained his own attitude:

> The character of the fair Jewess found so much favor in the eyes of some fair readers, that the writer was censured because, when arranging the fates of the characters of the drama, he had not assigned the hand of Wilfred to Rebecca rather than the less interesting Rowena. But, not to mention that the prejudice of the age rendered such a union almost impossible, the author may, in passing, observe that he thinks a character of a highly virtuous and lofty stamp is degraded rather than exalted by an attempt to reward virtue with temporal prosperity . . .

The expressions of praise and admiration bestowed upon the character of Rebecca might seem extravagant to those who are not familiar with Jewish history, but Scott has a host of historical examples to draw from. Dr. Philipson reminds us that in the real trials and afflictions of the bitter and troubled existence of the Jews in medieval times, there were many Jewish women who, like Rebecca, were willing to meet death rather than dishonor; "many of whom, maiden and wife, young and old, ascended the funeral pyre, or thrust the cold steel into their bosoms, or cast themselves into the flowing streams, when these were the only alternatives left to them rather than forsake the religion of their fathers."

It is evident that Scott attempts, through Rebecca, to express certain humanitarian sentiments with respect to the position of the Jews in modern society. For example, after healing Ivanhoe, Rebecca declares that the only reward she asks is that he shall

> believe henceforth, that a Jew may do good service to a Christian without desiring other guerdon than the blessing of the Great Father who made both Jew and Gentile . . .

and, later, in answer to the taunt by the Templar, that the Jews are degraded, being more conversant with ingot and shekel than with spear and shield, the gentle Jewess answers:

> Thou hast spoken of the Jew, as the persecution of such as thou art has made him . . . Industry has opened to him the only road to power and influence which oppression has left unbarred. Read the ancient history of the people of God, and tell me if those by whom Jehovah wrought such marvels among the nations, were then a people of misers and usurers! And know, proud knight, we number names amongst us, to which your boasted northern nobility is as the gourd compared with the cedar . . . Such were the princes of Judah. And there are those among them now who shame not such high descent, and of such shall be the daughter of Isaac, the son of Adonikam.

From our study of the Jew as he is presented in *Ivanhoe*, it is clear that, although the setting of the story is medieval, the pictures that Scott draws of Jewish character and aspirations are influenced in a measure by nineteenth century principles and ideas. As the novelist's sympathetic interpretation of the Jewish character arises in part from the growing tolerance of the age, so, too, does it stimulate the further spread of liberal sentiment toward the little known people. The romance, showing as it does the historical background of anti-Jewish prejudice, tends to enlist the sympathy of modern readers for the contemporary Jew. It serves as a model to other writers of fiction in whose stories the delineation of Jewish characters is more or less influenced by the magnanimous attitude of the romantic historian.

Among the many imitators of Scott in this particular respect was Horace Smith (1779–1849), who, in a novel entitled *Zillah, a Tale of the Holy City* (second edition, 1828), cast a romantic glamour on his Jewish characters. Zillah, the heroine, is a charming Jewess after the style of Rebecca. She sings beautifully, embroiders, and is instructed in Greek and Latin. As the daughter of a pious *Rav*, she is well read in the sacred books. Father and daughter go to Rome, where the Jew has been appointed to a high office in the government. By virtue of their superior culture and liberal outlook, these Jewish characters are able to overcome he prejudices of Roman society. Unfortunately, sentimentality rather than a passion for justice colors this novel, and the same is true of the works of many other imitators of Scott.

Miriam, a novel by Charlotte Anley, published in 1829, is written in the same sentimental vein as *Zillah*. The scene is laid on the northern borders of Westmoreland, in a romantic valley sheltered on every side by cliff and wood, and secluded from the noise and bustle of the gay world. Here lives a rich Jew named Imlah Durvan, "a sullen alien from mankind," and his daughter, Miriam.

> Naturally of a daring, impetuous temper, Imlah had early imbibed all those feelings of enthusiastic devotion to the cause of Israel, which tended so fatally to inspire those of passionate hatred against every class of the Christian people. . . . Thus did he begin life with a mind bent upon the restoration of his alienated race, believing in his mad enthusiasm that he could overthrow the Christian Church and frustrate the designs of an offended God.

But his cause having failed, he is forced to leave Germany and seek refuge in England, "where the Jew as well as the gentile may safely rove in unsuspected liberty, to enjoy all the privileges of peace and security." His daughter, Miriam, is instructed by a tutor, the faithful Mendez, in the faith of her fathers. The writings of Josephus become her delight and she dwells on the former greatness of her people.

> "O father," she one day exclaimed, "will not our Messiah soon retrieve the injuries of Judah, when he shall come, the mighty conqueror, to spill the blood of all our enemies! I am but young and surely I may live to see that glorious day . . ."
>
> Imlah turned aside to hide the tear which fell, on the remembrance of his own early ambition, and sighed to think that such a noble spirit was indeed confined within a woman's breast.
>
> "Miriam," he replied with a mournful tone, "Messiah tarries long . . . but we are his chosen people, and we must await the fulfilment of those righteous laws which alone ensure our deliverance . . .but remember, Miriam, that although we walk in a strange land, the very scoff of mankind, we need not stoop, that Chris-

tians may trample on the worms they hate. Be Imlah's
daughter, and rise above the narrow taunts by teaching them the dignity they want; but never, Miriam,
court their vile reproaches, by leveling yourself to their
society."

In the course of a few years, Miriam meets Jessie and Helen,
and through them becomes a favored and frequent visitor
in the home of the Stuart family. The Jewess soon learns
that the Christian girls and their parents are kindly and
sympathetic. Helen becomes Miriam's constant companion. This close association between Jew and gentile, both
characters of great refinement and sympathy, leads eventually to the conversion of the Jew, with the ultimate
happiness of all; and once more convention triumphs.

Negligible as these stories are from the standpoint of
literature, trite and emotional as they may be in conception
and performance, they are nevertheless of value to us as a
commentary on the changing attitude of English writers
and readers towards the Jewish character. The idea of the
conversion of the Jew was not, of course, a new one, but in
the specific treatment which it receives in many of these
stories, the reader will detect the influence of the contemporary Humanitarian and Evangelical movements.

The sympathetic presentation of Jewish character is again
evident in a novel entitled *The Village of Mariendorpt*, by
Anna Maria Porter (1780–1832), sister of Jane Porter, and
a story-teller who gained considerable celebrity in her own
day by "an exuberant fertility of invention and a quick and
accurate discrimination of character." *Mariendorpt* is not
among the best known of Anna Maria Porter's novels, but
it is written in her graceful style, and later supplies the basis
for Sheridan Knowles's play, *The Maid of Mariendorpt*, pro-

duced in 1838. In the novel, Joseph the Jew is an unselfish man of wealth, who, not only places his riches at the disposal of the daughter of Muhldenau, when the latter is condemned, but risks his own life to secure his friend's release. Lessing's note of brotherhood, taken from *Nathan the Wise*, runs through this English novel, and is expressed later by Knowles:

> Give me the Hebrew hand! The Christian's friend, His elder brother, tho' with difference.

Probably as a result of the popularity of *Ivanhoe*, and the tendency toward a sympathetic representation of Jewish character in fiction, a novel entitled *Theodore Cyphon, or the Benevolent Jew* (1796), by George Walker, went through a second edition in 1823 and was favorably received in London. The benevolent Jew in this novel is one Shechem Bensadi, who, like Isaac of York, has a daughter who also nurses a Christian hero. Shechem lends money to the improvident aristocracy of his day and devotes his gains to the relief of deserving men and women. His philanthropy is extended to Jew and gentile alike. In a remarkable scene, Walker presents Schechem surrounded by scores of poor Jews to whom he supplies goods, thus enabling them to earn a livelihood. In equally striking scenes the Jewish money-lender is shown in the role of benefactor and friend of gentiles.

In an equally sympathetic and popular novel of Jewish life, *Sophia de Lissau* (1840), by an author who signs herself as Amelia Bristow, there is a strong Christian bias in the handling of the theme, although the author assures the reader that the account she gives of the Jewish household in the nineteenth century is very real and "authentic." The Jewish characters are treated as "objects of peculiar interest

and sympathy to the Christian observer." It is to be re-
gretted, says the author, that the Jews are "separated from
all but casual intercourse with those among whom they
sojourn," and that "their domestic habits and relative duties
are but imperfectly known and lightly appreciated." The
reader is told that, although "it is too common to hear all
that is vile and abominable connected with the name Jew,"
it should not be forgotten that the Jews are "men of like
passions with others." The ancestors of Sophia de Lissau
are Polish Jews who have for many centuries resided at
Lissau, in Prussian Poland. After the division of Poland,
several Jewish families are expatriated, and the de Lissaus are
among those who seek a refuge in England. They become,
in a few years, prosperous merchants and fill a high place
in the Jewish community in London. Both Jews and Gentiles
bear witness to the de Lissau liberality in dispensing alms.
Sophia's mother, Anna de Lissau, is the object of universal
admiration. She is beautiful and endowed with an intellectual power of the highest order. Sophia, the younger
daughter, inherits the exquisite beauty of her mother, while
her benign and gentle spirit claims a relative resemblance to
that of her amiable father. Numerous offers of marriage are
made to her father for her hand, but in the end she is married
to Raphael Leoni, a Jew with a superficial understanding
and a narrow, selfish spirit. The marriage ceremony is an
elaborate affair which the author delights in describing at
length for the edification of her Christian readers. In the
final scenes of the story, Anna, the mother, dies, and Leoni
is unfaithful to Sophia. Sorrow and misfortune visit the
once-happy Jewish household. But, through it all, Sophia
preserves her native dignity and elegance. Unlike most
women in her community, we are informed that Sophia is

not "versed in the mysteries of the card table" and is not "wholly indifferent to eternal things." Sophia lives nobly and dies in the faith of her ancestors.

A second book on the de Lissau family, entitled *Emma de Lissau*, appeared shortly afterwards. In the preface to the third edition (1830), the novelist declares that she is certain that the details of her narrative are "affecting realities." She gives the reader a closer view of the Jewish household than was possible in the preceding study. In this novel we have a full-length portrait of the grandfather of Sophia and Emma de Lissau — the bigoted Jew, Eleazar de Lissau, who delights in assembling learned Jews of every country at the nightly meetings in his house, in order to discuss knotty points in the Talmud, and to make calculations respecting the advent of the promised Jewish Messiah. Of Emma, the heroine of the narrative, we learn that, on becoming an apostate and "worthy member of the Nazarene," she is cast out of her family and community, and, after many heart-affecting trials and tribulations, becomes the wife of a Christian, and attains to "ultimate happiness." The moral of Emma's story is contained in "Lines to a Converted Jew," by Maria Griffith, which we find published in *The Winter's Wreath* (1829); the last two stanzas reveal the sentiments of the Evangelical group towards Jewish converts:

> O snatch'd from error's gulf through grace,
> From Sin through Christ made free!
> Welcome, thou child of Israel's race,
> The Christian welcomes thee!
>
> Through thee may Israel seek the Lord
> And Jews prove Christians true;
> For Christians love the Jewish name,
> Their Saviour was a Jew!

In chapter XIII of the second volume, the author indulges in a discourse on the Jewish character, commenting favorably on Jewish philanthropists and worshipers in the synagogue who are "conspicuous for their alacrity in endeavoring to alleviate the sorrows entailed by the posterity of Adam, by the transgressions of their primogenitor."

Into these sketches of Jewish life, Amelia Bristow pours all the information that she has collected about the practical duties of a devout Jewish woman, the weekly preparation of the Sabbath, the feasts, and Jewish funeral rites and ceremonies. The two rabbis who make their appearance in the de Lissau home are new characters in fiction relating to Anglo-Jewish life. Rabbi Colmar, in *Sophia de Lissau,* represents orthodox Judaism; his presence helps to give reality to the religious life of the other characters.

> His spirit was haughty and dictatorial, and mirth and cheerfulness were a sin in his gloomy creed. His pale and interesting features rarely relaxed into a smile. He was a man of really profound learning and of unquestionable probity. He was treated with delicate respect, and was consulted on all important occasions.

A man of the same mould, and representing the same strict adherence to orthodox Judaism, is Rabbi Jonathan of Posen, in *Emma de Lissau.* He, too, is a man of eminent learning, peculiar devotion and profound cabalistic knowledge. But he is a kind and gentle shepherd of his flock, lacking the severity of Rabbi Colmar. An important comparison is made by the author between the English and foreign Jews. The de Lissau family, who retain their Polish costume and habits, engage in trade with, but are stricter in their ceremonial observances than, their English brethren, who, according to the author, unite religious superstition and bigotry with the most careless apathy and levity. Completely immersed as they are in traffic and commercial speculations, and quitting business only to relax their minds, they enter on all the fashionable amusements of the day; the theater, the ball-room, the card table — nay even the prize ring. They perform their cold and heartless synagogue worship, their daily use of the phylacteries and shemonahessrah, or prayer of the eighteen blessings. Their easy access to English society has greatly assisted to destroy their ancient character.

To the interest stimulated by the appearance of Polish Jews in England in the late 'twenties, we may attribute the publication in London of a story, originally written in Polish, and later translated from the German version, and published in English under the title of *Levi and Sarah, or the Polish Lovers*. The romance affords an admirable defence of the Jewish character at a time when the question of Jewish naturalization was before the House of Commons for discussion (1830). "Many of the severe remarks on our people," says the Jewish author, "have been partial, and many of the taunts and stigmas on our errors and crimes might with as much justice be directed towards the Christians... The crimes are those of the few, not of the whole... Believe me, among us there are honest and enlightened people." The story of the two lovers is presented in order to illustrate the virtues as well as the vices of a Jewish community. Levi and Sarah are secretly pledged to each other by mutual affection. Their union, however, is opposed by the father of the girl, partly because Levi is not an orthodox Jew, and partly because the father has already resolved that Sarah shall marry Jankiel, the son of a commercial agent at Berditschev. Through the influence of Jankiel, Levi is excommunicated on account of his liberality of sentiment and his intercourse with the *Goyim*, a term applied by Polish Jews to all who are not members of their own community. But Sarah, escaping the prison to which she has been consigned, joins her lover, and together they travel far away from their unsympathetic and fanatical families. In the characters of Levi and Sarah, the romancer endeavors to delineate the beauty and idealism of Jewish youth, just as in the portraits of Jankiel, the deformed and fiend-like son of the commercial agent, and of Moses, the strict and unsympathetic father of Sarah, an attempt is made to reveal "a Jew in the vulgar sense of the term." The sentence of excommunication pronounced on Levi is interesting to those who do not realize that the persecution of the Jew by the orthodox members of his community was as great as, and sometimes far more severe, than the persecution of the Jew by the world outside the ghetto. The offending Levi is cursed "by the Law and the superior Judges" and expelled without any mercy.

Among English writers of popular fiction, the information contained in this story of the Polish lovers had the effect of stimulating fresh interest in the internal ramifications of ghetto life. The vicissitudes and experiences of defenceless Jews and beautiful Jewish maidens once again became the theme of the short story, written for the New Year Gift Books and the Juvenile Souvenirs, the various Annuals, Keepsakes and Albums that were so popular in the 'thirties and the 'forties. For example, in the *New Year's Gift Book* (1830), there is a short story entitled "The Little Jew Merchant," by Mary Howitt (1799–1888), the popular writer of tales and poems, and editor, with her husband, of *Howitt's Journal*, in which the author takes up the theme of injustice to Jews, and shows how a fair-minded Christian household would behave when brought into association with Jews. The description given by the author indicates the degree of sentimentality with which the subject is treated:

> Our little merchant was an orphan Jew, about fourteen years of age, whose sole property was deposited in the few silver wares he was carrying in a flat mahogany box, slung across his shoulders . . . His countenance strikingly exhibited the characteristic physiognomy of his people, but without the sinister expression so often visible in it. Sorrow and unusual thought were deeply traced in every line of his face which, notwithstanding, was one of extraordinary beauty. He might indeed have furnished a model for the study of a painter. As he went on his often extensive rambles from village to village, he was called the handsome little Jew, and many a kind-hearted country-woman laid out her two shillings in a thimble, or bought a silver bodkin, out of pity for the solemn expression of grief which, she thought, had spoiled his beautiful face, while, in fact, we believe, it owed a great part of its charm to that very cause . . .

In later years, we shall find a Thackeray satirizing and burlesquing descriptions of this sort. But, on the whole, the conclusions which the reader can draw from these studies of the Jew in English fiction of the first third of the century seem fairly indicative of a change of attitude on the part of writers and readers in England towards the Jews. In the first place, the very number of the stories in which the Jew figures bears witness to the increase in public interest. The growth in numbers, wealth, and social position of the English Jewry, and the publicity which their fight for emancipation won for them, was beginning to command a public attention which they did not receive before. It is true that the interest in Jewish characters, shown in the stories we have examined, is still sentimental and romantic rather than realistic. There is little evidence of a direct repercussion in fiction of the fight for civil, religious and economic freedom. Such reaction can not be expected in the types of fiction in which the Jew has so far figured.

Yet, there is evidence, even in many of the novels and stories in which the Jew appears in the traditional role of villain, that he has been to some extent humanized, while in many of the novels of contemporary life in which he figures, he is a hero, noble and misunderstood. There is evidence, too, of some effort on the part of at least some of the writers to depict details of Jewish life and character with a truth and accuracy obviously based on first-hand study. The tolerance shown to the Jew, as a Jew, even in the most favorable cases, is of course not complete. The tolerance of the age was not complete. Yet it represents a decided advance over earlier times in liberal sentiment.

CHAPTER VIII

AMONG THE EARLY VICTORIANS

When Queen Victoria came into power in 1837, there were about 30,000 Jews in England. Of these, at least 20,000 lived in London. It was observed by a contemporary writer that a large proportion of the metropolitan Jews "had come to approximate very closely to their English neighbors in manners and customs," and that "some were discernible to an observant eye only by an oriental cast of physiognomy, or by occasional mistakes in the pronunciation of the *w* and the *y*." In a letter to a friend in Germany (July 26, 1835), a disinterested visitor, Frederick von Raumer, remarked about the Jews in England:

> I had a long discussion with Mr.— about the state of the Jews in England. He was very glad that a Jew had lately been elected an alderman of the City of London, which was the first instance of the kind. I believe that the indelible character of the Jews, which has been as often a subject of praise as of blame, will vanish sooner than is believed, when the legal and civil regulations, which draw so strict a line, shall be abolished . . .

The position of the Jews was benefited on the whole by the tremendous increase in wealth and financial power of some of the leading Jewish families, and by the philan-

156

thropies which, as a result, they were able to dispense on a magnificent scale. We have already seen how, during the Napoleonic wars, the House of Rothschild had succeeded in establishing itself as the leviathan of the English money-market. At the time of the Queen's accession, other Jewish families rose to eminence on the Stock Exchange and in the field of international finance; the Goldsmids, the Mocattas, the Phillips, the Salomons and the Montefiores. These families were reputedly generous to both Jews and Christians, and won many friends for their people in all walks of life in England.

Of course, there was also a negative side to the picture. It was inevitable that the great fortunes won by these families should lay them open to unfavorable criticism, even to harsh condemnation in some quarters. Especially was this true in the "Hungry Forties," when panics, famines and revolutions in Europe were the order of the day. In their confusion and misery, men of the laboring classes, thrown out of work through financial and industrial failures brought on by speculation and cheap money, looked askance at the concentration of capital in the hands of a financial oligarchy, and listened eagerly to all sorts of tales, true and false, concerning the commercial and financial world. It was inevitable that men who were idle against their will and despairing of better times should murmur against the capitalistic system, and, incidentally, against the Jewish financiers and brokers, for very naturally the reputation which the Jew bore for business acumen made him the target for blame and abuse in times of financial stress. However, in the period of expansion and financial prosperity on which England entered in the 'fifties, this temporary set-back, never very serious, was soon compensated for. The wealth of the Jews remained an asset, and the forces operating in Parliament and in English society in favor of liberalism worked markedly to the social and political advantage of the English Jews.

In the revolutions of 1848, the European Jews were in the very thick of the conflict. The names of Ludwig Börne, Heinrich Heine, Karl Marx, Ferdinand Lassalle, Johann Jacoby, Gabriel Riesser, Adolphe Crémieux, Henrietta Herz, and Rahel Levin stand high in the list of those who identified themselves with the social and political struggle in which the nations in this period were embroiled. Their influence was felt in England, especially among the younger generation, who believed that a new day had dawned.

Great changes were taking place throughout the world — changes that, it was hoped, would break down the walls of prejudice and misunderstanding that had long separated the nations. The invention and development of telegraphy (1837–1866), the laying of the great Atlantic cable (1857–1866), the extension of a system of railways throughout Europe and the British Isles (1830–1866), were to be the means whereby some of the ancient evils of bigotry, sectionalism and intolerance would be overcome.

As we have seen, the Jews of the upper and middle classes were year by year throwing off more and more of their foreign aspect and assuming the color of their English surroundings. They were, so it was reported, becoming less "stiff-necked" and more tolerant in their pride of race and religion. The need for religious reform had been recognized as early as 1812, and again in 1828, when Hebraic scholars in England first felt the influence of the historical research begun by such continental scholars as Zunz (1794–1886), Rapoport (1790–1867), and Luzzatto (1800–1865). In 1836 a petition was presented to the *Mahamad* by a number of the *Yehidim* asking for the introduction of such changes in the Synagogue service as had already been adopted by the Reform synagogue in Germany. Although the petition was rejected, preaching in the vernacular was adopted in 1838. What the reformers desired was a wider latitude in the interpretation of the Mosaic Law. They were willing to retain whatever in the talmudic tradition they considered to be the spirit of the Law, but they held that many usages of the synagogue had been rendered obsolete by the conditions of the times.

But the tenacity of life which had preserved the ancient faith through the persecutions of seventeen centuries was in the bones of the traditionalists. They opposed the new movement and rejected all suggestions of change. A split between what might be called "New Lights" and the traditionalists seemed inevitable, since the difference in the value which the Orthodox and the Reform factions severally attached to the teachings of tradition involved a hundred differences of the greatest moment in everyday social life. A closer intercommunion between those who profoundly venerated dogmatic authority, and those who desired to bring the ancient religion into harmony with the changing modes and attitudes of a new era, seemed impracticable. Therefore, in 1840, the organization of a new congregation led the way to the founding of other reform synagogues in Manchester, Bradford, and other centers. An important section of the English Jewry had set their faces toward liberalism and reform, and the indications pointed to changes within the ancient fold. This fact was sure in time to affect the standing of the Jews in the English community.

Although a feeling of uncertainty pervaded the country when the young queen ascended the throne, it was soon realized by both Whigs and Tories that Victoria's heart beat in sympathy with the cares and wishes of her people, and that it was her desire to be free from religious bigotry. In her first speech from the throne, she dispelled all fears by indicating that it was her purpose to raise the Crown above the turmoil of party strife, and to rule with justice. One of the first public acts of the new queen was the knighting of Sir Moses Montefiore, a Jew, and Sheriff of the city of London. In this liberality of sentiment she was in harmony with the majority of her subjects. The general cry of the times was for toleration and the abolition of political and social wrongs and injustice. As early as 1836, the People's Charter was drafted, demanding manhood suffrage, the ballot, annual parliaments, the abolition of property qualifications for members of Parliament, and equal electoral districts. In an atmosphere which could foster such an advanced program, the Jewish cause, too, might hope to flourish.

The feeling was growing stronger that the Jews, as actual tax-payers, landowners and industrialists, had established their claims on the grounds of national and personal merits to an equality with other subjects of the queen. Lord Holland, the famous Liberal peer, who was among the most persistent and devoted advocates of the Jew Bill, advised patience and fortitude on the part of the Jewish leadership, and looked hopefully forward to the ultimate triumph of their cause. The success which he prophesied was, in fact, not far off.

The political battle was yet to be won. The Reform Bill of 1832 had, as we have seen, by the enfranchisement of

220,000 voters, signified the recognition of a new democratic principle in government. Obviously this principle was certain, sooner or later, to react on the Jewish question.

Until 1847, the propriety of admitting Jews to Parliament had been purely an academic question; that is, since no Jews had been elected by a constituency, there was really no tangible case that could be presented to the House for decision. In order, therefore, to bring the Parliamentary issue to a test, the City of London, in the General Election of 1847, chose as one of its representatives a well known and popular Jew, Baron Lionel Rothschild. The voice of the electorate expressed itself in a practical manner by placing the Jew's name simultaneously with that of Lord John Russell, the Prime Minister, at the head of the poll. The matter was presented to the Commons by the Prime Minister himself, who moved that

> it is expedient to remove all civil disabilities at present affecting Her Majesty's subjects of the Jewish religion, with the like exceptions as are provided for Her Majesty's subjects professing the Roman Catholic religion.

In the autumn session, a resolution was introduced to seat Baron Rothschild, in accordance with the wishes of the London constituency. The measure was passed in the Commons by a substantial majority, but was rejected by the Lords. The Jewish member was refused his seat unless he should take the oath "on the true faith of a Christian."

Baron Rothschild was again elected in 1850, and for the second time prevented from taking his seat. At the conclusion of each session, the Jewish member would come forward to take his seat, shake his head when the oath was presented, and then return sadly to the visitor's gallery to wait patiently for the removal of the obstacle to his membership. The gentlemanly conduct of the Jewish leader won the respect and admiration of many of his colleagues. But it did not win him the coveted seat. The opposition resolutely attacked his election.

In 1851, David Salomon, the first Jew to become Sheriff, Magistrate, Alderman, and finally Lord Mayor of London, was elected Member of Parliament for Greenwich. But, as in the case of Rothschild, before taking his seat, the new Jewish member refused to take the oath "on the true faith of a Christian," and was therefore directed by the Speaker to withdraw from the bar.

As the question was debated pro and con in Parliament and press, its passage was like that of Samson's foxes through Philistine corn; it kindled every slumbering sentiment of sectarian hate.

When, in spite of the strong opposition, the Jewish Emancipation Bill came at last to its third reading (1853), the absurdity of the situation was clearly revealed by John Bright, who felt called upon to declare that the whole question of oaths in Parliament — oaths that prevented the Jew from taking his seat and being of service to his countrymen — was a ludicrous farce.

> Let us then get rid of this question, which has been discussed and decided year after year; and, above all, let us see that the Commons House of England is open to the Commons of England, and that every man, be his creed what it may, if elected by a constituency of his countrymen, may sit in this House and vote on all matters which affect the legislation of this kingdom.

Similarly, Lord Lyndhurst, in a speech before the House of Lords, took the opportunity, when the Bill came up for division, to "demolish every fallacy, unravel every intricacy," and treat the whole Jewish Question with the brilliancy, the apt illustration and the caustic wit of his best days. Ultimately, when the Palmerston ministry was swept out of office by one of those numerous gusts of popular wrath so frequent in political history, and when a stop-gap Conservative administration — of which Benjamin Disraeli was a member — came into power (March, 1858), a resolution was passed permitting Baron Lionel Rothschild to use the modified form of oath, and to take his seat for the City of London (July 26, 1858). The House was packed on that memorable occasion. In deep silence, the first Jewish member was led to the table by Lord John Russell. He bowed to the speaker and took the oath on the Hebrew Bible, substituting for the words "on the true faith of a Christian," the words "So help me, Jehovah!" Thus the long political struggle was ended. But what was of greatest significance was the fact that the presence of the Jewish member in the Commons served as a tangible symbol of the complete political emancipation of his people — it betokened the breaking down of the Christian exclusiveness of the state.

It was not to be expected, however, that the admission of a few prominent Jews to Parliament would at once efface all traces which centuries of oppression had left on the people. Yet a feeling of security and freedom was now shared by all classes of English Jewry.

In the literature of the early Victorian period, we may expect to find some reflection of the status of the Jew and of the public reaction toward the changes in his condition in society and politics. We shall see that the Jew appears in most of the varied types of literature of the time, sometimes with credit, sometimes with discredit, but always, or nearly always, with an increased humanity — that is to say, he becomes less and less a lay figure designed to arouse abhorrence or sentiment, and more and more a vital human being moved by passions not entirely alien to his gentile brother.

In this period, too, the literature of opinion in newspapers, periodicals, pamphlets and essays, echoes the views of the partisans of the Jewish cause, as well as the views of the opposition, with regard to all the movements, controversial and otherwise, in which the Jew is involved. An interesting sign of these new times is the establishment by the Jews themselves of the *Voice of Jacob*, a newspaper founded in London in 1841–1842, and devoted to the defence of the Jewish interests.

We have already noted that one of the features of this period was the growth of a greater tolerance on the part of the Jews themselves. In a pamphlet published in 1845, "An Israelite" expresses himself on this point:

> No chains are so heavy as those that shackle the mind; no slavery is so degrading as a moral one; no power is so despotic as that of ungoverned passions; no rule so tyrannical as that of our prejudice and bigotry.

Another writer (*Family Herald*, September 11, 1847), offers the opinion that the intolerant attitude of the Jews themselves has, in the past, been partly responsible for their unpopularity.

> . . . for many ages they would not eat at the same table with the Christians . . . we have seen them sitting by themselves at public dinners and eating their own dishes, because those of the Gentiles were un-

clean . . . they have kept themselves apart . . . . and the
Gentiles have naturally felt affronted by the estimate
which Jews put upon them, and resented it accordingly . . .

Benjamin Disraeli himself, in an impassioned exposition
of the unity of interests of Jew and gentile, declares (*Tancred*,
265 ff.), that there is no real opposition between Judaism
and Christianity; that the Jew is a proto-Christian, and
the Christian a completed Jew. He reminded his countrymen that

> The life and property of England are protected by
> the Laws of Sinai . . . Vast as the obligations of the
> whole human family are to the Hebrew race, there is no
> portion of the modern population so much indebted to
> them as the British people.

One seems to pass from the sublime to the ridiculous as
he turns from Disraeli's impassioned declaration of faith
in the destiny of the Jewish race, to the call of the Old
Clothes Man in the London streets. Yet, here is another
side of the Jewish picture, and the Old Clothes Man has
his meed of attention in the public press. In the *Oddities
of Real Life* (1838), Paul Pry describes at some length "the
industrious and dirty fraternity" of Old Clothes Men who
carry on a thriving business in Monmouth Street, "that
emporium of thrice-renovated garments." In this region
of London, half a dozen Jew "barkers" are wont to pounce
upon the unsuspecting countryman, each of them swearing
on the "Vord of a Shew," that the "pest bargains" are only
to be found in his shop.

On the other hand, the continued growth in financial
and social prestige of some of the leading Jewish families

during this period was receiving frequent notice in the contemporary press.

In the following stanzas (dated Saturday, May 18, 1833), Thackeray describes the head of the English house of Rothschild:

> Here's the pillar of 'Change! Nathan Rothschild himself,
>> With whose fame every bourse in the universe rings;
> The first Baron Juif; by the grace of his pelf,
>> Not "The King of the Jews", but the Jew of the Kings."
>
> The great incarnation of cents and consols,
>> The eights, halves and quarters, scrip, options and shares;
> Who plays with new Kings as young Missus with dolls;
>> The monarch undoubted of bulls and of bears!
>
> O, Plutus, your graces are queerly bestowed!
>> Else sure we should think you behaved *infra dig*!
> When with favors surpassing, it joyed you to load,
>> A greasy-faced compound of donkey and pig.
>
> Here, just as he stands with his head pointed thus,
>> At full-length, gentle reader, we lay him before ye;
> And we then leave the Jew (what we wish he'd leave us,
>> But we fear to no purpose) alone in his glory.

Two eminent Jewish financiers are described by an anonymous pamphleteer in 1851 in terms of appreciation.

Of Sir Isaac Goldsmid, we have this pen sketch in *City Men and City Manners*, published in London, 1851:

> There is little of the aristocrat in his dress. The royal blue surtout and the light waistcoat, overhung by a massive gold chain, gave the baronet the stamp of rank ... The Hebrews say that Sir Isaac Goldsmid is not sufficiently liberal to his own sect; they, however, award him the praise of being munificent to Christians.

More loyal to his own group, though not less respected by the general public, is the head of the great house of Salomons.

> To see him toddling down Bartholomew Lane towards his offices in Shorter's Court, Throgmorton Street, with his crutch stick, his bent back, and his close-cut grey beard, one would have thought, giving him credit for his decency of dress, that one of the more respectable of the class of Cutler Street or Rosemary Lane dealers was on a visit to his broker to invest a trifle. Although thus strange in his appearance, the elder Mr. Salomons was by no means parsimonious. He provided liberally for his friends, assisted many of the needy of his persuasion, and is esteemed as having been a kind-hearted and benevolent man.

Marriages between the daughters of rich magnates and scions of the English nobility were made the subject of satire and humorous verse. A parody on Anglo-Jewish unions, published in the *English Annual* (London 1863), runs as follows:

> Come, open your casement, Miss Moses;
> A fig for your father the Jew!
> No dream to the sleeper discloses
> My little flirtation with you.

He dreams of some plan by which copper
　　May soon be converted to gold;
Some diamond that lies in his shop, or
　　Some pearl that he yesterday sold.

*　*　*　*　*　*　*

Come down, then, my excellent Jewess;
　　Come down, lest my voice should be heard;
I'll show you how fond and how true is
　　The sensitive heart of a Lord!
Still cling to your Jewish persuasion,
　　Still weekly the synagogue view;
You'll learn, on some future occasion,
　　Some Lords are a sin-a-gog too!

Come, Zillah, I'll make you a Lady;
　　You can't think how pleasant it sounds;
Come, if your portmanteau is ready,
　　Slip in some additional pounds.
But do not suspect that I covet
　　The wealth of your father, good man;
Gold bores me, in fact, and I'll prove it
　　By spending as fast as I can!

In the early years of its existence (1841 ff.) the humorous weekly *Punch*, expressing the views of average conservative Englishmen, was manifestly unsympathetic towards the Jews. In a "prize preface" to the sixth volume (1844), the following paragraph was supposed to have been submitted by Benjamin Disraeli, under the motto "young Ben, he was a nice young man:"

It has been remarked by the surpassing author of the brilliant *Coningsby* that the world, although it dreams not of the glory, is at the present time governed by the Hebrew mind. *Punch* can bear testimony to the fact. Once *Punch* wanted money. Who lent it to him at

sixty per cent? A Jew. Who sued him on the bill?
a Jew. These are, however, common events. The
world will be startled to learn that *Punch* himself —
witness his nose — is a Jew!

With this truth made manifest, truly, indeed, did
the eloquent and deep-thoughted author of *Coningsby*
declare that the world was "governed by the Jewish
mind." We shall publish our next volume in Hebrew.

This was followed by other references to "Gentlemen
Jews," "The Jewish Mind," "A Jew Pig Dealer," and the
like. But sometime in 1847, Mr. Punch changed his attitude
towards the Jews to one of playful satire, as is indicated in
the following letter, supposedly written by "a Jew:"

To Sir Robert Inglis: Sir, Hath not a Jew brains? hath
not a Jew faculties, conception, memory, imagination,
judgment, reason? ruled by the same laws, liable to
the same punishments, open to the same action, entitled to the same remedy, condemned and acquitted
by the same judge and jury as a Christian is? If you
tax us, do we not pay? If you rate us, do we not cash
up? If you hang us, do we not die? If we obey your
Government, shall we have no hand in it? If we are
like you in the rest, we ought to resemble you in that.
I am, Sir Robert, your obedient servant, A JEW.

In 1856, when the Abjuration Oath was again up for
discussion before the Commons, *Punch* took up the question in the following characteristic manner: —

Are they (the Jews) necessarily excluded by the words
"on the true faith of a Christian"? Certainly not. One
of the most eminent of the original professors of Christianity declared, on a particular occasion, that he was
a Jew of Tarsus. He believed that the true faith of a

Jew was the Christian religion. Surely, any one holding that belief could quite consistently pledge himself
on the true faith of a Jew. Conversely, a Jew thinks
that all that is true in Christianity is just so much of
it as is retained from the law of Moses. We should like
to know what Dr. Pusey thinks about that. How many
exemplary and zealous persons are there who have
subscribed to the Thirty-Nine Articles in a sense very
considerably more unnatural than that in which
Abrahams may be supposed to vow that he would be
loyal to Queen Victoria on the true faith of a Christian?

Among the chief contributors to *Punch* was the popular
humorist and wit, Douglas Jerrold (1803–1857), whose "The
Barber's Chair" and "Hedgehog Letters" were as well known
as his famous "Caudle Lectures." In two letters addressed
to "Isaac Moss, slop-seller, Portsmouth" by Juniper Hedgehog (1847), the humorist comments on the Jewish question
as follows:

Dear Isaac,—
    What poor George the Third, Lord Eldon, and such
folk think of it, there's no saying, but in a twinkling
a Jew may be an alderman! Even the Bishop of London swallows the measure, although shuddering at it,
as if it was a black draught. However, Isaac, what
I write to you about is this. Mr. Ashwirt, in the common council of London, spoke about the Jews; and
after him the Duke of Cambridge in the House of
Lords. Both of 'em gave their reasons for what is called
Hebrew Emancipation; and it is to consider 'em one
with the other.— Mr. Ashwirt argues upon what are
called broad, wide and benevolent principles. He would
give liberty to the Jew because the man was born a
Jew: because he couldn't choose his father and mother,
his creed or color. It is his fortune to be a Jew, as it
may be the fortune of the Bishop of London to be a

Christian. Therefore the common councilman would give him equal freedom with the rest. Now, the Royal Duke would emancipate the Jew because "he contributes a large portion" to the funds of Christian charities. With the Duke, the Jew buys the favor with hard cash! Sir Moses ought to be an alderman, because he gave the Duke "a very handsome sum" for a charitable meeting.

. . . Now suppose, Isaac, that the Jews had been poor; that they never subscribed handsome sums, could the Duke, according to his own logic, have lifted up his voice in their behalf? I fear not . . . . .

And in letter XIX of the same series, as follows:

Dear Isaac,— Sir Robert Peel has stood your friend; and if you're out of money, and the freedom, and the luck, you may be Lord Mayor of London as soon as you like — You can't, as a Jew, sit in Parliament as yet, but time goes round, Isaac, and I shouldn't wonder if some day that was to come . . . .

One great writer of the times who viewed this economic and political advance of the Jews with the greatest distaste was Thomas Carlyle (1795–1881), who showed what Froude called "a true Teutonic aversion for that unfortunate race." He thought them lacking in humor — a fatal defect, in his eyes — and maintained that they had contributed nothing besides, to the wealth of mankind, being mere dealers in money, gold, jewels, or else old clothes, material and spiritual. He is said to have remarked, as he stood in front of Rothschild's great house at Hyde Park Corner:

I do not mean that I want King John back again, but if you ask me which mode of treating these people to have been the nearest to the will of the Almighty about

> them — to build them palaces like that, or to take the
> pincers for them, I declare for the pincers.

Then, says Froude, he imagined himself King John, with
the Baron on the bench before him.

> Now, Sir, the State requires some of these millions you
> have heaped together with your financing work. "You
> wont? Very well"— and the speaker gave a twist with
> his wrist —"Now will you?"— and then another twist,
> till the millions were yielded.

As for the great question of the day, the admission of the
Jews, Carlyle writes to Margaret Carlyle in 1848, that
"now they are for getting Jews into Parliament," and that
he will not give "half a snuff of tobacco" for or against the
Jew Bill. When the fate of the Jew Bill in Parliament
seemed uncertain, Baron Rothschild is reported to have
appealed to Carlyle to write a pamphlet in favor of the
measure, intimating that the sage of Chelsea might name
any sum which he liked to ask for payment. "Well," said
Carlyle, to Froude, "I had to tell him that it could not be;
but I observed, too, that I could not conceive why he and
his friends, who were supposed to be looking out for the
coming of Shiloh, should be seeking seats in a Gentile
legislature."

As in the early years of the century, so now, the question
of the admission of the Jews to Parliament aroused bitter
controversy. The chief opposition to emancipation came
from the formidable phalanx of Bishops who persisted in
holding to the old argument that "as long as Christianity
is part and parcel of the law of the land, a Jew should not
be permitted to legislate for a Christian state and a Christian
Church." In *Blackwood's Magazine* for December, 1847,

in an article entitled "Judaism and the Legislature," the following comment appears: —

> We cannot be silent when the intention is avowed to bring into a Christian legislature a sect which pronounces Christianity to be utterly a falsehood, its founder to be an imposter (we shudder at the words), and our whole hope of immortality dependent on his sacrifice and merits to be a wicked and blasphemous delusion . . . In England, Parliament rules everything. In making a man a member of Parliament, we in a certain degree make him our master . . . opening the doors of Parliament to the Jew is actually opening the doors of power, and of a power which, if he have a conscientious adherence to his own belief, he must use against ours. The question then is, not a mere municipal regulation, but the very life of our religion . . . What ought England to do at this moment? It ought to teem with petitions. Its clergy ought to meet and give their most solemn pledge to resist this most fatal innovation. Its bishops ought to take the lead in their meetings, and come forth to do their duty like men . . .

The following year (1848), another article in the same magazine avers:

> The whole and sole claim of the Jew is that some of his party are rich. How they have made their riches, or how they spend them, is beneath us to inquire. The measure must be thrown out by the awakened power of public opinion. We must not indulge our indolence in relying on the House of Lords. They may do their duty, but we must do ours. The Jew is not to enter the Christian legislature . . .

On the other hand, the advocates of Jewish emancipation felt equally convinced that "no other conclusion can be legitimately drawn, than that the full and entire emancipation of the Jews is the duty, as well as the interest of a Christian people." Not merely for the sake of the Jews, so the argument runs, but for the sake of religious truth itself, should enlightened and thoughtful men seek a settlement of the question by the removal of the last remaining civil disqualification of the English Jews.

Another interesting opinion was given by Archbishop Whateley in "Additional Remarks" to a printed copy of one of his speeches in the House of Lords (1833), in the course of which it is maintained that

> no one's religious opinions, so long as he does not molest his neighbors, ought to interfere with his civil rights; and as men we should employ our conscience to sit in judgment on ourselves, not on our own brother, whose religious errors, however great, and scruples, however foolish, should not prevent us as civil legislators from treating him as a good citizen, so long as he show himself qualified and disposed to act as such.

In response to the suggestion made by a Tory that Baron Rothschild, instead of having a seat in Parliament, should have one in the Pillory, a writer in the *Examiner* (1857), offers the following satirical "Plea for Persecution:"

> A little persecution, if not a dangerous thing, is a peddling, paltry thing. Persecute in earnest, or not at all. Turn it to profitable account, as your forefathers did. Much better than keeping Baron Rothschild out of the House of Commons, it would be to roast him whole, stuffed with sovereigns. Or, if that is objected to as rather partaking of the nature of cruelty, he might be offered the option of having his teeth drawn or ransomed at fifty-thousand pounds each, or some such moderate sum. If proscription and persecution are to

be, why then, in the name of common sense, not make something of it? Let there be profit as well as pleasure. The Jews are abominably rich and would stand a vast deal of fleecing. Why not vote a Jew, bodily goods, and all, now and then in supply?

A curious feature of the publicity given the Jews in the early Victorian press is the publication of reports from foreign lands, dealing with the treatment of Jews by other nations. A Jewish writer in 1851 makes the following comparison between continental and English Jews:

It is fair to say that, in reality, liberty of conscience prevails in England. And I, as a Jew, felt myself much more free in this country than I had in Prussia; and this circumstance, together with other advantages of English life, determined me to cast away every idea of ever leaving England again.

English travelers and workers in foreign mission fields offered favorable comments on Jewish life and character in other lands. For example, a visitor to the ghetto at Rome, concludes an interesting report with the statement:

The Jews, the venerable people, who ought never to be looked upon by Christians without some feeling of respect . . . still are these wandering children of Israel denied the rights of nature, the bonds of brotherhood, the claims of citizenship . . . .

and a traveler in Syria and the Holy Land, lamenting on the sufferings of this "despised, stricken and outcast nation," reminds his readers that "this extraordinary people" are "the favored of the Lord, the descendants of the Patriarchs and the Prophets, and the aristocracy of the Earth."

Among the most interesting commentators on the continental Jews is the versatile Thomas Hood (1799–1845).

In a volume of epistles entitled *Up the Rhine*, published in 1839, he gives a vivid picture of the wrongs suffered by the Jews in Prussia. In the course of a reported conversation between himself and a friend, Hood comments on an insult offered in his presence to a Jew:

But surely . . . such prejudice is rare, except amongst the most bigoted Catholics and the lower orders? Lower orders and Catholics! — quite the reverse . . . You will not rank the editor of the Public Journal, or his contributors, in the lower and ignorant class; nevertheless, my little Isaac the other day lent me a local paper, and the two very first paragraphs that met my eye were sarcastic anecdotes against the race. One of them was laughable enough, indeed I laughed at it myself; but in this country such stories are circulated more for malice and mischief than for the sake of fun . . .

. . . Von Raumer speaks of a Prussian liberal, who abused Prussia, as no better than a beast; — but he surely forgot this oppressed portion of his countrymen. As to love of country, in general he is right — but has the degraded inhabitant of Juden Gasse a country? To look for patriotism from such a being, you might as well expect local gratitude and attachment from a pauper without a parish! No, no, — that word, so dear, so holy, to a German, his Fatherland, is to the Jew bitter mockery. He has all the duties and burthens, without the common privileges of the relationship — he is as heavily taxed and hardly drilled, as any member of the family; but has he an equal share in the benefits — does he even enjoy a fair portion of the affection of his brothers and sisters?

. . . Yes — Heine abused Prussia, and he was a Jew. So did Börne, and he was a Jew too, born at Frankfort . . . whose inhabitants in the 19th century still amuse themselves occasionally, on Christian high days and holidays, with breaking the windows of their Hebrew townsmen. What wonder if the galled victims of such a pastime feel, think, speak, and write, as citizens of the world! As Sterne does with his Captive, let us take a single Jew. Imagine him locked up in his dark chamber, pelted with curses and solid missiles, and trembling for his property and his very life, because he will not abandon his ancient faith, or eat pork sausages. Fancy the jingling of the shattered glass — the crashing of the window frames — the guttural howlings of the brutal rabble — and then picture a Prussian Censor breaking into the room with a flag in each hand, one inscribed Vaterland, and the other Bruderschaft — and giving the quaking wretch a double knock over the head with the poles, to remind him that he is a German and a Frankforter! Was there ever such a tragi-comical picture! But it is not yet complete. The poor Jew, it may be supposed, has little heart to sing to such a terrible accompaniment as bellows from without; nevertheless, the patriotic Censor insists on a chaunt, and by way of a prompt-book, sets before the quavering vocalist a translation of Dr. Watt's Hymn of Praise and Thanksgiving for being born in a Christian Land!

. . ."In England," continued Markham, "we have seen a Jewish sheriff in London; but I verily believe if anything could excite a rebellion in these provinces, it would not be the closing of the coffee-houses and the suppression of the newspapers, but the making a Burgomaster of the race of Israel. However, all other brutal sports and pastimes are falling into decadence with the progress of civilization; Bear-baiting is extinct; Badger-drawing is on the wane; Cock-throwing is gone out; Cock-fighting is going after it; and Bull-running is put down; so, put on your hat, my dear fellow, and let us hope, for the sake of Christianity and human nature, that Jew-baiting and Jew-running will be the last of the line!"

There were press comments, too, on the obvious prosperity of the Jews in some parts of the world. For instance, in a letter dated May 25, 1833, Richard Ford, a traveler in the Mediterranean countries, gives the following descriptions of the Moorish Jews:

Their houses are more handsomely and abundantly furnished than those of the grandees of Seville ... the proof of the substantial prosperity of the sons of Israel, is in silks and jewels, the domestic comforts and luxuries, which are to be met with even among the poorest of them ... The Jewesses do not hide their faces as the Arab women do, and it would be a sin to do so, as they are truly beautiful ... Here we have to put up in the oriental dwelling of a respectable Jew who has two daughters, who make me think every day better of Moses as a legislator — fair complexions, dark black hair, and soft, mild, large, almond shaped eyes, rendered more oriental by a dark powder with which the lids are slightly blackened, which gives an indescribable soft expression to them ...

In his popular work on Palestine and the Holy Land, published in an enlarged edition in 1837, Dr. Michael Russell, after reviewing the antiquities, religion and manners of the Jews in their ancient land, takes the opportunity to observe that

to the eye of philosophy nothing can appear more striking than the effects produced upon the world at large by the opinions and events which originated among the Jewish people.

Another writer, who in this period commented volumi-
nously on the life of the continental Jew, was George Borrow
(1803–1881). The letters that he despatched to the officers
of the London Society for which he traveled, are to a very
large degree included in the pages of *The Bible in Spain*
(1843). Although no tourist "in search of the picturesque,"
Borrow finds it impossible to keep out of his reports the
many scenes and incidents of unusual interest to him as an
English missionary, and among these are many which concern the Jews. Being familiar with different dialects as
well as the slang of the Spanish language, he says he can
"discover a Spanish Jew by the sound of a particular word."
Several times this gypsy scholar is mistaken for a Jew, and
once for a rabbi, by the Jews themselves. But in view of
the fact that there were no Jews in Spain or Portugal since
1492 till very recently, his reports are open, to say the
least, to serious suspicion. In all his references to the Jews,
we find him, on the whole, sympathetic, liberal, and singularly free from prejudice and bigotry. Of the English Jew
he has less to say. In his *Lavengro*, however, a most interesting incident of his childhood is narrated.

One day a Jew — I have quite forgotten the circumstances, but I was long subsequently informed of it —
one day a travelling Jew knocked at the door of a farm-
house in which we had taken apartments; I was near
at hand, sitting in the bright sunshine, drawing strange
lines in the dust with my fingers, an ape and dog were
my companions; the Jew looked at me and asked me
some questions, to which, though I was quite able to
speak, I returned no answer. On the door being opened,
the Jew, after a few words, probably relating to ped-

lary, demanded who the child was, sitting in the sun; the maid replied that I was her mistress's youngest son, a child weak *here*, pointing to her forehead. The Jew looked at me again, and then said, " 'Pon my conscience, my dear, I believe that you must be troubled there yourself to tell me any such thing. It is not my habit to speak to children, inasmuch as I hate them, because they follow me and fling stones at me; but I no sooner looked at that child than I was forced to speak to it — his not answering me shows his sense, for it has never been the custom of the wise to fling away their words in indifferent talk and conversation; the child is a sweet child, and has all the look of one of our people's children. Fool, indeed! did I not see his eyes sparkle just now when the monkey seized the dog by the ear? they shone like my own diamonds — does your good lady want any, real and fine? Were it not for what you tell me, I should say it was a prophet's child. Fool, indeed! he can write already, or I'll forfeit the box which I carry on my back, and for which I should be loth to take two hundred pounds!" He then leaned forward to inspect the lines which I had traced. All of a sudden he started back, and grew white as a sheet; then, taking off his hat, he made some strange gestures to me, cringing, chattering, and showing me his teeth, and shortly departed, muttering something about "holy letters," and talking to himself in a strange tongue.

During his early wanderings, Borrow met an interesting old Quaker, Joseph Edward Guerney of Earlham Hall, at Norwich. It was through this genial Quaker that he made the acquaintance of a shelf-full of Hebrew books.

"I am fond of these studies (Zohar and Mishna, Toldoth Jesu and Abarbenel)," said he, "which, perhaps, is not to be wondered at, seeing that our people (the

Quakers) have been compared to the Jews. In one respect I confess we are similar to them: we are fond of getting money. I do not like this last author, this Abarbenel, the worse for having been a money-changer. I am a banker myself, as thou knowest."

Borrow's fondness for trailing all sorts of strange characters across his pages, leads him to associations with mystics and men versed in old-world learning. He reports a serious discussion between "a young man" and "an elder," touching, among other subjects, on the *Kiaempe Viser.*

"Ah, the Kiaempe Viser?" said the elderly individual...."there are singular things in that book, I must confess ... I thank you for making me acquainted with the book, and I thank the Jew Mousha for making me acquainted with you." "That Mousha was a strange customer," said the youth collecting himself. "He *was* a strange customer," said the elder..."I love to exercise hospitality to wandering strangers, especially foreigners; and when he came to this place, pretending to teach German and Hebrew, I asked him to dinner. After the first dinner he asked me to lend him five pounds. After the fifth dinner, he asked me to lend him fifty pounds; I did *not* lend him the fifty pounds ... "

We should like to know more about this Mousha. He is probably a "Schlemihl" who has failed at everything else, has taken up teaching, and, "being ignorant of German as of Hebrew," is obliged to transfer his pupil to someone else.

In all these sketches of Jewish character, Borrow is a sympathetic observer. If he has any prejudices, they are certainly not so deep as to blind him to the good points in the Jewish character.

One of the most important developments of the middle years of the century was the literary activity among the English Jews. "As the status of the Jew as a citizen improved," says Calisch, "so also his own share as author presented a brilliant advance over preceding centuries." Among the Jewish pioneers in the field of fiction was a Portuguese Jewess, Grace Aguilar (1816–1847). In *The Vale of Cedars*, written before 1835, and published in 1850, Miss Aguilar, whose forefathers fled from the persecutions of the inquisitors of Spain and sought refuge in England in the 18th century, takes up the story of her people in medieval Spain. In 1391, they were the victims of terrible massacres; 4,000 were slain in Seville, 2,000 in Cordova. In every trade center they were forced either to renounce their faith, or to meet a horrible death. Under the circumstances those who could not effect an escape, became Marranos. Almost always conversion on these terms was only outward and false. Although such converts accepted baptism and went regularly to mass, they still remained Jews in their hearts. Fanatical churchmen, when they realized this about the converted Jews, were frantic with pent-up rage. The monks who labored so frenziedly to convert the Jews, felt that they were fooled and cheated, and in their anger, instituted the unspeakable Inquisition. Using these historical facts as a background, Grace Aguilar transports the reader to a region known as the Vale of Cedars, in the very heart of Sierra Toledo where a Jew named Julien Henriquez finds a refuge and concealment from the secret power of the Inquisition, from which he has miraculously escaped. In the course of years the Vale becomes the safe and luxurious home of the Henriquez family. As the tale proceeds, we learn of the marriage of the grand-daughter Marie with a wealthy Spaniard, Don Ferdinand Morales, who loves the Jewess and believes her to be of his faith. At length when it becomes known that Donna Marie is a Jewess, the inquisitors, led by Torquemada, seek to sentence her to the rack or the flames, to pay the penalty for deceitfulness of her kind. But, with the gracious help of the noble Queen Isabella, the unhappy Jewess is enabled to escape to the home of her childhood, the Vale of Cedars, where she dies in peace and in the Hebrew faith.

In a Preface to a group of tales, the author informs her readers that her stories are

> . . . simply records of a people, of whose modern history so little is known, ... the word Jew is associated only with Biblical and ancient recollections, or as connected with characteristics, feelings and spiritual incitements wholly distinct from those which relate to man in general. The page of modern history, more especially of the middle ages, teems with the awful sufferings and martyrdoms of the Hebrews, yet the facts are passed over, with scarcely a notice, as the justly ordained punishment for our awful sin of rejection, when eternal salvation and temporal happiness were so mercifully proffered.
>
> We will only observe that if persecution and intolerance be always the signs of divine chastisement, how shall we account for the massacres and cruelties inflicted on the Protestants, and, in their early stages of supremacy, by them on the Catholics? Yet, in both cases, martyrdom has always been considered the proof of truth, fidelity, and divine support . . .
>
> Why then should not faithfulness to a religion far more persecuted than any other in the world, be considered in the same glorious light when applied to the children

of God? . . . . . Yet who draws example from the Jews?
Who lingers on the page of history when it is related to
them? . . . Although in these tales the incidents, even
as the actors, are fictitious, yet their originals may be
found many times repeated in the history of the Jews
during their secret existence in Portugal and Spain.
Their mode of living, the extraordinary means by which
their secret was preserved, the power which enabled
them through severest tortures and long imprisonment
so to retain that secret — all this is known to persons
living now, as having been encountered by their own
immediate ancestors, and hanging over their own
childhood . . .

In a story entitled *Josephine*, based on the edict issued
by Ferdinand and Isabella (1492) charging the Jews with
inducing Christian nobles of Andalusia to embrace Judaism, and banishing the Israelites from the realm, the song
of the Exiles expresses the woe of the persecuted people:

> Farewell! farewell! we wander forth,
>   Doom'd by th' Eternal's awful wrath;
> With nought to bless our lonely path,
>   Across the stormy wave.
> Cast forth as wanderers on the earth
>   Torn from the land that hailed our birth;
> From childhood's cot, from manhood's hearth,
>   From temple and from grave.

In a historical sketch, entitled *The Escape*, Grace Aguilar
tells of the experiences of Alvar Roderiguez, a Jew of high
intellect and indomitable spirit. He is one of many who in
Portugal and Spain observe the rites of their Jewish faith
in secret, but in public bow before the image saints of the
Catholic Church. The chain of deceit and concealment,
however, weighs heavily on the soul of Alvar. His troubled

spirit leads the Church authorities to suspect him. He is subsequently arrested and brought before the Inquisition. Every secret Hebrew is thrown into the greatest alarm, lest Alvar Roderiguez confess. If confession is made, the doom will be death. The reader is reminded that

> Again and again have the sons of Israel remained in the terrible dungeons of the Inquisition; endured every species of torture, during a space of seven, ten, twelve years; and then been released, because no proof could be brought of their being, indeed, that cursed thing — a Jew! And then it was that they fled from scenes of such fearful trial, to lands of toleration and freedom, and there embraced openly and rejoicingly that blessed faith, for which in secret they had borne so much.

The Inquisition applies the torture, but neither word nor groan is extracted from Roderiguez. Eventually, in the confusion caused by an earthquake, he escapes with his wife to England. The author assures her readers that

> to this very day, the merchant's descendants recall the providential preservation, by giving on every returning anniversary of that awful day, certain articles of clothing to a limited number of male and female poor.

The Fugitive is the story of Judah Azavedo, who settles in London. By successful commerce, in Holland, he has increased his wealth; and on arrival in England, is considered an eminent member of the proud and aristocratic Portuguese community. The story goes on to recount the experience of Judah Azavedo's son among Englishmen. Wherever he goes, he imagines that he is the object of derision and dislike. He shrinks from all social contacts, and, finally, with his father's permission, leaves England to travel in the East, visiting every scene endeared to him by the history of his persecuted ancestors. This experience frees his soul from fetters; thereafter he moves among his fellowmen, fearless and unabashed.

In nearly every story Grace Aguilar attempts to convey a message to her own people, calling upon them to remember the heroic sufferings and courage of their fathers in Spain and Portugal. Also, she desires to enlist the sympathy of English readers in the younger generation of English Jews. In a significant passage (*Essays and Miscellanies*, published 1851) she complains that

> by the multitudes, the Jews are still considered aliens and foreigners; supposed to be separated by an antiquated creed and peculiar customs from sympathy and fellowship — little known and still less understood. Yet, they are, in fact, Jews only in their religion, Englishmen in everything else. In point of fact, therefore, the disabilities under which the Jews of Great Britain labor are the last relic of religious intolerance ... Is it not discreditable to the commonsense of the age that such anomalies should exist in reference to this well-disposed and, in every respect, naturalized portion of the community?

Grace Aguilar's chief contention is that in externals and in all secular thought and actions, the English naturalized Jew is an Englishman, and that the Jewish families are deserving of the same education and accomplishments as other members of English society. Only in some private and personal characteristics and in religious practice are they different. In *Women of Israel* (1851) she says:

> The characteristics so often assigned to them in tales professing to introduce a Jew or a Jewish family, are

almost all incorrect, being drawn either from the impressions of the past, or from some special case, or perhaps from attention to some Pole, Spaniard or Turk, who may just as well be a Pole, or Spanish Christian, or Turkish Mussulman, as a Jew.

These great errors in delineation arise from the supposition that, because they are Hebrews they must be different from any other race.

They are different in feature and in religion, but in nothing else. Like the rest of the human race, they are as individuals, neither wholly good, nor wholly bad. As a people, their virtues very greatly predominate. Even in the most degraded classes, we never find those awful crimes with which the public records teem .... As members of a community, the Jews are industrious, orderly, temperate and contented; as the native denizens of Great Britain, ever ready to devote their wealth and personal service in the cause of their adopted land.

Working in the optimistic hope that a new era is dawning when persecution and intolerance shall cease to create unhappiness and injustice in England, and writing as a Jew about Jews, Grace Aguilar makes an important contribution to the literature on the Jew in England. It must be admitted that her work is of social rather than literary significance, but her tales, which had a considerable vogue during the middle years of the century, are designed to reveal the heroic elements in Jewish character and history.

In *Home Scenes and Heart Studies* (1843), for the first time in the century, English readers are able to enter a Jewish middle-class home in England, and under the sympathetic guidance of a friend of the family, learn about the conditions prevailing therein. The author presents the lights and shadows of Jewish home life in "The Perez Family." Simeon and Rachel Perez live in a small cottage in one of the close and melancholy alleys in the environs of Liverpool. Refinement and love are in this home; the *Mezuzot* (Deut. 6.9, 20) are carefully secured to every doorpost; and "the precepts of their God" are obeyed, "not only in word but in deeds," by this worthy couple, and are impressed upon their children. Joseph Perez tells his sister one day that Henry Stevens said the other day that, "Jews have no faith — and how can we trust them?" The boy's mother, who happens to overhear the conversation, answers in the most earnest terms:

> My dearest Joseph, do not let your companions so mislead you. I know that it is a charge often brought against us; but it is always from those who do not know our religion, and who judge us only from those who, by their words and actions, condemn it themselves. The Jew must have faith, not only in the existence of God, but in the sacred history our God inspired, or he is no Jew . . . .

In these sketches of Anglo-Jewish life, it is possible to detect the gradual invasion of the influence of environment. A little of English life is creeping into the home of the Perez family, just as it has crept into the Aguilar home. This process of adaptation is neither an easy nor a comfortable process in any class of society, and in the Jewish communities the process in the middle years of the century is at times attended by unusual hardships.

Following in the footsteps of Grace Aguilar, two other Jewish writers, the Misses Celia and Marion Moss, dared, in their own words, "the prejudice existing against us as a nation," to publish three volumes of tales entitled

The Romance of Jewish History (1840). The dedicatory
epistle, addressed to Sir E. L. Bulwer, is followed by a
preface explaining the circumstances which induced the
publication of the work:

> The English people, generally, although mixing with
> the Jews in their daily duties, are as unacquainted with
> their history, religion, customs, as if they still dwelt
> in their own land and were known to them but by
> name.
> With this view, we have endeavored to portray the
> Jews as they were while yet an independent people . . .
> We intend to trace the destinies of their children after
> they were scattered through every nation and bring
> down the history to the present year . . . . We wish
> this work to call the attention of the reader to the
> records of our people; to awaken curiosity, not to
> satisfy it.

The tales are of no particular value either as literary
works or as studies in Jewish character. Though the names
and scenes are derived from Jewish sources, the manners
and characteristics of the actors are not particularly Jewish.
Nevertheless, the attempt made by these young women to
present "greater instances of virtue, patriotism and self-
devotion" among their people, may be regarded as an
indication of the popularity of "propaganda literature,"
prepared by members of English Jewry, with a view to
winning middleclass opinion in favor of Jewish emancipation.

In a romance entitled *Neela, a Tale of the Jews in England*,
and another entitled *Jacob, a Tale of the Jews in Germany*,
Celia Moss makes a direct appeal to English readers to
investigate Jewish character, so that a better understanding
and sympathy might be established in Anglo-Jewish society.

Neela takes up "the old story of rapine, cruelty and oppression" in the romantic manner of Scott's *Ivanhoe*, and narrates the experience of a Jewish physician, Rabbi Ephraim, friend and benefactor of all who need his assistance, and of Neela, his daughter, who supports the feeble steps of her sickly and aged mother, and is the pride and joy of her father's heart. These worthy members of the ancient people, living in the perilous times of Henry III, are the victims of the same spirit that was driving the mobs to violence against the Jews of Damascus in 1840. A rapidly approaching multitude, whose fanaticism is announed by savage cries of "Down with the murdering Jew!" "Down with the sorcerers!" "Remember Hugh of Lincoln!" "Fire their houses!" seek to persecute and even destroy the good Jew of Chesterton and his household. The reader's heart goes out to Neela, the seventeen-year-old Jewess, who is another Rebecca. But the day is saved in the end by the gallant Sir Richard Falkner, who, with the aid of the Baron of Chesterton himself, rescues the victims of mob violence and takes them to his castle.

In the story of *Jacob*, the reader is transported to Munich, where Jacob, a young Jew, pleads for justice before the Duke of the city.

> "Who hath injured thee, Jew?" demanded the Prince, touched by the agony depicted in the upturned countenance of the suppliant.
>
> "Even he who sits at thy right hand, generous Prince . . . I accuse Ernest, Count of Wolstein, in the presence of God and man, of the murder of my father, Israel Herz Yusuf!"

Rage and astonishment appear to struggle in the breast of the Duke as he exclaimed "Begone, mad man!"— and, urging his horse forward, forgetful or regardless of the danger to the Jew who stood in his onward path, bids the procession to move on to the Palace.

"Are ye men, are ye Christians?" says a bystander, as the Hebrew is knocked down and nearly trampled to death by the steeds. No answer, until a woman, apparently of the humblest rank, steps forward and says, "My house is near; raise him in your arms, and I will conduct you to it . . . ."

Whether or not these tales, designed to strike home the inhumanity of Christian states in their treatment of the Jews, influenced other writers in the 'forties, the evidence points to the stimulation of popular sympathy for the human rights of these so-called "peculiar" people.

The greatest Jewish writer of the period was of course Benjamin Disraeli. His reactions to the prejudices of his day are to be found in the novels which gave him contemporary fame, and which came to be regarded as an expression of the author's political creed and philosophy of life. The portrayal of the Jewish character by Disraeli will be discussed in the next chapter.

CHAPTER IX

THE DISRAELIAN ERA

In the year of Victoria's accession to the throne (1837), Benjamin Disraeli (1804–1881) won his first election to Parliament. From 1837 to the day of his death, forty-four years later, he was never out of Parliament. And, during the entire period of his parliamentary career, he was constantly reminded of his Jewish origin. When he stood up to make his maiden speech before the Commons as member for Maidstone, that august assembly did not take very kindly to the livid countenance, black curls and flashing eyes of the "Hebrew member." His appearance, not less than his flamboyant personality and his aloofness from the rest of his fellows, marked him out as a "foreigner." The speech was interrupted with hisses and laughter, and the young Jewish orator cried out in defiance:

> I have begun several times, many things, and I have often succeeded at last; aye, sir, and though I sit down now, the time will come when you will hear me!

In later years, O'Connell denounced him as "the heir-at-law of the blasphemous thief who died impenitent on the Cross;" Lockhart, the son-in-law of the author of *Ivanhoe*, referred to him as a "superlative Hebrew conjurer." But it is not known that Disraeli ever mentioned to his friends the pangs

which he was made to suffer. He never flinched before a
taunt; sufferance seemed to be the badge of all his tribe. "Ah,
my dear Dorothy," he said to his sister, "it is not my politics they dislike, it is myself." This was as far as he went.
He had learned the patient humility of his race. No tempest
of ridicule could shake his imperturbable calm. One wonders what his feelings were when Sir Robert Inglis, the leader
of the opposition, declared in the course of a vigorous debate
in the Commons that "the Jews were a class who could never
regard themselves as Englishmen, or as belonging to any but
a foreign people;" when Gladstone opposed the third reading of the Jew Bill on the ground that the profession of the
Jewish faith was a disqualification for office in a Christian
country; and when Macaulay, in reply, asked "How would
Mr. Gladstone himself be content to be excluded from that
House on account of his creed?"

In the year when Benjamin Disraeli remained silent in
Parliament during the debate on the removal of Jewish disabilities (1849), *Punch* published "The Jew Bailiff's Com-
plaint," addressed to the Jewish leader:

> Since you thought our race so clever,
>   What's your motive, may I ask,
> From the "peoplish" cause to sever,
>   When to aid us was your task?
>
> Curly locks and dark complexion
>   Can not alter nature's claim;
> Though you cut us, your connection
>   Is apparent all the same.
>
> Why did you, in novels flashy
>   For our elevation toil?
> Promises are poor and trashy
>   From us if your acts recoil.

In the opinion of Justin McCarthy, Disraeli's whole manner was "that of the typical foreigner whom English people regard as the illustration of all that is vehement and unquiet;" and Lord Bryce sums up Disraeli's position in English society in *Studies in Contemporary Biography* (1903), as follows: "Imagine a man of strong will and brilliant intellectual powers, belonging to an ancient and persecuted race, who finds himself born in a foreign country, amid a people for whose ideas and habits he has no sympathy and scant respect . . . . To achieve success, he must use the language and humor the prejudices of those he has to deal with, while his pride avenges itself by silent scorn or thinly-disguised irony . . ."

Benjamin Disraeli came of an ancient Jewish family which had traveled through many centuries, by way of Spain, Portugal and Italy, to England. Isaac D'Israeli, Benjamin's father, was the popular author of a collection of stories and anecdotes about authors and their works, published under the general title of *Curiosities of Literature* (1823), and a work on the *Genius of Judaism* (1833). Initiated into the Covenant of Abraham in infancy, Benjamin grew up in an atmosphere that was inevitably race-conscious. When he reached his twelfth year, it was deemed advisable, mainly for social reasons, to enroll him as a member of the English Church. Accordingly, he was baptized (July 31, 1817) at St. Andrew's, Holborn, and passed the rest of his life as a supporter of the Anglican creed. Nevertheless, renegade though he apparently was to the faith of his fathers, at heart Benjamin Disraeli never ceased to be influenced by the thought of Judaism and the glory of the Jewish people. In every act of his brilliant career, as he moved among Englishmen, he seemed to give evidence of his distinctly Jewish

heritage. It has been said that his fine fancy which, soaring
at intervals to great heights, established his kinship with a
nation which produced Isaiah, Ezekiel, Solomon, and Job,
and his "racial mind," so steeped his utterances in the colors
of the East that occasionally they seemed to blaze forth in an
oriental rhetoric which, according to his detractors, reminded
one of the passages that might come from any professional
penman in an Eastern bazaar. Not only in this exuberance
of oriental imagery was Disraeli's racial strain perceptible,
but also in the eccentricities of pose and costume with which
the young dandy created so much sensation in the circle of
the most flamboyant set of fops that ever appeared in English society. He preferred his peacocks to birds of less color-
ful plumage. His was the exotic air of the East.

In 1833, Disraeli developed his "ideal ambition" for the
Jews in the oriental romance entitled *Alroy*. The romance
is based on the comparatively modest tale of David Alrui,
or Ibn Alruhi, who appeared with a rousing summons to
revolt in the Jewish settlements of Azerbaijan (c. 1160), and
was murdered in his sleep by his father-in-law. Disraeli
idealizes Alrui beyond recognition, transfiguring him into a
warlike genius who, after nearly restoring the royal house of
Judah, with Bagdad as his capital, dies a martyr's death.
In the preface to the edition of 1845, the author says:

> Being at Jerusalem in the year 1831, and visiting the
> traditionary tombs of the Kings of Israel, my thoughts
> recurred to a personage whose career had, even in boy-
> hood, attracted my attention ... and I then commenced
> these pages that should commemorate the name of
> Alroy.

This romance, based on the exploits of a Jewish national
leader, expresses the young enthusiast's faith in the Jewish

national ideal. The prose is highly colored; there are occasional lyrics, and sometimes cadences upon the waving of banners, the flourish of trumpets, the neighing of steeds, and the glitter of spears, that drop into rhymed verse. In the final scenes of the novel, Alroy is defeated and taken captive. But he redeems his fame and wins the crown of martyrdom by refusing life and liberty as the reward of apostasy from his faith. The patriot's beloved sister, Miriam, in an endeavor to console him in his failure, declares:

> You have done great things for Israel; no one in these days has risen like you . . . You have shown what we can do and shall do. Your memory alone is inspiration. A great career, though balked of its end, is still a landmark of human energy. Failure, when sublime, is not without its purpose. Great deeds are great legacies, and work with wondrous usury. By what man has done, we learn what man can do, and gauge the power and prospects of our race . . .

If, as is supposed by commentators, the character of Alroy is drawn partly from Disraeli himself, and that of the lady Miriam is modeled after his sister, the question is naturally raised whether or not Disraeli in 1831 dreamed that the legacy of Alroy had descended upon him, so that he felt the inspiration of the Jewish leader's example and heroic memory? The vision of Alroy is not of a mere restoration of the throne of David. It betokens the universal domination of the race of Abraham:

> Warriors of Judah! holy men that battle for the Lord! The land wherein your fathers wept and touched their plaintive psaltery . . . March, onward march, ye valiant tribes; the hour has come, the hour has come! All the promises of ages, all the signs of sacred sages, meet in this ravishing hour . . .

From the outset it is clear that the novelist, looking back upon his own origin, finds glory enough and to spare in the thought that he is unchangeably a member of the superior Hebrew race. With a poet's mind he takes a sweeping view of history and conjures up gorgeous visions of human progress and national triumphs. It is also evident that, consciously or not, having absorbed the spirit of patriotism of his people, the author of *Alroy* desires that his readers should see the glory of the Hebrews who, though scattered, banished, plundered and humiliated for thousands of years, by Pharaohs, Assyrians, Roman Emperors, Scandinavian crusaders, Gothic chiefs and Spanish inquisitors, still continue to hold their own in modern life, inexhaustible, indispensable, and full of the energy and genius that God has given his "Chosen People."

Consciously or not, Benjamin Disraeli absorbed the spirit of the patriotism of his people, and for this reason his novels assume a special significance for us. The delineations of character and scene contained in them correspond to the changes in politics and society which, as a result of the Reform Bill of 1832 and other legislative measures, extended the bounds of national democracy. A great part of the novelist's material is of an autobiographical nature, depicting aspects of the author's own complex and varied experiences as a Jewish patriot in Victorian England. In at least two of his romances, much space is given to an exposition of what Disraeli believed to be the political dreams and aspirations of the House of Israel in the British Empire.

Starting with his *Vivian Grey* (1826), the youthful and romantic novelist provides his readers with an audacious and brilliant description of an England largely under the old aristocratic regime. Well-known men and women of contemporary society fill the scene. In the words of the publisher's notice of the book, "Everybody who is anybody is in it." There is hardly a man of his time that the novelist has not presented in the guise of a character in this and succeeding tales. Of course, keys to the characters were distributed by the publisher, in spite of the author's protest that his creations were all imaginary figures! However, by placing his scenes in English society and weaving his tale around the political history of the day, Disraeli embodies the national consciousness of his generation and extends his investigations into the modes and manners of the various classes that are engaged in parliamentary politics. Furthermore, by a singular trick of his own, he interprets events in such a way as to further the interests of his own party, incidentally indicating what attracted the critical eye of an "alien patriot" as he views the scene from the outside.

While neither *Vivian Grey* nor *Contarini Fleming* (1832) may be used literally for autobiographical details, it is possible to see in these novels glimpses of the author's recollections of his own school days. There is a strong suggestion in them that at school young Disraeli, like Vivian and Contarini, was taunted with his birth, was resentful of the insults flung at him on account of his foreign appearance, and was compelled to fight his way through school as an outsider. It will be remembered that the usher at school calls Vivian "seditious stranger," and the charge is taken up by his school-fellows who cry out, "No Stranger! No Stranger!" Likewise the companions of Contarini do not seem disposed to favor his "southern appearance and descent." Says Contarini:

> They were called my brothers, but nature gave the lie to the reiterated assertion. There was no similitude be-

tween us. Their blue eyes, their flaxen hair, and the white visages, claimed no kindred with my Venetian countenance. Wherever I moved, I looked around me and beheld a race different from myself. There was no sympathy between my frame and the rigid clime whither I had been brought to live.

A sense of detachment from the English scene shows itself in his descriptions of Victorian life and manners. Disraeli takes the view of one who watches the antics of his generation undisturbed by party cries and contemporary prejudices. He moves among Englishmen without being of them. He deals with their affairs as one who is accustomed to watch the habits of bees and ants — that is, with a cool scientific view of a student of natural history. He understands English society and English politics with a sort of external intellect.

Nobody seems to have realized more completely than Disraeli himself that much of his success was due to a reliance upon "the sublime instincts of an ancient race." The Tory party needs the imagination of which it was the Jew's good fortune to be in possession. Hence "Young England" was conceived in Jewry!

As we have already indicated, the political novelist's reaction to the prejudices of his day is to be found in *Coningsby* (1844), *Sybil* (1845), and *Tancred* (1847), which came to be regarded as an expression of the author's political creed and philosophy of life. Cast in the form of a romance, there is little attempt to conceal the fact that these works contain a gospel of moral and political reform for the English people. In the name of the "Young England" party, the Jewish politician seeks to inaugurate a policy that would effectively revive old England, and put spirit into the Tory party. According to Disraeli himself, (Preface to *Coningsby*, 1849),

> the Conservative triumph of 1841 had set the youthful mind of England searching for an answer to the question, what, after all, they had to preserve.

The spirit of old Toryism, recently shaken from its seat by the Reform Act of 1832, is losing ground. If England is to be saved, the aristocracy must alter its ways and infuse life into the fast crumbling institutions of the realm. The Eastern mind suggests therefore that politics be lifted into the realm of romance!

In *Coningsby or The New Generation*, while setting forth the essential principles that should guide the Young Englanders, Disraeli flings a challenge to the whole orthodox political system. Coningsby, the hero, in expressing the temper of his associates, declares that he desires to see

> authority once more honored; a solemn reverence again the habit of our lives ... Let me see property acknowledging, as in the days of old faith, that labor is his twin-brother, and that the essence of all tenure is the performance of duty.

How is this to be realized? At a party given by Lord Monmouth, it so happens that Coningsby meets a Jew by the name of Sidonia, who is described by the novelist as

> A great Hebrew who has exhausted, like Solomon, the sources of all human knowledge; who, at thirty, is acquainted with all languages, all arts, all literatures; has traveled everywhere, knows everybody.

Through Sidonia, the novelist attempts to voice his own idealized notions on politics, race and religion. To some it may seem ironical to have England explained to Englishmen by a Hebrew financier; somehow that becomes the function of the Jew in romance, as it later becomes Disraeli's in real life. To instruct the ruling classes in England to look for the future happiness and welfare of their country in National Character, is, in the novelist's opinion, more powerful than laws and institutions. By means of briliant word analysis and rapier-like wit, the fine gentlemen who are ruling England are exposed as pompous fools at the best and something much more evil at the worst. The responsibility of leading the people and of offering to them an ideal of honor, virtue, courage, thrift, refinement, manners, such as is the birthright of every freeborn Briton, can not be entrusted to a corrupt section of the governing body, to the Mr. Tadpoles and the Mr. Rigbys, who live on the corpse of Westminster as lice live on the parent host. They are the toadies who sit round the dinner tables of wealthy political peers and haunt the boudoirs of Lady St. Julians and Lady X, Y, or Z, who in turn take up politics instead of cards or the fine arts. And Lord Monmouth is represented as summing them all up in an expression of his own ambitions: "After all, what is the end of all parties and politics? To gain your object." His Lordship is aspiring to a ducal coronet.

Having called the attention of the public to these creatures who are, to all intents and purposes, engaged in a gigantic game of bluffing the nation, Disraeli shakes the sawdust out of the dummy figures who pretend they are statesmen, and declares that only by a sound aristocracy, aided by the quickening power of an energetic middle class, can England hope to be saved.

Partly through Sidonia's suggestions, partly from his own musings, Coningsby at length works out a political creed which involves faith in a free monarchy, faith in the church, and faith in a party. But character is to be the supreme force in the whole scheme of government. It must not be forgotten however that, although Sidonia is a person of excellent qualities — versed in the wisdom of all ages and lands, and wealthy as the Rothschilds — he is not a citizen of his native land. The anomaly of his position as a Jew is offered by Disraeli as a criticism of the contemporary situation. The civil disabilities of the Jews have not as yet been removed, and certain of the aristocracy are still protesting against the admission of the Jew to Parliament. For the benefit of these noble lords who stand in the way of Jewish emancipation, Disraeli avails himself of the opportunity to hold the English Jews up for Tory inspection as the trustees of tradition and the conservators of all that is spiritual in human nature. Through Sidonia, the Tories learn something about an English Jew's intense pride of race.

In *Sybil, or The Two Nations*, Disraeli expounds the popular side of his new policy. While exposing an age of political materialism and confused purposes, he lays stress on the conviction that Toryism will rise again, to "bring back strength to the Crown, liberty to the subject, and social welfare to the people." He also reminds Englishmen who have manifested much concern for the injustice done to Negro slaves in Africa, and the persecution of Jews in Damascus, that English men and women are being enslaved in coal pits, laboring sixteen hours a day, naked to the waist and with iron chains fastened to their belts of leather, and that there is persecution among the masses in the fair land of England. As a son of the East, he carefully examines the civilization of Western Europe, and finds it revolting. The leaders of English life have forgotten their history; they have wandered far from any solid ground of stable principles in public life;

it is therefore imperative that they be reminded of their forgotten national wisdom. "Unless we bring man nearer to heaven, unless government become again divine, the insignificance of the human scheme must paralyze all effort." That is the wisdom of the East, offered by a Jew for the solution of the ills of English society.

The climax of Disraeli's propaganda is reached in *Tancred, or The New Crusade*, in which the young hero, Tancred, weary of the shams that surround him at home, goes on a pilgrimage to the East. On the summit of Mount Sinai it is revealed to him that the revolt and blind discontent of the European nations are due to their having followed after other gods than Him of Sinai and Calvary, and that the spiritual values of the Eastern world should be set up in the place of the materialism of the Manchester school. The new Crusade, like its historical predecessor, must move on to Jerusalem.

Sidonia, the Jew, presiding more enigmatically than ever over the money-market, turns up again to guide the Crusade. He advises Tancred:

Well, when you arrive at Jerusalem, you will naturally go to the Convent of Terra Santa. You will make there the acquaintance of the Spanish prior, Alonza Lara. He calls me cousin ... We are pure Sephardim ... he is master of the old as well as the new learning; this is very important; they often explain each other. Your bishops here know nothing about these things. How can they? A few centuries back they were tatooed savages. This is the advantage which Rome has over you, and which you never can understand. The Church was founded by a Hebrew, and the magnetic influence lingers. But you will go to the fountain-head ... I shall give you a note to Lara; cultivate him, he is the man you want ...

Armed with letters of introduction to Lara and to the Hebrew banker Besso, who, it will be remembered, is the friend of Contarini Fleming, Tancred arrives in the Holy City.

What need of nature to be fair in a scene like this, where not a spot is visible that is not heroic or sacred, consecrated or memorable; nor a rock that is not the cave of prophets; nor a valley that is not the valley of heaven-anointed kings; not a mountain that is not the mountain of God!...a city which Mahomet seized to rule, and over which the Creator alike of Assyrian kings and Egyptian Pharaohs and Roman Caesars, the framer alike of the desert and of Christendom, poured forth the full effusion of his divinely human sorrows...the View of Jerusalem is the History of Earth and Heaven!

Here the hero meets the beautiful and young Eva, the daughter of Besso.

"You Franks love Bethany?" inquired Eva.

"Naturally," answered Tancred, "a place to us most dear and interesting."

"Pray, are you of those Franks who worship a Jewess, or of those others who revile her, break her images and blaspheme her pictures?"

"I venerate, though I do not adore, the mother of God," said Tancred, with emotion.

"Ah! the mother of Jesus!" said his companion. "He is your God. He lived much in this village (Bethany). He was a great man, but he was a Jew; and you worship him!"

"And you do not worship him?" said Tancred, looking up to her with an inquiring glance, and with a red-
dening cheek.

"Sometimes it seems to me that I ought," said the lady,
"for I am of his race, and you should sympathize with
your race."

"You are, then, a Hebrew?"

"I am of the same blood as Mary whom you venerate,
but do not adore."

In the course of the discussion that follows, Eva hints that
she might very well accept Christianity, were it not for the
outrages habitually inflicted by Christians on the people of
their own redeemer.

> The Christianity which I draw from your book does
> not agree with the Christianity which you practice . . .
> in this perplexity it may be wise to remain within the
> pale of a church much older than all others, the church
> in which Jesus was born, and which he never quitted,
> for he was born a Jew, lived a Jew and died a Jew;
> as he became a Prince of the House of David, which you
> do and must acknowledge him to have been . . .

Eva then combats the doctrine that the whole Jewish people
bears the responsibility of the crime of the crucifixion, and
concludes passionately with the words:

> There was a great party in the country not disinclined
> to Jesus at the time, especially in the provinces where
> he had labored for three years, and on the whole with
> success; are they and their children to suffer? . . . My
> grandfather is a Bedouin sheik, chief of one of the most
> powerful tribes of the desert. My mother was his daugh-
> ter. He is a Jew; his whole tribe are Jews; they read
> and obey the five books, live in tents, have thousands

of camels, ride horses of the Nedjud breed, and care for nothing except Jehovah, Moses and their mares. Were they at Jerusalem at the Crucifixion, and does the shout of the rabble touch them? Yet my mother marries a Hebrew of the cities, and a man, too, fit to sit on the throne of King Solomon; and a little Christian Yahoo with a round hat, who sells figs at Smyrna, will cross the street if he see her, lest he should be contaminated by the blood of one who crucified his saviour; his saviour being, by his own statement, one of the princes of our royal house. No; I will never become a Christian, if I am to eat such sand. He is not to be found in your book ... Persecute us! Why, if you believed what you profess, you should kneel to us! You raise statues of the hero who saves a country. We have saved the human race, and you persecute us for doing it."

"I am no persecutor," said Tancred, with emotion; "and had I been so, my visit to Bethany would have cleansed my heart of such dark thoughts."

"We have some conclusions in common," said his companion, rising. "We agree that half Christendom worships a Jewess, and the other half a Jew. Now let me ask you one more question. Which do you think should be the superior race, the worshipped or the worshippers?"

Tancred looks up to reply, but the lady has disappeared.

Thus would Disraeli point out to the Tory debaters in the Commons and the Lords, and all others who are opposed to the emancipation of the English Jew, that the greatness and the morality of the Christianity which Lord Eldon and Gladstone claim are the foundation of the English constitution, are derived from the Jews and founded upon Hebrew principles. The Jews and the Christians worship the same

God; they habitually use the same religious poems (the Psalms) in their public worship; and there is really no opposition between the ultimate purpose of the two faiths.

Almost within sight of Sinai, Tancred broods over the fact that

> The life and property of England are protected by the laws of Sinai ... The hard-working people of England are secured in every seven days a day of rest by the laws of Sinai. And yet they persecute the Jews and hold up to odium the race to whom they are indebted for the sublime legislation which alleviates the inevitable lot of the laboring multitude.... Vast as the obligations of the whole human family are to the Jewish race, there is no portion of the modern population so much indebted to them as the British people. It was the "Sword of the Lord and Gideon" that won the boasted liberties of England; chanting the same canticles that cheered the heart of Judah amid the glens, the Scotch, upon their hill-sides, achieved their religious freedom.

> Then why do these Saxon and Celtic societies persecute an Arabian race, from whom they have adopted laws of sublime benevolence, and in the pages of whose literature they have found perpetual delight, instruction and consolation?

"*That*," says Tancred, in very much the same manner as Disraeli, as he hears the opposition speeches on the third reading of the Jew Bill in the Commons —

> that is a great question which, in an enlightened age, may be fairly asked, but to which even the self-complacent nineteenth century would find some difficulty in contributing a reply.

Disraeli's object in *Tancred* is to show the absurdity of denying full emancipation to a people that has given so much to

modern civilization. The novelist takes pride in the achievements of the Jewish group. In a day when the study of
Anthropology was in its infancy, he tells his readers that
Race is everything, nationality negligible in comparison.
The individual is great only as he combines in himself all
the great qualities of the race. The Hebrew race is an
unmixed race; it has defied exile, massacre, spoliation; it
has defied Time. Unfortunately, Disraeli is so ardent in his
desire to make good the claims of the Jews to superiority
of birth, that he permits his theory of race to run away
with him. He proceeds to show that everything that is
noteworthy is Jewish: that Jewish blood might be found in
the veins of Mozart, Rossini, and among the leading diplo-
mats of Europe; that the most popular poet in England is
not Wordsworth, nor Byron, nor even Shakespeare, but
"the sweet singer of Israel;" that the Jews are the firm
upholders of tradition and stable government; and that
from the East, the land of their fathers, will come the
wisdom which alone could save the nations.

In the Jewish characters presented by Disraeli to English readers, it is possible to see a daring insistence on a new
attitude toward the Jew as a member of society. Both *Coningsby* and *Tancred* are designed to reveal the importance of
Jewish personality. No longer is the Jew to be regarded in
literature merely as a fence, a greedy money-lender, an unscrupulous usurer, or an old-clothes-man. Disraeli insists
that the members of his race are leaders of thought, philosophers, the upholders of cherished tradition. Through Sidonia,
he reveals the Jew acting according to "the sublime instinct
of an ancient race," and ultimately succeeding. Nobody
seems to realize more completely than Disraeli himself that
much of the success of the Jewish character is due to in-

domitable energy, unhesitating self-confidence and indefat-
igable perseverance, combined with the rebelliousness of a
proud heart and the ancient idealism, which are distinctive
characteristics of the Jewish heritage.

Disraeli's novels were received with mixed feelings by contemporary reviewers. While some paid tribute to the high
literary merit of the gifted author's art and style, and some
recognized the importance of these records of current views
on political and social questions, there were others who refused to accept the political manifesto set forth by the Jewish
politician.

Punch (1847), commenting on Disraeli's Jewish propaganda, retorts with propaganda of the opposite kind:

> After reading his last work, *Tancred,* we took quite
> a fresh view of all the itinerant sons of Israel, whom we
> met in the streets of the great Metropolis. "Look at
> that Old Clothes Man," said we to ourselves. "Who
> would think that the unmixed blood of the Caucasus
> runs through the veins of that individual who has just
> offered his nine-pence for our penultimate hat, and is
> refusing to give us ten-pence for our preter-plu-perfect
> or rather more than finished-and-done-for high-lows?"
>
> It is evident that Mr. Disraeli has determined in his
> own mind that until there is a Mosaic Parliament, sit-
> ting in Rag Fair, the object of his great mission will
> be unaccomplished. We shall begin to suspect that
> Mr. Disraeli is the poet of Messrs. Moses and Son's
> Establishment, and that "Costume Castle" is to be the
> foundation-stone of the New Jerusalem, removed from
> over the way, that is to say, from the other side of the
> world, for the convenience of business.

In the 'forties and the 'fifties, when Disraeli was among
the most popular authors of the day, there was a demand

for what the *Athenaeum* described as "taffeta books, hybrid volumes in which writers were wont to weave a tissue of fiction for the painter to embroider with pictorial fancies, and the engraver to adorn with gems of art." This fad encouraged the writing of tales and romances which, though they possessed little or no literary value, made use of materials from medieval and modern Jewish life. The spectacular siege of Granada toward the end of the fifteenth century, when the Spanish Jews gave wealth and an eastern exoticism to the kingdom of Ferdinand and Isabella, furnished many a glamorous historical setting for Jewish romances. Among the writers in England who availed themselves of this material to produce stories for the "taffeta" books, Edward Lytton Bulwer, afterwards Lord Lytton (1803–1873), was the most able, showing an aptness that almost amounted to originality for exploiting any novel suggestion or subject of popular interest. Bulwer wrote a tale about the siege of Granada entitled *Leila* (1838) and dedicated to the Countess of Blessington, in which the interest depends upon a love passage between Leila, a Jewess, and Muza, the superb champion of the Moorish cause, whose manly and self-sacrificing fidelity to the king, despite unworthy usage, is only equaled by his tenderness to the fair Jewish maiden. Leila is another Rebecca, although in the end she is converted to Christianity with a facility the more wonderful because the act severs the only ties that bind her to earth. Her father, Almamen, though a Jew, passes for a Mussulman and an enchanter and, when he learns of his daughter's rejection of the faith of her fathers, stabs her at the altar, just as Leila is about to take the veil. The heroine falls dead into the arms of her Paynim lover. Though the plot is of ordinary quality, Bulwer has enriched it with several picturesque scenes; and the portraiture of the Jewish maiden and her revengeful father is done in the romantic manner of Scott.

In *The Jew's Daughter*, the Countess of Blessington (1789–1849), like Bulwer, falls into the Scott tradition of romantic tale, recounting the experiences of a rich Jew, Abraham Solomon, and his only child, the beautiful Jessica, who, as the heroine of this tale, eventually takes her place in English society as the wife of Lord Levendale, and becomes the happy mother of two fine boys and a lovely girl. This is the sort of conclusion which Scott regarded as bad taste in his medieval romance; but the aristocratic author of *The Jew's Daughter* seems to feel that conditions having changed in the relationship between Jew and gentile, the union of Jew and gentile need not be attended by any disagreeable results, provided the young couple are attracted to each other by the strong bonds of love and admiration.

In the same spirit of tolerant philosophy, though somewhat more skillfully constructed, another novel, *Joseph the Jew* (1857) by Mrs. Scott, tells the story of a Jewish orphan, who, destitute and weary, arrives at the gate of a German town, where a Christian burgomaster becomes his benefactor. In the house of this excellent Christian gentleman is a graceful little girl, who also befriends the Jew. At length, Joseph goes to Berlin to study and gain a livelihood. There he meets the Jewish philosopher Mendelssohn and a certain golden-haired Jewess, Sarah, to whom he becomes betrothed. The years that follow bring prosperity to Joseph's home. Thrown once more into the society of the burgomaster's daughter, both Joseph and his wife are influenced by her faith and good-will. Joseph witnesses an evident change in the mind of his golden-haired Sarah. When she dies, he too becomes a Christian.

This constant insistence upon conversion in the ending of a story would seem to indicate that the spirit of good will had achieved only partial results; the Jews were, indeed, pointed to as acceptable human beings, but that which makes the Jew a Jew, his religion, was still undesirable. Whatever may have been the feelings of other English romancers on this question, it is interesting to note that William Makepeace Thackeray (1811–1863) gives his opinion in a "romance upon a romance," a delightful extravaganza entitled *Rebecca and Rowena* (1850), the purpose of which, says the author, is to show what an ill-assorted marriage is that of Ivanhoe, the hero of Scott's romance. "Receive it kindly, you gentle readers of novels, who love poetical justice," says Thackeray, to indicate that the union of Jew and gentile can not be any worse than the union of two gentiles who are not really soul-mates. This clever and witty travesty comes as a fresh breeze dispelling the tedious sentimental vapors of the Taffeta School.

In another characteristic work, entitled *Codlingsby*, Thackeray parodies Benjamin Disraeli's *Coningsby*, taking occasion to burlesque certain characteristics attributed to the Jews by Disraeli and others. The satirist describes the Jews as "a vast brotherhood, suffering, silent, scattered, sympathizing, waiting — an immense Freemasonry," spreading over the entire world.

> The Jewish city is lost to Jewish men; but have they not taken the world in Exchange?

Thus muses Godfrey de Bouillon, Marquis of Codlingsby, as he "debauches from Wunch Street into the Strand." He goes in the direction of the London Ghetto, where he discovers that the occupants sit on their porches, basking in the evening sunshine, with numerous children playing on the steps.

Ringlets, glossy and curly and jetty — eyes black as night — midsummer night, when it lightens; haughty noses bending like beaks of eagles — eager quivering nostrils — lips curved like the bow of love — every man or maiden, every babe or matron, in that English Jewry bore in his countenance one or more of these characteristics of his peerless Arab race.

"How beautiful they are!" mused Codlingsby . . .

"D'you vant to look at a nishe coat?" a voice said, which made him start.

"Rafel Mendoza!" exclaimed Godfrey.

"The same, Lord Codlingsby," the individual so apostrophised replied. "Will it please you to enter?" . . .

All traces of the accent with which he first addressed Lord Codlingsby had vanished. It was disguise. Half the Hebrew's life is disguise. He shields himself in craft, since the Norman boors persecuted him.

"How many castles, palaces, houses, warehouses, shops, have you, Rafel?"

"This is one," Rafel answered, "Come in."

With Codlingsby we enter the Jew's apartment, and Thackeray enjoys the fun of burlesquing the Jewish propensity for display and magnificence.

The carpet was of white velvet, painted with flowers, arabesques and classic figures. The edges were wrought with seed pearls and fringed with Valenciennes lace and bullion. The walls were hung with cloth of silver, embroidered with gold figures, over which were worked pomegranates, polyanthuses, and passion-flowers, in ruby, amethyst and smaragd. The drops of dew which

the artificer had sprinkled on the flowers were diamonds
. . . The hangings were overhung with pictures, yet more
costly. "Welcome to our snuggery, my Codlingsby,"
said Rafel.

Since it is necessary that the scene should include a beautiful Hebrew maiden, Rafel is provided with a charming sister,
Miriam.

She had been seated at an ivory pianoforte, on a
mother-of-pearl music stool, trying a sonata of Herz.
Miriam the Hebrew was fair! Her hair had that deep
glowing tinge in it which has been the delight of all
painters and which, therefore, the vulgar sneer at. It
was burning auburn. Meandering over her fairest shoulders in twenty-thousand minute ringlets, it hung to
her waist and below it . . . She had three necklaces on,
each of them would have dowered a princess; her fingers
glistened with rings to their rosy tips, and priceless
bracelets, bangles, and armlets wound round an arm
that was whiter than the ivory grand piano on which
it leaned . . .

Codlingsby swoons almost in the brightness of her beauty!
It is well the Hebrew maiden speaks — her voice, so sweet
and kind, restores him to consciousness.

Muttering a few words of incoherent recognition, he
sank upon a sandal-wood settee, as Goliath, the little
slave, brought aromatic coffee in cups of opal, and ala-
baster spittoons and pipes of the fragrant Gibelly. "My
Lord's pipe is out," said Miriam, with a smile, remark-
ing the bewilderment of her guest — who, in truth,
forgot to smoke — and taking up a thousand-pound
note from a bundle on the piano, she lighted it at a taper,
and proceeded to reilluminate the extinguished chibouk
of Lord Codlingsby . . .

This burlesque of the romantic elements in Disraeli's novel in particular, and of all novels in which the oriental and Jewish characters and scenes are treated with unrestrained imagination, serves no doubt as a clever criticism of the manner and methods of contemporary fiction. The satirist calls our attention to the fact that the wealth of the Jew is very much overrated — just as his virtues and villainies are usually considerably exaggerated.

In a work of fiction that enjoyed a wide and merited popularity, *My Novel, or Vanities of English Life* (1853), Bulwer-Lytton again introduces a Jewish character which may have been an attempt to represent the popular conception of the Baron Rothschild type of English Jew. Mr. Levi, in consequence of some services toward the negotiation of a loan, is a money-lender who has been created a baron by one of the German kings. The wealth of Mr. Levi is said to be equaled only by his own generosity to all who are in want of a temporary loan and who have sound expectations of repaying it some day or other. One seldom sees a finer looking man than the Baron — so well-preserved, such magnificent black whiskers, such superb teeth. Despite his name and his dark complexion, he does not, however, look like a Jew. If the truth must be told, he is not a Jew on his father's side, but the natural son of a rich English grand seigneur, by a Hebrew lady of distinction. After the boy's birth, this lady marries a German trader of her own persuasion, and this may account for the fact that Levi is on good terms with both Jew and Christian, and, being neither one nor the other, resembles (to use Sheridan's incomparable simile) the blank page between the Old and the New Testaments. No man has more friends, no man sticks by them more firmly — so long as there is a pound in their pockets — than does the Baron. Towards the end of the narrative, Lytton gives us several intimate glimpses of the drawing-room scenes in which the Baron plays an important role, especially among the New Men who are seeking office in the new ministry. His luxurious business-room is furnished with Axminster carpets, three inches thick, *portières à la Française* before the doors; Parisian bronzes on the chimney-piece; and all the receptacles that line the room contain title-deeds and post-obits and bills and promises to pay — sepulchers of departed patrimonies veneered in rosewood that gleam with French polish and blaze with ormolu. The Baron is reported to be a respected and responsible man of business, and rather liked as a friendly accommodating species of Sir Epicure Mammon, who very often does what is thought handsome and liberal and "in short," says one of these experienced referees, "he is the best fellow going — for a money-lender!"

In examining the fiction of the middle years of the century, the reader cannot fail to observe that the years of struggle for political emancipation witnessed an increase in the popular interest in the Jew as a literary character in novels by both Jewish and gentile writers. The novels of Disraeli, in particular, in their passionate glorification of the Jewish race, helped to advertise the fact that Israel could still produce idealists, patriots and saviors, even though these were hidden under the sober livery of the nineteenth century "city" man.

CHAPTER X

CHARLES DICKENS AND THE
REALISTIC SCHOOL

It was while the Jews were struggling desperately for a recognition of their civil rights that Charles Dickens (1812–1870) took the City by storm with his story of *Oliver Twist*, begun in the second number of *Bentley's Miscellany*, February, 1837, and continued in monthly parts till completion in October, 1838. The second edition of the novel in book form was issued soon after the first in 1838, and the third edition (1841) and the first cheap edition (1850), each contained a preface by the author. There is no doubt that in writing the story of Oliver, the great-hearted novelist intended it as an exposure of the poor law system and the miseries silently borne by the thousands of unfortunate children in the crowded cities. Unfortunately at the time to which the story refers, the class of criminal operating in the manner of Fagin was frequently composed of persons commonly designated as Jews. Therefore when the author calls Fagin, "the Jew," we feel that the reference is not to the Jew's religion, but to his group. Unquestionably Fagin belongs to the dens and the stews of London which Dickens desires to expose and clean up, just as Squeers and Pecksniff belong to another scene of criminal and corrupt English life which calls for similar treatment. It is absurd, therefore, for critics like Hilaire Belloc, for instance, to say that Dickens dislikes Jews, and that, in creating Fagin he shows a prejudice unworthy of a humanitarian novelist. Dickens has no intention of maligning the Jewish people. He is merely describing a reprobate in the dens of London who makes pickpockets of his "young friends," and who, it so happens, is of Jewish origin. Of course, it is unfortunate that Fagin's appearance on the scene coincides with the time when English Jews were petitioning Parliament for a recognition of their rights as English Citizens. Thoughtful readers, however, will see that, although Fagin belongs to the Jewish people, he retains no distinctive peculiarities of his religion. In fact, he is just as much an outcast Jew, as Bill Sykes is an outcast Christian. Fagin belongs to no synagogue, he has no feeling for anything Jewish; and when, in the final scenes, some rabbis visit him in prison, he drives them away. As a Jew he lacks actuality. He has so completely broken with his people and their ways that he possesses scarcely a trace of their peculiar diction and manners, being un-Hebrew even in his fondness for sausages.

There can be no objection to Fagin as a vivid, though perhaps somewhat melodramatic presentation of a possible type of underground criminal. His diabolical leer and red hair (for which the novelist is indebted to the stage Jew), and the mystery surrounding the reprobate creature, are designed to strike terror in the heart of the reader, and effectively drive home certain facts in ways characteristic of this particular type of sensational novel. The reader is taken to Fagin's "den" near Field Lane, where he meets the hideous creature face to face:

The walls and ceiling of the room were perfectly black with age and dirt. There was a deal table before the fire; upon which were a candle, stuck in a ginger-beer bottle, two or three pewter pots, a loaf, and butter and a plate. In a frying-pan, which was on the fire, and which was secured to the mantle-shelf by a string, some sausages were cooking; and standing over them, with a toasting-fork in his hand, was a very old shrivel-led Jew, whose villainous-looking and repulsive face was obscured by a quantity of matted red hair. He was dressed in a greasy flannel gown, with his throat bare; and seemed to be dividing his attention between the frying-pan and the clothes-horse, over which a great number of silk handkerchiefs were hanging.

"We are very glad to see you, Oliver, very," . . . said the Jew . . . "Ah, you are a-staring at the pocket-handkerchiefs — eh, my dear! There are a good many of 'em, aint there? . . . Ha! ha! ha!"

Later, Oliver — who is supposed to be fast asleep in his dark corner — sees the villainous Fagin examining the various stolen articles that have been brought to him by his "pupils."

"Ah!" said the Jew, shrugging up his shoulders and distorting every feature with a hideous grin. "Clever dogs! Clever dogs! Clever dogs! Staunch to the last! Never told the old parson where they were. Never peached upon old Fagin. And why should they? It wouldn't have loosened the knot, or kept the drop up, a minute longer . . . What a fine thing capital punish-ment is! Dead men never repent; dead men never bring awkward stories to light. Ah, it's a fine thing for the trade! Five of 'em strung up in a row, and none left to play booty, or turn white-livered!"

In answer to a letter of protest addressed to him by Mrs. Eliza Davis, a Jewish lady, the wife of Mr. J. P. Davis, who purchased the novelist's London residence, Tavistock House, on his retirement to Gad's Hill, Charles Dickens writes (July 10, 1863):

.... I must take leave to say that if there be any general feeling on the part of the intelligent Jewish people, that I have done them what you describe as "a great wrong," they are a far less sensible, far less just, and a far less good-tempered people than I have always supposed them to be. Fagin, in *Oliver Twist*, is a Jew, because it unfortunately was true of the time to which the story refers, that that class of criminal almost invariably *was* a Jew. But surely no sensible man or woman of your persuasion can fail to observe — firstly — that all the rest of the wicked dramatis personae are Christians; and, secondly, that he is called "the Jew," not because of his religion, but because of his race. If I were to write a story in which I pursued a Frenchman or a Spaniard as a "Roman Catholic," I should do a very indecent and unjustifiable thing; but I make mention of Fagin as a Jew because he is one of the Jewish people, and because it conveys that kind of idea of him, which I would give my readers of a Chinaman by calling him a Chinese ... I have no feeling towards the Jewish people but a friendly one. I always speak well of them, whether in public or in private, and bear testimony (as I ought to do) to their perfect good faith in such transactions as I have ever had with them. And in my *Child's History of England*, I have lost no opportunity of setting forth their cruel persecution in old times.

This letter clearly expresses the sentiments of the author toward the Jews. In subsequent letters to Mrs. Davis (November 16, 1864, and March 1, 1867), Dickens reiterates the "hope to be, as I have always been in my heart, the best of friends with the Jewish people;" "a people for whom I have a real regard, and to whom I would not wilfully have given an offence or done an injustice for any worldly consideration."

An interesting explanation of the origin of Fagin is given in a letter to the *London Times* (December 29, 1871) by George Cruikshank, the original illustrator of *Oliver Twist*, who claims that he not only suggested much of the plot and many of the scenes to Dickens, but actually helped to create the monster Fagin. Cruikshank says:

> I had long time previously to this directed Mr. Dickens's attention to "Field Lane," Holborn Hill, wherein resided many thieves and receivers of stolen goods, and it was suggested that one of these receivers, a Jew, should be introduced into the story; and upon one occasion Mr. Dickens and Mr. Harrison Ainsworth called upon me at my House in Middleton Terrace, Pentonville, and in the course of conversation, I then and there described and performed the character of one of these Jew receivers who I had long had my eye upon (sic) and this was the origin of Fagin. Long before Oliver Twist was ever thought of, I had by permission of the city authorities, made a sketch of the condemned cells in Newgate prison; and as I had a great object in letting the public see what sort of places these cells were, and how they were furnished, and also how to show a wretched condemned criminal therein, I thought it desirable to introduce such a subject into this work ... I had the greatest difficulty to get Mr. Dickens to allow me to carry out my wishes in this respect, but I said I must either have what is called a Christian or what is called a Jew in a condemned cell, and therefore it must be Bill Sykes or Fagin; at length he allowed me to exhibit the latter.

The terrible picture drawn by Cruikshank of Fagin in his cell has been thought by some to be a masterpiece and by others a gross exaggeration. But it is singularly impressive as a portrait, and almost impossible to banish from the memory. With reference to Cruikshank's statement, Forster in his *Life of Dickens* (vol. I, 183), quotes a letter from the novelist to the artist, showing that the artist's claim is false. But the artist restated his claim in 1872.

Fagin is generally supposed to have been modeled on a certain disreputable pickpocket and receiver of stolen goods who was tried at the Old Bailey before Mr. Sergeant Arabin in July, 1830, found guilty and sentenced to seven years' transportation. Dickens may possibly have been present at the trial. But why should he have kept Ikey in his memory for seven years? Landa, in his *The Jew in Drama*, offers another theory of the origin of the character, based, he says, "not on conjecture, but on facts discovered by careful research." He maintains that Dickens received his ideas for his creation of Fagin from a stage-Jew named Barney Fence, a minor character in a melodrama entitled *Van Dieman's Land*, produced in 1830, at the Surrey Theater. The play probably would have passed out of existence, but for the subsequent trial of Ikey Solomons that same year. After the conviction of Ikey, the play was revived, and Barney Fence — a Jew, and a receiver of stolen goods — was renamed *Ikey Solomons*. Says Landa: "Barney Fence, subsequently Ikey Solomons, was played as a conventional stage-Jew, and it is the regulation stage-type that is delineated by Dickens in Fagin . . . Dickens was afforded an opportunity of setting on record the source whence he drew Fagin, but, unfortunately did not avail himself of it. The obvious inference is that it would have meant a confession that the character was not drawn from life." This conclusion is scarcely so obvious as Landa would have us believe; but the reader may take the suggestion for what, to him, it is worth.

To sum up the discussion on Dickens and his creation of Fagin, it must be admitted that there is neither forethought nor malice as far as the novelist's attitude towards the Jewish community is concerned, in calling Fagin a Jew. Other Jewish characterizations by Dickens are found in *Pickwick Papers*, where Mr. Leo Hunter informs Mr. Pickwick that he could secure a fancy dress from Solomon Isaacs, the Jew in High Street, who has thousands of them; in *Sketches by Boz*, where several ghetto types are presented, especially in the vicinity of Holywell St., "red-headed and red-whiskered Jews . . . who forcibly haul you into those squalid houses and thrust you into a suit of clothes, whether you will or not;" and in *Martin Chuzzlewit*, where Poll Sweedlepipe has "the beard of a Jewish rabbi," and where Solomon Jacobs, in Chancery Lane, is the keeper of the debtor's jail, and retains "Ikey" as top-boots.

At a later date, perhaps in an attempt to make *amende honorable* before the world for the villainies of Fagin, Dickens in *Our Mutual Friend* (1863) produced Mr. Riah, "the gentle Jew in whose race gratitude is deep." A compromise between the romantic and the realistic treatment of the Jewish character is evident in the creation of Mr. Riah, a set-off to Fagin, perhaps, and an apology to the Jewish community. "Thus they stand," says Dr. Philipson, "Fagin, the Jew of Dickens's youth, and Riah, he of later years. Was it experience that taught him better? Had he met with such whose characters and doings impelled him to the thought that he had done wrong in naming one of his blackest creations a Jew? ... A later judgment must always be supposed to subvert an earlier one, and we are justified in concluding that Dickens's opinion of the Jews underwent a complete change, as we may learn from this novel."

Notwithstanding the comparatively small part that he plays in *Our Mutual Friend*, Mr. Riah is presented as an amiable character, and, with his benevolent smile and generous actions, helps to correct the popular view that all Jews follow the scent of gain, and that all Jews are villains. Mr. Riah illustrates the fact that there is much poverty and kindness of heart among his coreligionists. Through him the reader learns of the many hundreds of Jewish poor in London, enduring tribulation in silence and seeking relief only among their own people. Mr. Riah says:

> Men find the bad among us (Jews) easily enough. They take the worst of us as samples of the best; they take the lowest of us as presentations of the highest; and they say 'All Jews are alike'.

Perhaps, as Dr. Philipson observes, Dickens desired Mr. Riah to make amends for the annoyance he had caused certain Jewish readers by the creation of Fagin. But if the portrayal of Fagin sins in one extreme, the creation of Mr. Riah sins in the other. No man, whether Jew or gentile, can be as faultless as Mr. Riah. Both Fagin and Riah are open to the same objection; they are not particularly Jewish in their faith or in their racial characteristics.

A number of other novelists attempted, in the middle years of the century, to make use of sensational material from the life of the day, in order to effect the removal of prevailing social wrongs. Among these writers of the novel of purpose was Frances Milton Trollope (1780–1863), the mother of Anthony Trollope. Our interest in her work has to do with her treatment of Jewish character in her novel entitled *A Romance of Vienna* (1839), in which she sets herself "to show up Judaism in Austria." The materials for this story were gathered in July 1836, during a trip through central Europe, where the novelist says she found an opportunity "to view the Jewish situation" in an interesting setting. The mainspring of the story is the runaway marriage of an Austrian noble with a young British woman, whom he soon tires of, and spirits away to the castle of a Jewish banker, Imlar Balthazar. The cruel husband secures the unfortunate woman's silence by threatening to take away her child.

Imlar Balthazar is represented as a sort of "amatory agent," an Israelite blessed with a sycorax of a mother, who spouts the language of the Prophets on common occasions, and a lovely Jewish wife whom he treats with cruel indifference. Mrs. Trollope paints the portrait of the Jewish wife with gusto, entering into detailed description of her listless life and neglected situation. Whenever the Jewish characters appear on the scene they reflect much discredit on themselves and on their people. It is not certain where the author gained her knowledge of Jewish home life, but it is evident that she leads these unfortunate victims of her bigotry and prejudice into some absurd situations.

Another author with a purpose was Charles Kingsley (1819–1875), the fiery leader of Christian Socialism, who advocated a Christianity that would be known by its works rather than by its lip-worship. In *Alton Locke* (1850), Kingsley gives realistic pictures of the sweated poor in London at the time of the Chartist agitation, and makes the charge pretty plain that both Jews and Christians are responsible for the misery and inhumanity of that situation. Among those who aid and abet in the immorality, the insanitary conditions, the tyranny and the poverty of the vicious system of industry and among the "sweaters," many belong to the Jewish persuasion.

In *Hypatia, or New Foes with an Old Face,* first published in *Fraser's Magazine* (1852), and in book form (1853), Kingsley chooses that particular time in history, the dawn of the fifth century, because he conceives that the elements of decay and demoralization in the Church, and the forms of unbelief, doubt, difficulty and despair which hold riot beyond the ecclesiastical pale of Alexandria in the days of Cyril, are the same as those which prevail in 1853.

> I wish to show you your own likenesses in toga and tunic, instead of coat and bonnet... The same devil who tempted the Egyptians tempts you. The same God who could have saved these old Egyptians, if they willed, will save you, if you will...

The scene of *Hypatia* is laid in Alexandria in the year 413, and the struggle in which Kingsley finds the springs of dramatic and ethical interest is not that between Goth and Roman, but between expiring paganism and growing Christianity. No description of Alexandria and her opinions in the fifth century, however, is complete without the Jewish element, and this the novelist presents in a number of vivid portraits, of which one of the most striking is that of Raphael Aben-Esra, a type of the highly cultivated, subtle, sarcastic, fearless Jew, in whom the faith of his Fathers is extinct, and who has found nothing to replace it in the jargon of the cabalists or the vague theosophy of Philo.

Through Raphael the Jew we obtain a view of the workings of Christian belief and practice from a new point of view. He can see very little that is commendable in the sort of Christianity professed by Orestes the prophet, and his circle, to whom power and wealth secured at any price are the end of religion. Nor is Raphael favorably impressed by the sort of Christianity practiced by the Patriarch Cyril, in whom the avarice and ambitions of a strong ecclesiastical organization find satisfactory leadership. The profound skepticism of Raphael the Jew pierces through the lofty pretentions of prefect and patriarch. As the story proceeds, however, the Jew comes into contact with Majoricus, an adherent of Heraclian of Africa, and his daughter, Victoria, whom Raphael has just rescued from destruction in the rout of Heraclian's army near Ostia. Raphael sees in these two persons a new Christianity, an active and practical life of helpfulness and good-will. In other words, the Jew who can clearly see through the selfish ambition of Cyril, who despises and loathes the vulgarity and crudeness of an Orestes, is now overcome by the active goodness and the unpretending self-sacrifice of Victoria and her father. And when he finds that the root of all this is in their faith, he at once acknowledges the supremacy of the real Christianity. He is willing to embrace the faith of Majoricus and Victoria.

In Raphael, as a character in fiction, we have a contemplative and intellectual type — something that we have not had outside of Disraeli's novels — a Jew who appreciates the Christianity which lives up to its social obligations to all humankind in the spirit of the nameless Samaritan who ministered to his fellow man, irrespective of color or creed.

"Kingsley has created a noble Jew," says Baldwin; "but on the advice of his friend Maurice, he had the Jew converted to Christianity, through the influence of St. Augustine. When he did so, Kingsley, writing for his day, valued purpose more than art."

Before the conclusion of the story, the reader feels a great sympathy for the Jewish characters in the narrative, even for the old Jewess Miriam, who is led into a life of wickedness by certain Christian priests. Before her death, she reveals her true identity, and makes the startling confession that she is the mother of Raphael.

> A king's daughter I am, and a king's heart I had ...
> It made me dread and scorn to be a slave, a plaything, a soulless doll, such as Jewish women are condemned to be by their tyrants, the men. I craved for wisdom, renown, power, and my nation refused them to me; because, forsooth, I was a woman! So I left them. I went to the Christian priests ... They pampered my woman's vanity, my self-will, my scorn of wedded bondage, and bade me be a saint ... the bride of God! Liars! Liars! — and so, Miriam the daughter of Jonathan — Miriam of the house of David ... I found them out that day ... Then I found out their blasphemy ... And I shook off the dust of my feet against those Galilean priests, and went back to my people — and palmed you, (Raphael) my son, on Ezra as his son, I and his wife ... And then I did live for you ... For you I toiled, hoarded, lied, intrigued ... You are the richest Jew south of the Mediterranean!"

There are some pathetic scenes that draw our sympathy for every section of life in that old pagan world. Kingsley manages to enlist the reader's sympathies with Jew and pagan.

The credit for creating a vivid picture of a contemporary Jew, on the very eve of Jewish emancipation in England, goes to Charles Reade (1814–1884), who, like Dickens in dramatic method and social purpose, presents Mr. Levi in a novel entitled *It is Never Too Late to Mend* (1856). While harboring the prejudices of a Tory squire, Reade has a strong sense of justice which prompts him to take the part of the oppressed. He describes Isaac Levi as an oriental Jew of authority and learning in his tribe who has traveled as a young man in India, and later journeyed, to engage in business in St. Petersburg, Rome, Paris, Vienna and Lisbon. Now, he lives in a rented house at Farnsborough. The two children born to him have died in this house; and his wife, Leah, has died there too. Then John Meadows, who has just bought the house, loses no time in giving the Jew notice to leave instantly. Not that Meadows needs the house; but he hates Jews and wishes to have no dealings with any member of that people.

"Have pity on me, sir, an aged and lonely man," said Isaac; "tear me not from the shadows of my dead."

"No," was Meadows' stern answer.

"No? Then you must be an enemy of Isaac Levi?"
"Yes," was the grim reply.

"Ah!" cried the old Jew, with a sudden defiance, which he usually suppressed. "And what have I done to gain your enmity, sir?"

"You lend money."

"A little, sir, now and then — a very little."

"That is to say, when the security is bad you have no money in hand; but, when the security is good nobody has ever found the bottom of Isaac Levi's purse."

"Our people," said Isaac apologetically, "can trust one another — they are not like yours — we are brothers, and that is why money is always forthcoming when the deposit is sound."

"Well," said Meadows, "what you are, I am; what I do on the sly, you do on the sly, old thirty-per-cent."

"The world is wide enough for us both, good sir."

"It is!" was the prompt reply. "And it lies before you, Isaac. Go where you like, for the little town of Farnsborough is not wide enough for me and any old man that works my business for his own pocket..."

"It is a frail policy," said Isaac Levi..."I tell you what these old eyes have seen in every nation and read in books that never lie. Goliath defied armies, yet he fell like a pigeon by a shepherd boy's sling.... No man can defy us all, sir!... Be advised, then, do not trample upon one of my people. Nations and men that oppress us do not thrive. Let me bless you. An old man's blessing is gold. See these grey hairs; my sorrows have been as many as they. His share of the curse that is upon his tribe has fallen upon Isaac Levi."

Age and sorrow plead in vain, for they are wasted on the strong will and vulgar soul of John Meadows. Says the novelist, "I am almost ashamed to give the respectable brute's answer!"

In this novel we see much of the realism which it is the novelist's unvarying ambition to secure. Like the French naturalist, Émile Zola, Reade is reported to have checked his material by his own investigation, and the result in this description of the Jewish money-lender is at least free from the sort of unpleasant caricature that makes so many portraits of the Jew repulsive. Isaac Levi's righteousness in business transactions, his active benevolence towards those whom he can serve without hurting his own interests, the grave and lofty tones of his rebukes to foolish wrong-doing, his faith in the destinies of his people — all these aptly combine to make him more real than any of the superb heroes of Disraeli. Keenly resentful of injury, astute, able and patient, the Jewish money-lender follows his long-cherished revenge with terrible ingenuity and persistency; and yet, at the end of the narrative, we see that Isaac Levi can be softened towards a fallen foe who asks of him justice tempered with mercy. In the final scene, there is a certain grandeur, a sort of scriptural majesty about Isaac Levi. On the whole, the effect of Charles Reade's novel is in the direction of fair and just judgment of the people to which Isaac Levi belongs.

During the period of the Russian persecutions (1840), when the finer sensibilities of many English writers were naturally outraged by stories of rapine, massacre, and the destruction of property suffered by the Jews in the Czar's dominions, Thomas De Quincey (1785–1859) wrote what may seem like a sensational long-short-story, entitled "The Avenger," revealing an unpleasant aspect of the Jewish situation in Europe. In this story the author of *Confessions of an English Opium Eater* details a series of startling murders in a German town in 1816, committed by a young man, whose mother and sisters have been pub-licly scourged and insulted simply because they were Jews, and who has vowed to avenge his mother's death on all concerned in the outrage. More journalistic than literary, this tale is interesting merely as a piece of literary propa-ganda. In his *English Opium Eater*, published in the *London Magazine* (1821), De Quincey indicates his fairness to the

Jews in telling of his dealings with money-lenders, and particularly with a Jew named D—. He says:

> Like all Jews with whom I had negotiations, he was frank and honorable in his mode of conducting business. What he promised, he performed; and if his terms were high, as naturally they could not but be, to cover his risks, he avowed them from the first.

The year 1847, which saw the publication of *Tancred*, is also marked by the publication of a number of short stories presenting aspects of the Jewish character, some favorable and others detrimental to the Jewish cause in England. One of these entitled "Zeky Naashon, the Jew of Portsmouth," by William H. G. Kingston, appears in *Ainsworth's Magazine*.

Zeky Naashon, according to the testimony of a yachtsman who tells the story, is a Jew in the Captain Marryat tradition.

> Well, sir, there wasn't such a Jew in all Portsmouth . . . There wasn't a thing in the universal world Zeky hadn't got to sell, always except a little honesty . . . No sooner did a ship from a foreign station drop her anchor at Spithead, and shoreboats was allowed to come alongside, then Zeky was to be found with his wares spread out between two guns on the main deck driving a brisk trade with all on board. He'd got everything among his goods, from a sou'wester to a shoe-string for the men, and from a ear-ring to a petticoat for the gals . . . Now I don't say on any manner of account, that all Jews are like Zeky; for I've known several very decent, Christian-like chaps among 'em, so I means nothing disrespectful to any on 'em; but you knows, sir, there are rogues among all nations; . . . Howsomever, with respect to Zeky, if there was a big rogue, he was

one to a sartenty . . . His nose was a rummish-looking ornament, stuck in the middle of his face, for all the world like a hawk's beak, with a twinkling eye on each side of it, which looked so black and piercing that one couldn't help thinking that he'd filched 'em from the same bird . . . I don't know where he got his teeth from except out of the jaws of a mangy cat. . . . yet he contrived to have dealings with everybody, and everybody courted his favor, though he spit upon 'em and they hated him . . . but the truth is, they were afraid of him . . . .

When Zeky, however, in the final scenes, falls overboard, the sailors let him drown and divide his money. But the money is soon gone and the evil-doers are haunted by dreadful memories of the wretched Jew whom they refused to save.

Simultaneously with the revival of parliamentary discussion on the Jew Bill in 1853, there was an evident demand for stories with Jewish characters taken from real life.

Among these appeared a story entitled "Jacob Bendixen the Jew" (1852), adapted from the Danish of Goldschmidt by Mary Howitt, in which the attempt is made to present a "faithful transcript of the life and feelings" of the English Jews. The story is designed to afford the Jewish and the Christian reader alike some grave and important lessons of tolerance. The narrative opens with a picture of the Jewish hero's boyhood, and goes on to show the effect of a series of domestic and social persecutions on his sensitive spirit. A love engagement into which the hero enters closes the narrative in mortification and despair. Another story of the same type is "The Jew's Legacy;" and a third, "The Jew," taken from the Russian, presents an Israelite who, by his intellectual gifts and sincere nature, wins the heart of the daughter of a German landowner. In other periodicals appeared fiction in which the sentimental vein, so characteristic of the 'fifties, seemed to prevail. For example there was the "Jewess of Pisa," concerning Ruth, the daughter of the merchant Zakiel Kilverino of Pisa, who plunges into the moonlit water of the Arno rather than surrender herself to the man she does not love; "The Jewish Heroine," a literal translation of Don Eugenio Maria Romero's "El Martiria de la Jevon Hachnel; La Heroina Hebreal;" and a novel, *Leila Ada, or the Jewish Convert* (1853), and *The Relatives of Leila Ada, or the Persecutions of the Jewess* (1854), by Osborn W. Trenery Heighway.

Leila Ada in particular, while purporting to be "an authentic memoir," deals sentimentally and melodramatically with the difficulties that beset a Jewess who is converted to Christianity. It is again evidence of the smug, unspoken hope that, in return for being treated like human beings, the Jews would become Christians, like the author and, presumably, the reader. In the last scenes, Leila Ada settles in a little English village and lives in the company of simple, earnest Christian folks. Chapters VIII and IX of the novel contain a long letter written by the Jewess to her father, explaining her position and expressing hopes for a bright day for her people.

> A brighter day is to dawn upon our ancient people; a day which, by their conversion to Christianity, shall recover them from their fallen and ruined condition . . .

Though ostracized by her people and ill-treated by her uncle, Leila remains loyal to her new faith. The reader is given an opportunity to watch at the bedside of the dying convert.

As in the preceding period, so in this, the familiar figures of the heroic Jew, the comic Jew, and the villainous Jew appear in many of the dramatic productions which meet with public approval. A popular representation of the heroic Jew is afforded in the character of the self-sacrificing Joseph, in the *Maid of Mariendorpt*, Sheridan Knowles's adaptation of the novel *The Village of Mariendorpt*, to which reference has been made in a preceding chapter.

Dion Boucicault (1822–1890), a prolific playwright of this period, was responsible for supplying the Victorian theater with a varied assortment of stage Jews, mostly money-lenders, turf rascals, and the like. In a vivacious comedy, *London Assurance* (Covent Garden, 1841), he presents a Jewish writ-server, Solomon Isaacs; and in another play of a burlesque type, *A Legend of the Devil's Dyke* (1838), a money-lender named Levy Lewis. Throughout the Victorian era, contemptuous and degraded Jews of this type are common on the stage. They are frequently earmarked for opprobrium. Usually they figure as smugglers, receivers, and escaped convicts, and there is much of Fagin in them.

Long before the last instalment of *Oliver Twist* was published in *Bentley's Miscellany*, Fagin and his associates were thrust upon the boards. The first stage adaptation of the novel was produced at the St. James' Theater, March 27, 1838; and the other versions were prepared in a hurry before the end of the year. Dickens himself was most anxious that *Oliver Twist* should succeed as a play, and before October 1838 offered a dramatization of his own to Macready. But the most notable *Oliver Twist* play was written by John Oxenford, dramatic critic of the *Times* (1868); it kept the boards during the greater part of the second half of the century.

In making a final survey of the English writers of the realistic school, including Dickens and his followers, it may perhaps be noticed that these writers are not only quick to recognize the value of the Jew as a literary type, but also, in their deep sense of the novelist's obligation to give a truthful representation of contemporary life, they succeed to a great extent in breaking away from the old patterns, and in giving a less unjust and more tolerant delineation of Jewish character. Stories showing the devotion of the Jews to their religion, and their unflinching loyalty in the face of centuries of persecution, rather than tales of their wickedness in usury and trickery, are becoming more the rule than the exception in the late 'fifties.

CHAPTER XI

THE VICTORIAN COMPROMISE

When Baron Rothschild, as the first Jewish member, entered the English Parliament in 1858, it was estimated that there were about 30,000 Jews in Great Britain, of which number at least 25,000 lived in London and its suburbs. This number was to be greatly increased, as we shall see, when, in the 'seventies and 'eighties, a new wave of bitter anti-Semitism swept through continental Europe and caused thousands of Jewish refugees from Germany and Russia to seek safety among their coreligionists in England. Gradually it became evident that there were at least four classes of Jews in the larger English cities. First, there were the Jewish aristocracy, in whose princely homes brilliant society assembled, and invitations to whose parties were regarded as a social distinction. The connection maintained between the Hebraic patrician and his coreligionists of the bourgeoisie was either official or philanthropic. The advantages reaped by England from this Hebrew aristocracy were not only material, but intellectual and artistic. Consequently, the presence of this class did much to prevent the outbreak of any anti-Semitic demonstration in English society during the latter part of the century.

The second class of English Jews differed from the patrician class chiefly in a resolute rejection of assimilation that so often ended in intermarriage. The pride of race and the teachings of Judaism combined to maintain among these highly educated religious Jews the aloofness which was at times objectionable to Christian Englishmen. But these Jews, represented by Grace Aguilar in *Home Scenes and Heart Studies* (supra, 195), having sprung from two or three generations settled in England, were as proud of the traditions of England and of the fame of Shakespeare as any of the descendants of the Conqueror. This "older English Jewry," of which the Perez Family are a good example, retained the spirit of the Victorian era in manners and thought to a very marked degree, and, playing conspicuous parts in the learned professions, made a valuable contribution to the national life of the century.

The third class, though fairly common, is less easy to describe. It was made up of the cosmopolites who were not much more than self-centered individualists. As a rule they were Jews by origin who had worked themselves into wealth, and who had given up the restraints of Jewish tradition. Describing a member of this class, a Jewish writer in the *Westminister Review* (1893) says:

In his kitchen hang samples of well-flavored Westphalian (or Wiltshire) hams. His cellars are well-stocked with wines that do not often bear the official rabbinical seal. His cook is not educated in the niceties of distinction between "meat" and "milk" utensils, and, perhaps, would be obliged to confess to an utter ignorance of the meaning of the word *Kosher* . . . . Rarely indeed is he moved to the contemplation of things spiritual. Business and pleasure absorb his whole being. The age in which he lives suits him excellently well . . . he is the incarnation of the modern spirit of indifference.

The Jews of this class emancipated themselves from the slavery of what they believed was an "antiquated orthodoxy," and although having a strong pride in the Jewish group, they lost all sympathy with the forms of its ancient worship.

The fourth class of English Jews was composed of the newly-arrived alien immigrants who were commonly regarded as "foreign undesirables," driven to England by the persecutions on the continent. A writer in *Blackwood's* (CLXIX, 279 ff.), forgetting that he could not predict what the third generation of these immigrants would be like, and not bothering to discover what his ancestors had said about the Portuguese Jews of the first generation a century or two earlier, complains that

> The Jewish aristocracy, the Sephardin of Portugal and Spain, who gave us a Disraeli in the third generation, have ceased to arrive. The Dutch Jews, with their long pedigrees, are stationary. Even the more plebeian German Jews are fast giving place to the outcasts of Russia and Poland — the wild, hunted-looking creatures, with fur caps and baggy, greasy clothes, who may be seen gaping about them most days at the London docks.

In the higher circles, the prosperity and progress of the Jewish merchants and bankers still kept them in the best of English society. The influence and ability of the Rothschilds, the Montefiores, the Goldsmids, and the Salomons were recognized and duly rewarded. In 1885, Sir Nathan Meyer Rothschild was raised to the ermine and woolsack as Lord Rothschild, thus indicating that even the portals of the once hostile Upper House were now open to the English Jews. The daughters of the House of Rothschild married members of the English aristocracy, one of them becoming the wife of a future Prime Minister. It was hardly a secret at court that the Prince of Wales (later Edward VII) regarded his Hebrew friends "with conspicuous favor;" and, since His Royal Highness in this, as in other matters, set the fashion in English society, the innumerable host of his satellites followed his example.

While this social amalgamation was steadily advancing in the higher ranks, the feeling between Jew and gentile among the other levels of English society was not altogether harmonious. At least there still existed a certain mutual disinclination on the part of middle-class Jew and gentile to fraternize. Some of the English resented their Jewish neighbors, and preferred that these should occupy themselves with purely Jewish affairs. They looked upon the culture of England as a purely Christian culture.

There was a considerable party in the British Jewry which, while it accepted what the parliamentary acts of 1858 and 1866 had to offer, insisted on guarding more closely than ever its own peculiar cultural identity, considering their religious life quite distinct from their loyalty to England and its culture. Some went to the extreme of seeking to sublimate, as it were, the sense of membership in "The Chosen People" group into a sense of the superiority of race. The Jew, they felt, must not be disloyal to his community. He had ultimately won his citizenship on the "true faith of a Jew," and he should be proud of his heritage. This rejection of complete assimilation could not but be disappointing to a large number of even liberal Christians.

These then were some of the factors that still tended to prevent the development of a true understanding between the groups. However, economic and social developments during the remaining years of the century were to aid materially in modifying these differences. The spirit of examination and questioning which followed the publication of Darwin's *Origin of Species* (1859), the tremendous expansion in commerce (1859–1865), and a series of revolutionary events in the political and social world, stimulated the growth of democratic interests among men and nations. In these years, the relationship between Jew and gentile was considerably changed. The presence of Jews in nearly every profession and their rapid progress in all fields of commercial and social activity in the British Empire placed them more and more in a position of equality with other subjects of Her Majesty's Dominions.

Partly on account of the free exchange encouraged by the abolition of the Corn Laws (1845), partly on account of the more general world movements, there was, at the beginning of the 'sixties, a great commercial activity in England and signs of prosperity everywhere. Railways and ocean liners created a world market on a vast scale. The volume of English exports rose from about forty millions a year in the first decade of the century to nearly sixty millions a year in the 'fifties. The English Jews were ready and eager to enjoy their share of what Lord Morley termed "the steady splendour of the economic era." Availing themselves of the advantages accruing from their newly-won rights and opportunites, they grew in importance and influence throughout the realm. In London, for instance, Sir David Salomons became one of the founders of the London and Westminster Bank, the Goldsmids secured a controlling interest in the London docks, Sir Moses Montefiore and his brother-in-law, Nathan Rothschild, assumed a large measure of responsibility in the creation of the Alliance Insurance Company. These and similar business activities brought Jewish economic interests into ever widening relations with the rest of the Empire. The great organization of investment by company promotion, the chief economic event of the last century, was undoubtedly a Jewish achievement.

In the late 'sixties, when, as a result of the headlong speculation in commerce and banking, Jews and gentiles alike suffered in a tremendous crash which paralyzed trade and convulsed the centers of industry, an effort was made to point the finger of reproof at the Jewish merchants and speculators, and blame them for the catastrophe. Similarly, in the 'seventies, when a season of prosperity was followed by a wild orgy of speculation, leading inevitably to a prostration of trade and a slump in business, the clash of interests and the inevitable reaction, provoked a revival of prejudice and ill-will against the Jews in business. But now that the English Jews were legally citizens of the state, their position was unassailable, and there was no fear of persecution, as in the days of King John and Edward I. In this respect they were much more fortunate than their kinsmen in Russia, whose growing financial strength aroused a violent hostility which resulted in brutal dispossessions and massacre that stirred the whole English nation.

Even if she had wished to do so, England could not have ignored the Russian situation in the second half of the century. She was inescapably involved in the economic aspect of the persecutions, at least, because of the unusual number of Russian Jewish immigrants who sought the shores of Britain as a refuge from the storms of persecution. The number of immigrants attracted to the East End of London in particular was considerably larger than could easily be handled, so that fears were entertained as to the sufficiency of work, food and accommodation for so unexpected an influx of aliens. It was estimated that, as a result of the Russian persecutions of 1881–1882, 50,000 impoverished Jews fled to England. Again in 1890–1891, after similar outrages, 20,000 other refugees poured into England from Russia and Poland. Most of these immigrants settled in London, Leeds and Manchester. In London, they formed 30 per cent of the Mile End population, and 19 per cent of the Whitechapel community. The way in which they congregated in a few trades — shoe and slipper making, tailoring, and other branches of the clothing trade, cigar-making and peddling — indicated the changes in Jewish occupations among the lower classes in recent years. It was not long before the cry was raised that these immigrants were injuring the English workman by unfair competition and by lowering the rate of wages. Socially, too, these immigrants were regarded by the Sephardim and the Germans as a a detriment to the older Jewish communities. The preponderance of alien and strange-mannered families in any community is by no means advantageous to the reputation of that community. Here was a horde of neglected "poor relations," with all the old-world fears and superstitions and prejudices in their hearts, intrenching themselves in "tribal exclusiveness" in modern England. Different in outlook and unusually staunch in their orthodoxy, they distrusted not only all who belonged to other faiths, but even those of their own brethren of the Reformed synagogues. Sir Walter Besant, historian of London, describes these Jewish immigrants as follows:

They are the poorest of the very poor; when they come over they have nothing . . .Their ranks are always recruited by new arrivals. There is talk of their taking work away from English workmen. Yet there seem to be no signs, as on the continent, of a *Judenhetze* or any such wide-spread, unreasoning hatred of the Jew as we lately saw in France, and as we have seen in Russia and Germany. The newly-arrived Jews have their own colony . . .They now occupy, almost to the exclusion of others, a triangular area of East London, lying north of the Whitechapel Road immediately without the city limits; it has a base of nearly half a mile, and an altitude of three-fourths of a mile. Here for a time the poorer Jews are all crowded together. It is alleged that they have ingenious ways of sweating each other; as soon as the Polish Jew has got his head a little above water, he begins to exploit his countrymen; he acquires the miserable tenements of the quarter, and raises the rent and demands a large sum for the "key." These Jews all succeed, unless they are kept down by their own favorite vice of gambling . . . they succeed partly because they are extremely industrious, patient, orderly and law-abiding.

These immigrants evidently of necessity remained for a generation an isolated and self-centered people, within their narrow limits, and fundamentally alien in their aims and ideas to the rest of their fellows. This of course was understandable to those who had some knowledge of their sufferings and persecutions in Germany and Russia and Poland. But it did not help the Jewish cause in England. On the contrary, these new aliens were sure to engender friction and provoke new misunderstandings and hostilities. English Jewry at the end of the century was faced with a serious problem.

The eviction of Jews from Russia and the wave of anti-Semitism that caused it served to remind Jewish leaders in Germany, France and England that, despite all the long years they had fought for social and political liberty, the Jews still had not gained security and complete emancipation. They had been telling themselves that they were at home everywhere, but now it was evident that they were not wanted, at least in the dominions of the Czar. Thousands were still in *Galut*, in exile. As if in response, therefore, to a desire on the part of the masses of homeless Jews, a movement, which had remained merely a dream for many years, was organized for the purpose of promoting the return of Jews to their ancestral homeland in Palestine.

Independent of any European propaganda appear to be the efforts of the English philanthropist, Sir Moses Montefiore, who, early in the century turned his attention to the ideal of restoring Palestine to his brethren. In 1827, accompanied by his wife, he made a trip to Palestine. Eleven years later he made a second trip, to obtain concessions from Mohammed Ali, and to establish several hundred families in that region. The Damascus Affair (1840) took Montefiore to the East again, and while there, he became more convinced than ever that the solution of the Jewish question in the East could be accomplished only by establishing Jewish agricultural colonies in Palestine. The first "Zionist" organization was called the Montefiore Society.

It will be remembered that when the young Benjamin Disraeli traveled in the East in 1831, he became not only an ardent lover of Zion, but a strong believer in Jewish nationalism. In his romance *Alroy* (1833), he pictured the Jewish vision of the return of the ancient race to the home of their ancestors. Later, in *Tancred* (1847), the desire of his people was set forth in the words:

> The vineyards of Israel have ceased to exist; but the Jewish eternal law enjoins the Children of Israel still to celebrate their vintage. A race that persists in celebrating their vintage, although they have no fruits to gather, will regain their vineyards. What sublime inexorability in the law! But what indomitable spirit in the people . . .

If Disraeli, when he came to power, failed to realize the visions of his youth about his people, he encouraged and supported the efforts of another English man of letters, who, though not of his group, shared the Jewish patriot's belief in the ultimate restoration of Zion to the Jews. Lawrence Oliphant, diplomat and member of Parliament, abandoned a brilliant career in England, and, acting under the inspiration of a religious idea, obtained a charter for Jewish agricultural colonization in the land of Gilead, on the east side of the Jordan, thus launching what may be regarded as the second "Zionist" movement. Though Oliphant met with no success, the scheme for the Jewish colonization of Palestine received fresh impetus as a result of the persecutions in Russia.

The feelings of a section of the English Zionists found expression perhaps in a poem entitled "Pro Patria" by Paul Newman, published in the *Yellow Book* for April, 1895. After praising the beauty and charm of England, the Jewish poet proclaimed his love for the home of his people:

> A little longer and the inhabitants
> Of exile shall re-echo to thy call,
> "Return, my children, from among the nations,
> Forget the years of banishment and thrall!"

Land of the Prophets! in the Prophet's vision
Thy future glory far transcends thy woes;
And soon, in spite of hatred and derision,
Thy wilderness shall blossom as the rose!

In 1895, Theodor Herzl, a journalist of Vienna who had till then regarded the assimilation of the Jews as a natural and desirable way of solving the Jewish question, openly admitted that the anti-Semitic feeling revealed in the Dreyfus Affair (1895) made it clear to him and other Jewish leaders that a latent and dangerous hatred of the Jews, ready to burst into flame at the slightest provocation everywhere, called for the organization of a national movement, for the establishment of a state in Palestine. Herzl looked to the English Jews for support. Through the instrumentality of Israel Zangwill, Herzl visited England in 1896, and addressed a mass meeting in East Side, London. It was not unreasonable to suppose that to thousands of Jewish immigrants the idea of a settlement where they might find an assured home and peace, seemed like the fulfillment of prophecy. Among those English-Jewish leaders who partly agreed with the Zionists was Baron Rothschild, who, as chairman of the Royal Commission to consider the restriction of alien immigration in 1896, felt that a radical solution of the Jewish problem could be found in the institution of agricultural colonies in the ancestral home of Israel. The response of English Jewry to the call of the Zionists was not as enthusiastic and hearty as the leaders had reason to expect. The answer of individual English Jews was only too obvious. They did not feel attracted to Zion; they were satisfied with the prospect of remaining as citizens of a New Jerusalem on the banks of the Thames or the Hudson. However, the Zionist movement had this effect on Jewish communities everywhere; it proved a reaction against the process of assimilation, and, by the return of some fraction of the people to Palestine, served to make communities conscious of that "self-respect which every Jew loses in some degree when he strives to become what he is not."

In a comment on a series of lectures on "The Jews in Relation to the Church and the World," published in 1879, the London *Spectator* (LI, 252) declared that it was "curious in what differing forms a subject which has come to the surface of the general thought crops up. Now it is our greatest novelist who gives to her latest prose work a completely Jewish atmosphere; then articles regarding the Jews, or written by their foremost men, appear in our periodicals, and now again, we have this series of lectures, full of sympathy which must be appreciated by a people of such intensity of feeling." It was indeed a noticeable fact that, since 1859, many papers and articles on Jewish matters had appeared in the principal English periodicals and newspapers. At random the reader could pick out a variety of papers, written with the idea of stimulating interest in the English Jews, on such subjects as the Jewish homes and synagogues in London, Jewish feast days and religious observances, the Jews in England, and Hebrew legends and folk-tales. "It is to be hoped," observes the editor of *Leisure Hour* (XV, 825) in 1866, "that explanations of Jewish life and manners may prove instrumental in removing prejudices that are still entertained by some against the ancient people."

In his papers entitled *The Jew, the Gypsy, and El Islam* (1869–1871) the famous traveler and explorer, Sir Richard Burton, has the following account of the Jews, with strong evidence of the gentile standpoint:

Physically and mentally, the Jewish man and woman are equal in all respects to their Gentile neighbors; and in some respects are superior to them ... We visit him (the Hebrew), we dine with him, and we see him at all times and places, except perhaps at the Sunday service. We should enjoy his society but for a certain coarseness of manner, especially an offensive familiarity, which seems almost peculiar to him. We marvel at his talents, and we are struck by the adaptability and the universality of his genius. We admire his patience, his steadfastness and his courage, his military prowess and his successful career in every post and profession — statesman and senior wrangler, poet and literato, jurist, surgeon and physician, capitalist, financier and merchant, philosopher and engineer; in fact, everything that man can be. When we compare the Semite Premier with his Anglo-Saxon rival, it is much to the advantage of the former; while jesting about the Asian mystery, we cannot but feel there is something in the Asiatic which we do not expect, which eludes our ken, which goes beyond us ...

The Jew of popular English fiction is no longer *Mosheh*, a wretch who believes in one God and in Shentper-shent as his profit; whose eyes, unlike those of Banquo, are brimming full with "speculation." The Fagin of young Dickens, only a quarter of a century ago, has become "the gentle Riah" of the old Dickens — a being remarkable for resignation and quiet dignity ... *Tancred or the New Crusade*, to mention nothing of meaner note, teaches us to admire and love the modern "Rose of Sharon." Miriam has become in fact a pet heroine with novel writers and novel readers, and thrice happy is the fascinating young Christian who, like "that Boy of Norcott's," despite his manifold Christian disabilities, can win her hand and heart.

Of the middle and lower classes of Jews, the Englishman only hears that they are industrious, abstinent, and comparatively cleanly in person; decent, hospitable and as strict in keeping the Sabbath as the strictest Sabbatarians could desire. He is told that they are wondrous charitable in their dealings with those of the same faith, always provided that some mite of religious difference does not grow to a mountain size . . .

To my mind, there are few things so admirable and wonderful as the "getting on" of the Hebrew race. Most Jews seem to rise . . . The young man with the banner in Mr. Longfellow's ballad, was, depend upon it, an Israelite of the Israelites. Only, I think the poet was wrong, as poets generally are, in his climax. The young man was not frozen to death. He made an immense fortune at the top of Mt. Blanc, by selling Excelsior penny ices . . .The average Englishman smiles at their intense love of public amusements and their excessive fondness for display . . . Knowing this, however, he supposes himself to know the worst. He has heard little of the excessive *optimism* of the Jews.

Another writer, J. Mills (*The British Jew*, 1862), remarks:

Although a variety of causes may cooperate to modify the character, still the great agents of all moral change are religion and education . . . After much inquiry and reflection, we verily believe that the British Jews are not guilty of any habitual vice peculiar to themselves; but, on the other hand, that they are less addicted to the immoralities that so frequently disgrace their Gentile neighbors . . .

The cultivation of these social virtues (geniality and sociability) gives to the Jews advantages over the thousands of their Gentile neighbors who so shamefully neglect them . . . It is a well-ascertained fact that the Jews residing in London have suffered less in proportion to the population than other inhabitants (from disease and sickness).

It became customary for most English observers to pay
tribute to the Jewish group and to speak of the English Jews
as naturally genial and social companions, famed for their
hospitality.

Punch, or the London Charivaria, to whose pages we have
referred in the preceding chapter as being unsympathetic
towards the Jews in the early 'forties, was now among the
English journals willing to admit that "every country has
the Jews it deserves." In 1882, in a cartoon on the Jewish
pogroms in Russia, *Punch* depicted Humanity as Portia
pleading *for*, and not *against*, the Jews. How would it read,
asked Mr. Punch, if our papers contained accounts of the
murdering of Jews, and the burning of their houses in
Houndsditch, with the police looking on in amused indifference, and the Home Secretary sending messages of thanks
to the murderers? In a poem published in 1882, entitled
"A Cry from Christendom," against the old anti-Semite
cry of "Hep! Hep!", Mr. Punch indignantly denounced
the hounding of Hebrews in the name of the Cross:

> Out, out on the Tartuffes of Creed!—Let the spirit
>   of Christendom speak
> Plain words of unfaltering truth for the cause of
>   the helpless and weak.

In general, it may be said that the British press was in
sympathy with the Jewish communities during the years
of European anti-Semite propaganda and Jewish persecution. Soon after the Paris convocation (1876) of leading
Jews of Europe, when the attention of all governments was
drawn to the wrongs inflicted on Israel in Turkey, the
Saturday Review (1877) observed that

> the tendency of all the western nations has long been,
> not only to relieve the Jew from all actual oppression,

> but to put him on the same civil and political level
> as the Christian. Yet even in western countries, even
> where the Jew is a citizen, and very often as good a citi-
> zen as any other, something of his old historical posi-
> tion still clings to him;

and, later, felt it necessary to point out that even the English "who are not at bottom a tolerant race," were distinctly
in advance of other European races in their attitude towards
the Jews.

The persecution of the Russian Jews in the 'eighties became a matter of deep concern in England. The wholesale
eviction of thousands of Jewish residents stirred up considerable sympathy among the churches. "All our sympathies," declared Rev. Charles Haddon Spurgeon, the eminent English preacher and writer in 1882, "are aroused for
the Jews who are being brutally treated in Russia. One is
made to blush for the name of Christian when we see it
mixed up wth murder, plunder and ravishment. The large
catalogue of Russian atrocities is enough to move a heart
of stone . . . The House of Israel knows assuredly that all
real followers of Jesus of Nazareth desire the good of their
nation and lament their persecution." The *Edinburgh Review* (1883) was even more severe in its denunciation of the
Russian situation:

> Persecution is one of the fevers of society . . . In former
> times the chief incentive to persecution was religious
> bigotry and fanaticism; in our own it is popular ignor-
> ance and intolerance, moved by the baser passions of
> envy and fear . . . The victims of persecution to whom
> the following pages are to be devoted, are, however, of
> a lowlier caste, though of the most ancient lineage. But
> they have suffered all the more from cruelty and in-

justice; and surely the spirit of persecution is never more detestable than when it inflicts incalculable suffering on the humblest members of society ... Jew-baiting, as it exists at this moment, is not only a monstrous injustice, but it is an outrage on decency, a darkening of the fair face of Christendom; and as such it cannot fail to retard the progress which, as Christians and as citizens, we most desire .... Equality before the Law, charity and good-will, are solvents which nothing can resist. By their influence the celebrated "Jewish Question" which has cropped up at intervals ever since the time of Exodus, has been solved, or rather has solved itself in England and America ...

One of the most important literary expressions with reference to the social and political welfare of the English Jews was the outspoken and sympathetic essay entitled *The Modern Hep! Hep! Hep!* by George Eliot, who, speaking as an English citizen, claimed that "our affinity with them (the Jews) is only the more apparent when the elements of their peculiarity are discerned." In summing up the case for the Hebrew character, the essayist remarked on the "predominant kindliness" of the Jews ... "a trait which must have been deeply ingrained in the constitution" to have outlasted the ages of persecution and oppression.

The concentration of their joys in domestic life has kept up in them the capacity of tenderness; the pity for the fatherless and the widow, the care for the women and the little ones, blent intimately wth their religion, is a well of mercy that cannot long or widely be pent up by exclusiveness. And the kindliness of the Jew overflows the line of division between him and the Gentile. On the whole, one of the most remarkable phenomena in the history of this scattered people, made for ages "a scorn and a hissing", is, that after being subjected to this process, which might have been expected to be in every sense deteriorating and vitiating, they have come out of it (in any estimate which allows for numerical proportion) rivaling the nations of all European countries in healthiness and beauty of physique, in practical ability, in scientific and artistic aptitude, and in some forms of ethical value . . . They are among us everywhere; it is useless to say we are not fond of them . . . If we wish to free ourselves from the inconveniences that we have to complain of, whether in proletaries or in Jews, our best course is to encourage all means of improving these neighbors who elbow us in a thickening crowd, and of sending incommodious energies into beneficent channels . . .

In the course of the discussions pertaining to Jewish persecutions, it seemed inevitable that an inquiry be made into the actual cause of bitter feelings between Jew and gentile in modern Europe. Were they different from the people among whom they lived? A writer in the *Spectator* (1880) ventured the opinion that if the Jews were successful in business, their idea of luxury, apart from a certain love of splendor which the East thinks magnificent and the West vulgar, differs very little from that of their competitors. Failing to realize that he was urging the Jewish people to self-destruction as Jews, he says:

The rich German, or Frenchman, or Englishman has not much right to talk about Jewish profusion, or of the Jew's hunger after material comfort, or even the Jew's fondness for display. Still, the Jew is disliked, as his rivals living like him are not disliked, and in all Western countries things are pardoned to successful natives which in successful Jews arouse the bitterest resentment . . . The main reasons for the dislike, we believe, are two: The first being that the Jews in all countries remain Jews, that is, distinctive, and thereby acquire the dislike with which any foreign race whatever similarly successful would be regarded; and the second, that they are an exceedingly pushing people . . . The Jews say, of course, everywhere that they are merely citizens with a distinctive creed; but citizens with a distinctive creed rarely refuse to intermarry, do not live so completely among themselves, do not help each other so markedly, and are not separated from the majority by so unmistakable a difference of appearance. They are separate, and, with the mass of mankind, separation implies hostility, more especially when, as in this case, separation is not accompanied and palliated by seclusion.

It was the conviction of Professor Goldwin Smith that the separatist character of the Jews was not the effect, but the cause, of their persecution. He attributed to the "tribalism" of the Hebrew race the qualities which he condemned and which he declared made them bad citizens. In 1881, in a paper on the Jewish question in England, (*Nineteenth Century*, X, 494 ff.) the historian says:

If patriotism means merely a willingness to perform all social duties and to do good to the community, nobody can deny that it may be possessed in the largest measure by the kinsmen of Sir Moses Montefiore. But if it means undivided devotion to the national interest, there is difficulty in seeing how it can be possessed without abatement by the members of a cosmopolitan and wandering race, with a tribal bond, tribal aspirations, and tribal feelings of its own . . . All other races profess at least allegiance to humanity; they all look forward, however vaguely, to a day of universal brotherhood . . . The Jew alone regards his race as superior to humanity, and looks forward, not to its ultimate union with other races, but to its final ascendancy under the leadership of the tribal Messiah.

The era of Aryan and Nordic racialism was still fifty years away.

Supporting Goldwin Smith in this view of the modern Jews was Arnold White, who, after an investigation of conditions in Russia and among the Jewish immigrants in England, felt strongly that, by refusing to assimilate with their neighbors, and by openly expressing a repugnance to the ways of the Anglo-Saxon, the average orthodox Hebrew immigrant "created a condition of friction and conflict which was detrimental to the welfare of the English commonwealth."

From these explanations, however, there was dissent. The *Spectator* (1891) again ventured to assert that the bad qualities of the Jews were directly due to oppression and ill-treatment; and, on the other hand, that many of the accusations brought against them could be applied with equal force to classes which in the rest of Europe are deemed worthy of all respect.

This examination of the literature of opinion of the period 1859–1900 shows that, on the whole, the attitude of the British press and of English contributors to periodical journalism was somewhat divided on the Jewish question. The majority however seemed convinced that "this martyr people, who for thirteen centuries had confronted all that fanaticism could devise," were entitled to fair play at the hands of Christian governments and communities. The general attitude of the more liberal writers may be summed up in the words of W. E. H. Lecky, who, in his *History of Rationalism in Europe* (1865), paid the following tribute to the Jewish people:

.... Persecution came to the Jewish nation in its most horrible forms ... But above all this the genius of that wonderful people rose supreme. While those around them were grovelling in the darkness of besotted ignorance; while juggling miracles and lying relics were the themes on which almost all Europe was expatiating; while the intellect of Christendom, enthralled by countless superstitions, had sunk into a deadly torpor, in which all love of enquiry and all search for truth were abandoned; the Jews were pursuing the path of knowledge, amassing learning and stimulating progress with the same unflinching constancy that they manifested in their faith. They were the most skilful physicians, the ablest financiers, and among the most profound philosophers; while they were only second to the Moors in the cultivation of natural science. They were also the chief interpreters to Western Europe of Arabian learning.

Any mention of the Jew in connection with the poetry of the Victorian age inevitably calls up the name of Robert Browning (1802–1889). The sarcasm of such a poem as *Holy Cross Day*, the philosophical exaltation of *Rabbi Ben Ezra*, reveal a passionate nature protesting against the stupidity born of religious bigotry and honoring true goodness irrespective of race and creed. *Holy Cross Day* (1855), suggested by a certain regulation in 17th century Rome which forced Jews once a year to attend a particular church and hear a special sermon, is prefaced by a quotation from a Diary by the Bishop's Secretary, 1600, in which it is recorded that "as it was of old cared for in the merciful bowels of the Church, that, so to speak, a crumb at least from her conspicuous table here in Rome, should be, though but once yearly, cast to the famishing dogs, under-trampled and bespitten-upon beneath the feasts of the guests ..." and headed by the remark of the poet, "Though what the Jews really said, on thus being driven to church, was rather to this effect...." With pathos and irony, the narrator tells how the Jews were herded into the church:

> Higgledy piggledy, packed we lie,
> Rats in a hamper, swine in a sty,
> Wasps in a bottle, frogs in a sieve,
> Worms in a carcass, fleas in a sleeve.
> Hist! square shoulders, settle your thumbs
> And buzz for the bishop — here he comes.
>
> — — — — — — — —
>
> Aaron's asleep — shove hip to haunch,
> Or somebody deal him a dig in the paunch!

They ridicule the entire proceeding, but then take on a solemn note as they silently bewail Israel's bereft glories. They chant under their breath "Ben Ezra's Song of Death", the while receiving new strength into their hearts from a contemplation of the prophetic promise that

> The Lord will have mercy on Jacob yet,
> And again in his border see Israel set.
> When Judah beholds Jerusalem,
> The stranger shall be joined to them;
> To Jacob's House shall the Gentiles cleave,
> So the Prophet saith and his sons believe.
>
> — — — — — — — —
>
> By the torture, prolonged from age to age,
> By the infamy, Israel's heritage,
> By the Ghetto's plague, by the garb's disgrace,
> By the badge of shame, by the felon's place,
> By the branding tool, the bloody whip,
> And the summons to Christian fellowship,-
>
> We boast our proof that at least the Jew
> Would wrest Christ's name from the Devil's crew.

> Thy face took never so deep a shade
> But we fought them in it, God our aid!
> A trophy to bear, as we march Thy band
> South, East, and on to the Pleasant Land!

Browning manifests a knowledge of the tradition and literature of the Jewish people in several other poems. His longest poem, *The Ring and the Book* (1868–1869), shows again and again the persecution and abuse to which the medieval Jew is subjected through Christian intolerance and bigotry. In *The Privilege of Burial,* the gentile rowdies are described as resenting the law that forbids them to pelt with stones the Jews who have gathered to bury their dead in the cemetery. The poet's themes are medieval, but his attitude towards the Jews is decidedly sympathetic. According to Stopford Brooke, "no English poet, save perhaps Shakespeare, whose exquisite sympathy could not leave even Shylock unpitied, had spoken of the Jew with compassion, knowledge and admiration, till Robert Browning wrote of him. The Jew lay deep in Browning." The poems of Jewish interest written by Browning during the period now under review were *Rabbi Ben Ezra* (1864), *Filippo Baldinucci* (1876), and *Jochanan Hakkadosh* (1883). Of these, *Rabbi Ben Ezra,* dealing with the philosophical wisdom of one of the most eminent Jewish literati of the Middle Ages, Abraham ben Meir ibn Ezra, is perhaps the most popular. The distinctive features of the rabbi of the poem are drawn from the writings of the real rabbi, whose advocacy of freedom of thought and research, whose views concerning the immortality of the soul, and whose attitude towards his fellow men, while not specifically Jewish, seemed to Browning to emphasize those traits in the Hebrew character which had made occasional contributions to the wisdom of modern civilization. In *Jochanan Hakkadosh*, the poet does full justice to the elevated nature of Rabbi Judah the Holy, who was probably the original of the character, and makes excellent use of his knowledge of the Talmud. Commenting on Browning's Hebraic sympathies, a Jewish critic in 1891 observed that "it may be held a blessing that one of England's greatest poets has shown such intelligent comprehension of the claims of the Jewish people... The value of the Hebrew element in Browning's poems is that it does much to remove prejudice, and to place the philosophy of the Jew in its true place among the world's Credos. A Ben Ezra and a Jochanan may supplant a Shylock and a Fagin in public estimation. This is an effect much to be desired."

A similar friendly attitude towards the Jews was exhibited by two other English poets of this period. Matthew Arnold, who in his essay on Heine and elegiac poem, *On Heine's Grave*, paid high tribute to Hebrew culture and learning; and Algernon Charles Swinburne, who, at the time of the Russian persecution of the Jews (1882) expressed a deep sympathy for the unfortunate victims of the Czar's inhumanity, in a poem entitled *On the Russian Persecution of the Jews*.

Other poems of Jewish interest by English poets in the second half of the century deal with the Jews of remote times: *Israel in Egypt*, in twenty-two books (1861), *The Fall of Nineveh*, in two volumes (1868), by Edwin Atherstone; poems on Jewish themes in *The Song of the Reed* (1887), by Edward Henry Palmer; and three poems by Sir Edwin Arnold, *The Feast of Belshazzar* (1852), *Potiphar's Wife* (1892), and *The Wonderful Adventure of Phra the Phoen* (1890).

Bitter criticism was aroused by a poem entitled *The Wandering Jew*, *A Christmas Carol*, by Robert Buchanan, which ran through two editions in 1893. The living Christ is pictured in this poem as a weak, aged and helpless Wandering Jew, who goes feebly through the cities, ever suffering afresh, and never prevailing. The Wandering Jew, so the poet believes, had utterly failed to convince the world of his godhead. Yet, he survives, and continues to survive, as the divine ideal — a pathetic figure searching Heaven in vain for a sign, for a token that he has not wholly failed. As he walks the streets of the city, he asks himself, after 1800 years of weary effort, the terrible question: After all, are men worth saving?

A considerable part of English poetry dealing with the Jews, 1880–1900, was more or less inspired by the compassion aroused by the persecutions on the continent and by the new movement for the restoration of the Jews to their ancient home in Palestine. The bulk of this verse appeared in minor periodicals and has little literary merit. In *The Minor Poet*, published in 1882, Amy Levy, the gifted Jewish poet and novelist, who attracted favorable notice during her brief career, gave evidence of the discontent and restlessness of her generation of Jewish idealists. Her last volume of poems, *A London Plane Tree*, appeared posthumously (1900). Another gifted Jewish writer, Mrs. Henry Lucas, published two volumes of metrical translations of Hebrew poems under the title of *Songs of Zion* (1894) and *The Jewish Year* (1898). Commenting on the first volume of poems, which contained twenty-five translations from a selection of medieval Hebrew singers, an English reviewer observed that "the aristocratic contempt with which too many Christian theologians regard Judaism is difficult to maintain in the presence of the religious poetry of the Jews. Reading the old medieval hymns, we feel how much we are at one with their authors in our deepest thoughts and aspirations . . . If this book should do something to diminish the prejudice which still keeps Christians and Jews asunder, and hinders them from learning from each other, it will have done even better than merely adding to the store of fine religious poetry."

The drama, too, maintained its interest in the Jew during the period under review. In the year following the admission of English Jews to Parliament (1858), Tom Taylor, editor of *Punch* and a popular playwright of mid-Victorian days, wrote a play, *Payable on Demand*, in which Reuben Goldsched, a banker, was the chief Jewish character. The plot was based on the experiences of Meyer Rothschild, who, entrusted with the wealth of the Landgrave of Hesse, came to London in 1806, made a fortune by staking his entire wealth on the campaign against Napoleon, and was able to lend money to the British Government. Another play of Jewish interest by Taylor was the well-known *Ticket-of-Leave Man* (1863), with Melter Moss, a Jewish receiver of stolen goods, as the hero's evil genius. This play set the fashion for stage Jews for the rest of the century. Melter, according to Landa, was bodily transferred to innumerable other plays.

In the last quarter of the century, the second-rate theaters capitalized on melodrama of the flimsiest character. Stage Jews were dragged in, as they had always been, to supply the comic relief, or to heighten the melodramatic effects. A good example of extravagant melodrama is furnished in *The Stolen Jewess* (1872), a play by Colin Hazelwood, which proved to be a veritable lumber-room of current ideas on Jews. Landa gives us the following interesting summary of the play:

> The period is 1807. In a Spanish valley near the French frontier, where a Jewish family is accused of being in league with the enemy, the daughter is stolen by Don Carlos, who has no heir, and treasonable papers are secreted in the house ("O, Great Father of my race, direct my steps and enable the poor Israelite to regain his che-ild"). Tableau, end of Act I, sc. i. The che-ild is taken to a convent, the Jew is saved from the block ("Talk not to me of the usury of the Jew; look at the usury practised by Christian attorneys, the greediness of Christian bill discounters, the cruelty of men in office like you, and then call the Israelite an inferior if you can.") Rapturous applause, and eighteen years elapse. Don Carlos tries to marry his supposed daughter to the son of an English nobleman, but he is recognized by the Wandering Jew and Jewess, in search of their che-ild, and in a cathedral there is a Revelation . . . The English nobleman turns out to be a Jew, Jacob Vonstein, and so the young people can marry ("a good Hebrew is better than a bad Christian.")

In 1889, at the Adelphi Theater, London, Chester Bailey Fernald produced a Jewish play, *The Ghetto*, a drama in four acts which he had translated and freely adapted from the Dutch of Herman Heijerman. Since it was a play in which the Jewish interest was strikingly sympathetic and suggestive of a new trend in dramatic treatment of Jewish character, it merits examination at some length. The action of *The Ghetto* takes place in the ghetto of Amsterdam, in the 'eighties. Into the shop of the blind old Jewish miser, Sachel, enter Samson and Daniel.

"See old Sachel," says Daniel, "there in the gloom like a spider waiting in its web — he would keep open all night for two cents."

Old Sachel suspects everybody and is hard to live with. Mordecai, a neighbor, curses him for a "black hearted miser." It happens that Sachel's son, Rafael, is a dreamer, a composer of music, and in love with Rosa, the Christian maid in Sachel's house. Rosa is the handsomest girl in Amsterdam, high or low, and believes in "the God of all peoples, of all faiths, the God who knows no ceremony but the way of living, and no creeds but what He plants in the hearts of everyone." Sachel is well aware of the advantage of having a Christian maid to help him, because being a Christian, it matters not what Rosa does on the Sabbath. Rafael cannot endure his miserly father's dishonest ways. The young idealist complains:

"On the platform of the scales, when your client stopped to balance them, I had seen a foot go out — go out and press down — so that the scales read false — so that the man who bought our goods was tricked and robbed of the money we had not earned from him. And again I saw it, and again and again, father! And the man whose foot went out and did that crime, the man who was stealing my respect, my honor, my youth, before my eyes, — was it Jacob? No, it was you — you, my father, my father whom I loved and pitied, and they had trusted because you were blind!"

Sachel: (hoarsely) "have I been different from the others? Aaron, Levy, Isaac, would they not have done the same? . . . no; business is business!"

Rafael: "Business — Aaron, Levy, Isaac — God! How I have despised them all my life!"

When Rafael declares his love for Rosa, and proposes marriage, the Christian maid answers:

"Your wife — here in the ghetto — here among your people? No, to them I am a Christian — to them I cannot be your wife — to them I am a sacrilege — an insult in their teeth .... what is your love ... the love of a Jew!"

Rafael: "And now *you* say *Jew*! *Jew*, as they say it in the streets, among the mob, when I go beyond the ghetto. It sounds strange from lips that I thought loved me; it sounds strange from the daughter of your father. Such a man he was! ... You told me of the noble deeds your father had done in behalf of the Jews; I couldn't help loving you for his sake; and now you call me *Jew*. I am a Jew. Never forget that I am a Jew! ... And I shall still be a Jew, proud of my race, proud of my fortitude, of the great triumphs which shall come to us Jews when we have shaken off the material shell which hides our spirit and makes us no better and no worse than the Christians."

At the end of the play, Rafael confesses in public, amid hisses and groans from the Jewish crowd, that Rosa has been his wife for many months past. When Rosa realizes the danger Rafael is in, she jumps into the canal; but Rafael leaps in to save her, and with her in his arms rushes out of the Ghetto — "out of the ghetto into the air!"

In the final years of the century, as might be expected, Russian pogrom plays were much in evidence. Among these, *Siberia* (1887), a play by Bartley Campbell, was perhaps the most successful. Other plays of Jewish interest were *The Old Jew* (1894), *The Degenerates* (1899), by Sidney Grundy, *Sam'l of Posen* (1895) by G. H. Jessop, and the *Cabinet Minister* (1890), by A. W. Pinero. As a general thing, these plays fell between farce and comedy, as far as the Jewish character was concerned. "To the end of the century," observes Landa, "the Jews of the stage were compelled to run the gauntlet of the jeering crowd along the theatrical highway, led by folly, pursued by bovine blundering, impelled ever onward by the callous thongs of the dramatist." The explanation for this, however, appears to be, not as Landa believes, "in the thoughtless excitement of the chase," wherein the mob rarely paused to ponder over the possibility of the Jew being a human being, but rather in the fact that the dramatists fell easily into the old stage tricks which required no originality to imitate. The laughter was for the comic character, and not for the Jew.

The production of a dramatic version of Israel Zangwill's *Children of the Ghetto* in 1899, was expected by sympathetic readers of the novel to win a favorable reception by the English public. But, though admirably acted at the Adelphi Theater, the play was criticized as "offensively Jewish in tone," and withdrawn after a brief run of six weeks. In his presentation of the Whitechapel ghetto of 1867, Zangwill no doubt insists on the aloofness of the Jews from ordinary humanity, and there is perhaps too much in the play that has to do with the strange customs and quaint ways of the ghetto community. It was felt at the time that the dramatist laid too great a stress upon the superficial peculiarities of his kindred, while passing over those deep and essential characteristics which really constitute the Jewish group.

CHAPTER XII

THE END OF AN ERA

"One of the most marked characteristics of our age," observed a literary critic with reference to the trend of the English novel at the close of the century, "is a certain spirit of scepticism, or let us say, a spirit of enquiry. We cannot or will not accept a dogma unless we have no alternative. Rules of conduct and of society which have been accepted throughout the history of civilization to-day require defence. Consequently the novelist has developed a new method. An institution or a custom is taken, and a story is told in which its defects are made apparent . . . The life exhibited must be true. Thus again, we find the tendencies of the age reflected in its literature." How well and how effectively the novelists of the second half of the century were able to apply and develop their "new method" with reference to the delineation of Jewish character and Jewish life, is the subject of investigation in this section.

As a result of the increasing immigration of European Jews during the dark days of Russian pogroms, new questions concerning the Jews in England and the Jews in every other part of the world began to interest writers of novels and short stories. Since public attention was being focused on the miseries of thousands of individuals of this most romantic people, writers of fiction were quick to realize the literary value and possibilities of materials pertaining to the adventures and experiences of homeless and wandering Israelites far and near. The fallacy of the assumptions that the Jews of one country were identical with those of other countries added to the interest of the problems to be exploited by the writer of realistic fiction. Also, it was natural that the wave of persecution should fasten the attention of English writers upon the position of the continental Jew, so different from that of his English brother.

Among the first novels in the 'sixties to deal with the conditions prevailing among Jews in central Europe was *Nina Balatka* (1879) by Anthony Trollope (1815–1882), published in serial form. Trollope takes the general problem of interracial marriage, in its most modern shape, making Prague, where old distinctions between Jews and Christians still linger in very much of their old intensity, the scene of his story. "A Christian here will hardly walk with a Jew," the novelist says, "unless it be from counter to counter or bank to bank. As for living together — or even eating in the same room — do you ever see it?" Under such circumstances, the marriage of the beautiful Christian girl, Nina Balatka, to the Jewish hero, Anton Trendellsohn, inevitably brings tragedy in its wake. The Christian aunt cries,

> Marry a Jew, Nina . . . it cannot be possible. There has been no girl connected with decent people who has ever so degraded herself!

The Jewish father, on the other hand, protests:

> Then, my son, you will live to rue the day in which you first saw her. She will be a bone of contention in your way that will separate you from your friends . . .

and will be odious alike to both . . . Do you think
that you have the strength to bear the contempt of
those around you? . . . As for me, I must look for another
son to bear the burden of my years.

But the younger generation look wistfully toward the more
tolerant countries of the West.

"We hear," says Rebecca, the young Jewess who befriends the heroine, "that in other countries the prejudice against us is dying away, and that the Christians
stay with Jews in their houses, and Jews with Christians, eating with them and drinking with them. I fear
it will never be so in Prague."
"And why not in Prague?" said Nina. "I hope it may.
Why should we not do in Prague as they do elsewhere?"
"It must take long first — very long," said Rebecca.

The mental conflict of the hero is vividly and sympathetically portrayed:

He had thought much of his position as a Jew before
he had spoken of his love to the penniless Christian
maiden . . . To be a Jew, always a Jew, in all things a
Jew, had been ever a part of his dream. It was as impossible to him, as it would be to his father, to forswear the
religion of his people . . . How could a Jew among Jews
hold up his head as such who had taken to his bosom a
Christian wife? . . . He would show the world around
him, both Jews and Christians, how well a Christian
and a Jew might live together. To crush the prejudice
which had dealt so hardly with his people — to make a
Jew equal in all things to a Christian — this was his desire; and how could this better be fulfilled than by his
union with a Christian? One thing at least was fixed
with him — one thing was fixed, even though it should
mar his dreams. He had taken the Christian girl to be
part of himself, and nothing should separate them.

In the end, to avoid separation, the Jew and his Christian wife leave Prague, bound for one of the great cities of the west, where, in a more liberal atmosphere, we are to suppose they live happily ever after.

As a picture of Jewish life in a foreign city, this novel reveals an inadequate knowledge of actual conditions. It is important, however, because it is obviously written to throw light on subjects of contemporary interest to the English reading public — the contrast between English tolerance and continental hatred of the Jew, and the question of the possibilities of success in inter-racial marriages, which was, as we have seen, a pertinent one in English society. Trollope shows us both the Jewish and the Christian feeling of alienation in its decadence, changed from its old persecuting fervor and its religious fanaticism, to social prejudice and religious scruple. That may have been true for some Jews and gentiles; but the impression is unavoidable that Trollope failed to realize the implications of inter-marriage to the Jewish group as a whole. By making opposition to his hero's plan a manifestation of nothing more than narrow religiosity, the author missed an opportunity to show a conflict between the powerful emotion of love and a sense of group loyalty which a ghetto youth was bound to feel. Intermarriage was more than a breach with convention: it was, and still is felt to be a blow at the vitality of an ancient people and its broad ideals. Such, at any rate, would have been the reaction of a hero of flesh and blood. Trollope varies the tale to make a Christian girl, a Bohemian, fall in love with a Jewish merchant and money-lender of Prague, with whom her father has business, and so interferes with the hopes of the Jewess, our author's

Rebecca, to whom the fathers of both had intended that he should engage himself.

In another novel entitled *Count Teleki* (1869), by an anonymous author, in the same sympathetic manner as Trollope's, the scene shifts from Europe to England. The story is one of modern Jewish life and customs and told by one who claims a familiarity with life within the ghetto. It is not certain whether the author, who signed himself "Eca," is a Jew or a Christian. Internal evidence would seem to point to Jewish origin. The story starts off with a realistic scene on the quarter-deck of a night mail packet. A party of young Englishmen, returning from the Paris races, are laughing and talking.

"And so, Dizz is to be Prime Minister?"
"So the papers say — who are going to form the Ministry?"

"Oh, all kinds of reports — Moses and son have been offered the Board of Trade, I hear — latest intelligence from the Minories."

"They say that Rothschild is going to be King of Jerusalem as soon as he wins the Derby, — in fact, that he has bought the Plains of Mamre already, as exercising ground for his horses."

"Quite correct, my boy, as your information always is. A race-course is going to be made between Jaffa and Jerusalem. The Passover Cup is to be run before Goodwood; the Lebanon stakes and the Houndsditch Steeple Chase in the October meetings . . ."

"But I say, it's an awful thing to think that the head of the Government — the first man in Europe — is a Jew — a "Ebrew Jew," as they say on the stage. Shades

of former Premiers, can ye rest in your graves and see
your parliamentary descendants so insulted!"

"Not at all — I'd far rather see Dizzy in than Gladstone and these reformers. Conservatism and the Cau-
casian mystery for ever! *Le Jew est Fait; Vive le Jew!*
as they say in Baden."

These Englishmen are outspoken and sportsmanlike. They
feel free to discuss politics and to face the realities of the
day, each as he pleases. Daniel Teleki, the hero of the
story, who has met many Englishmen in the course of his
travels, heartily approves of the outspokenness and the
manly independence of the average Englishman. Teleki
is the only son of Count Solomon Teleki, a wealthy Jewish
merchant and banker of Warsaw, who wishes the young
man to grow up like his sire, a thorough Jew, proud of his
religion, proud of his ancestry, a pillar of the Synagogue in
Warsaw. To this end, Daniel has been instructed in French
and English, and he is well acquainted with the Hebrew
scriptures and instructed in the Talmud. But, a few weeks
after his marriage, the young man loses his wife, and in the
bitterness of his grief, banishes all interest in life and sets
out on a prolonged trip — the Wandering Jew in search of
consolation and a new interest. He visits Rome and sees his
people surrounded by superstition and sunk in degradation.
At Constantinople he intercedes for the hapless Israelites
there. In Russia, he finds his people branded as 'accursed
and suspect of the empire'. Hearing of the liberality of the
English government, the freedom of English subjects, and
the independence of the English press, he decides to visit
England. What he wishes to see now is the effect of the re-

gime of toleration upon his own people. Are the English
Jews appreciative of their political freedom, are they hap-
pier? Above all, are they better Jews? In the third chapter
of the narrative, we have an account of Teleki's visit to the
Chief Rabbi of Great Britain, Dr. Hermann Bauer, who,
like Teleki, is a Polish Jew. From the Rabbi the count
learns that

"Parliament is open to us; we are free from all Jewish
disabilities; high civil offices in the state are occupied by
these of our faith. The clouds of oppression are fast
rolling past, and, as a race, I say we have much to be
hopeful for. But, as a sect — rigid and exclusive — we
have much to fear."

"To fear?" said the Count.

"Yes; to fear — not from without, but from within — not from Christians, but from ourselves. The very
liberality we enjoy is detrimental to the purity of our religion . . . Formerly, when persecuted and oppressed,
our people clung together, united in one bond. There
was sympathy in our seclusion . . . But now that the
arena of life is open alike to Hebrew and to Christian,
the result is that the former is rapidly losing that exclusiveness of his religion which is the very essence of
Judaism. Surrounded as we are by Christian influences,
social, moral and spiritual, — dwelling in a Christian
atmosphere — our habits of thought and feelings have
unconsciously become much modified. Our race has in
this country studied Christianity more than ever it has
done before . . . In many instances we are Christian-
izing our Judaism."

"Impossible!" said the Count, horror-struck.

"True, my son. Here you will see that in many of our
communities, the mode of Christian work has influenced

them. We have opened Sabbath schools and infant schools, like the Christians. We employ Scripture readers, cottage lecturers, and tract distributors, like the Christians. In many of our synagogues you will see pulpits and organs, and hear sermons in the vernacular tongue, and singing, like the Christians. We have adopted the title of the Christian clergy and their dress. All this is new."

As a chronicle of changing conditions, the novel contains interesting information that confirms current reports of a gradual transformation of English Jewish life. The reader accompanies the Rabbi and the Count as they go through the Jewish quarter investigating the changes; and from what the Rabbi tells the Count, it is possible to note indications of a slow but inevitable anglicization of the Jewish communities that live within the bounds of Houndsditch, Bishopsgate Street and Aldgate.

The delineation of the Count in this novel is of particular significance to the readers of the day. No one sees him without recognizing at a glance that he is a Jewish character new in English fiction, "surpassing the Sephardim Jews in all the glorious and choicest qualities of the race." The author emphasizes the point that "the Polish Jews are regarded by all as the most highly gifted of the Hebrew race, both in intellectual power and mental cultivation." "Here, in Count Teleki," says the reviewer in the *Athenaeum*, (1869), "is the charming picture of what young ladies, more enthusiastic than refined, are wont to call *a duck of a man!*"

In *That Boy of Norcott's* (1869), by Charles Lever (1806–1872), another attempt is made by an English novelist to present the Jew as he appears in contemporary life. It is

said of Old Ignaz Oppovich of the firm of Hodnig and
Oppovich, that he is a Jew who "could teach many a Christian the virtues of his own faith — a Jew that never refused
an alms to the poor, no matter of what belief, and that he
never spoke ill of his neighbor." He is a widower with two
children, a son and daughter. The son, Adolph, an irre-
claimable scamp and vagabond whose debts are paid over
and over again, is turned out of the army in disgrace, and
wanders about Europe trading on his father's name for
small loans. The daughter, Sarah, is, according to current
report, not much more likable than her brother. She is
proud and insolent to a degree remarkable in a princess
of a reigning house, and, from the clerks in her father's
establishment, exacts a homage that is positively absurd.
According to Hanserl, who, like old Thady in Maria Edgeworth's *Castle Rackrent*, describes the Jewess and expresses
the prejudices of a devout Roman Catholic towards a
member of the ancient race, Sarah is an insufferable representative of her people. It is not enough that the clerks
should always stand uncovered as she passes by; she even
demands that if any of them have occasion to address her,
he should preface what he has to say by kissing her hand
—"an act of vassalage that in Austria is limited to persons
of the humblest kind." When asked if the young Jewess
is handsome, Hanserl retorts, "How can she be handsome
when she is so over-bearing?"

We have seen that, in the 'seventies, the influence of rich
Jewish financiers in London increased by reason of their
activity and success in international trade throughout the
British Empire. In his only novel with a distinct social purpose, *The Way We Live Now* (1875), Anthony Trollope attempted to satirize the more malignant social tendencies of

the day, and presented, as the most important figure in the scene, Melmotte, a grotesque and nauseating monstrosity, in whose character the author personified the commercial corruption of the 'seventies, with all its brutalizing effects upon human character. Augustus Melmotte carries about him a certain suggestion of the ostentatious Jewish financier, Baron Albert Grant, a German Jew whose real name, according to Baring Gould, was Gottheimer. Men of the Gottheimer type are, in the opinion of the novelist, merely international financial adventurers who have settled in London with no other intent than to fleece the country gentry of England. They are the wrong kind of Jew, for whom success is wealth, and wealth is God. To such lovers of England as Trollope, this alien tarnishing of the bright shield of English manners, this betrayal of the land in the interests of commercialism, is just as bitter as it was to William Cobbett and other English yeomen in the early years of the century. Therefore, Trollope flays Melmotte, the alien millionaire, company promoter and swindler.

The bloated and ferocious alien plutocrat has a fat woman for a wife, and a Jew, Breghert by name, for an aide. Marie, the vulgar but otherwise unobjectionable daughter of Melmotte, does not dare to cross her father's will or stand in the way of his villainies. Whenever she does, the brute does not hesitate to "cut her to pieces" — in plain English, to horsewhip her within an inch of her life. Marie's associates are other young women as unattractive as herself, who expend their energies and innocence in intrigues to get husbands, not for love, but for the enjoyment of greater freedom and more pocket money.

The novel contains several different kinds of English

life — the great world in London, the young club life in London, the genteel English country life and humble country life, the journalistic and commercial life of London. Nearly all the characters are seeking mean ends — working, playing, intriguing, making love, with the simple object of obtaining cash or social position of the most vulgar and flaunting kind. The central figure is Melmotte who gives enormous dinners, entertains the Emperor of China, gets elected for Westminster, bullies and seeks people with titles. Concerning this novel a commentator says, "Trollope is so rarely inaccurate that we suppose there is somewhere a world like that he describes; and so somewhere among the marshes there is a sewage-farm, and we would as soon go there for a breath of fresh air as to the *Way We Live Now* for entertainment."

In later years, Trollope is reported to have expressed regret for this description of the alien financier and his Jewish family, declaring it to be ill-natured and over satirical. But, in the opinion of Hugh Walpole, *The Way We Live Now* is one of the most remarkable of all English novels published between 1860 and 1890. It is a novel of London life, with the colossal figure of Melmotte as a kind of symbolic character — a dirty, bullying, greedy, ignorant charlatan, representing a familiar type of exploiter who dominated the scene in those days.

Among the contemporary critics of Benjamin Disraeli's theory of races was Mary Ann Evans, who, as "George Eliot" (1819–1880), was to treat the Jewish question in a novel of her own. Because her last novel, *Daniel Deronda* (1876), was so essentially based on the philosophy which inspired her criticism, we have chosen to present her comments on Disraeli's theory here, rather than in the literature of opinion, where at first glance, they might seem more logically to belong.

The period of George Eliot's girlhood corresponded with the early stages of the controversy over the Jewish Disabilities Bill, and it is probable that she followed the speeches of Lord Macaulay, Lord John Russell, John Bright and others, in support of the measure. Also, no doubt, she came under the influence of some of the literature that poured forth from the opposition press. With Disraeli's share in the controversy, however, she was not pleased. From letters written by Mary Ann Evans at the time when Disraeli's trilogy was being widely read and discussed, we get some idea of her feelings regarding the "Jewish adventurer," whose sincerity as a novelist remained, in her opinion, as much in question as his sincerity as a politician. She felt that Disraeli wrote "much more detestable stuff than ever came from a French pen," that *Tancred* was "very thin" and inferior in the working up to *Coningsby* and *Sybil*, and that his "theory of races has not a leg to stand on and can only be buoyed up by windy eloquence." Commenting further on the Jewish statesman's theory of races, Mary Ann Evans says:

> My gentle nature kicks most resolutely against any assumption of superiority in the Jews, and is almost ready to echo Voltaire's vituperation. I bow to the supremacy of Hebrew poetry, but much of their early mythology and almost all their history is utterly revolting.

At the time when Mary Ann Evans wrote these letters, she herself had no theory of race, such as later took so great a hold on her. She shared the general feeling of distrust in

Disraeli's political and social principles. It is interesting, however, to observe that both Disraeli and George Eliot, though so divergent in their outlook and spirit, wrote almost at the same time of the same ancient race, in the hope of bringing about almost the same results — namely an appreciation of the great gifts and contributions of the Hebrews to the progress of Western civilization.

It was a part of George Eliot's purpose as a novelist, as it was of Disraeli's, to criticize the social life of England because of its deficiency in spiritual power, moral purpose and noble sentiment. In spite of her opposition to Disraeli's theory of an unmixed and superior race, she was attracted by the Disraelian dream of the restoration of a national center for the Jewish people, and by a desire to protest against the conventional conception of the ancient race in English life and politics. While she disagreed with Disraeli's inordinate love of lineage and his glorification of the Jewish nation, she felt certain that the opposite representation of the Jew as a Shylock, a scheming loan-shark, and a despicable old-clothes man, was equally unfair. The mission of Israel, she believed, was neither to govern the earth, nor to wander over the face of it as a condemned criminal. There were men and women in the English Jewry who were neither devils nor saints. What was needed was a fair statement of the many sides of the complex group character of the Jews. "There is nothing I should care more to do," she says, "if it were possible, than to rouse the imagination of men and women to a vision of human claims in those races of their fellow men who most differ from them in customs and beliefs." And towards the Hebrews, she believes that the western people, who have been raised in Christianity, have a peculiar debt.

There is little information in George Eliot's published journals and letters relating to the origin and development of her sympathy for the Jewish people. Perhaps this interest arose from her friendship with Emanuel Deutsch, the great talmudic scholar, who died just prior to the publication of *Daniel Deronda*. As a young woman, the novelist read considerably in the histories and literature of the "fine old race who have done great things for humanity," and, reading Hebrew with ease, delved extensively into the traditions and poetry of the Chosen People. Moreover, she is reported to have visited the synagogue and familiarized herself with the religious customs and services in vogue, and taken the greatest pains in inquiring into the home life and peculiar social habits of the Jewish communities in London. "Her knowledge of things Jewish," says Dr. Calisch, "is full and thorough." Thus, led by a cordial inclination to the study of Jewish national and domestic life, and after years of preparation for the undertaking, the novelist felt justified in championing the cause of the English Jews in her last novel. It is, of course, in this Jewish aspect of the book, rather than in its more frequently discussed exposition of the positivist philosophy, that we are here interested.

When *Daniel Deronda* appeared in 1876, the English Jews had already been eligible for election to Parliament for a decade and a half, and were making considerable headway in municipal and parliamentary affairs. The theme of the novel, therefore, does not concern itself so much with the recognition of the political rights of the Jew in the English commonwealth, as with the development of the Eastern dream — pointing to the East as the *fons et origo* of the spiritual values of culture and advancement. The novelist is interested in presenting the contrast between the traditions and conventions of the western world and those of the more ancient oriental peoples, particularly the Jewish. To this end, full expression is given to the ideas then current concerning the mighty moulding influence of heredity and race, and the ultimate union of racial and national ideas. On the old folk fable of the scullion who, a prince by birth, discovers his origin at the end of the story by some indelible mark, George Eliot bases her plot, presenting as the chief character a man of some importance among the gentiles, who discovers that he is a Jew. The fact that he is a member of the ancient race becomes important. Immediately upon the realization of his lineage, he enters into full spiritual and intellectual maturity and devotes the rest of his life to the advancement of his people.

What is Daniel Deronda's history in the novel? A foreign singer who wishes that her only child might be spared what she considers the miseries of the Jewish race, determines to break all family ties and give her infant son to an admirer, Sir Hugo Mallinger, who, so it is agreed by both parties, is to spare the boy all the sorrows and the humiliation that inevitably fall to the lot of Jews. Sir Hugo is faithful to his pledge. He brings up the boy in luxury and kindness, but in ignorance of his race and parentage. From the start Daniel is destined to be kind to his fellows; at school he befriends Hans Meyrick, and, later, saves a beautiful young Jewess named Mirah from drowning, and offers assistance to a poor Jewish workman named Mordecai, who, by sheer force of enthusiasm inspires the young hero with a desire to serve a great cause. Taught from boyhood to be courageous in his opinions and sufficiently independent in mind to examine things for himself, Daniel Deronda grows up to be a man free from the cowardice usually attributed to the Jews. In the course of his search for Mirah's lost relatives, he is led to a close contact with the Jewish communities in the city. At first, he is indifferent about the inhabitants of Jewry, but in time he becomes interested in their daily struggles and aspirations, in Judaism and its professors. His gravity of manner and many-sided sympathy are meant by the author to be taken as hereditary traits which incline him to take up passionately the cause of wronged individuals as of oppressed races.

Daniel Deronda's meeting with Mordecai on the bridge near Chelsea is the beginning of a remarkable friendship. In the poor Jewish watchmaker, Daniel finds the first man for whom he has admiration and reverence. At times, after long philosophic conversations with Mordecai, Daniel wishes he were a Jew. Mordecai's dreams and aspirations are chiefly concerned with the Jewish people; he has long been seeking a coreligionist to whom he can impart the mission which fate will not permit him, a poor consumptive in the final stages of the disease, to fulfill. Later, at a meeting of the "Hand and Banner," a club composed of "poor men given to thought," Mordecai reviews the position of the Jews among the nations:

> Let their history be known and examined; let the seed be sifted, let the beginning be traced to the weed of the wilderness — the more glorious will be the energy that transformed it. Where else is there a nation of whom it may be as truly said that their religion and law and moral life mingled as the stream of blood in the heart and made one growth; where else a people who kept and enlarged their spiritual store at the very

time when they were hunted with a hatred as fierce as
the very forest fires that chase the wild beast from his
covert? There is a fable of the Roman that swimming
to save his life he held the roll of his writings between
his teeth and saved it from the waters. But how much
more than that is true of our race? They struggled to
keep their place among the nations like heroes — yea,
when the hand was hacked off they clung with the
teeth... hooted and scared like the unknown dog, the
Hebrew made himself envied for his wealth and wisdom and was bled of them to fill the bath of Gentile
luxury; he absorbed knowledge, he diffused it... The
native spirit of our tradition was not to stand still, but
to use records as seeds and to draw out the compressed
virtues of law and prophecy...

While on a visit to Frankfort, Daniel Deronda is recognized by a Jewish banker as the grandson of his old friend,
Daniel Charisi. This leads to the climax of the narrative.
At once, the banker communicates with Deronda's mother,
who, after remaining for nearly a quarter of a century without seeing her offspring, appears on the scene, and in a
dramatic scene discloses the secret of the hero's birth and
family. The young man, however, has been elaborately prepared for the melodramatic revelation of his real parentage.
He has already fixed both love and fellowship upon members of the Jewish people. Therefore, he is not altogether
displeased by his mother's revelations. On the contrary,
when the fact that he is a Jew is disclosed, he is able to
say:

..... for months, events have been preparing me to
be glad that I am a Jew... It is no shame to have Jewish parents — the shame is to disown it.

Later, he adds:

> I shall call myself a Jew. But I will not say that I shall profess to believe exactly as my fathers have believed. Our fathers themselves changed the horizon of their beliefs and learned of other races. But I think I can maintain my grandfather's notion of separateness with communication. I hold that my first duty is to my own people, and if there is anything to be done towards restoring or perfecting their common life, I shall make that my vocation.

Daniel Deronda accepts his race in the spirit of one who has entered into the possession of an inheritance for which he has yearned. He returns to Mirah and Mordecai with something that is better than freedom; with a bond of loyalty and duty to race which fills him with great joy and satisfaction. He confesses to Mordecai that he has wonderful news, that he, Daniel Deronda, is a Jew!

> We have the same people. Our souls have the same vocation. We shall not be separated by life or by death ... And it is not only that I am a Jew ... but I come of a strain that has ardently maintained the fellowship of our race — a line of Spanish Jews that has borne many students and men of practical power ... and it is through your inspiration that I have discerned what may be my life's work.

Through Mordecai, whose passion centers in a dream of a glorious future for the Jewish race, Daniel Deronda receives the call to service. The hope for the future is conveyed in the following speech by Mordecai.

> ... The soul of Judaism is not dead. Revive the organic center; let the unity of Israel which has made the growth and form of its religion be an outward reality.

Looking towards a land and a polity, our dispersed people in all the ends of the earth may share the dignity of a national life which has a voice among the peoples of the East and the West — which will plant the wisdom and the skill of our race so that it may be, as of old, a medium of transmission and understanding. Let that come to pass, and the living warmth will spread to the weak extremities of Israel; and superstition will vanish, not in the lawlessness of the renegade, but in the illumination of great facts which widen feeling and make all knowledge alive as the young offspring of beloved memories . . .

There is a store of wisdom among us to found a new Jewish polity, grand, simple, just, like the old — a republic where there is equality of protection, an equality which shone like a star on the forehead of our ancient community, and gave it more than the brightness of western freedom amid the despotisms of the East. Then our race shall have an organic center, a heart and brain to watch and guide and execute; the outraged Jew shall have a defence in the court of nations, as the outraged Englishman. And the world will gain as Israel gains . . .

I know there are difficulties. But let the spirit of sublime achievement move in the great among our people. and the work will begin . . . I shall cherish nothing for the Jewish nation, I seek nothing for them, but the good which promises good to all nations. The spirit of our religious life, which is one with our national life, is not hatred of aught but wrong . . . *the vision is there; it will be fulfilled*.

The establishment of a Jewish polity, in the true sense of the word a theocracy, where the Infinite Holiness reigns supreme, in justice, purity and love, is a task which appeals to the highest aspirations of the hero. His readiness to undertake a national mission most improbable of realization only proves George Eliot's belief in human possibilities, which all who achieve difficult enterprises must share.

In Daniel Deronda, a Jewish hero after the Sidonia type reappears; a man who is to teach more than an ordinary lesson to his fellows. He is a type of Jew who is willing to devote the best years of his life to the loftiest national aims of his people. In the end, he goes to the East, to become better acquainted with the people of his race there. Daniel marries Mirah, and together they journey to the land of their fathers.

The story of Mirah, who turns out to be the heroine of the Jewish part of the story, presents another purely aesthetic side of Jewish life. The epithet "Jewess," hurled at her on various occasions, strengthens her resolve to remain Jewish. She yearns for the mother she has lost and for the brother whom she believes she has lost; and when she is reunited with them, her joy is as great as Deronda's when he discovers he is a Jew. Mirah's sad, humble complaints that she has not been a good Jewess, because she has been cut off from the use of Jewish books, and restrained by her scoundrel of a father from attendance at Jewish worship, find their answer in her deep and unfailing sense of her share in the national doom of suffering. She inherits in a surpassing degree a wonderful musical talent — the only art which the Jewish race pursues to perfection.

On the other hand, Deronda's mother represents the unbelieving and wordly side of Jewish character. Her desire is to spare her son what she considers the miseries of her race. She remains for a quarter of a century away from her son. When at last she meets him, in one of the strangest meetings between parent and child ever recorded, she offers what she regards as an adequate explanation of her conduct.

She has always regarded Judaism, with all its rules and for-
malities, as an oppressive burden. Her stern father resolutely
opposed her in all her artistic inclinations, and forced her to
marry the man of his choice. Therefore, when father and
husband die, she determines to free her son from all racial
ties, and endeavors to break away from all associations with
her people. Having communicated these facts to her son,
she passes out of his life, and out of the novel, as drama-
tically as she enters them.

Another un-Jewish Jew in the novel is Pash, who is represented as having neither faith nor reverence. "I don't
see why our rubbish is to be held and saved," he says, "any
more than the rubbish of Brahmanism or Buddhism." Like
Pash is Gideon, a Jew by birth but not by temperament.
Says Gideon:

> I'm a rational Jew myself. I stand by my people as a
> sort of family relations, and I am for the keeping up of
> our Worship in a rational way. I don't approve of our
> people getting baptized, because I don't believe in a
> Jew's conversion to the Gentile part of Christianity.
> And now we have political equality, there's no excuse
> for a pretence of that sort. But, I'm for getting rid of
> all our superstitions and exclusiveness. There's no rea-
> son now why we shouldn't melt gradually into the pop-
> ulation we live among. That's the order of the day in
> point of progress. I would as soon my children married
> Christians as Jews. And I'm for the old maxim," A man's
> country is where he is well off."

In the Cohen family, the author portrays a Jewish household of the humbler class with almost photographic accuracy.
Ezra Cohen, a pawnbroker in Holborn, is the embodiment of
the qualities usually attributed to the Jewish tradesman.
He is described as being keen in the pursuit of gain and

hard in driving a bargain. Also he is reported to be a good father and husband, and a strict follower of the practices of his faith. He is an odd compound of calculation and sentiment. His son, Jacob, bids fair to become what his father is — a brisk and prosperous merchant, blessed with much of the trading spirit of his group, boastful of his success and proud of his business. The old mother carries beneath a rough exterior the affections that fill a big place in all Jewish hearts.

Whatever may be the faults of *Daniel Deronda* as a novel, there is little doubt that, as a study of Jewish life in England, it reveals the sympathetic attitude of the novelist towards the aspirations of a section of the Jewish community. It also reveals a whole-hearted interest in the Jewish problem in English society. As we have already pointed out the novel is reported to have played a considerable part in predisposing certain elements of European Jewry in favor of a Zionist movement.

The publication of *Daniel Deronda* in 1876 is believed to have made a stirring impression on certain Jewish leaders who had their thoughts turned toward Zion. "It (*Daniel Deronda*) came as a precursor," says an American Jewish writer, "to the political Zionism proposed by Theodor Herzl (1860–1904) in his Jewish State twenty years later." George Eliot put into the mouth of Mordecai Cohen, an important character in her novel, the ideas and aspirations of a national Jewish policy, "so powerful in its claim that all differences of opinion must be set aside in order to make the restoration of Israel to Zion a reality."

It is reported that four years after the appearance of *Daniel Deronda*, a new school of theorists composed of

Peretz, Gordon, Smolenskin, and Lilienblum, arose in Russia and that to them the national-political restoration at once became the only road to human salvation. They at once made George Eliot's novel their own; translating it into Hebrew, and supplementing it by their own views on the recolonization of Palestine. In the opinion of a writer in *The Jewish Forum* (V, 368), "the prophecies of Mordecai were set on foot" by this new school of theorists.

George Meredith (1828–1909), who, like George Eliot, treated the novel as a form of art which should offer not only a representation of human life, but also an interpretation of the forces that regulate human conduct, dealt with Jewish character in *The Tragic Comedians* (1880), a novel based on the love story of Ferdinand Lassalle, the Jewish socialist leader, who was hailed by Heine as "the Messiah of the Nineteenth Century," and Helena von Dönniges, the eighteen-year old daughter of a Bavarian aristocrat. In 1879, a volume of memoirs entitled *Meine Beziehungen zu Ferdinand Lassalle* by Princess Von Racowitza, giving the princess' own version of her fateful meeting with Lassalle and its tragic result, laid bare one of the great love stories of the world. There was more of tragedy than love in the confession, and, in its dramatic aspect, the story appealed to Meredith, whose method was to paint the portraits of actual people as characters in fiction. The details of the romance which he determined to use in his novel were as follows: In 1862, Lassalle first met Helena von Dönniges. He fell in love with her at first sight, and his affections were returned by the beautiful daughter of Bavarian aristocracy. But the father of the girl objected to the origin and religion, the political views and past reputation of the Jewish socialist. Helena, however, was willing to sacrifice everything for her lover; she fled from her home, went to Lassalle in his hotel, and, if he had then married her, all would have been well. But the wayward temperament of the young radical forced him to egotistical and quixotic decisions. He, the superman, would conquer the objections of the Dönniges family; and he, the past profligate, would wed a wife in the conventional manner, out of her parent's home. So he sent the girl back to her father, and thus lost her forever. The father, a typical German officer, broke Helena's spirit by confinement and terrorism. He actually compelled her, against her will, to send letters of renunciation to her Jewish lover, and ultimately had her betrothed to a Roumanian noble named Janko von Racowitza. In the tempest of his wrath, Lassalle promptly sent a challenge to Helena's father and to his rival Janko. It was Janko who accepted the challenge, and in the duel that was fought on the morning of Sunday, August 20, 1864, in a suburb of Geneva, Lassalle fell mortally wounded. He died within three days. Thus did "the Messiah of the Nineteenth Century" blindly and recklessly sacrifice his life on the altar of love. A few months later, Helena was married to the man whose hands were stained with the blood of her lover.

In *The Tragic Comedians*, Meredith sets down the story as he got it from Helena's confession. Ferdinand Lassalle becomes Sigismund Alvan, the Jewish leader of a socialist party, and Helena von Dönniges is renamed Clotilde von Rüdiger, a member of the small German aristocracy. When Clotilde sees Alvan for the first time, she sinks on a sofa. "*That* the man?" she asks. "Oh! Jew, and fifty times over Jew! nothing but a Jew!" Which was indeed true, for Alvan's face had the characteristics of the Hebrew profile. But, as the girl listens to the conversation between Alvan and the other men in the room, and grasps the socialist leader's ideas, she gradually revises her opinion of the race of Ahasuerus. Indeed she grows in time to respect and even love "the demagogue and Jew." When Clotilde's father learns that his daughter has gone to Alvan's hotel and has been sent back to her home, he rages and storms at the "dirty Jew, the notorious thief, scoundrel, gallowsbird." He locks his daughter up, so that she might have nothing more to do with "the despicable Jew." What follows merely enhances the tragic quality of the love between the Christian maiden and the Jewish lover. Alvan is killed in a duel, and much of the fault, Meredith would say most of it, is Clotilde's. Yet so godlike a figure is Alvan, that to be claimed for his mate makes Clotilde immortal. The final word about the Jewish hero raises him above his fellow men:

> He was neither fool nor madman, nor man to be adored; his last temptation caught him in the season before he had subdued his blood, and, amid the multitudinously simple of this world, stamped him a tragic comedian.

There is little in this novel to indicate Meredith's attitude towards the Jewish question. However, it is a significant fact that this story of the love affairs of a Jew and a German aristocrat appeared at a time when the anti-Semitic agitation in Germany was bitter and widespread, and when one of the pretexts for popular clamor against the Jews in Europe was "the large share which Jewish leaders were supposed to take in the new ultra-liberal social and political movements" of the day. In *The Tragic Comedians*, the novelist seems to stress the fact that the chief objection to Alvan's suit was his origin, and that he was a radical in public affairs.

The novelist also makes it clear that Alvan, in resenting the insults hurled at his people and himself, takes the opportunity to proclaim with pride the superiority of his race. He tells Clotilde:

> We Jews have a lusty blood. We are the strong of the earth . . . We have truly excellent appetites. And why not? Heroical too! Soldiers, poets, musicians; the Gentile's masters in mental arithmetic — keenest of weapons; surpassing him in common sense and capacity for brotherhood. Ay, and in charity; or what stores of vengeance should we not have nourished! Already we have the money-bags. Soon we shall have the chief offices. And when the popular election is as unimpeded as the coursing of the blood in a healthy body, the Jew shall be foremost and topmost, for he is pre-eminently by comparison the brain of these latter day communities. But that is only my answer to the brutish contempt of the Jew. I am no champion of a race. I am for the world, for man!

At the moment when *The Tragic Comedians* appeared, the Jews were more or less the subject of two opposite crazes, not equally innocuous but almost equally irrational. While they were denounced and persecuted on the continent, they were petted in England by a group of enthusiasts who, according to a contemporary journal, "with strange disregard to the most obvious indications of character and physiognomy, are pleased to identify the English people with the ten lost tribes of Israel." The novelists of the final years of the century, like the contemporary music-hall singers, obeying without question the mandate of their audience, sought to study their clients with diligence and insight, and, as far as it was possible, to crystallize the prevailing taste. When the persecution of the Jews was extended to Russia in the 'eighties, the interest of readers shifted to the trials and tribulations of the Jews farther east, and the sordid conditions to which Israelites were condemned in Roumania, Galicia and Lithuania served as background for fiction of dramatic and sensational adventure. The tragic story of the Polish Jews is told in the novels of Dorothea Gerard with ability, vigor, but with scant sympathy. For example, in a full-size novel entitled *Orthodox* (1888), the novelist treats of life among orthodox bigots in a little Polish settlement. The Jew who figures in this study differs greatly from the mild-mannered, honorable, tolerant gentleman portrayed in some recent fiction. These Polish bigots are very far from the Jews that George Eliot drew. On the contrary, Miss Gerard introduces the reader to an abhorrent set of rascals, chief among whom are the Marmorstein household and their friends. Berisch Marmorstein, dealer in bones and skins in Yoratyn, has two daughters. Salome, the elder, is a magnificent creature with "pure red-gold hair," classical features and a superb figure. Surchen, the younger, is a "pretty, but revolting little baggage," full of low cunning and preternatural sharpness of wits. When the young and credulous Count Ortenegg joins his regiment at Yoratyn, he easily falls in love with Salome, and the pretty but weak-minded Jewess as readily promises to abandon her orthodoxy at his entreaties. Ortenegg confesses to a friend that he knew nothing about Jews — not until he came among these Polish bigots.

Since I came here their wretchedness and misery have awakened my pity . . . When I ask, 'Why do you abuse them? Why do you cuff and beat them?' you say 'Because they are Jews.' You shut them out from every employment you can, and call them rapacious because they grasp at what is open to them. You ill-treat them at every turn, and then call them spiteful because they don't love you. You force them to live in wretched hovels and call them filthy because their houses are not like yours. And when I ask again, 'Why?' you answer 'Because they are Jews,' as though Jews and scum and dust were just different words for one identical thing.

At the end of his experiences with these Jews, the Count changes his mind. He learns that Berisch Marmorstein, for example, has two consciences, one for his fellows, and one for Christians. He learns also that the intensity of the fanatical abhorrence with which these bigots look upon the baptized knows no limits. Yet the author does not have the Count offer to marry Salome as a Jewess, let alone change his faith and brave the hostility of his own group. He plans to convert Salome and marry her, but is cheated by the "filthy Hebrew" of a father. The lying scoundrel has the girl married at once to a dirty and disreputable dealer in clothes. The disillusion of Count Ortenegg is complete, and he retires to a monastery.

In a second novel, *Recha* (1890), Dorothea Gerard returns to the theme of romance between a Jewish maiden and a gentile youth, crossed by the passionate avarice and by the yet more passionate fanaticism of a paternal rascal. Gedeile Wolf, the father, is merciless, cruel and fanatical, yet with as passionate a love for his beautiful daughter, Recha, as his prototype had for Jessica. The hero is a young officer of the Austrian army. The unhappy experiences of the lovers makes as somber and tragic a tale of Jewish fanaticism as any could be. In this, as in other novels of intermarriage achieved or intermarriage thwarted, what seems fanaticism to the Christian might have seemed loyalty and noble sacrifice had the situations been reversed. Nevertheless the novelist is praised very highly for her portrait of Recha. "This Jewess," says the *Academy*, "is almost without a sister in literature, for she is as distinct from Jessica of Venice as from Rebecca of England. She is as real, perhaps more real, than them, though a rarer type."

The tragic story of another Jewess, Anna Klosstock, the Queen of the Ghetto, is related by Joseph Hatton in a novel entitled *By Order of the Czar* (1890). It is a ghastly record of horrors, revealing the distress of Jewish communities during the pogroms against the Jews in southern Russia. Anna, the beautiful daughter of the chief Jewish merchant of the little town of Czarovna, not only witnesses the seizure of her father and lover, the latter being knouted to death, but herself suffers outrage at the hands of General Petronovitch, the Governor of the district, and is also condemned to the knout in the public square. Almost miraculously she survives the punishment under which so many of her coreligionists have died. Thereafter she vows her life to vengeance on Petronovitch and on the government of the Czar. Being given out as dead, she escapes from Russia and joins a secret society of Nihilists. Finally, in London, she succeeds in her vengeance on the malignant Petronovitch.

Another novel which deals preëminently with Russian scenes was entitled *The Limb* (1896). The author, who signs himself "X. L.," reveals in his descriptions of Jewish

manners and customs, an exceptional familiarity with the
religious persecutions among the Jews themselves in the
small towns of White Russia. The plot of the narrative is
based upon the experiences of a Christian who is brought up
as a Jew in the midst of Jews who are ignorant fanatics,
strongly attached to Hasidism. The first important character is Faivel Ravouna,

> a Jew such as you see in London, Paris, or Vienna — a
> very rich scoffer, unbeliever, cynic, skeptic; not hesi-
> tating, whenever it suits his purpose, to conform to the
> most extraordinary rites of his congregation.

He lives only for revenge and is grotesquely wicked. In the
course of time, he obtains a child, the son of Lotta Czapak,
a Roumanian gypsy musician, and brings him up as a Jew.

The second important character is the adopted boy, Michael, or Mishka, who thinks he is Faivel's nephew and a
Jew. He is delicate, refined, gentle, and receives the strictest
education in religious matters from the rabbi, who happens
to be "a half-mad mystic."

In the details of the narrative, the author seizes every opportunity to communicate all the knowledge at his command
on Jewish laws and usages. Many references are made to
commentaries on the *Halakah*, the *Agada*, the *Gemara*; to
the Prayer Book, the school of Hillel, of Shammai, and so
forth. Altogether, the author seeks to get at the heart of the
problems involved in the intolerant and persecuting Jewish
community in the remote regions of the Czar's empire.

Taking up the same theme of Jewish trials and tribula-
tions, but in another part of the intolerant world, Hall
Caine wrote the story of a Jewish family in Morocco, in
The Scapegoat (1891).

In a prefatory note, the novelist expresses his thanks to Chief Rabbi Adler, "for opening to my observation the homes and lives of the Sephardic Jews of Morocco;" to Israel Abrahams, editor of the *Jewish Quarterly Review*, and to another Jewish scholar, "for guidance in Jewish ceremonial law;" and to certain friends in Morocco, "for important help in nearly all that concerns the local atmosphere of my story." The chief Jewish character in the story is Israel Ben Oliel, the son of a Jewish banker at Tangier. His mother Sarah is the daughter of a banker in London. When the boy is eight years old, his father marries a second wife, his first wife being still alive. The new marriage, which is only another business transaction to the banker, is a shock to Sarah. Nevertheless, she supports its penalties through three weary years. When a second family begins to share her home, and the rivalry of the mothers makes domestic life troublesome, Sarah leaves the banker and returns to England, taking Israel with her. Twelve years go by, and the boy grows up to be a tall, silent, sedate young man, clear-headed on all subjects, and a master of figures. On his return to Tangier, however, he discovers that as a Jew he has no right in Mohammedan law to present a claim to his father's property. He is without standing, whether as a Jew, a Moor, or an Englishman. He is a stranger in his father's country. Being a man of indomitable spirit, he refuses to return to England. From this point on, the career of Israel Ben Oliel repeats the experience of his group. In intellectual interests, in a strong and unflinching sense of God, in love for wife and daughter, in invincibility of spirit, and in his dignity which defies humiliation, he is an example of the highest type which Judaism has produced.

His little daughter, Naomi, shares with him the hardships and misfortunes to which Jews in Morocco are subjected. She has been born deaf, dumb, and blind; but as she grows to womanhood, a skillful doctor gives her the sense of hearing and restores the power of speech. Eventually, she gains her sight. But the fearful experiences she goes through at the hands of the Moors, both as a Jewess and as a one-time hostage in the hands of the wicked Sultan of Morocco, are matched only by the sufferings of Israel Ben Oliel himself. Both father and daughter know what suffering is; their loneliness and heroism inspire the love and admiration of those who know their story. In the end, they determine to return to England, "free, mighty, noble England, the white island of the sea;" but fate intervenes, and Ben Oliel, an epitome of his people, dies in exile.

While the population of English Jewry was rapidly increasing in the 'eighties, through the arrival of refugees from Russia, among those who became specially interested in conditions under which the immigrants lived and labored, was Sir Walter Besant (1836–1901), who met many of the newcomers and studied them at firsthand. A novel from his pen, depicting Jewish life, was therefore certain to contain realistic pictures of actual conditions. In *The Rebel Queen* (1893), he manifests an unusual interest in Jewish philosophy and manners. The chief Jewish character, Madame Elveda, has one of the largest drawing rooms in Cromwell Road, and, with her daughter, Francesca, entertains in royal style. The madame's face is of the oriental type, her nose somewhat aquiline. Referring to mother and daughter, one of the guests at Madame Elveda's party says:

"Humph! I hear they call themselves Moors. But surely —." "They come from the Lord knows where," said Lady Risinge, "and the papa Elveda was the Lord knows who. They *are* Jews — look at the mother — as plain as can be written on any face —"

The fact of the matter is that Madame Elveda is a Jewess who has made a deliberate effort to renounce her people, but without success.

"I renounce the people," said she to her husband, "I belong to them no longer. Your old traditions, your jumble, and jargon of ceremonies and superstitions, I will follow no longer. I throw them off."

But Emanuel Elveda knows better. He is a man of ancient lineage as well as a man of intellect. His ancestry is far more ancient than that which any Christian family, even the Bourbons, can boast. In Spain, his people have pretended for generations to conform to the Christian faith; they cannot, however, give up their Jewishness. He shakes his head, as his wife speaks.

"You cannot renounce your people," said he with conviction. "Any other man or woman may renounce his race and enter another nation; you cannot. None of us may renounce our people. On our faces there is a mark set, — the seal of the Lord, by which we know each other and are known by the world."

This opinion of the Jewish merchant is further confirmed by the Man of the Turf.

"You cannot separate yourself from your people," said he, "You cannot . . . We are stamped with the seal of the race, so that everybody as we pass along the streets may cry out if he likes, 'Jew, Jew, Jew'."

This novel contains many graphic descriptions of Jewish life among the poorer classes, showing the novelist's sociological interest in the East End communities. Besant feels friendly and well-disposed towards the immigrants, and, in his novel, seeks to render the same service to the Jews that George Eliot did in *Daniel Deronda*.

In the 'nineties, the presentations of the Jewish character changed with the quick shifts in literary fashions. Writers of stories of passing interest were wont to follow their trade with no special independence of spirit. For them, what interested the public was the important thing. Still, while fashions shifted and changed, the mysterious element in the Jewish character was sure to meet with popular approval.

It was in 1892 that George Du Maurier (1834–1896), who had already made a name for himself as a pictorial satirist on the staff of *Punch*, thrilled English readers with his story of *Trilby*. This novel is of interest to us because, into the studio of the three young British artists — Taffy, Sandy, and Little Billie — there enters a tall, bony individual, of any age between thirty and forty-five, of Jewish aspect. This is the mysterious Svengali — another version of the immortal Wandering Jew. Through him, Du Maurier infuses the element of magic and hypnotism into the narrative. Nobody knows exactly where the "monster" lives, or where he originally came from. He is a musical genius who, throughout the story, holds the attention of his audience by his strange manners, his devilish leer and penetrating eyes. Svengali, walking up and down the earth, seeking whom he may cheat, betray, exploit, borrow money from, make brutal fun of, bully if he dares, cringe before if he must — is, says Du Maurier, "as bad as they make 'em." By his hypnotic influence Svengali holds Trilby in thrall, making her produce wonderful notes at his command. She who, as an artist's model, was "tone deaf," becomes the possessor of the finest voice in Europe. Du Maurier's uncanny, unkempt, and mysterious Svengali became just as universally known as Dickens's mysterious Fagin.

Du Maurier produced a second novel, entitled *The Martian* (1897), in which he presented the portrait of a lovely Jewess, perhaps to offset the crudeness of Svengali. In Leah, the high Sephardic type is more marked than in her mother, Mrs. Bletchley, a most magnificent and beautiful old person with large eyes as black as night. Says the novelist,

> In Leah the term Jewess brings to my mind some vague, mysterious, exotically poetic image of all I love best in woman. I find myself dreaming of Rebecca of York, as I used to dream of her in the English class at Brossard's, where I so pitied poor Ivanhoe for his misplaced constancy.

Every respect is paid by Du Maurier to the admirable Hebraic qualities and character of Leah, and there is no stint of praise for her grandmother, "the splendid old Jewess."

Towards the last of the century, several minor novels of the realistic type included Jewish characters which, to all intents and purposes, were used simply for the purpose of adding local color, as though English life in the 'eighties and 'nineties would be incomplete without some representation of the modern son of Shem. For instance, in *Mrs. Keith's Crime* (1885), by Mrs. Lucy (Lane) Clifford, the rich Mr. Cohen appears on the scene, simply to glory in the fact that he is a Jew:

> The Jews are the finest people in the world, and the oldest ... It is the best thing in the world to be a Jew, and the wisest to be proud of it.

Similarly, in *Count Royal* (1886), by S. Baring Gould, an attempt is made somehow to bring in a Jewish pawnbroker, Emanuel Lazarus, whose absurd portrait is reminiscent of the old Jew-baiting tradition. In *Sir George Tressady* (1896) by Mrs. Humphry Ward, a Jew comes forward at a meeting of workers, to tell about the sweating system among his people in the East End of London:

> Why, why, they use us up cruel in the sort of shop I work for. Ten or twelve years, and a man's all to pieces. It's the irons and the heat, and the sitting — you know what it is ... If my master gives me the sack for speaking here, I'll have nothing but the Jewish Board of Guardians to look to ...

Benjamin Disraeli appears in *The School for Saints* (1897) by John Oliver Hobbes (Mrs. Craigie), for just a moment, to add an air of reality to the narrative:

> ... walking slowly, but with rather long strides through the public drawing room. His worn and livid countenance had lost the romantic beauty to which he owed much of his early fortune, but neither illness nor anxiety had dimmed the piercing brilliancy of his expression. It was impossible to see him without observing the conspicuous details of a costume which was certainly not the least uncommon part of his picturesque and amazing personality. He wore a light overcoat, grey trousers, a white hat, and lavender gloves.

In the brief conversation that follows this description, the novelist, who is evidently a great admirer of the Jewish statesman, makes him talk like his own books, with that mixture of mysticism and mystification, of eastern poetry and West-end persiflage, of which one would think Disraeli had the exclusive secret, if a clever novelist does not thus prove her power of finding it out.

Other novels of the last decade which turned the attention of readers to the riddle of Jewish character, and were of passing interest as works of fiction, were *Ivan Graham* (1896), by Louisa Thompson, presenting a story of the medical mission to the Jews in Russia; *Tristram Lacy, or The Individualist* (1899), by William Hurrell Mallock, in which Mr. Halbeckstein, a Jew who is "equally out of place in polite society and in clean linen," receives sympathetic notice; and *The Circle* (1900), by Katherine Thurston, in which one receives glimpses of the sordid environment to which Jews in Europe are condemned.

Victorian novelists in general were biased against the trading class in England. Few novelists made the excitement of business life the theme of a novel, and, whenever possible, they attacked the spirit of commercialism that was playing an important part in the last decade of the century. To the Jewish financiers in particular were ascribed the evils associated with the materialistic life. They were represented, as in the days of William Cobbett, as fattening on profits secured at the expense of the unprotected and unwary masses. The new novels of the 'nineties dealt with the emancipated Jews in various sections of the British Empire, and in South Africa, in particular, where they were the bankers who financed the gigantic trading companies and supplied the world with "sequins, Naples soap, horses and intelligence." From the novelist's point of view, when the Jew got rich, he

seemed to get much too rich and to get rich much too quick-
ly, finally exercising far too much power through his wealth.
This seemed to be the view of Marie Corelli (1864–1924),
who, in *Temporal Power* (1897), described the Jewish plutocrat with much severity.

David Jost, the principal character in the novel, is the
sole proprietor of the most influential newspaper in the land,
and the largest share-holder in three other newspaper companies in the metropolis, all apparently differing in party
views, but all in reality working for the same power and the
same ends. In other words, Jost governs the press and what
is euphoniously termed "Public Opinion." He secures all
the advertisers, and, as a natural consequence, can well
afford to be "The Voice of the People" *ad libitum*.

Quite apart from any works of realistic fiction, stands a
strange and satirical "fantasy" on the materialism of the
Jews, entitled *The Story of a Famous Old Jewish Firm* (written in 1876, and published in 1883), by James Thomson (B.V.).
It describes the beginning of Judaism in terms of the establishment of a mercantile firm. It shows unmistakably
the influence of German anti-Semitism current at that
time.

During the period under consideration, several works
of fiction, most of them based on historical and biblical
episodes, treated with Jewish character in a romantic and
imaginative manner. Some of these works continued the
tradition of regarding the Jews of the time prior to the
Christian era as the chosen people of God, and of looking upon
the Jews of the Christian era as objects of divine wrath. The
earliest of this group, *Strength of Judah* (1862), by Charles
Stokes Carey, deals with Jewish life in the time of Isaiah.

The dress, habits and customs of the people, the settings and details of historical interest, are minutely treated by the sympathetic author. Similarly, in *The Gladiators* (1863), by G. J. W. Melville; *Exiles in Babylon, or The Children of Light* (1867) by Charlotte Tucker; *Ephraim and Elah, a Story of the Exodus* (1879), by Edwin Hodder; *Rescued from Egypt* (1883), by Charlotte Tucker; *The Spell of Ashtaroth*, a story of the time of Joshua and the conquest of Palestine (1888); *Raphael Ben Isaac*, a tale of 20 C. E. (1887), by John Bradshaw; *Son of a Star*, a romance of the second century (1888), by Benjamin Ward Richardson; and *For the Temple*, a tale of the fall of Jerusalem (1888), by G. A. Henty — there is a great amount of information relating to Jewish life and manners, and they all follow the general style of romantic treatment of the Jewish character. In *Nobly Won* (1888), by B. Pullen Burry, a more serious attempt is made to grapple with the complexities of Jewish life, and the novelist, in his endeavor to be thorough, cites for authority the books of the Old Testament, Cassell's *Bible Dictionary* and *Illustrated English History*, sundry articles in the London *Times*, and the *Banner of Israel*. The story has to do with an old Hebrew prophet who accompanies Jerusha, the daughter of King Zedekiah, in company with her attendant, Miriam, and the scribe, Baruch, from Jerusalem to Ireland; and there witnesses the Hebrew princess's marriage to Eochaid, a prince of Dan, who dwells in the halls of Tara.

Literature of this romantic genre, at once popular among church workers and middle-class readers of all ages, came to be written more and more by women writers. In reviewing *The Heart of Sheba, the Story of a Great Queen* (1890), by Ethel May Hewitt, the *Athenaeum* made an observation that may very well be applied to the majority of the romances of Jewish interest written in the 'nineties:

> We have had enough and more than enough in the last few years of the history of the old times, retold from parchments and the like. It is most difficult to make such books interesting, and Miss Hewitt in "The Heart of Sheba" has certainly not been successful . . . it is dull, deadly dull.

Jewish characters in these romances appeared and went through their parts like figures in a village pageant, and for the most part were Jewish only in name. *Acte* (1890), by Hugh Westbury, a story of the time of Nero, presents Judith, "the Jew maiden" who refuses to marry Titus; *Masters of the World* (1888), by Mrs. Mary A. M. Marks, has a little to do with the Jews in the reign of Domitian; *The Young Macedonian* (1891), by A. J. Church, and *The World's Desire, a Story of the Exodus from Egypt* (1891), by Henry Rider Haggard and Andrew Lang, — all make use of Jewish characters of no special distinction.

Of a more highly romantic and melodramatic nature than any of the works of fiction just mentioned was a full-length novel entitled *Barabbas, A Dream of the World's Tragedy* (1895), by Marie Corelli. The narrative, based on the Gospel account of the crucifixion, takes up the career of Barabbas, the thief, who was released in place of the Man of Nazareth. Through Barabbas, the reader is introduced to the Iscariot family. The robber is in love with Judith, the sister of Judas, the betrayer of his friend and master. The suicide of Judas is described as the beginning of a series of woes that descend upon those who participated in the cruel treatment of Jesus. Judith, the beautiful Jewess, is presented as being but a tool in the hands of the arch-traitor, Caiaphas.

The faithful Barabbas, perhaps the most admirable character in the story, is judged guilty of connivance with the followers of the Nazarene in a plot to steal his body from the tomb, and, on the order of Caiaphas, is led back to prison. There is nothing particularly Jewish in any of the Jewish characters, except their names and their relation to the biblical narrative. But the endeavor made by Marie Corelli to present a new interpretation of the tragedy of the crucifixion, in which all Jews are held to have a share of responsibility, may be taken as an indication of the modern tendency to discredit the wholesale condemnation of the Jews for the death of the founder of Christianity. The author assigns new motives to human action and deals very sympathetically with Barabbas, the notorious Jewish criminal.

Shortly after the publication of *Barabbas*, another woman writer, Olive Schreiner, described the return of the crucified Jesus to South Africa, to flay the greedy and turbulent agents of the Chartered Companies there. In *Trooper Peter Halket of Mashonaland* (1897), the tall figure, clad in a loose linen garment, his heavy locks of hair hanging on his shoulders, and carrying no weapon of any kind, is indeed "The Jew from Palestine." His feet and hands are "scarred with the traces of old wounds."

In summarizing the work of the non-Jewish novelists of the second half of the nineteenth century, it is possible to see that there was no better example of the closeness of the connection between the Jewish communities in England and English literature than was supplied by works of fiction. Every change in the public attitude towards the Jews, nearly every aspect of Jewish life in the centers of England and in the ghettos of Europe yielded a greater amount of literary material for the writer of fiction than in earlier years. Whether or not the information contained in these later novels and short stories did justice to the Jewish character may be open to question, but the evidence points to an increased interest on the part of the writer and the reader in contemporary Jewish life and Jewish problems. Perhaps it seemed obvious to most Englishmen that wherever there were Jews, there was a Jewish problem of one sort or another. Discussions in the English press on questions pertaining to Jewish assimilation, Jewish separatism, Jewish nationalism, the Jew in politics, in business, and the place of the Jew in modern life, pointed to the ever-widening field of incessant activity occupied by the Jews in modern life. "It is pretty certain," said Arnold White, "that, unless a great war submerges lesser questions in the welter of international conflict, the Jew will engage the close attention of Europe during the next score of years." Consequently, it was to be expected that much space should be allotted to the contemporary Jew in fiction that attempted to deal realistically with contemporary problems. As we have already noted, from 1859 to the end of the century, at least twenty popular novels, among them two by Trollope, and one each by Charles Lever, Dickens, George Eliot and George Meredith, took up questions regarding Jewish life and manners, and in several of them, George Eliot's *Daniel Deronda* in particular, the attitude of the author indicated the tendency of modern British writers to give the Jew fair treatment. In the majority of these novels, the purpose of the realistic descriptions of Jewish home life and manners is to convey to the reader a strong sense of things actual in experience and within the range of observation of the average man. In the main, therefore, as novels of purpose, they distinctly subordinate the amusement of the reader to his improvement or information. Some of these novels may in truth be said to have been written in the interest of the Jewish people, just as Kingsley wrote his *Alton Locke*, and as Mrs. Gaskell wrote her *Amos Barton*, to enlist the sympathies of English readers in the problems of the manufacturing classes. The point we should like to make is that, even though the number of these Jewish studies may seem slight in comparison with the great stream of fiction produced during the second half of the century, the fact that writers of high reputation, ability, and pronounced opinions did find the Jews of sufficient popular interest to devote whole novels to the treatment of their problems, indicates that the Jewish claims to literary consideration were by no means slight.

CHAPTER XIII

"THE OLD ORDER CHANGETH —"

The removal of civil disabilities in 1858 enabled the English Jews to participate in the national life in a fuller way than ever before. It was natural to expect, therefore, that this new freedom would give certain members of their community fresh inspiration in the expression of their hopes, ideals and experiences. At no time in their history had the Jews been accused of intellectual weakness, nor had they ever lacked imaginative power. Their mental vigor, occasionally thwarted by the daily grind of their confinement in ghettos, had not degenerated into a commercial cunning and a search for material success. There were some members of the ancient people who, in spite of degrading circumstances, or as a result of them, cultivated the traditional liking for literature and the works of the spirit; and who, as the status of the Jews improved, particularly in England, entered the field of journalism and fiction writing. Yet, according to Joseph Jacobs, one of the foremost Jewish literary commentators and editors of the century, the favorable condition of the English Jews did not result in any very widespread display of Jewish talent. Only a few important writers produced works of any distinction in the field of fiction. On these the *London Quarterly Review* (CLXXV, 35) commented:

> Perhaps it is only to-day, when some children of Israel have taken the pen and written true words of their people, that the English Jew is beginning to be rightly understood by his neighbor, the English Gentile.

Benjamin L. Farjeon (1833–1903) was perhaps the most prolific of the Jewish novelists of the nineteenth century. His first work, *Grif* (1870), was favorably received by the reviewers and attracted the notice of Charles Dickens. In all, Farjeon produced some forty-odd novels, several of which dealt with Jewish life and manners. The first of his Jewish novels was *Solomon Isaacs* (1877). Isaacs, for whom the novel is named, is an old clo' man, who, by driving shrewd bargains and by miserly saving, amasses a considerable fortune. As a devout Jew, he goes to the synagogue regularly, mumbles through the form of prayers of whose meaning he has as much knowledge as does the man in the moon, and commands the respect of his brethren. Like him is another old clo' man, Moses Levy, who started in business by going forth into the English countryside "like a tortoise with his warehouse on his back." Never once in his life has Moses neglected the performance of his sacred duties as an orthodox Jew. He rises at seven, washes, and binds his forehead and arm with leathern straps, and says his prayers with his face to the East, swaying his body gently backwards and forwards, as he fervently mumbles his words. The heroine of the story is his daughter, Rachel, a pure, lovable and lovely Jewess, who earns a little money as a waist-coat maker. On a certain cold and bitter Christmas night, Rachel finds a Christian mother and infant in distress. The child is "a child of shame." But, says the author, "Charity, thank God! is a heavenly, not a theological crown;" and Rachel ministers to the need of the Christian mother and takes the infant under her care. "God bless you!" are the dying mother's last words, while the Christmas bells ring the tidings of "Peace on Earth and Good Will among Men!" What interests the reader in this novel is the delineation of Jewish characters born in England. They sojourn, not in Canaan or in Palestine, but in Spitalfields; and, though Moses Levy is given to murmuring under his breath in Hebrew, "May Jerusalem soon be rebuilt and established," and though another character has but recently arrived from a pilgrimage to Jerusalem, the interests of these Jewish folk are pretty well established in England.

In his second novel of Jewish interest, *Aaron the Jew* (1894), Farjeon presents what might be described as a Hebrew Aristides. Aaron Cohen is a miracle of amiability and generosity. His devotion to his wife, his loyalty to his friends, and his conduct in business, afford the author ample opportunity for the portrayal of all the solid virtues of his people. But Farjeon has sought to produce his effects solely by the use of various "properties" of the writer of Jewish stories, and by recourse to long extracts from a Jewish manual of devotion. In a desire to exalt the Jewish character in Aaron, he adopts a process of white-washing, but with so little moderation and judgment that, instead of attracting sympathy or compelling good-will, he inspires dislike for this namby-pamby man of straw. "There never was such a Jew," says a reviewer in the *Saturday Review*, "and we sincerely hope that we shall never meet such a Christian." Like Mr. Riah, in Dickens's *Our Mutual Friend*,

Aaron is much too good, and a Jew in name only. In fact, the Judaism which he professes is merely external, and but for the terminology extracted from the Jewish manual of devotion, might as well be a Quaker or a Mohammedan. There is humor in the portrait of Mr. Moss, the good-natured money-lender, who goes about always chanting snatches from Gounod's *Faust*, and in the sketch of the little street arab, Prisay, who is rescued from the gutter by the Cohens. On the whole, however, it may be said in defence of this novel that, even if it is difficult to reconcile the roseate delineation of the Jews portrayed by the novelist with the Jews of actual life, the study affords a most pleasant set-off to the caricatures of the comic papers and the Adelphi melodrama.

The Cohen family appears also in Farjeon's *Fair Jewess* (1894). The childless Aaron and his wife, Rachel, have moved from London to Gosport. The symbol of Aaron's business stands over his shop door; the familiar device of the Three Golden Balls. There is some objection to Aaron settling himself in Gosport, and Mr. Edward Whimpole, the corn-chandler and church warden, a large-framed and fleshy-faced man, is not graciously disposed toward the Jew.

"I am not mistaken," said Mr. Whimpole, with a flush of resentment, "in believing you to be a Jew?"

"You are not mistaken," replied Aaron with exceeding urbanity. "I am a Jew. If I were not proud of the fact, it would be folly to attempt to disguise it, for at least one feature in my face would betray me."

"It would," said Mr. Whimpole, dealing a blow which had the effect of causing Aaron to lean back in his chair and laugh for fully thirty seconds.

"Excuse me," said Aaron, drawing a deep breath of enjoyment. "I beg you will not consider me wanting in politeness, but I have the instincts of my race, and I never waste the smallest trifle, not even a joke — even the thinnest joke! We are at once both thrifty and liberal."

Mr. Whimpole, coming to the real purpose of his mission, offers to buy Aaron's house. Aaron will not accept less than five hundred pounds for it.

"You are a— a—," stutters Mr. Whimpole.
"A Jew," says Aaron, "leave it at that. Can you call me anything worse?"

In the weeks that follow, life is made very miserable for the Jew at Gosport. His business is ruined, the children of the market-place are instructed to call out "Jew! Jew! Jew!" as Aaron passes by. The Jew soon learns that he can get no credit in the little town.

"I saw Mr. Whimpole today," he remarks to his wife, "and I made a bow which he did not return. My Jewish nose offends him. How unfortunate!"

In the course of time, a Jewish friend, Mr. Moss, drops in. He comes with an extraordinary offer from a lawyer, Gordon. Would Aaron and Rachel be willing to care for a child? The offer is as wonderful as it is startling. After much deliberation and discussion, the poor couple consent to receive the child of strangers into their home. Ruth, the adopted child, her parentage unknown to the rest of the town, becomes the daughter of the Cohens, and to the friends and acquaintances of the household, she is "the lovely and gracious Jewish maiden who shall in time become a mother in Judah."

At one point in the book there is an interesting discussion of the work done among Jews by Christian missionaries. A gentleman comes to Aaron's home for a contribution to "an old established society known all the world over," the Society for the Promotion of Christianity among the Jews. Aaron smiles, as he says:

"But, my dear sir, I am a Jew."

"I am aware of it," says the gentleman, "and the reason I make the appeal is that you have been quoted to me as a man who has no narrow prejudices, and who in no sense of the word could be called dogmatic."

Aaron is pleased, but he takes the opportunity to voice the sentiments of Farjeon on the matter.

I cannot but consider the matter seriously, for there can be no doubt of your sincerity. Still it occurs to me that if we were both equally sincere in our advocacy of objects of a similar nature, it would be as well that we should pause to ask ourselves the question, instead of endeavoring to convert Jews and Christians to a faith in which they were not born, would it not be better to employ ourselves in making those who call themselves Christians true Christians, and those who call themselves Jews better Jews?

Aaron ends the discussion by giving the gentleman a check for twenty pounds, and the gentleman in turn gives Aaron a check for ten. In the final scenes of the novel, a lawyer, Mr. Dillworthy, arrives to put a very serious matter before the Cohens. It seems that Lord Storndale's son is in love with Ruth Cohen, and that his lordship, who has an invincible dislike for Jews, is shocked to think that his son has contemplated marriage with a Jewess. This is Aaron's opportunity to speak out:

You speak of the pride of race as affecting Lord Storndale. We have also that pride, and if we were so far forgetful of the obligations of our faith as to admit your client's son into our family, it is upon him and upon Lord Storndale, not upon us, that the honor would have been conferred. Such an alliance will never, with my sanction, be entered into; and I will endeavor to guard my daughter from the peril with which she is threatened.

As for Ruth herself, the author states that, though she is brought up as a Jewess, she has an instinctive aversion to Jewish society. "It is in her blood," Aaron says to himself. The man Ruth loves is a Christian of good family, and, in the end, in order to bring about a satisfactory termination to what might otherwise result in tragedy, the novelist contrives to have Aaron reveal the secret of Ruth's Christian origin, and bring about the union of the happy lovers. In this conclusion, the plot resembles that of Maria Edgeworth's *Harrington*, but one wonders why, in this work by a Jewish writer, it should be necessary to dodge the issue.

In two other novels, *Miriam Rozella* (1897), and *Pride of Race* (1900), Farjeon includes several Jewish characters, all of whom seem consumed with a desire to advertise the virtues of their people. The importance of these works lies in the novelist's opportunity to convey to English readers first-hand information concerning Jewish home-life.

Pride of Race, the story of an illiterate who becomes a millionaire and marries his son to a girl of the English nobility, though filled with melodramatic incident, serves as an exposition of certain conditions in English society, wherein the social status of the Jew and the attitude of the gentiles to wealthy Jews, make such a union both possible and desirable to Jews and Gentiles alike. According to Farjeon's story, there is an exchange of social good-will and a steady development of understanding between the educated members of both communities.

Referring to Jewish manners and customs described in these novels, Calisch reminds us that "even though the barriers of physical ghettos have been demolished, there is a certain social aloofness, partly objective, and partly subjective, in which the Jews live. The inherited traditions and customs of centuries are not uprooted in a generation." An intimate understanding of the circumstances that surround the Jewish home and its members is something that the outsider cannot realize in all its fullness. Such an understanding, if possible at all, can be shared only by those who participate in the fellowship and obligations of the Jewish family. Therefore, the disclosures made by Jewish authors have a peculiar value and are of special interest for the general reader. Among the authors who, as members of the Jewish group, revealed the conditions and the domestic scenes within their exclusive social circle, were three gifted women, Amy Levy, Julia Frankau ("Frank Danby"), and Mrs. Alfred Sidgwick (Mrs. Andrew Dean).

In the one important novel which she wrote, Amy Levy attempted to describe English Jewish life as viewed by one who was a member of a Jewish household. *Reuben Sachs* (1889) is a study of the everyday life of a cross-section of Victorian Jewry, by a poetic spirit, sensitive to all the injustice and the coarseness of a materialistic society. Amy Levy is apparently conscious of a lack of soul and of ennobling ideals in the character of the Jew of her day. She deplores her kinsmen's sordid devotion to material interests. The principal character of the novel, Reuben Sachs, is the pride of his family. After a successful career at one of the great London day schools, he goes to the University, where he is equally successful. The fact that he is a Jew proves no bar to his popularity. He gains many desirable friends, and to some extent shakes off the provincialism inevitable to one bred in a small community. In due course, he is called to the bar, and with his usual good fortune prospers as a legal luminary. "He will never starve," says his mother, shrugging her shoulders with a comfortable consciousness of safe investments. "He must marry money — but Reuben can be trusted to do nothing rash." Mrs. Sachs, an elderly woman, short and stout, with a wide, sallow, impassive face, lighted up by occasional gleams of shrewdness from a pair of half-shut eyes, is proud of her brilliant son. Her daughter, Adelaide (Mrs. Cohen), a thin, dark woman of twenty-eight or twenty-nine, with restless, eager face and an abrupt manner, is, like the mother, always fashionably dressed, and never seen without a great array of jewels. Adelaide's husband (Mr. Cohen), lives with her in average contentment.

The reader soon observes that the Jewish community to which the Sachses belong, has "its innumerable trivial class differences, its sets within sets, its fine-drawn distinctions of caste, utterly incomprehensible to an outsider." In this community however, the Leuniger family hold a good, though not the best, position, and their drawing-room — spacious and hung with primrose-colored satin, and lighted with incandescent gas from innumerable chandeliers and sconces — is the frequent scene of parties. Here the cream of Jewish middle-class society assembles. Israel Leuniger, who began life as a clerk on the Stock

Exchange and after successful speculation on his own account became a partner of the great brokerage firm of Sachs and Company, is the head of this household. His wife, Ada, is beloved by all. The daughter, Rose, is a fat woman with red hair and light eyes, a *fleur de tête* of her charming little brother, Leopold Leuniger, a short, slight boy of one and twenty. A third member of the firm of Sachs and Company, Kohnthal, is never present. He has been shut up in a madhouse for ten years. But his only daughter, Esther, a gnome-like creature with small glittering eyes that outshine the diamonds in her ears, is the biggest heiress and the ugliest woman in all Bayswater. She tells everyone quite frankly that her father is in a madhouse — and why not?

The older generation of this circle represents the orthodoxy that is gradually passing. Samuel Sachs cannot understand the spirit of indifference and levity which prevails among the younger generation. When old Solomon Sachs, the patriarch of the family, with flowing beard and skull-cap, starts to perform his "incantations" in Hebrew, the young folk assume airs of aggressive boredom, lifting their eyes, or even permitting themselves to yawn, at family worship. The younger generation attend the synagogue under protest. One of them, Leo, is known to have revolted against a people who, as far as he can see, live without ideals and are given up body and soul to the pursuit of material gains.

The Sachs and the Leunigers have their gentile acquaintances, chiefly people of the sham "smart," pseudo-fashionable variety, whose parties at Bayswater or South Kensington they attend. But, as a rule, the business of the Jewish households, their chief interests, lie almost entirely within the tribal limits. As Hebrews of the Hebrews, the older folk prefer to assemble in patriarchal fashion at the Sachs home; and, so it appears, the younger members assemble out of a sense of duty, and grumble all the way home after the party. The sad-eyed elderly women, unsatisfied and heart-hungry amid the wealth and gorgeousness which are esteemed as the chief ends of existence, and the richly-gowned women, pledged to the pursuit of fashion and fortune, are indeed a pathetic group. They are representative of the kind of society in which Amy Levy finds herself.

It is at one of these tribal gatherings that Reuben Sachs, on a certain occasion, breaks the news that his friend, Lee Harrison (Lord Norwood's cousin) has "gone over body and soul to the Jewish community." He has come round to thinking Judaism the one religion, and has been duly received into the synagogue. The novelist gives us an excellent report of the conversation that follows:

> "He has a seat in Berkeley Street," said Reuben, "and a brand new talith; but still he is not happy. He complains that the Jews he meets in society are unsatisfactory; they have no local color. I said I thought I could promise him a little local color. I hope I have the pleasure of introducing him to you all."
> "What do his people say to it all?"

Later in the evening, when Lee Harrison arrives, he is presented by Reuben Sachs to the family.

> "I wonder," cried Rose, "what Mr. Lee Harrison thought of it all?"
> "I think," said Leo, "that he was shocked at finding us so little like the people in *Daniel Deronda* . . . I have

always been touched at the immense good faith with which George Eliot carried out that elaborate misconception of hers."

"Now, Leo is going to begin," cried Rose, "he never has a good word for his people. He is always running them down."

"Oh, I have nothing to say against us at all," answered Leo ironically, "except that we are materialists to our fingers' ends. That we have outlived, from the nature of things, such ideals as we ever had."

"Idealists don't grow on every bush," answered Reuben, "and I think we have our fair share of them. This is a materialistic age, a materialistic country."

"And ours the religion of materialism. The Corn and the Wine and the Oil; the Multiplication of the Seed; the Conquest of the hostile tribes — these have always had more attraction for us than the harp and the crown of a spiritualized existence."

"It is no good to pretend," answered Reuben, in his reasonable, pacific way, "that our religion remains a vital force among the cultivated and thoughtful Jews of to-day. Of course, it has been modified, as we ourselves have been modified by the influence of western thought and western morality . . ."

"That does not alter my position," said Leo, "as to the character of the national religion, and the significance of the fact. Ah, look at us," he cried with sudden passion.

Amy Levy would have the reader understand that these characters in her novel are no mere wire-worked puppets, who, while made to act and express themselves in such a melancholy fashion, work out the tragedy of their little circle. They are representative of a section of her own people, the materialistic and socially unsatisfied group with whom she came in touch. Some of them are ignorant and unthinking, some are afflicted with genius and an impatient disgust with their associates, and there are some (like Reuben) who, with practical philosophy, hold the Jewish religion in affection for the sake of the Jewish people.

The novelist points to Reuben as the Jewish man of the hour — a hero who, after enjoying all the opportunities of culture afforded by English institutions, as embodied in Oxford, the Inns of Court, and the House of Commons, nevertheless remains the slave of inherited instincts, and deliberately breaks away from the grand passion of his life from mercenary and ambitious motives. By way of contrast, the novelist presents Joshua Quixano, who is regarded as a nobody among Israelites by his fellows, because he is incapable of appreciating the might of Mammon. All the rest of the characters, the women more than the men, are Mammon worshipers.

On the whole, it is evident that the women characters in the novel are more skillfully delineated than the men. The portraits of Mrs. Sachs, Adelaide Sachs Cohen, and Rose Leuniger, in particular, are a distinct contribution to the gallery of Jewesses in fiction. In *Reuben Sachs*, for the first time, we have an intimate description by a Jewish writer of certain types with whom gentile writers do not often have the privilege of meeting in a social way. The lazy untidy Jewess, for instance, who is sated with wealth all her life, and who goes on idolizing it, in spite of its joylessness; the fat, pretty daughter, who admits with a sigh that she is certain not to like the man she marries, but who is quite too rich to marry the man she likes; the rich, malicious, gnome-like daughter of a father, who proclaims aloud that there is always either an idiot or a ne'er-do-well in every Jewish family; the greedy, dyspeptic devotee of fashion, who knows herself to be distinctly second-rate and yet cannot control her desire to force her way to the circles where she is well aware she will be snubbed — these, and several other such Jewish women of the middle-class English community, are dashed off with the vigor which, in spite of the slightness of the sketching, greatly impress the reader.

Amy Levy's brooding and melancholy interest in the problems of her people, especially in the disappointments and yearnings of her intellectual friends, is revealed in fragmentary sketches contributed to various publications in the last years of her brief and tragic career. For example, in a sketch entitled "Cohen of Trinity," published in the *Gentleman's Magazine* (CCLXVI, 417) shortly before her death, she tells the story of a gifted young man whose experiences in University circles are supposed to represent the hopelessness and despair of a sensitive and lonesome Jewish genius in the 'eighties. According to the author, Cohen is at Trinity on a scholarship, and is desperately unapproachable. He is misunderstood by everybody, even by Leuniger, a fellow Jew.

> A desire to stand well in another's eyes, to make a brave show before one another, is, I have observed, a marked characteristic of the Jewish people. As for little Leuniger, he went his way, and contented himself with saying that Cohen's family were not people that one "knew."

On the subject of his family, Cohen himself, at times savagely reserved, at times appallingly frank, volunteered little information, though on one occasion he had touched in with a few vivid strokes the background of his life.

I seemed to see it all before me; the little new house in Maida Vale; a crowd of children, clamorous, unkempt; a sallow shrew in a torn dressing-gown, who alternately scolded, bewailed herself, and sank into moody silence; a fitful paternal figure coming and going, depressed, exhilarated according to the fluctuations of his mysterious financial affairs; ... but naturally enough, it was as an individual, not as the member of the family, that Cohen cared to discuss himself ... Of his failure at his work he spoke often enough, scoffing academic standards, yet writhing at his own inability to come up to them ... What I had foreseen as inevitable at length came to pass. Cohen disappeared at a short notice from the University, no choice being given him in the matter.

Some time later, Cohen attracts public notice as the author of a much-discussed book, *Gubernator*, and, as a result of the fame of the work, a feeling grows among Cambridge men that he has been unjustly treated by the University. Shortly after a club dinner at which he is present, the news of his suicide comes as a shock and a surprise to his friends. The author concludes:

I have confessed that I was astonished, that I was wholly unprepared by my knowledge of Cohen for the catastrophe. Yet now and then an inkling of his motive, a dim, fleeting sense of what may have prompted him to the deed, has stolen in upon me ...

Using the same methods and almost the same point of view, Julia Frankau (1860–1916), in a novel entitled *Dr. Phillips, A Maida Vale Idyl* (1887), sketched the life of the orthodox and well-to-do middle-class Jews with vigor and daring. It is, according to one English critic, "the most uncompromisingly honest presentation of Jewish life in English fiction," although the *Athenaeum* believed that the "animus which pervades every allusion to the West End Jewish community in this novel is rather suggestive of a personal grievance than a conscientious effort after impartiality." The book aroused a storm of indignation that brought from the author a preface to the second edition, in which she denied that she had attacked the people whom she described, and of whom she was one. As a matter of fact, unsparing as is the exposure of the narrow, sordid life of this successful middle-class Jew, yet it leaves the reader not only with pity but with real admiration for Dr. Phillips, whose Hebraism is the essence of his success and his failure.

Mrs. Frankau produced several other novels, which, despite the brutality of the Jewish characters and the vulgarity of the settings, were significant as revelations of a section of Jewish life in the metropolis, and manifested the author's interest in the variety of new types in the English Jewry. In *A Babe in Bohemia* (1889), the singer Antonelli is described as an "Italian from Whitechapel;" in *Pigs in Clover* (1904), which Israel Zangwill praised very highly for its realism and its daring delineation of Jewish life, there are several full-length portraits of British Jews. The main problem with which the book deals is that of the eligibility of the modern Jew to be received on a footing of social equality with gentiles. The title, with brutal directness, suggests the pushing droves of unsavory and unwelcome intruders among the "emancipated" Jews, who seek to feast upon the forbidden social clover. The novel contains two types of Jews: the full-blooded Hebrew who, like Karl Althaus, is the self-made multi-millionaire, proud of his success, conscious of his shortcomings, and good-naturedly amused by the pointed snubs he receives in English society; and the mongrel type, "the veneered cad in a gilded frame" who, like Louis Althaus, is a sinister creature, a man so contemptibly mean, selfish and cruel, that he seems to have no moral standard at all. The author gives a glimpse of the origin of the two brothers — the squalid chamber in the wretched *kosher* provision shop near Houndsditch where they grow up. The mother of Karl is a fat repulsive old woman with a greasy black fringe above her forehead, lying paralyzed and helpless in her bed, dead already except for the haunting pathos of her questioning eyes. The father is a Jew of Polish origin, who, not satisfied with having drained his wife of her last penny and her last ounce of strength, heaps upon her the crowning insult, the final degradation, of bringing in a girl from the London streets to share his bed. In an unforgettable scene in this early tragedy, the author reveals a dying Jewess, a dying English girl, a new-born child, and Karl Althaus, a lad of twelve, solemnly promising to be a brother and a protector to the bastard son of his father. From this scene, we grasp the secret of the life-long difference between the half-brothers. The story emphasizes this difference, and shows the powerlessness of Judaism to help either. According to Karl Althaus, Judaism is not a religion at all, it is a thing of forms and food, a race habit.

The third in this group of women novelists, Mrs. Alfred Sidgwick (Cecily Ullman), dealt with characters and scenes from Jewish life among the more prosperous class, handling Jewish problems with a certain quality of "mental uprightness" that gave potency to her portrayal of conditions in English Jewry. Among her earliest stories of Jewish life, Mrs. Sidgwick, writing under the name of "Mrs. Andrew Dean," produced a lively sketch, *The Powder Bloom Baron*, in which it is possible to notice a trace of the satirical manner of Thackeray. The narrative describes the experiences of Esther Schon, whose father wants her to marry Reuben Adler, a good-looking man of brains and humor. The Jewish blood in Esther's veins, we are informed, lends a touch of the exotic and supplies a reason for her cleverness, her delicate beauty and her wealth. In London, where "no one cares whether you are a Christian or a Jew," Esther is aware that "lots of Christians want to marry a rich Jewess." However, she is not ready to marry. "I have not had enough fun yet," she says; "I want to go to Eberheim." So she goes to Eberheim and tastes life in a German Jewish community. In German towns, the better Jewish families form an artistic center. They gather in their rooms to entertain the intellectual aristocracy, whose recruits come from every quarter and whose qualifications are not those of creed or station. Unfortunately for Esther, her uncle and aunt, not being in a set of that kind, occupy a respectable position in a dull corner of the Jewish society in Eberheim. They are absorbed all the year round in their business responsibilities and obligations; the husband in making an income, the wife in squeezing the utmost value out of it.

"Well," said Esther, after a month of strict discipline at Eberheim, "I've grown up in London, and I'm not orthodox; but if I stay in Eberheim a month, I shall want to marry the Chief Rabbi."

She soon discovers that anti-Semitic feelings are common in German society.

"I object to people who label themselves anti-Semites," said Esther. "If I lived in Eberheim I should not admit anyone with such opinions to my house."

"Then you would have no intercourse with Christians," said Major Brown.

"They would have themselves to blame," said Esther.

"Do you mean to say that in England there is no prejudice against Jews?" asked Herr Freese in a solemn voice . . .

"They are such boors," said Esther afterwards. "What a question to ask at your table!"

Baron Amsing admires Esther, but his prejudice against the Jews makes it difficult for him to decide what to do. She is a Jewess, and he, Reinhold von Amsing, is a Major in a Regiment of Hussars, and good-looking to boot. However, the Baron at length goes to London, and, presenting himself before Esther's father, asks for the young lady's hand.

"Baron," said Mr. Schon, "as far as the matter lies with me, I have the honor to refuse it."

"On what grounds?"

"Nothing would induce me to let Esther go to Eberheim," said Mr. Schon. "If she is silly enough to want to marry you, she must persuade you to live in London and adopt her faith."

The Baron sprang to his feet. "Do you want to insult me . . ." he cried.

"Not at all," said Mr. Schon. "Here is Esther, and she shall speak for herself."

Baron Amsing turned round hastily, and saw that Esther had come into the room with Reuben Adler. They both looked radiantly happy, and so did Mr. Schon the moment he beheld them.

So Esther's problem is solved by her marriage to the English Jew.

In a novel entitled *Isaac Eiler's Money* (1889), Mrs. Sidgwick presents another intimate sketch of community life, of Frankfort Jews in London. This squalid crowd of money-grabbers, and their less repulsive women folk, contemptuous and ignorant of anything better than the material interests of life, are put on exhibition before the English reading public, and criticized from the point of view of a cultured English woman. "It cannot be said," writes George Saintsbury with reference to Mrs. Sidgwick's delineation of Jewish characters, "that these sketches have usually presented a very pleasant picture of the Chosen People." The worship of the Golden Calf, and the observance of no very exquisite standard of taste and manners, are the chief crimes charged against the Eiler and Goldberg families, the "latter of which does not behave more cruelly or insolently than Christians might."

Another novel dealing with the London Jews of the better class is entitled *Lesser's Daughter* (1894), in which Mrs. Sidgwick reveals an aspect of the Jewish character in mixed marriages, and presents a delicate and sympathetic sketch of Lesser Bremen, a wealthy but insignificant person, a stranger in his own home, who is unable to win the affection of his own child until the moment of his death. The heroine, Aline Bremen, is described in a manner that indicates a departure from the usual romantic delineations of Jewesses in literature.

> She had inherited her father's insignificant stature... She had thick, fair hair, lively eyes of no particular shade, and an unremarkable nose and mouth. But the general effect of her features distinctly showed her Jewish descent, and this, in her mother's opinion, destroyed their charm.

Mrs. Bremen has never learned to feel at home in England. The climate depresses her, the people excite her derision. The friends who amuse her drop in on Sunday afternoons, and most of them confess to a dislike of the Jews. The subject of race comes up for discussion with a frequency unusual in England, and stories are told and opinions expressed that grate cruelly on the feelings of the master of the house. But Lesser Bremen does not protest much. If he were a log of wood, his wife's acquaintances could not pass him over more completely. Mrs. Bremen has little use for her husband's friends, the Granger-Yorks.

> "Their names, their manners, their style! Most of their friends are Jews too."
> "You always talk of Jews as a white man talks of niggers," said Lesser, indignantly. "As you have married one, I call that bad style."

> ... His wife's tone, when she alluded to the race from which he sprang, always offended him sorely. The fact that her marriage was not recognized by her own Church had deepened her prejudice and quickened her dislike. She held aloof from her husband's people with a violence that in England was unusual... Corona had married Lesser's money; but she turned from him with aversion. She had never cast off the prejudice her race harbors against his. Even London,

so tolerant, hospitable and quick of appreciation, could not teach her better. Her real objection to her husband was that he had Jewish blood in his veins.

In another novel, *Grasshoppers* (1895), in which the villain is half-Jewish, there is further study of the manners of mixed nationalities, and in *Scenes of Jewish Life* (1904), a group of every-day stories of Jewish life and manners, originally printed in the *Cornhill*, the *Pall Mall Magazine*, *Temple Bar*, and *The Sphere*, we find an additional group of realistic scenes and first-hand studies, all of which point to a new treatment of the Jewish character in English literature.

In the winter of 1882, a reviewer in *Blackwood's Magazine* commented on the fact that "the recent persecutions of the Jews in Russia, the grievances of the same race in Roumania, and the *Judenhetze* of Germany, have called special attention to the position occupied by this people .., and the ready sale the works of Sacher Masoch, of Bernstein, of Kompert, and of Franzos have met with, shows that an interest has been excited among Christians as well as the Jews of the West, in the political, moral, and material condition of their Eastern coreligionists, which, had the facts of the case been known sooner, would doubtless have been long since evoked." In the same year (1882), a collection of studies of Jewish life entitled *Scenes from the Ghetto*, by Leopold Kompert, was translated from the German, and published in London. These studies, drawn from the life and experiences of a Jewish writer who, having been born in the ghetto district of Münchengrätz, Bohemia, knew from close observation the various institutions peculiar to the ghetto manner of living, present in strong colors the strange conditions produced by centuries of seclusion and exclusion. The reader is introduced to Jewish characters and scenes different from any that have existed elsewhere. These ghetto dwellers, shut off as they are from communication with the rest of the community, develop from one generation to another certain distinctive traits and qualities. Maltreated and oppressed, they cling to one another and suffer their tribulations uncomplainingly. Hard as their life certainly is, unbearable as it sometimes becomes, they continue to fall in love, to dream of relief and redress, and to make the best of their opportunities and aspirations.

Also in 1882, *Jews of Barnow* by Karl Emil Franzos, admirably translated by Miss M. W. Macdowell of Garthland, was published in London, and afforded a vivid and pathetic picture of life among the Jewish population in a small Podolian town. Animated by a sincere love of his people, Franzos reveals in this collection of ghetto studies the benighted condition of his coreligionists in distant corners of Eastern Europe; and he portrays with touching pathos the terrible injustice and the self-inflicted miseries to which a combination of ignorance, credulity, and intense devotional sentiment has given rise.

To what extent these translated stories of European ghetto life influenced English writers, it is not possible to say; but it is probable that the romantic style and fresh outlook of a writer like Kompert, and the pathetic characters delineated by Franzos and others, may have suggested to the younger Jewish writers in England the feasibility of making similar literary studies of the London ghetto. The social background of the Jewish district of the East Side became the special subject of investigation of several Jewish authors, but none made such capital use of their observations and wrote with as much distinction as did Israel Zangwill (1864–1926), a scholar and thinker, who had transcended by sheer capacity the limits of the "London ghetto," and had found time in his scanty leisure to graduate at the London University with honors, and turn the lighter side of his pen to account.

The London ghetto which Zangwill presents in his numerous short stories and novels, unlike the ghetto of Kompert and Franzos, is not enclosed by walls. It has grown up as the result of a natural tendency of the Jewish people to live with their own kind. The recent arrivals from Russia and Poland, especially, feel the necessity of segregating themselves, for in large homogeneous groups they can practice more easily their distinctive way of living in accordance with Jewish laws and traditions. The ghetto dweller regards himself as belonging to the "we" group; everybody else belongs to the "they" group. The chief conflict, therefore, in the lives of these simple ghetto folk, and especially in the lives of their children, has to do with the process of a painful transition from the old order to a new. The older generation have brought with them certain fixed conceptions of life and conduct, firmly established in the traditions of their fathers. The younger generation, brought up in orthodox homes, and attending English schools, feel, on the one hand, the deep influence of the Jewish faith, and, on the other hand, the forces of a new democratic spirit in a progressive world. On the whole, the task of compromising between the old and the new, to bring harmony between the orthodoxy of their fathers and the liberal tendencies of their associates, often leads to difficult situations. And the theme of the conflict between the two forces, receives the chief emphasis in the studies of ghetto life by Zangwill. He shows the sorrows of the disrupted home, of children leaving their parents, of parents disowning their wayward offspring. He pictures Jewish life at a crucial period of transition and difficulty. He discovers a Judaism transplanted by the fathers from the secluded ghettos of Europe to the free atmosphere of modern London, and describes the inevitable struggle between the talmudic world and the forces of Western culture.

In the *Children of the Ghetto* (1892), Zangwill presents what has been called "an epic of London Jewry." The stories, which concern the Jews who crowd the East End of London, reveal the manners, customs, and intimate relationships of a section of humanity little known to the world in general. In this remarkable series of studies, there are, on a rough estimate, about fifty different Jewish characters, whose evolution is traced from Petticoat Lane to the West End. Zangwill knows these characters, not as George Eliot knew them, through a process of philosophic induction, but at first hand, because he is a Jew by birth and breeding, and has lived among them. In his character-drawing, therefore, there is a sympathy and intimate knowledge beyond the power of an outsider. In the *Proem*, he says:

> This London ghetto of ours is a region where, amid uncleanness and squalor, the rose of romance blows yet a little longer in the raw air of English reality; a world which hides beneath its stony and unlovely surface, an inner world of dreams, fantastic and poetic as the mirage of the Orient where they were woven, of superstitions grotesque as the cathedral gargoyles of the Dark Ages in which they had birth. And over all lie tenderly some streaks of celestial light shining from the face of the great Lawgiver.

The *Children of the Ghetto* opens with "The Bread of Affliction," a gloomy picture of the ghetto in the dull winter twilight. A strange group is gathered in one of the meanest thoroughfares, before a building where soup and bread are to be dispensed to the poor. The group is made up mostly of women, but a number of men "stunted, swarthy, hairy creatures, with muddy complexions, illumined by black, twinkling eyes" hover in the neighborhood.

The occupations of the inhabitants of the ghetto are varied. Many are keepers of small shops, others have merely stalls or barrows from which to dispense their wares. A familiar character of the streets is the old-clothes man, timid, grimy, often with a worn-out book of the sacred law tucked away in his pocket, for although he is forced to menial service, he sometimes occupies a position of honor and dignity befitting his scholarship.

Zangwill endeavors to show how the ghetto dwellers, struggling in a difficult environment, find consolation and comfort from the harsh realities of the day in the ceremonies and sanctifications of the religious life. The law of Moses regulates the lives of the people from the moment of birth to the inevitable hour of death. The Jewish calendar is full of fasts and feasts.

Friday night ushers in the Sabbath. We see the Rabbi on his way from the synagogue to his house, anticipating the welcome that awaits him there. Thus Zangwill describes his arrival:

> The rabbi kissed the *mezuzah* on the outside of the door and his daughter on the inside. Everything was as he pictured it — the two tall wax candles in quaint heavy candlesticks, the spotless tablecloth, the dish

of fried fish decorated with parsley, the Sabbath loaves covered with a velvet cloth, the flask of wine, and the silver goblet.

"Good *Shabbos*, Simcha," said Reb Shemuel to his wife.

"Good *Shabbos*, Shemuel," said Simcha. The light of love was in her eyes, and in her hair, her newest comb.

The father then blesses the various members of his family with the traditional blessing. The *zemirot* are sung, the meal is over, and grace is chanted.

A like observance of the Sabbath evening takes place in the house of the lowly. When the feast of the Passover comes round, there is a general celebration of the holiday, even in the home of the Ansells who are the poorest family in the ghetto. Esther Ansell, the "little mother" of thirteen, has assumed the full duties of the household since the death of Mrs. Ansell, and we see her making preparations for the ceremonials on *Seder* night. Her father, Moses Ansell, is sitting at the head of the table with an air of majesty. The table is attractive with new dishes and novel food. These are the settings for the stories of "Elijah's Goblet" and "The Seder Night." It would be a mistake, however, to think that all Jews in the ghetto respond to these occasions in the same religious spirit. To many these customs are dear because they are customs. To others, especially among the younger generation, the whole system of Judaism is a heavy burden. Just what the novelist's own views on ritualistic Judaism are it is difficult to say, so thoroughly objective is his treatment of the scenes.

However unattractive and bare of comforts the houses described by Zangwill may be, love and devotion invariably make up for the lack of material things. The story of the

Ansells, who live in a single attic room, demonstrates that there can be "much love in a little room." Often, when the father comes home in the evening from his quest for work, the old book of legends and wonderful stories is read aloud, and the final thought of the day is always of "God who forsaketh not his people Israel, and who even for us will likewise work miracles and wonders, and send us the righteous Redeemer speedily in our days."

In the chapter on "The Silent Family," there is a picture of another kind of home life. The grown son and daughter, through different interests and the new influences of English manners, become estranged from their old parents. Miriam Hyams, the pretty but rather snobbish daughter, is a teacher, and feels that her family must live up to her position. Daniel, a silent, uncommunicative boy, loves "Bonnie Bessie," a daughter of Sugarman, the *Shadhan*, but he realizes that his support of the home makes it impossible for him to marry. He keeps his love a secret. Silently, each member of the family goes about his duties. Then, suddenly, the parents realize what has happened. Mutual distress draws the father and mother together. They become aware for the first time that they are standing in the way of their children. So the old couple decide to go away to America, where old Mendel will begin anew to earn a living for his wife. In order to obtain their children's consent, they tell a story of a new relative who has offered them a home in America.

Among a host of interesting Jewish characters, Zangwill introduces several unusually striking individuals: Birnbaum, the young second-husband to his old mother-in-law; Malka, the self-willed, self-contradictory, vain, tyrannical, but kindly mother-in-law; Pinchas, the ghetto poet, a living blend of self adoration, intellectual restlessness, low cunning and ecstasy; Sam Levine, the jocose commercial traveler, engaged to be married to Malka's daughter; David Brandon, the up-to-date Jew from the Cape; Hannah, the daughter of Reb Shemuel, who falls in love with David, and, though attached to her faith, complains of its rigidity, and is tempted to elope with her lover to America; Simon, who, with Pinchas, is a leader in the Socialist Club, and makes a demonstration for better conditions; Mrs. Belcovitch, the imaginary invalid who "can hardly crawl around" with her ill-matched feet; and Shossi Shendrik, the shy lover of the sick woman's daughter. Altogether, the *Children of the Ghetto* is a masterly presentation of an interesting section of English Jewish life. "To the Jews themselves," says S. L. Bensusan in *The London Quarterly Review* (1926), "perhaps one of the most interesting aspects of the story is its study of changing conditions."

In 1893, Zangwill published *Ghetto Tragedies* and *Ghetto Comedies*, chips from the workshop in which the larger work was fashioned. Essentially poetic in treatment, the artistic presentation of these stories of ghetto life was more satisfactory than that in the *Children of the Ghetto*. In a story entitled "They who Walk in Darkness," are two interesting characters, the good wife, Zillah, who after many years of yearning and praying, has a boy-child born to her; and her husband, Jessel, who is overcome with gratitude. In the *King of Schnorrers* (1894), Zangwill portrays one of the most humorous and grotesque figures in ghetto life. One has to go back to a humorous conception like Wilkins Micawber to find the equal of that luxuriously named Jewish mendicant, Menasseh Bueno Barzillo Azevedo da Costa, the King of the Schnorrers, who, though a beggar, is not to be confounded with the ordinary tramp. This kingly beggar is a dignified and learned man. He considers himself the special agent of God, inspiring men to charity, for how are his well-to-do neighbors to acquire deeds of virtue if beggars do not afford an opportunity for generous conduct? Menasseh graciously extends this opportunity to his many friends, and lives the life of dignified leisure, happy in the thought that he is the humble instrument of so many good deeds; the ladder, as it were, on which men climb to heaven. The characterization is of course deliberately exaggerated, but the study of the oldest and most exclusive section of the Jewish community, the Sephardim, whose synagogue is in Bevis Marks, is based on much that is historically interesting.

Zangwill's stories reveal to the English public the tragedy and the comedy of Jewish experiences in a changing world. Knowing the Jews to be human, not only because they have "hands, organs, dimensions, senses, affections and passions," but because they are capable of the same virtues and vices, the same splendors and the same trivialities, that help and hinder other human beings, the novelist succeeds in giving his readers a more convincing idea of London ghetto life than any other writer in England. Zangwill shows, too, that though Jews may be different from other people, this difference goes hand in hand with a unique genius for adaptation.

Far different in tone and treatment is Zangwill's next publication, *Dreamers of the Ghetto* (1898), a series of short stories based on historical fact, describing the spiritual experiences of Israel's great dreamers. "My object," says the author, "is mainly to exhibit what contributions to human thought and aspiration Jewish thinkers in every age have made. The minds of the Jews have always been playing about the problems of the Universe." The book includes sketches of "Joseph the Dreamer," "Uriel Acosta," "Maimon the Fool," "Nathan the Wise," "The Palestine Pilgrim," and the "Conciliator of Christendom."

In the interval between the writing of *Children of the Ghetto* and *Dreamers of the Ghetto*, Zangwill turned his attention to Zionism, and his views of the destiny of Judaism became profoundly pessimistic. He convinced himself that "the time had come for a new religious expression, a new language for the old everlasting emotions, in terms of the modern cosmos," and that "the safe alternative is the return to nationalism." Consequently, he transferred the Jewish problem from the field of spirited and palpitating activities to the romantic canvas of Jewish history. In the lives of typical revolters, men like Uriel Acosta, Spinoza, Heine, Lassalle, and even Disraeli, who sought in one direction or another to burst the bonds of the synagogue, or expressed its spirit "in terms of the modern cosmos," Zangwill endeavored to bring out or explain their motives by a process of dramatic idealization. As romance, the work is brilliantly successful, but as history, even on the author's own principle that "fiction is the highest form of truth," its value is doubtful. None the less, from the point of view of art, Zangwill's great achievement is the seemingly sincere portrayal of the eternal tragedy of Israel in the light of modern experience and modern culture, and, as Holbrook Jackson observes, "he has done this with fitting seriousness and a most gracious and refreshing sense of humor." The same critic also says, "By writing in English, Israel Zangwill has not only revealed the tragedy and the comedy of Jewry to the English speaking members of his race, he has also revealed them to a nation which still takes its knowledge of the Jew from the *naiveté* of Shakespeare's Shylock and the buffoonery of the comic papers . . . . Zangwill is adapted by birth, experience, gifts and temperament to communicate between ineradicable Israel and absorbing England."

The approval that Zangwill's work received at the hands of the English critics was, from the start, most encouraging to the author, and, in a great measure, indicative of the popular interest in the subjects he chose to present. *Children of the Ghetto* woke all reading England to applause. Never before had the Ghetto been seen in light so penetrating; never before had the romance associated with a strange people and an unfamiliar faith been realized. Readers were astonished to learn that a district some knew by sight and others only by name, held a life so varied, so picturesque, so wonderfully upheld by faith of which the foundations were strengthened by misrepresentation and persecution. It is reported that the book did much to advance the cause of the Jew throughout the world; certain anti-alien legislation submitted to the British government for consideration was dropped because of the sympathy aroused by the work. Zangwill's courage was highly commended by the critics. Says the *Academy* (LIII, 405 ff.):

He does not flatter or spare, but shows us all the squalor, the sordid narrowness, the perverted ingenuity of his people. Those are the very things indeed which give him his artistic opportunity. For, in pathetic contrast to them all, he reveals to us the peculiar glory of Israel — the obstinate patience, the undying hope, the strange beauty of an immemorial ritual, the passion of a despised kinship, and somewhere in the heart of the race that unsatisfied hunger for God.

In the opinion of some critics, Zangwill's interpretation of Israel to the gentiles is a work "well worthy to be done, and a work urgently needed to be done, if one is to judge by the rapidity with which modern nations drop back into a blind medieval hatred of the Chosen People." The *Spectator* (LXXX, 44 ff.), discussing the peculiar contributions of the Jewish novelist to literature, describes Zangwill as an interpreter and medium between his people and the unsympathetic outside world.

> He has felt their sufferings so acutely and has understood so completely the conditions of their separateness, that he has longed to make them intelligible, if not to the world, at least to the English people, who, in their coldly just way, accord the Jews, without liking them, so complete a toleration. While painting his people realistically in their squalor and their narrowness, their fierce industry and their desire to accumulate, he contrives, without even descending to fine language, to give them the impression of their poetic dreaminess, their steadfast obedience to a burdensome law, their admirable household discipline, and their undying hope of a lovely future which would yet be a future on this earth and in this present state. He paints nothing in rosy colors and does not shrink from describing absurdities.

In summing up this appraisal of Zangwill's ghetto studies, it may be said that it is owing to *Children of the Ghetto*, *Dreamers of the Ghetto*, and *The King of Schnorrers* that the Jew in English literature is no longer treated as a conventional type, either very good (rarely), or very bad (more often). The Jew has become a human being — a living type which Jewish writers and (by contagion) non-Jewish writers attempt to delineate with sincerity and passion. In the words of M. J. Landa, in the *Contemporary Review* (1926), Zangwill led the child of the ghetto into the front rank of the novelists. "He did for the Jew what Dickens did for so many victims of the world's coarse thumb, with unfailing humor, with irresistible pathos."

Zangwill's children of the ghetto live more or less in the traditions of the past. Their grandchildren live in the present. The story of these grandchildren is told in the novels of other Jewish writers at the end of the century, particularly in the works of Samuel Gordon (1871–1927), who, like Zangwill, recognizes that the ghetto is not all that it should be, but, unlike Zangwill, is not so sure that the problems of the ghetto can be solved by Zionism. Gordon believes that the hope of Israel in modern life lies in orthodox Judaism. He feels that the ghetto, too crowded and too restricted in trades, calls for the help of the social worker and the philanthropist. Hundreds of ghetto children need the advantages of modern education, many of them should not be permitted to start work at an early age. The wages that most ghetto workers earn are hardly sufficient to support their homes. Something should be done in a practical way to alleviate their economic misery and their spiritual depression. In a novel, entitled *Sons of the Covenant, a tale of London Jewry* (1900), Gordon presents an environment which is practically the same as that of Zangwill's ghetto studies. But, being less of a philosopher than Zangwill, Gordon sees nothing beyond the sociological and sentimental aspects of the scene and situation. The story of the novel has to do with the experiences of two Jewish boys, Phil and Leuw Lipcott (said to be Gordon and his brother), who assume the responsibility of doing something for the welfare of the people of the ghetto. They analyze the situation as follows:

> There are hundreds, thousands of us who, as the cant phrase has it, have risen superior to their surroundings. They have emerged from the teeming, struggling depths of their kindred in race, flattering themselves that they did it by their own native mother-wit, and sublimely ignorant that the capital they started with was their portion of the national inheritance, which our people had accumulated during the years wherein their oppressors thought they were beggaring them inevitably in hope and health and the will to live. And thus, few, very few, have returned to give tithe or toll of their success where it is due.

The boys devise a "decentralizing scheme" for the amelioration of the conditions of the Jewish families in London's East End. The chief obstacle in their way is the inertia of the ghetto.

> "The walls, which were at once their prison and their barricade," said Phil, in explaining the psychology of the ghetto people, "have fallen, but they do not yet know what to do with their liberty. They have still to be taught that their huddling together like sheep in a storm is happily — with scarcely any qualification — an anachronism. This congestion has bred a sort of economic cannibalism which devours, without digesting, the best energies of the workers; it has perpetuated a monopoly — one might almost call it a monopoly — of trades with well nigh internecine results . . . ."

The two reformers concentrate their efforts on "the younger growth of the East End Jewry," and, bound together by the highest ideals of the Jewish covenant, they minister to the needs of their people.

In other sketches of Jewish life — "The Fourth Dimension," "An Alien Immigrant," "The Redemption of the Serpent," "Out of the Land of Bondage," "Rabbi Elchanan's Guest," "The Mordecai of the Serfa," and "The Cossack and the Chorister"— Gordon deals with problems of the ghettos of Russia. The purpose of these tales, as stated by the author, is to "depict the Russian Jew in his native surroundings as a creature possessing organs, dimensions, senses, affections, passions, actuated in his dealings both with his brother in faith as well as with his Gentile neighbor, by the same motives, good and bad and indifferent, which actuate those of his fellow beings to whom the Providence of history has been less than a step-mother."

This mass of fiction, written by Jewish writers about their own people during the final years of the nineteenth century, is obviously of great significance. The life of the modern Jews, even in London where, according to the *Bookman* (XXXI, 144), "they are more absorbed in the population than anywhere else," has recesses and sanctuaries which few gentiles guess. Not only in the East End, among the poor and the wretched, are their religion and ritual a great fact, but behind the complacent comfort of Jewish villadom, there lingers still a wealth of ceremony and sentiment, a picturesqueness of custom out of which the spirit has not all died, and a tenacity of group habit without parallel in a shifting age. In the works of these Jewish writers we find the reaction of the individual Jew towards the problems of the day as they affect the particular needs of his community. And, as we read these first-hand studies and reports, it becomes clear that emancipation has not solved all the difficulties of Jewish life in modern England. Some of these writers cry out against the materialism of the group, others show the persistence of the Jewish spiritual values among those who lack all material things. Some believe in the saving power of an orthodox Judaism, and others feel strongly that Zionism offers the way out for Israel in modern life. All of them, however, hope to find some solution that will bring about a better understanding between Jews and the rest of the world.

CHAPTER XIV

CONCLUSION

In the preceding chapters we have followed the progress of the English Jews through several centuries of tremendous social, economic and political changes. We have seen how the new economic forces which transformed England from an agricultural into an industrial nation awoke the national consciousness to the need for political and social reorganization. We have watched the gradual breaking up of old forms and conventions, and the corresponding increase of freedom of thought and action, and noted the growing attention to the claims of the masses against those of the privileged few. We have seen, too, how, as the Jewish communities in England advanced in numbers and in prestige, they attracted the notice, sometimes of the liberal forces, and at other times of the reactionary groups in English society. Eventually, late in the nineteenth century, through the influence of the liberal and more tolerant elements among both Jews and gentiles, the English Jews emerged into political emancipation and social acceptance.

In 1800 there were about 8,000 Jews in England; in 1900 there were about 160,000 in London alone, and at least 270,000 in the British Isles. At the beginning of the century the Sephardim, or Spanish-Portuguese community, was still predominant, and the Ashkenazim, or German community, constituted the bulk of the "ghetto" Jews of the industrial centers. But, by the end of the century, the character of English Jewry had been considerably changed by the fresh arrivals from Germany, Russia, Poland and other parts of Europe. At the beginning of the century, the English Jews were excluded from the learned professions, and labored under severe political and social disabilities; by the end of the century, they achieved equality with other Englishmen in the professions and governmental service, and manifested an astonishing aptitude for identifying themselves with the nation in which they cast their fortunes. Dean Milman, in the 1870 edition of his *History of the Jews*, comments on the change as follows:

> In 1829, I wrote thus: 'They (the Jews) are excluded from the higher branches of the learned professions . . . from the lower chiefly by popular opinion of their own habits. In the city of London they are prevented by municipal regulations from exercising their freedom'. Since that time, all the higher offices of the city of London have been filled by Jews. A Jew, Mr. Salomons, has been Lord Mayor; it may be said that few have maintained the office with greater dignity, liberality or popularity.

In the course of the years the English Jews passed from a position of insecurity to one of security and influence in the British Empire, and were transformed from an immured community of aliens into an integral part of the body politic. The attitude of the English people in general towards the Jews changed with all these changes. "It is difficult to realize," says the *Westminster Review*, "that barely half a century ago, the Jews as a people were denounced by members of the House of Commons — Cobbett among them — as nothing more than a miserable set of grovelling money-grabbers." At the end of the century, it was acknowledged that the alliance of Jew and gentile in England was "based upon an identity of interests; it was cemented by similarity of tastes, pursuits and needs; it was confirmed by reciprocal obligations." As early as 1868, the *Spectator* made the observation:

> We call them (the Jews) the "unchangeable people," but did any other people change so quickly, has any other or could any other remain as separate, yet be more English than the English? So far from being the unchangeable, they are the most adaptable of mankind; and as persecution ceases everywhere, this very quality will tend to merge them in the people among whom they live and with whom they have at last found that they have sympathies . . . Day by day families drop away, inter-marry, subside, often half consciously, into the mass, and we see no guarantee that in a couple of centuries more, if the world advances on its course, the Jews will be in any way a separate or a noticeable people, more distinct than Unitarians among ourselves, or Protestants in France, or Catholics in America . . .

Whether or not this expression can be substantiated by fact, does not concern us here any more than the question whether or not the Jews would welcome such complete assimilation. What we are interested in is the attitude of a section of the English public toward the change in the status of the English Jews. The same journal observes that the Hebrew community is at last able to take a part, and a leading part, in the general interests of humanity, in politics, in social life, and the great sequence of movements which we term the progress of civilization.

Side by side with the liberalizing and humanizing spirit from the outside, we have observed the growth of liberalization among the younger members of the Jewish community within the ghetto. Jewish youth at the close of the century is seen occupying a more formidable and strategic position than in former years. In the struggle between fathers and sons, the latter are gradually cutting themselves loose from the anchor of their religious heritage and centuries-old tradition, and drifting towards the new educational centers, where they are becoming imbued with foreign ideas of social relationships, art and literature. "These young men and women," observes a Jewish critic, "whether they stayed abroad and remained outside the ghetto, or returned to their native heath as spiritual guides and instructors, became the apostles of a new era."

We have already seen that, with the development of the realistic school, nineteenth century literature began to mirror with increasing truth and accuracy the circumstances and attitudes of English society; and we have studied in detail the many and varied portraits of the Jew reflected in the stream of this literature, observing the changes in color and form made by the shifting currents of thought. Now, as we look back on these studies in the mass, it is apparent that certain well-defined types emerge, and we may, perhaps, observe, in a final examination of these types as they shift and alter with the changes in contemporary thought, even more clearly than can be done in the study of individual cases, the close interrelation between literary and social trends.

Among the Jewish types which stand out conspicuously in English literature of the nineteenth century, there naturally appear those modeled on the conventional patterns inherited from earlier times. The Shylock tradition had persisted since the Tudor age, and it still admirably met the demand of the early nineteenth century reader for the exotic and the unusual. The Jew of this type was a swarthy, hook-nosed merchant, money-lender and usurer, always gesticulating, bowing and fawning; he was versed in mystic lore, magic, sorcery, and the healing art; in learning, he was usually somewhat in advance of the rest of the community. Almost invariably, he was a widower, and fond of an only daughter. If old, he was shriveled and hawk-eyed; if young, he was red-lipped and showy. Young or old, he was coarse, vulgar, rapacious, with seldom an ennobling trait to redeem the repulsive picture. No attempt was made, of course, to model such characters from life. "The delineation," says James Picciotto, "was as faithful as if a Whitechapel costermonger had been held out as a type of British merchant."

In what ways was this pattern altered by the changing currents of nineteenth century thought? As the century progressed, writers began, as we have seen, to turn to life itself for their models, and swayed, sometimes consciously, sometimes unconsciously, by the liberal spirit of the age, to inject something of real humanity into these lay figures, to allow them even some virtues, and to view their faults with some degree of tolerance. There is a world of difference between Maria Edgeworth's presentation of Solomon, the rapacious money-lender in *Belinda* (1801), Solomon, the art-dealer in *The Prussian Vase* (1801), and Mr. Carat, the jeweler, in *The Good Aunt* (1801) — to cite typical examples of the old pattern — and the same author's portrayal of the Jewish man of business who is also a philosopher and a gentleman, in her later novel, *Harrington* (1816). Likewise, Charles

Lever's presentation of Ignaz Oppovich in *That Boy of Norcott's* (1869), a Jew of whom it was said that he could teach many a Christian the virtues of his own faith, and Charles Dickens's portrait of Mr. Riah in *Our Mutual Friend* (1864), a Jew who, though a man of business, is benevolent and gentle,— reveal a tendency to humanize the traditional stage-Jew of the seventeenth and eighteenth centuries. In the *Rebel Queen*, Sir Walter Besant adds another of this type in the character of Emanuel Elveda, a man of intellect, for whom the things of the spirit are more important than the possession of money or power. These examples suggest what happened in the course of the nineteenth century to the Shylock type which was reproduced so faithfully according to the old pattern at the beginning of the period.

Sir Hall Caine, in an address in 1892, stated that, if the Shylock and Fagin types continued to prevail in literature, it was because writers copied each other, having no knowledge of better types. The novelist continued:

> And, if so, is their ignorance altogether their fault, or partly their misfortune? Do the Jews in their old inveterate distrust of the imaginative writer, in their dislike and fear of the novelist or dramatist who has pursued them through centuries with odium and ridicule, shut themselves up from him, and so make it difficult to see the nobler qualities which no man carries on his sleeve? . . . May I dare to say that it would be well if the Jews came oftener into the light and free air of the world that is common to all men. The Jew is notoriously assimilative and clubable, and it would be easy for him — in England at least — to laugh the grotesque Jew out of all claim to be regarded as a Jew.

Another type of Jewish character which curiously persisted in English literature from an early age was that of the

Wandering Jew. He had his appeal to early nineteenth century readers whose prejudices were perhaps nourished by contemporary discussions on "the conversion of the Jews," "the mission to the Jews," "the Jews as objects of divine wrath," and the like. The image of the doomed wanderer, kept alive by William Godwin's version of the legend in *St. Leon* (1779) and by M. G. Lewis's *The Monk* (1795), was implanted more firmly in the public mind by John Galt's popular romance, *The Story of the Wandering Jew* (1818), and George Croly's lengthy tale of *Salathiel* (1828). In the middle years of the century, the hoary legend was still further popularized by the translation into English of Eugene Sue's *Wandering Jew*, after which, according to Landa, "there was a glut of wandering Jews on the English stage." However, this type, too, was altered under the inspiration of the new humanitarian and evangelical movements. We find that this nineteenth century Wandering Jew is wont to do good as he passes along the way, and that it is possible for human compassion to proffer some light mitigation of the divine sentence. Eventually, after the removal of civil disabilities in England, when the Jews are permitted to become fixed members of society and occupy public office and a seat in Parliament, the tragic wanderer of tradition seems more or less of an anomaly in modern life and in current fiction.

So much for the nineteenth century treatment of the time-honored Jewish types. We have already had occasion to observe that new social, economic and political developments during the century gave rise to new literary characters. The old-clothes-man and the itinerant peddler, for instance, appeared in English fiction as the direct result of the presence of thousands of Jewish immigrants from the

Rhine districts and Russia. These fresh arrivals from continental ghettos, outlandishly dressed, speaking a strange gibberish, and resorting to every available means of earning a penny or two until they could find their place in the land of their adoption, became a familiar sight in every English town and hamlet. Writers of fiction were quick to recognize their literary possibilities and to make use of them in the creation of two new types. By some writers these uncouth aliens were depicted as beings of a different world, to be viewed with distrust and fear. The *London Mirror* in 1827 described one of these unfortunates as possessing "the head of a fox on the body of a mastiff," and living a life which was "a long game of verbal and periodical lies, of substitution and sycophancy . . . a vile slinking principle curling about his lips, a fitful puckering-up of his eyes, a thrilling of chicane at the very tip of his nose." Little actually was known by English writers about these ghetto Jews in the early years of the century, and therefore much villainy was attributed to their mysterious appearance and uncouth ways. It was customary, as we are told by Maria Edgeworth in *Harrington*, to make use of them in literature as "bogies", to scare children and to make the adult flesh creep. Also, according to Besant, it was the usual thing for school boys to run out on the streets and pelt these tragic-looking creatures whenever they passed by. On the other hand, this same class of Jews appealed to the comic spirit in other writers. The strange lisp, the long beard, the gesticulations, struck many as being grotesque. For purposes of comic relief, they were soon introduced into the music-hall skits and fiction, their success as mirth-provokers being increased by an exaggeration of the incongruous elements of their speech, manner and dress. The comic type persisted throughout the century with little change, except that, as the ghetto Jew became more "anglicized" and lost his peculiarities of dress and manner, the comedy which he afforded became predominantly psychological rather than sartorial. The "bogey" type, on the other hand, was inevitably softened and modified, as, with the passage of years, ignorance gave place to knowledge, and fear and distrust to familiarity and human understanding. The Jewish peddlers of Captain Marryat's stories and those of Israel Zangwill's ghetto stand worlds apart, but the nineteenth century covered the distance in its stride.

Another new Jewish type which the portrait gallery of the period offers is that of the Jewish hero. The Jewish group in England proved itself worthy of recognition by producing leaders of the type of Sir Moses Montefiore, Sir David Salomons, Baron Lionel de Rothschild, and Sir Francis Henry Goldsmid, men of wealth, culture and character. Now a literary champion appeared on the scene to glorify the Jewish race and to champion the Jewish cause. It was the part of Benjamin Disraeli to set forth with magnificent courage and eloquence his declaration of faith in the destinies of his race. In *Alroy* (1833), he conceived what novelists up to this time had refused to conceive — a noble Jewish character, far removed from the Shylocks and Isaacs of romantic fiction. In *Coningsby* (1844) and *Tancred* (1847), he presented the Jewish Sidonia, a fine gentleman, adroit in politics, profound in scholarship, and gifted with the wisdom of his race. Through Sidonia, the novelist pictured the industry, temperance, energy and vivacity of the Jewish mind. He showed that in every great intellectual movement in Europe the Jews had played leading parts; that they were of the true nobility of the earth, possessing a lineage so splendid and so ancient that, in comparison, the oldest English families were but of yesterday.

Beside these portraits we may set Grace Aguilar's heroic pictures of the little understood and persecuted leaders of medieval and Renaissance Jewry in Spain and England, of the ghetto dreamers and scholars of the historic past.

But the Jew was not portrayed as a hero only by writers of his own blood. In *Daniel Deronda*, George Eliot presented Mordecai, whose dreams and aspirations were all for his people, and Daniel himself, who, although brought up as a gentile, was prepared, on discovering that he was a Jew, to lay aside every personal consideration, all feelings of selfishness and aggrandizement, and to devote the rest of his life to the loftiest national aims of Israel.

Alongside the portraits of the Jew as a hero, we may place the more conventionalized pictures of the Jewess as heroine. It may be set down as a general rule that the Jewish woman in fiction is almost invariably treated with a sense of chivalry by English writers. The Abigails, Nerissas, Rachels and Miriams, are all of one type — they are all endowed with beauty, grace and charm. Be she angel of purity or courtesan, the Jewess retains her fascinating and almost magical loveliness of face and form. Paying tribute to the charm of Scott's Jewess, Thackeray in his *Roundabout Papers* says:

Rebecca, daughter of Isaac of York, I have loved thee faithfully for forty years! Thou wast twenty years old (say) but I was twelve, when I knew thee. At sixty odd, love, most of the ladies of thy orient race have lost the bloom of youth, and bulged beyond the line of beauty; but to me thou art ever young and fair, and I will do battle with any felon Templar who assails thy fair name.

As a rule too, the Jew's daughter is accomplished; she is well read in the Hebrew scriptures, acquainted with magic and the art of healing, and able to sing and play on some instrument of music. She is loyal to her faith, and, if she becomes a Christian, it is for deeply religious reasons, and not for any social benefits that she may derive from the change.

There are of course some departures from the traditional delineation of the Jewess, especially in the latter part of the century when realistic portraiture became more the fashion. For example, in George Eliot's *Daniel Deronda* (1876), the Princess Alcharisi, and in Sir Walter Besant's *Rebel Queen* (1893), Madame Elveda, are as worldly as their masculine prototypes. In the pages of Amy Levy's *Reuben Sachs* (1888), the English reader is given a close view of other Jewesses who are "sad-eyed elderly women, unsatisfied and heart-hungry amid the wealth and gorgeousness which are esteemed as the chief good in existence." In the stories of Frank Danby and Mrs. Andrew Dean too we found others of this type, a pathetic and futile group, so unlike the Rebeccas and the Miriams of the romantic tale. These modern Jewesses are pledged to the pursuit of fashion and fortune and manifest as little interest in the traditions of Israel as possible.

The unbelieving and worldly Jew and Jewess are new types in English fiction, appearing for the first time in this period. That there were certain Jews who protested against the intolerance and the rigidity of the Jewish system of conduct and ceremonial was a fact well-known to the Jewish and and the gentile world for many centuries, but this rebel Jew was not presented as a character in English fiction before the nineteenth century. In Kingsley's *Hypatia*, there is a suggestion of rebelliousness in the character of Miriam, the Jewish procuress. She is an apostate to her faith, fallen and vile, but she does not openly rebel against Judaism as does Deronda's mother, whose desire to spare her son the miseries of her race and religion lead her to have him brought up as a Christian. The Princess Alcharisi protests against the forms and "oppressive burdens" of her stern father's faith, and, once free of husband and father, she resolves to have no more to do with Jews and Judaism. Similarly, the sole object of Madame Elveda is to renounce her people. "Your old traditions," she says to her husband, "your jumble, and jargon of ceremonies and superstitions, I will follow no longer. I throw them off." To these individuals, as to Heine, Judaism is a misfortune. They are so mortified by their social position as Jews that they resent the humiliations brought upon them by their faith.

In the nineteenth century gallery of masculine portraits there are figures like Baron Levi, in Bulwer Lytton's *My Novel*, who, straying further and further away from Jewish associations, belong in fact among the modern "emancipated" Jews who are ready to break old home ties and forget their Jewishness. Pash, in *Daniel Deronda*, is perhaps a fair representative of this new class of un-Jewish Jew. He declares that he is not in sympathy with the "rubbish" in Judaism and is not interested in the future of Israel. He is on good terms with both Jews and gentiles. With him stands Gideon, who believes that it is time to get rid of "superstitions and exclusiveness." These characters represent the assimilationists who are willing to melt into the population. "A man's country is where he is well off," sums up Gideon's philosophy of living. A typical example of the Jew who completely throws aside his Jewish interests and becomes a law unto himself is given in the character of the plutocrat, David Jost, in *Temporal Power*. Jost is described as a Jew by birth but not by temperament. "He kept his Hebraic colors flying for the King," says the novelist, "judging that to flatter royalty was always a safe course for Jews."

The process of transition from orthodoxy to rebellion is best illustrated in the pictures of Jewish life in *Reuben Sachs*. The white-haired, shrewd, prosperous grandfather Sachs, who, his fortune won, fills up his leisure hours with constant, mechanical muttering of Hebrew prayers, belongs to the passing order. His grandchildren still conform outwardly to the exactions of the old religion, but in devious ways; some ignorantly and unthinkingly, some with reverent mockery, and some with practical philosophy, holding the Jewish religion in affection for the sake of the Jewish group, but none with deep, intelligent conviction of the heart. Material success becomes the real god of Reuben Sachs, and he deliberately breaks away from the grand passion of his life from mercenary and ambitious motives.

In Israel Zangwill's pictures of the talmudic Judaism crumbling under the pressure of modern culture, we find almost every type represented, from the *schnorrer* to the rich merchant, from the pious peddler to the radical who shares Heine's belief that "Judaism is a misfortune." Under the sway of centrifugal impulses, we see the more progressive characters move out of the ghetto to form new colonies, moulting their old feathers, and replacing them by finer. Zangwill describes the various stages of transition, as only one who has watched the process with an intimate knowledge of the Jewish heart could describe it. In the work of Samuel Gordon, also, we find a sympathetic and vivid portrayal of these same types of a transitional period.

In this study of the presentation of Jewish characters in English literature, it is of passing interest to note the type of English characters who are opposed to the Jew, and to observe the novelist's attitude toward them. In the historical romances, the traditional enemies of the Jews in England are members of the established Church. For example, in *Ivanhoe*, Christian society as a whole resents the presence of "the unbelieving Jew." The Abbot feels free to insult Isaac of York, and the Templar will not tolerate "a dog Jew" under any circumstances. The Pilgrim and the Palmer and all the servants of Cedric's Saxon household oppose the Jew on religious grounds. For his part, the Jew realizes the danger of living in the domains of Philip de Malvoisin and Reginald Front de Boeuf, and knows perfectly well that from these Christians he can expect no sympathy and protection.

This attitude of medieval Christian society towards Jews is carried into nineteenth century society by certain representatives of the church-going classes. "These Christians," says Imlah Durvan to his daughter, "have been taught to dread the contamination of a Jew . . . and we walk in a strange land, the very scoff of mankind." Another Jewish character, Joseph Perez, tells his sister, "Henry Stevens said the other day that Jews have no faith, and how can we trust them?" In *Fair Jewess* by Farjeon, the medieval Christian attitude is clearly shown by Mr. Pointer, "the true Christian, regular in his attendances at church," who hates Aaron Cohen because he is an unbeliever. Manifestly the novelist has very little sympathy for these un-Christian

Christians and invariably shows them up as hypocrites and fanatics. In the case of Mr. Poynter, Farjeon does not hesitate to reveal the fact that this man who sought to "find something in the Jew's past that would bring shame upon him," is the man who betrayed the mother of Ruth Cohen.

A second type of English character expresses hate for the Jew because he is a foreigner. The turn of the head, the carriage of the back, the glance of the eye, the oriental coloring, the Jewish nose; these are the unmistakable signs in the Jew that are resented. Not even an English hat, coat or manner can disguise these foreign characteristics. Concealment is useless; the Jew's very being breathes another race. And so, although Harrington's father cannot explain his anti-Semitic feelings, he simply opposes the Jew Bill in Parliament and warns his son to keep away from the Jews. Similarly, in *Fair Jewess*, the chief objection to the Jew, as expressed in the speech of Mr. Whimpole, is "There is a prejudice against your race."

"Am I not aware of it?" says Aaron. "Is not every Jew aware of it? . . . Your use of the word 'prejudice' is appropriate, for, as I understand its meaning, it represents a judgment formed without proper knowledge. Yes, sir, it is not to be disputed that there exists a prejudice against our race."

"Which, without putting any false meaning upon it, will make this ancient and respectable town — too hot to hold you," said Mr. Whimpole.

In *The Tragic Comedians*, Meredith makes it clear that the only reason why the von Rudiger family are opposed to the marriage of their daughter to Alvan is the young man's origin. When the story opens, we are informed that Clotilde herself shared her family's "abhorrence of Jewry." "The Jew was to Clotilde as flesh of swine to the Jew ... One of the favorite similes of the family for whatever grunted in grossness, wiggled with meanness, was a Jew."

In the majority of the novels, however, as far as we are able to determine, the chief objection to the Jew in England seems to be the notion that he is a usurer, an unscrupulous man in business and given to driving a hard bargain against the natives who are unfortunate enough to get into his clutches. It has been a strangely persistent notion, carried on from generation to generation until long after moneylending had ceased to be a fairly common Jewish occupation. John Meadows, in *It is Never Too Late to Mend*, evicts old Isaac Levi from his house, for just that reason.

> "What have I done to gain your enmity, sir?" asks the Jew.
>
> "You lend money."
>
> "A little, sir, now and then — a very little."
>
> "That is to say, when the security is bad you have no money in hand; but when the security is good nobody has ever found the bottom of Isaac Levi's purse."

Perhaps the chief objection Fledgeby, in *Our Mutual Friend*, has to Mr. Riah is that the Jew is in business. "Now, Judah," says the Englishman, "What are you up to there? ... You mean mischief, Jerusalem, yes, you do. Oh, you sinner, Oh, you Jew." And so, the gentle Mr. Riah is believed to be "the bitingest and tightest screw in London."

It is significant to note that in whatever form they may appear, these English characters who obstruct the progress of the Jew in England and in one way and another insult, injure or show resentment against Israelites are in general represented by the novelist (with the possible exception of Charles Dickens in *Oliver Twist* and Anthony Trollope in *The Way We Live Now*) as belonging to an ignorant, or cowardly or even degraded class of citizen.

In concluding this study of the Jew in the literature of England, it may seem appropriate to add a word of final comment on the work of the Jewish writers of the period. What the Jew has to say about his own people is obviously of great significance. "Perhaps it is only today," says the *London Quarterly Review* (1897), "when some children of Israel have taken the pen and written true words of their people, that the English Jew is beginning to be rightly understood by his neighbor, the English Gentile." In the Jewish fiction of later years we see the reaction of the individual Jew towards the problems which the question of emancipation raise and answer, as well as towards those more persistent problems which only the passage of time and perhaps countless generations in the future can solve. All these writers show an interest in the difficulties facing the contemporary Jew and seek to find a way out. All points of view are represented in their work. We have the sugared sentimentality of a Grace Aguilar and a Farjeon, in whose representations nearly every Jewish character is made to figure as a peaceful, unoffending saint, with hardly any blemish to mar his character or to explain his maltreatment. We have the passionate cry against materialism of an Amy Levy, a Frank Danby or a Mrs. Andrew Dean, who, as severe critics of their people, deal with the local history of their day. We have the eloquent presentation of the political situation and a remarkable championship of the glory of Israel in the studies of a Disraeli. We have the understanding compassion of a Zangwill, whose profound pessimism sees in Zionism a possible way out, and the optimism of a Samuel Gordon, who hopefully turns to the saving grace of orthodox Judaism for the future happiness of Israel. Which is right, which is wrong? Only the future can answer.

"The Jew is now a great figure in literature," says an English novelist, "both as creator and the subject of it. No base tyranny can be perpetrated on the Jews with the old impunity. The pen is the sword of modern warfare, and it is the friend and champion of the Jew."

NOTES

I. IN MEDIEVAL ENGLAND

In his *History of the Jews*, 1829, Book XXV, 236, Henry Hart Milman main tains that the Jews were in England under the Saxons. The first reference to them is in Bede's *Ecclesiastical History*, written in 731, in connection with the controversy of the tonsure and the constitution of Egbright, Archbishop of York.

Edward A. Freeman, *History of The Norman Conquest of England*, revised American edition, 1876, V, 547, states that, although Jews are mentioned in the ecclesiastical laws both of Theodore and Ecgbert, the canons forbidding Christians to have intercourse with Jews, and the like, are, on the face of them, "copied from the decrees of ancient councils . . ."

In Tovey's *Anglia Judaica*, no case of a Jew in England earlier than the Conquest is mentioned.

G. M. Trevelyan, *History of England*, 1929, 187, does not believe that the Jews were able to engage in business in England before the Conqueror had instituted law and order. "Saxon England," says Trevelyan, "was so primitive that there was hardly any need for money-lenders."

Holinshed, *Chronicles of England*, 1578, III, 15, refers to William the Conqueror inviting the Jews of Rouen to settle in England.

It is true that usury was contrary to the strictest Rabbinical teachings, (M. Lazarus, *The Ethics of Judaism*, I, 281) but such teachings were not, in fact could not, be enforced, since money-lending was practically the only way to make a living left open to the Jews in Medieval England (Hyamson, *History of the Jews in England*, 4). Rowland Strong (*Academy* LXXIV, 614) disagrees with this view.

For description of the prosperity of English Jews under Henry II, consult H. Graetz, *History of the Jews*, III, 409, and L. F. Salzmann, *Henry II*, 199.

An interesting sketch of Aaron of Lincoln is given by Joseph Jacobs in *Transactions of the Jewish Historical Society of England*, III, 157 ff.

The financial transactions of the Exchequer of the Jews in the reign of Richard I are described by Madox, *History of the Exchequer*, I, 150–178; and in *The Jewish Encyclopedia*, V, 284–285.

Kate Norgate, in *John Lackland*, 137, says: "At the opening of 1210, all the Jews in England, of both sexes, were by the King's order arrested, imprisoned and tortured, to make them give up their wealth. It is said that the King wrung ten thousand marks from one Jew at Bristol, by causing seven of his teeth to be torn out, one every day for a week." *Vide* Joseph Jacobs, *The Jews of Angevin England*, 222, 228–230, 239–240.

The *Domus Conversorum*, opened by Henry III in London for Jewish converts, was in Chancery Lane, on the site now occupied by the Rolls Court. *Vide* Rev. Michael Adler, "The Domus Conversorum," *Transactions of the Jewish Historical Society of England*, IV 1896, 16 ff.

In 1290, the Order of Expulsion was issued by Edward I. Vickers, *England in the Later Middle Ages*, 34 ff., supports the report that the King was probably influenced by his mother who had expelled all Jews from her dowry towns (*Calendar of Patent Rolls*, 1281, 67) and by an excess of religious zeal.

Also consult B. L. Abrahams, *Expulsion of the Jews from England in 1290*, 82 ff.; and Lionel Abrahams, "Condition of the Jews of England at the Time of their Expulsion in 1290," *Journal of the Jewish Historical Society of England*, I, 76 ff.

According to Green, *Short History of the English People*, Revised edition, 1916, 205, "no share in the enormities which accompanied the expulsion of the Jews can fall upon Edward I, for he not only suffered the fugitives to take their wealth with them, but punished with the halter those who plundered them at sea. But the expulsion was none the less cruel."

Vide Graetz, *History of the Jews*, III, 645; and G. H. Leonard, "The Expulsion of the Jews by Edward I," *Royal Historical Society Transactions*, 1891, 135–136.

The Ritual Murder of Hugh of Lincoln: in Child's *English Ballads*, 1882, II; no less than eighteen versions of the story of the martyred Christian boy have been collected.

The modern attitude toward the case of Hugh of Lincoln is pointed out in Cecil Roth's *Medieval Lincoln Jewry and its Synagogue*, Jewish Historical Society of England, London, 1934.

In *The Jewish Encyclopedia*, III, 266, may be found a list of the cases of ritual murder, beginning with William of Norwich.

It should be noted that Chaucer uses the word "Jew" as a national name without any offensive connotation, as in the *Pardoner's Tale* (*C. T.*, C 351). The Pardoner says that he has among his relics "a sholder boon, which was that of an hooly Jewes shape," probably referring to a Jew before the time of Jesus. The Merchant (*C. T.*, E 2277) calls Solomon "this Jew." *Vide* Carlton Brown, "The Prioress' Tale and its Analogues," *P. M. L. A.* XXI, June 1906, 486 ff.; and J. L. Cardozo, *The Contemporary Jew in Elizabethan Drama*, 23 ff.

In *Piers Plowman*, the references to Jews are to be found in C. V. 194; C. VII, 241; C. XX, 96. *Vide Piers Plowman*, edited by J. J. Jusserand, translated by M. E. R., 1894, 17, 52, 113, 121, 131, 161, 166, 184, 205, 210, 216.

Gower's reference to Jews is in *Confessio Amantis*, Book VII, 3207.

The ballad of the Wandering Jew is included in Percy's *Reliques of Ancient English Poetry*, edited by Rev. George Gilfillan, Edinburgh, 1858, II, 236 ff. *Vide* H. Graetz, *Papers of the Anglo-Jewish Historical Exhibition*, 1–4; Nelson Sherwin Bushnell, "The Wandering Jew and The Pardoner's Tale," *Studies in Philology*, XXVIII, 1931, 450–460; and David Hoffman, *Cartaphilus, The Wandering Jew*, Chronicles selected from the originals, 3 vols, London, 1853.

Matthew Paris's version of the story of the Wandering Jew, *Chronica Majora*, ed. Luard, London, 1880, V, 340–341.

Reference to Jews in Medieval drama is discussed by M. J. Landa, *The Jew in Drama*, 1927, 38. *Vide* also A. W. Pollard's Introduction to *English Miracle Plays*, Oxford, 1909; and K. L. Bates, *English Religious Drama*, London, 1893, 83.

II. THE TUDOR RENAISSANCE

M. J. Landa, *The Jew in Drama*, 1927, 15, points out that Shakespeare and his contemporaries were obviously influenced by Lyly's *Euphues* in their attitude toward the Jew as a character in drama.

With reference to Marlowe's *Jew of Malta* and the original of Barabas, consult C. F. Tucker Brooke, *Times Literary Supplement*, London, June 8, 1922.

In the discussion on Shakespeare's treatment of Jews, consult Dr. David Philipson, *The Jew in English Fiction*, 1889, 38–39; Gerald Friedlander, *Shakespeare and the Jew*, London, 1922; and Cardoza, *The Contemporary Jew in the English Drama*, 1925.

It is pointed out by Landa, *The Jew in Drama*, 82–83, that the one incident of a Jewess exciting interest in Shakespeare's time was of an absolutely opposite character to that of Jessica in *The Merchant of Venice*. Maria Nunes, a crypto-Jewess, was reported to have fled from Spain, and was captured by an Elizabeth captain, a nobleman. The Jewess refused the hand of the English commander in marriage and may have experienced cruel treatment as a result of her refusal, had not her beauty and romantic story created a great stir in London. She was befriended by Queen Elizabeth, who drove through the streets with her, and helped the Jewess, under royal protection, to reach Holland, where she remained faithful to the Jewish faith. *Vide* Graetz, *History of the Jews*, IV, 664–7.

For discussion on character of Shylock, consult Solomon Hurwitz, *Jewish Forum*, V, 1922, 198 ff; Sir Sidney Lee, *Elizabethan England and The Jews*, 1888, 159 ff; Lucien Wolf, *Publications of the Anglo-Jewish Exhibition*, I, 71; E. N. Calisch, *The Jew in English Literature*, 81 ff.; E. E. Stoll, "Shylock," *Journal of English and Germanic Philology*, X, 241–243; and *Shakespeare Studies*, 1927, 311 ff.

Other references to Jews by Shakespeare may be found in *Two Gentlemen of Verona*, II, 5, 58, where Launce says to Speed,

> "Go with me to the Alehouse; if not
> Thou art an Hebrew, a Jew, and not
> Worth the name of a Christian;"

in *Much Ado About Nothing*, II, 3, 272, where Benedick says, "If I do not love her, I am a Jew —;" in *Henry IV*, part I (II, 4, 198), where Falstaff says, "They were bound, every man of them, or I am a Jew else, an Ebrew Jew;" in *Love's Labour's Lost* (III, 1, 136); in *A Midsummer Nights' Dream* (III, 1, 97), etc.

III. THE RETURN OF THE JEWS TO ENGLAND

Vide References to Jews in Burton's *Anatomy of Melancholy*, revised edition, 1893, I, 242; II, 81, 370, 401, 412.

For satisfactory accounts of the return of the Jews to England, consult Lucien Wolf, "The Jews of the Restoration," *Transactions of the Jewish Historical Society of England*, V, 12 ff.; "Manassah Ben Israel's Study in London," *Ibid*. III, 144 ff.; and *Manassah Ben Israel's Mission to Cromwell*, 1901.

In "Bishop Barlow on the Case of the Jews," *Transactions of the Jewish Historical Society of England*, III, 1896, 151–156; Rev. S. Levy enumerates the conditions on which Jews were to be admitted into England. Bishop Barlow declared that "no toleration should be given them to speak blasphemously or impiously against the Gospels; let them profess, but not propagate, their religion; they be not permitted to carry any office or indignity in the Christian common weal; they never be permitted to make marriages with Christians . . . ."

Spence, *Anecdotes*, 1858, 58, states that the first public toleration of the Jews was granted by Oliver Cromwell, for which concession he received sixty-thousand pounds. It is stated on the authority of the *Thurloe State Papers*, II, 632, that the Jews offered to pay five-hundred thousand pounds to the Commonwealth, on the following terms: (1) that the laws against the Jew should be appealed; (2) that the Bodleian Library should be assigned to them; and (3) that the Jews should have permission to use St. Paul's Cathedral as a synagogue. *Vide* Francis, *History of the Bank of England*, 24; and *Notes and Queries*, First Series, I, 1850, 401, 474.

In the early days of the Restoration, a petition drawn up by the London merchants and tradesmen, praying for the Expulsion of the Jews, was read before the Privy Council (December 7, 1660). The petition was referred to Parliament for consideration, but no action was taken. "There is no entry," says H. S. Q. Henriques, *Return of the Jews to England*, 1408, 2–3, "in the journal of the House of Commons, and a few days after, Parliament was dissolved."

Cartaret Webb, in an appendix to his question "Whether a Jew can Hold Land?" *Jewish Quarterly Review*, XVII, 205; gives a list of 105 Jews who obtained letters of denization in the reign of Charles II and James II. *Vide* Lucien Wolf, "The First English Jew (Antonio Fernandez Carvajal)," *Journal of the Jewish Historical Society of England*, II, 1894, 14–23.

In 1668, Sir Joshua Child, the millionaire governor of the East India Company, pleaded for the naturalization of the Jews, on the score of commercial utility. The City of London felt itself obliged to "connive at the Jew's illegal representation on the Exchange," and to violate its own rules, so that the Israelites might act as stockbrokers without previously receiving the freedom of the city. *Vide Encyclopedia Britannica*, XV, 406.

By the end of the reign of Charles II (1685), the legal recognition of the Jews in England was practically complete. The order of Council, dated November 13, 1685, granting protection and the free exercise of their religion to the English Jews, establishes the date of the legal settlement of the community in Engl.nd. *Vide* Henriques, *Return of the Jews to England*, 2–3; C. Duschinsky "Rabbinate of the Great Synagogue in London," *Jewish Quarterly Review*, IX, 103–137, 371–408.

IV. THE EIGHTEENTH CENTURY

The views concerning the Jews, expressed by Joseph Addison in the *Spectator*. it may be observed, are similar to the views held by his father, the Rev. Lancelot Addison, who, according to Macaulay, "enjoyed an excellent opportunity, as chaplain at Tangier, of studying the history and manners of Jews and Mohammedans; and of this opportunity he appears to have made excellent use," being the author of a work entitled *The Present State of the Jews*, London, 1675.

For Joseph Addison's observations on the Jews, see *Spectator Papers* for November 3, 1711; September 27, 1712; and November 8, 1712.

The chief names of interest in Anglo-Jewish history of the 18th century, in addition to those of Sir Solomon Medina and Sampson Gideon, include David Nieto, the *Hacham* (*Jewish Encyclopedia*, IX, 302–303); Moses Hamburger, founder of the Hambro' Synagogue; Sarmento Castro (*Jewish Encyclopedia*, III, 612); and the two brothers Da Castro, one the secretary of the Royal Society, and the other the founder of the Hebrew section of the British Museum. A quaint figure is presented in the person of Baron d'Aguilar, the eccentric miser (*Jewish Encyclopedia*, I, 274).

Even as late as 1780, when the *Belle's Stratagem*, produced at Covent Garden, was popular, the name of Sampson Gideon aroused some resentment. One of the characters in the play exclaims: "Why, you testy Israelite; go back to Duke's Place, and preach your tribe into a subscription for the good of the land on whose milk and honey ye fatten" — Act IV, 1.

The names of the Jews naturalized in the colonial plantations in America (1740–1761) are given in the *Colonial Office Records*, LIX, LXVI.

For the political status of the Jew in England in the Eighteenth century, consult Gerald Berkley Hertz, *British Imperialism in the Eighteenth Century*, 1908, 60 ff.; William Cox, *Memoirs of the Administration of Pelham*, 1829, II, 245 ff.; *Extract from an Appeal to the Throne against the Naturalization of the Jewish Nation*, 1753; and Sir Walter Besant, *History of the Eighteenth Century*, 1902, 177, 180, 262.

Dr. H. R. S. Van Der Veen, *Jewish Characters in the Eighteenth Century Fiction and Drama*, 1935, 23 ff., gives an authoritative account of Defoe's associations and views of the Jews.

For references to Jews by Defoe, consult *Works of Defoe* (Bohn Standard Library), II, 314, 346; IV, 392, 402, 433; VII, 328.

An investigation of the plays produced in the last quarter of the Eighteenth Century — several of which are still extant in manuscript form in the Huntington Library at San Marino — would provide the reader with evidence of a change in the treatment of the Jew in English drama.

For information about Jewish peddlers in the Eighteenth Century, *Vide* Maurice Myers, "Jewish Calendars of the Coaching Days," *Jewish Historical Society of England*, V, 1905, 219–225; *Gentleman's Magazine*, 1754, p. 44; 1758, 91; 1760, 40.

An interesting account of Lord George Gordon, the English nobleman who became a Jew, is contained in Israel Solomon's paper, *Jewish Historical Society of England*, VII, 1913, 260 ff.; and in Justin McCarthy's *History of the Four Georges*, 1901, III, 289.

For a detailed report on the career of Daniel Mendoza, consult his *Memoirs*, printed by D. Mendoza and G. Hayden, Bridges St., Covent Garden, no date; and Louis Berg's article on Mendoza, *Menorah Journal*, XVI, 1929, 122 ff.

The quotation from Rabbi Hart Lyon's sermon is taken from the article on the Reform Movement by Dr. C. Duschinsky, *Jewish Quarterly Review*, IX, 11 ff.

V. THE DAWN OF A NEW ERA, 1800–1833.

According to F. A. Wendeborn, *A View of England towards the Close of the 18th Century*, 1791, II, 468; the number of Jews in England at the close of the century was 12,000. But the *Jewish Encyclopedia*, V, 174, sets the figure at 8,000.

The increase in the ranks of the Jewish community at the beginning of the nineteenth century is recorded in the minute books of the Jewish Board of Deputies (1802) wherein it is stated that great numbers of the poorer classes came from all parts of Germany. *Vide* Charles H. L. Emanuel, *A Century and a Half of Jewish History*, London, 1910, 10–11.

A fairly representative view of Jewish life among the upper classes is presented in *The Diaries* of Sir Moses Montefiore and Lady Montefiore, edited by Dr. L. Loewe, London, 1890, I, 60–65; and in Corti's *The Reign of the House of Rothschild*, New York, 1928, 182 ff.

At one of the parties given by the Rothschilds at Piccadilly, the guests included Sir Moses and Lady Montefiore, the Duke and Duchess of St. Albans, Lady Luisa Beauclerk, the Hon. Shaw Stewart, Lord and Lady Kinwell, Sir William and Lady Bowley, the Spanish Ambassador and his Lady, the Brazilian Ambassador, Sir Charles Beresford, Sir William Abdy, Mr. George Harrison, and others.

It is not possible to estimate the value of the work done by the London Society for Promoting Christianity among Jews (founded in 1807) in the first quarter of the century. Many Jews are reported to have been baptized and hundreds of Jewish children educated through this agency. Rev. W. T. Gidney, *Jews and Their Evangelization*, London, 1899, 91 ff., calls attention to the "four great achievements" of the early years, namely (1) the translation of the New Testament into Hebrew in 1817; (2) into Yiddish in 1821; (3) the publication of the Liturgy of the Church of England in Hebrew, in 1837; and (4) the establishment of the first Medical Mission in 1824. Among the many indirect results of the missionary work for Jews in London, the "decay of Jewish prejudice, the disintegration of Judaism, and the acquaintance with the New Testament," are mentioned.

Vide J. S. C. F. Frey, *Narrative of the Minister of the Gospel to the Jews*, London, 1809; James Picciotto, *Sketches of Anglo-Jewish History*, London, 1875; and Gabriel Festing, *John Hookham Frere and his Friends*, London, 1899, 274–293.

The protests against the London Society's activities were more or less caused by the proselytizing of the Jewish young people by methods that were open to question. Among these protests was a pamphlet by Thomas Witherby, *A Vindication of the Jews*, 1810, in which certain facts were "humbly submitted to the consideration of the Missionary Society and the London Society." *Vide* the *Anti-Jacobin Review*, XXXV, 1810, 242–243.

Dean Henry Hart Milman was attacked for his position on the Jewish question, and defended himself in a preface to the third edition of his *History of the Jews*, 1829. *Vide* "A Letter to the Rev. Henry Hart Milman, M. A., reputed author of the History of the Jews, deprecating the re-publication of that work; by One who is also an Elder," Oxford, 1830.

William Cobbett's attack on the Jews was continued in his *Rural Rides*, I, 318, 401; II, 45, 177; and in his pamphlet entitled *Good Friday, or the Murder of Jesus Christ by the Jews*, published by the author, London, 1830.

Although in his "Imperfect Sympathies," Charles Lamb confessed his dislike for the Jews as a class, on other occasions he expressed an appreciation of certain individual Jews. For example, in a letter, dated February 26, 1808, he declared that "The Little Jew"— the singer Braham —"has bewitched me. I follow him as the boys followed Tom the piper. He cures me of melancholy as David cured Saul; but I don't throw stones at him as Saul did at David in payment. I was insensible to music till he gave me a new sense." Two years later, on the death of Braham, Lamb wrote again (January 2, 1810), "That glorious singer, Braham, one of my lights, is fled. He was for a season. He was a rare combination of the Jew, the gentleman, and the angel." *Vide* Charles Lamb's *Letters*, edited by Ainger, 1913, I, 296, 314.

John Brahms (or Abrahams), born in London about 1774, was left an orphan at an early age. He sold pencils in the streets, until he was adopted by Meyer Lyon, and given an appointment as *Meshorer*, or singing boy at the Great Synagogue. As a singer of Handel, Brahms was incomparable. The critics declared there was no tenor to approach him. *Vide* F. L. Cohen, "Some Anglo-Jewish Song Writers," *Jewish Historical Society of England*, I, 1894, 1–7.

It is interesting to note that Sir Robert Peel, in his speech on the Disabilities of the Jews (House of Commons, April 17, 1833), quoted the words of Dr. Thomas Arnold, the famous headmaster of Rugby: "For the Jews I see no place of justice whatever; they are voluntary strangers here, and have no claim to become citizens but by conforming to our moral law, which is the Gospel." *Vide* Dean Stanley's *Life and Correspondence of Dr. Thomas Arnold*, 1844, for Arnold's expression of feeling against the Jew Bill.

Macaulay's Essay on the subject of The Jewish Disabilities was published in the *Edinburgh Review*, 1831, 363 ff.

A marginal note scribbled in the copy of Hazlitt's essay on Jewish Disabilities, owned by Bertram Dobell, the book-seller, states that Isaac Goldsmid caused the essay to be written. The pamphlet by Francis Henry Goldsmid, to which Macaulay and Hazlitt are supposed to have gone for information, was entitled *Statement of the Civil Disabilities and Privations affecting the Natural Born Subjects of His Majesty's Professing the Jewish Religion, commonly called Jews*, London, 1829.

VI. THE ROMANTIC REVIVAL

In *The Friend*, Coleridge published three *Talmudic Tales* in verse, and translated two of Professor Hyman Hurwitz's Hebrew poems, "Israel's Lament" and "The Tears of a Grateful People." It is interesting to note that Coleridge referred to Hurwitz as "My Christian friend of the Jewish persuasion." *Vide* Israel Abrahams, *By-Paths in Hebraic Bookland*, 1920, 214.

Isaac Nathan, in his *Fugitive Pieces,* 1829, records the fact that Byron wrote the lyrics in *Hebrew Melodies* for the Jewish singer's tunes, and reports many conversations between the poet and the Jewish cantor during the progress of the collaboration. We learn, however, that the poet was never satisfied with his share of the work. *Vide* Leon Spitz, "The Hebraic Note in Byron," *Jewish Tribune* (February 26, 1926), 22 ff.; Maurice Myers, "Byron and Heine," *Jewish Chronicle Supplement* (October 26, 1923), iii ff.

Richard Cumberland's play, *The Jew,* successfully held the stage well into the nineteenth century. It ran through many editions, was translated into several languages, including Hebrew and Yiddish, and had a considerable vogue on the continent.

Thomas Wade's tragedy, *The Jew of Aragon,* 1830, was literally "howled" off the stage, on account of the partiality shown to the Jews. But, nothing daunted, the dramatist, who was an advanced liberal in politics and religion, published his play with a dedication "to the Jews of England," and restored in capitals the passages deleted by the licenser on political grounds. *Vide D. N. B.* LXVIII, 1899, 419.

VII. THE REGENCY NOVELISTS AND SIR WALTER SCOTT

Two years after the publication of Lewis's *The Monk,* 1795, a farcical play entitled *The Wandering Jew* was produced at Downy Lane. It was humorously announced at that time that "The Wandering Jew is certainly at this moment in London . . . He predicts the hour of his dissolution to be within a twelve-month and the object of his journey to London is to wed some British beauty by whom he may leave an heir to his longevity."

There seems to be little doubt that the original of Isaac's beautiful daughter in *Ivanhoe* was Rebecca Gratz of Philadelphia, a close friend of Matilda Hofman, whom Washington Irving loved ardently and whose untimely death he mourned so long. It is reported that Irving, who had often met Miss Gratz, admired the Jewess's nobility of character and person, and, on his visit to Sir Walter Scott in 1817, could not refrain from describing her to his host. It is from the American writer's description that the novelist drew his Rebecca of York, "even to the name," says Calisch, "as the name Rebecca was not common among the Jews of England before the expulsion." *Vide* Calisch, *The Jew in English Literature,* 125; and Lockhart, *Life of Scott,* 1861, V, 294–295.

When *Ivanhoe* was published in 1819, Scott sent a copy of the novel to Irving, with a personel note in which he asked: "How do you like your Rebecca? Does the Rebecca I have pictured compare with the pattern given?"

A reviewer in the *London Magazine*, I (January 1820), 82, observes that "it is a fine touch of characteristic historical truth to confer on a Jewess that heroic character which reflects back glory from an individual to a people . . .Jewish women have been always famous for their patience, courage and religious enthusiasm." *Vide* S. T. H. Hurwitz, "Jews and Jewesses in English Literature," *Jewish Forum*, V, 243 ff.; and Wilson Brewer, *Shakespeare's Influence on Sir Walter Scott*, Boston, 1925, 297–298.

VIII. AMONG THE EARLY VICTORIANS

Although Thomas Carlyle was critical of the Jews in England, it may be of some interest to observe that one of the men who acted as his secretary was Joseph Newberg (1809–1867), who accompanied the historian on the trip over the battle-fields of Frederick the Great. Newberg translated *On Heroes and Hero Worship* into German, and died while at work on the translation of *Frederick the Great*.

David Goitein, in his comments on the Hebrew books mentioned in Borrow's account of the Quaker's Library at Norwich, points out that the *Zohar* is a collection of mystical writings which deal with Jewish theosophy, exegesis and philosophy, apart from pure mysticism; and doubts whether the Quaker banker could have made very much of this exceedingly difficult work, which does not come under the heading of "Hebrew books" at all. The *Zohar* is written in Aramaic. Also, Goitein points out that the *Mishna* is the codification of the Jewish law, and in pure Hebrew. The *Toledot Jeshu* is, no doubt, entirely unknown; a medieval life of Jesus of Nazareth, and extremely scurrilous. As for Abarbanel, he is the author of a biblical commentary.

Vide: The Jewish Chronicle Supplement, London, November 28, 1924, vi.

IX. THE DISRAELIAN ERA

Just how young Benjamin Disraeli looked in those early days of the Victorian dandies may be guessed from his portrait done by "Alfred Croquill" (Daniel Maclise, R. A.) for *Fraser's Magazine*. There he stands with the ambrosial curls, the poetic eyes, decked in ruffles, rosettes, and rings.

The cadences in the composition of *Alroy* tempted an irreverent parodist to apostrophize "The curly hair and forehead fair, the nose so high and gleaming eye, of Benjamin Dis-ra-e-li."

Vide Philip Guedalla, Introduction to *Alroy*, 1927, v-vi.

Although the "Key" supplied by the publishers of *Coningsby* asserts that the original of Sidonia was Baron A. de Rothschild of Naples, it is believed by several critics that Sidonia was drawn from Nathan Meyer de Rothschild, the man who financed half of Europe after the battle of Waterloo, established one brother as a banker in Paris, another in Vienna, and himself became a naturalized Englishman in 1804.

Other critics suggest that the Sidonia of the novels is readily recognized to be Nathan Meyer's son, Baron Lionel de Rothschild, who in 1844 was about thirty-six years old, and, since his father's death in 1836, was head of the banking house in England.

As it may be granted that in circumstances and in outline, Rothschild may have been the original of Sidonia, so there is a half-truth in the view that Disraeli may have meant to delineate, under a thin veil, himself in the character of this hero. The early misfortunes of the Sidonia family in Spain, their migrations to Italy, and their coming to England, were very much like the experiences of the Disraeli family.

However, we feel that much of the evidence points to the fact that the novelist is endeavoring to present, if not a portrait of Rothschild or of himself, at least "The ideal Jew" in the character of the political hero of a new day.

Disraeli is pointed to as a patent instance of one whose change of faith altered hardly at all his Jewish characteristics. In discussing whether or not Disraeli was a representative Jew, Emma Lazarus, *Century Magazine*, I, 939 ff., observes that the author of *Alroy* remained a Jew, though not of the faith, just as a man born in England and belonging to the established church does not cease to be an Englishman if he ceases to be a Christian.

Vide G. R. Sterling-Taylor, *English Political Portraits of the Nineteenth Century*, Boston, 1929, 205 ff.; and Dr. David Philipson, *The Jew in English Fiction*, Cincinnati, 1889, 103 ff.

X. CHARLES DICKENS AND THE REALISTIC SCHOOL

It is likely that the anxiety of Dickens to see his novel, *Oliver Twist*, dramatized justifies the contention that "the character of Fagin was invented with an eye to the theater." Oxenford's dramatic version of the novel was produced at the old Queen's, Longacre (1868) with John Ryder as Fagin, Henry Irving as Bill Sikes, and J. L. Toole as the Artful Dodger. *Vide* M. J. Landa, *The Jew in Drama*, Chapter XII, "On the Origin of Fagin," 159 ff.

Dickens' letters to Mrs. Eliza Davis, November 16, 1864 and March 1, 1867, are referred to by John Forster, *Life of Dickens*, edited by J. W. Ley, London, 1928, 740.

XI. THE VICTORIAN COMPROMISE

Theodor Herzl's *Jewish State*, published in 1896, was accepted by the Zionists as the basis for the Zionist Movement. The book was revised and translated into English, with a preface and notes, by J. de Haas, New York, 1904.

Besides Nathan Meyer Rothschild who was raised to the Woolsack, the other Jewish members of the House of Lords were: Henry de Worms, created Lord Pirbright; Sir Henry Samuel, who was made Lord Swaythling; and Sir Rufus Isaacs (later Lord Reading), Lord Chief Justice, and Viceroy of India.

A daughter of Meyer Amschel Rothschild married Archibald Philip Primrose, Earl of Rosebery, who succeeded Mr. Gladstone as Prime Minister in 1894.

With reference to the persecution of the Jews in Europe, consult *Contemporary Review*, LXIII, 1893, 699 ff.; Bernard Lazare, *Anti-Semitism, its History and Causes*, translated from the French, New York, 1903; C. K. Salaman, *Jews as They Are*, London, 1882; and S. M. Dubnow, *History of the Jews in Russia and Poland*, Philadelphia, 1916.

Robert Browning's interest in the Jews is discussed by Mary Cohen, "Browning's Hebrew Sympathies," *Poet Lore*, III, Boston, 1891, 254 ff.

It is reported that a feeling of mutual respect existed between Matthew Arnold and Benjamin Disraeli, and that the relationship between the poet and the Rothschild family was particularly cordial. *Vide* George W. E. Russell, *Letters of Matthew Arnold, 1848–1888*, London, 1895, I, 143, 151, 180, 196, 202, 210, 218 ff.; and L. I. Newman and R. B. Morris, "The Jewish Interest of Matthew Arnold," *American Hebrew*, CXII, 1922, 185, 189, 191.

XII. THE END OF AN ERA

S. Baring Gould is of the opinion that Augustus Melmotte, the ostentatious Jewish financier in Trollope's novel, *The Way We Live Now*, is none other than the German Jew of the name of Gottheimer, who came to England as a company promoter and assumed the name of Grant. Later, he became M. P. for Kidder-minister! Heaven and the Austrian court only know how and for what services he obtained his title of Baron Grant. But the Epigram concerning him circulated freely:

> Kings may a title give,
> Honor they can't —
> Title without Honor
> Is a barren grant!

The fellow died in 1899. The Napoleonic wars had all but made Austria bankrupt. If titles of Baron could be sold, and if Jewish bankers were desirous of purchasing, why not sell? Accordingly titles were sold. A successful Jewish tailor retires from London to Vienna, and struts the streets as *Hochwohlgeborener Herr Baron*, and puts a coronet on his visiting card! *Vide*, S. Baring Gould, *Early Reminiscences*, London, 1923, 52–53.

It is suggested by James Picciotto, author of *Sketches of Anglo-Jewish History*, London, 1875, that Colonel A. E. W. Goldsmid, an English Jew whose romantic career is presumed to have given the idea of Jewish restoration in Palestine, may have been the original of George Eliot's Daniel Deronda. Goldsmid's parents, in the interest of his career, had concealed from him the fact that he was a Jew until the time when he wished to marry a gentile girl. Then they revealed the facts concerning their son's origin. Luckily for the lovers, it was discovered that the girl, too, was really of Jewish blood. The marriage was celebrated, and the happy pair sailed for Palestine on their honeymoon, determined to devote themselves to the study of the Hebrew language, history and traditions. Their daughters, Rachel and Carmel, were born there.

Vide: B'nai B'rith Magazine, XL, November 1931, 40 ff.

In an endeavor to fix the real personalities of the other Jewish characters in *Daniel Deronda*, Joseph Jacobs observes that the original of Mordecai was one Cohen or Kohn, the hero of a philosopher's club described by George Henry Lewis in an article on Spinoza, in the *Fortnightly Review*, April 1866. *Vide* Joseph Jacobs, *Jewish Ideals and Other Essays*, London, 1896, 68–70.

It has been suggested that the original of Leonara, Princess of Halm-Eberstein, born Charisi, may be found in the grandmother of Benjamin Disraeli. In the life of Isaac D'Israeli by his son, we read ". . . My Grandmother, the beautiful daughter of the family that had suffered much from persecution, had imbibed for her race that hatred which the vain are too apt to adopt when they find that they are born to public contempt . So mortified by her social position was she, that she lived until eighty without indulging a tender expression. She never pardoned her husband for his name, and resented the humiliation of Judaism." *Vide: Temple Bar*, XLIX, 1877, 542 ff.

The resemblance between George Eliot's *Daniel Deronda* and Sir Walter Besant's *The Rebel Queen* is clearly seen in the characters of the Jewish mothers in each novel. These mothers separate themselves from their people, and bring up their children as Christians. Both Daniel and Francesca finally become aware of their Jewish origin and welcome the revelation.

In connection with George Eliot's attitude toward the Jews, read her essay, "The Modern Hep! Hep! Hep!" in *Impressions of Theophrastus Such*. The traditional cry against the Jews in Germany was "Hep!". The word has been explained as being made up of the three words *Hierusalem est perdita*. It is perhaps nothing more than a corruption of *Heb, Heb* ("Stop, hold him!"), still used in this sense in the Rhenish lands.

XIII. THE OLD ORDER CHANGETH

Information about Amy Levy, the poet and the novelist, is scarce. The best sketch of her life is by Dr. Richard Garnett, in the *D. N. B.* XXXII, 1889, 417 ff.

On the subject of the public indignation in England at the expulsion of the Jews from Russia (1891), E. A. Freeman, the historian, wrote: "The Lord Mayor and the Archbishop and the Cardinal did not care a bit, as long as it was only Russia; but, when they heard the blessed word *Jew*, then they jumped up and said, 'We must protest.' Well, I do rejoice in the snub the Tsar gave them. As I said aforetime, 'Let every nation wallop its own Jews!'." *Vide* E. A. Freeman, *Life of Letters*, edited by W. R. W. Stephens, Dean of Winchester, II, 428.

For an interesting treatment of the ghetto in literature, consult Dr. David Philipson, *Old European Jewries*, Philadelphia, 1894, Chapter IX., 221 ff.

XIV. CONCLUSION

Every Parliament since the time of Baron Lionel Rothschild and Sir David Salomons has had its professing Jewish members; Sir George Jessel, Solicitor General and Master of the Rolls, Lord Pirbright, Parliamentary Undersecretary of the Board of Trade, Sir Julian Goldsmid, deputy speaker of the House of Commons, Sir Herbert Samuel, Undersecretary of The Home Department, being among the most conspicuous Jewish leaders.

BIBLIOGRAPHY

1. Historical and Social Background

ABBOTT, GEORGE FREDERICK, Israel in Europe, New York, 1907.

ABRAHAMS, B. L., Expulsion of the Jews from England in 1290, Oxford, 1895.

ABRAHAMS, ISRAEL, Jewish Life in the Middle Ages, London, 1896.

ABRAHAMS, LIONEL, "Condition of the Jews of England at the time of their Expulsion in 1290," *Journal of the Jewish Historical Society of England*, II (1894), 76 ff.

————, "Admission of the Jews of England to Parliament," *Journal of the Jewish Historical Society of England*, IV, 116 ff.

ADLER, DR. HERMANN, Chief Rabbis of England, London, 1887.

————, "A Homage to Menasseh ben Israel," *Journal of the Jewish Historical Society of England*, I (1893), 25–54.

ADLER, ELKAN NATHAN, History of the Jews of London, Philadelphia, 1930; 189–196, 199 ff.

————, Jews in Many Lands, London, 1905.

————, Auto da Fé and the Jew, Philadelphia, 1908.

AGUILAR, GRACE, History of the Jews in England, London, 1847.

————, Women of Israel, 2 volumes, London, 1851.

ANDREADES, A., History of the Bank of England, 1640–1903, London, 1924.

ASHTON, JOHN, Dawn of the Nineteenth Century in England, 2 volumes, London, 1886.

————, Social England under the Regency, 2 volumes, London, 1890.

————, When William IV was King, London, 1892.

————, Gossip in the First Decade of Victoria's Reign, London, 1903.

AYERST, REV. W., The Jews in the Nineteenth Century, London, 1846.

BARBER, MARY ANNE SERRETT (died 1864), Redemption in Israel, a Narrative of Conversion among the Jews, London, 1844.

BARON, DAVID, The Jewish Problem, London, 1892.

———, The Ancient Scriptures and the Modern Jew, London, 1900.

BATTERSEA, LADY, Reminiscences, London, 1922. The autobiography of Constance de Rothschild of the Montefiore family on her mother's side.

BAYNES, NORMAN H., Israel among the Nations, London, 1927.

BELLOC, HILAIRE, The Jews, London, 1922.

BENJAMIN, L. S. (LEWIS MELVILLE), "The Passing of the English Jew," Nineteenth Century Magazine, LXXII, 491 ff.

BENNETT, SOLOMON, The Constancy of Israel, London, 1812.

BENTWICH, NORMAN, England in Palestine, London, 1932.

BERNARD, HERMAN H., The Creed and Ethics of the Jews, London, 1832.

BERTHOLET, ALFRED, History of Hebrew Civilization, New York, 1927.

BESANT, SIR WALTER, London in the Eighteenth Century, London, 1909.

———, London in the Nineteenth Century, London, 1927.

BEVAN, EDWIN ROBERT, and SINGER, CHARLES, The Legacy of Israel, Oxford, 1927.

BIGHAM, HON. CLIVE, The Prime Ministers of Britain, London, 1923.

BLEASE, W. LYON, A Short History of Liberalism, London, 1913.

BLOCH, JOSEPH SAMUEL, Israel and the Nations, English translation by Dr. Leon Kellner, Berlin, 1927.

BLUNT, JOHN ELIJAH, The History of the Jews in England, with an Enquiry into their Civil Disabilities, London, 1830.

BONAR, ANDREW ALEXANDER, Narrative of a Mission of Inquiry to the Jews from the Church of Scotland, Edinburgh, 1842.

BRANDES, GEORG, "The Jew and the Christian World," Menorah Journal, VI (1920), 124.

BRIGHT, JOHN, M. P., Speeches on Questions of Public Policy, edited by J. E. T. Rogers, London, 1869.

BRINTON, CRANE, English Political Thought in the Nineteenth Century, London, 1933.

BROWN, REV. DAVID, The Restoration of the Jews, Edinburgh, 1861.

BROWN, P. A., The French Revolution in English History, London, 1918.

BROWN, WILLIAM, Antiquities of the Jews, carefully compiled from authentic sources, London, 1820.

BROWNE, LEWIS, Stranger than Fiction, New York, 1925.

BRYCE, LORD (JOHN), Studies in Contemporary Biography, New York, 1903.

BUTLER, J. R. M., The Passing of the Great Reform Bill, London, 1914.

CHRISTIE, O. F., The Transition from Aristocracy, 1832–1867, London, 1928.

CLARK, G. KITSON, Peel and the Conservative Party, a study in Party Politics, 1832–1841, London, 1929.

CLARKE, SIR EDWARD, Disraeli, London, 1926.

COHEN, ISRAEL, Jewish Life in Modern Times, New York, 1929.

———, "The Jewish Community and Social Isolation," *Sociological Review*, III (1910), 216–218.

COLE, JOHN, Observations on the Civil Disabilities of the British Jews, London, 1834.

CORTI, COUNT EGON CAESAR, The Rise of the House of Rothschild, 1780–1830, translated from the German by Brian and Beatrix Lunn, London, 1928.

———, The Reign of the House of Rothschild, 1830–1921, translated from the German by Brian and Beatrix Lunn, London, 1928.

COXE, WILLIAM, Memoirs of the Administration of William Pelham, 2 volumes, London, 1829.

CROKER, JOHN WILSON, The Croker Papers, edited by Louis J. Jennings, second revised edition, 3 volumes, London, 1885; III, 138, 140, 159, 160.

DA COSTA, ISAAK, Israel and the Gentiles, translated by Mary J. Kennedy, London, 1850.

DAVIES, H. C. W., England under the Normans and the Angevins, 1066–1272, London, 1905.

DAVIES, M. D., Shetaroth; Hebrew deeds of English Jews before 1290; London, 1888.

DAVIES, R. TREVOR, Mediaeval England, 1066–1500, London, 1924, description of the Jewish money-lenders, 165–172.

DAVITT, MICHAEL, Within the Pale; the true story of the anti-Semitic persecution in Russia, Jewish Publication Society, Philadelphia, 1903.

DAY, REV. EDWARD, The Social Life of the Hebrews, New York, 1901.

DE CASTRO, DON ADOLFO, History of the Jews in Spain, translated by Ed. D. G. M. Kirwan, Cambridge, England, 1851.

D'ISRAELI, ISAAC, Genius of Judaism, London, 1833.

DISRAELI, BENJAMIN (LORD BEACONSFIELD), Biography of Lord George Bentinck, fifth edition, London, 1852.

———, "The Disraeli Family," by Lucien Wolf, *Journal of the Jewish Historical Society of England*, V (1905), 202–218.

DOWSETT, F. J., "Both Sides of Jewish Character," *Westminster Review*, CXXX (1888), 47–154.

DUBNOW, S. M., History of the Jews in Russia and Poland, translated from the Russian by I. Friedlander, 3 volumes, Jewish Publication Society, Philadelphia, 1916–1920.

———, An Outline of Jewish History, 3 volumes, translated from the Russian, New York, 1925; III, Chapter 8.

DREYFUS, ALFRED, Five Years of My Life, New York, 1901.

DUNSCOMBE, T. S., The Jews of England, their History and their Wrongs, London, 1866.

EDERSHEIM, REV. D. ALFRED, Sketches of Jewish Social Life, American Edition, New York, 1881.

EGAN, CHARLES, The Status of the Jews in England, from the time of the Normans to the reign of Her Majesty Queen Victoria, impartially considered, London, 1848.

ELBOGEN, ISMAR, History of the Jews after the Fall of the Jewish State, Cincinnati, 1926.

English People are the Ten Lost Tribes:— *vide* article on "Anglo-Israelism" in *Jewish Encyclopedia*, I, 600 ff., and books by Rev. J. Leyland Feilden, London, 1876; Rev. Joseph Wild, London, 1880; and the Rt. Rev. Bishop Titcomb, London, 1879.

EMANUEL, CHARLES H. L., A Century and Half of Jewish History, London, 1910.

ESCOTT, T. H. S., England, Her People, Polity and Pursuits, London and New York, 1880, 475–479.

———, Social Transformations of the Victorian Age, London, 1897.

———, King Edward and his Court, London, 1903.

EWALD, ALEX CHARLES, Historical Sketches, London, 1885.

Exchequer of the Jews:— Calendar of the Plea Rolls of the Exchequer of the Jews, preserved in the Public Records Office; edited by J. M. Rigg, London, 1902.

FARRER, J. A., The Monarchy in Politics, London, 1917.

FINN, JAMES, Sephardim: or the history of the Jews in Spain and Portugal, London, 1841. A collation of anti-Jewish legislation during the Inquisition.

FINKELSTEIN, LOUIS, Jewish Self-Government in the Middle Ages, New York, 1924.

FISHBERG, MAURICE, The Jews, New York, 1911.

FRAZER, JOHN FOSTER, The Conquering Jew, New York, 1915.

FREEMAN, E. A., History of the Norman Conquest of England, revised American edition, Oxford, 1876, V, 547 ff.

FREEMANTLE, A. F., England in the Nineteenth Century, 1801–1805, London, 1929.

FRIEDLANDER, ISRAEL, The Jews of Russia and Poland, New York, 1915.

FREY, S. C., Narrative of S. C. Frey, Minister of the Gospel to the Jews, London, 1809.

GASTER, REV. MOSES, History of the Ancient Synagogue of the Spanish and Portuguese Jews, London, 1901.

GIDNEY, REV. WILLIAM, The Jews and their Evangelization, London, 1889.

GLADSTONE, W. E., Speech in Favor of Jewish Emancipation, House of Commons, December 16, 1847. Published with a Preface, London, 1847.

GOLDSMITH, SIR FRANCIS HENRY, Two Letters in Answer to Objections Urged against Mr. Grant's Bill for the Relief of Jews, London, 1830.

———, The Arguments Against Emancipation of the Jews Considered in a Series of Letters, London, 1831.

———, A Few Words Respecting the Enfranchisement of the British Jews, addressed to the New Parliament, London, 1833.

———, Remarks on Civil Disabilities of the British Jews, London, 1839.

———, Reply to Arguments against the Removal of the Remaining Disabilities of the Jews, London, 1848.

GOLLANZ, D. HERMANN, Sermons at the Bayswater Synagogue, London, 1894.

———, "Anglo-Judaica," *Journal of the Jewish Historical Society of England*, VI (1910), 56–88.

GOODMAN, PAUL, A History of the Jews, New York, 1930.

GOODMAN, TOBIAS, Pamphlet Protesting against the London Society for the Promotion of Christianity Amongst the Jews, London, 1809.

GOSSE, PHILIP HENRY, History of the Jews, London, 1851.

GRAETZ, HEINRICH HIRSCH, Geschichte der Juden, eleven volumes; English translation, five volumes, Philadelphia, 1891–1892.

GRANT, JAMES, The Great Metropolis, Fourth Edition, London, 1837, 263 ff.

Graphic (London), XXXII (1885), 177, 180–181; "Sir Moses Montefiore," tribute on the death of a great English Jew.

GRAVES, C. L., Mr. Punch's History of Modern England, London, 1921.

GREENE, JOHN R., A Short History of the English People, revised edition, London, 1916.

GREVILLE, C. G., Journal of the Reigns of George IV and William IV, fourth edition, London, 1875.

GREVILLE, C. G., Diary, edited by P. W. Wilson, 2 volumes, 1927, II, 402 ff.

GRONOW, CAPTAIN REES HOWELL, Recollections and Anecdotes, London, 1877, 131–133.

GROSS, CHARLES, The Exchequer of the Jews in England in the Middle Ages, London, 1887.

GUEDALLA, PHILIP, The Duke, London, 1931. Published in the United States as, Wellington.

HALEVY, ELIE, History of the English People in 1815 (translated), New York, 1924.

———, History of the English People, 1815–1830 (translated), New York, 1927.

———, History of the English People, 1830–1841 (translated), New York, 1927.

Hansard, XVII, 205; for Robert Grant's original motion for the Removal of Jewish Disabilities. House of Commons, 1833.

HEARNSHAW, F. J. C., Prime Ministers of the Nineteenth Century, London, 1926.

HENRIQUES, H. S. Q., The Return of the Jews to England, London, 1905.

———, "The Political Rights of the English Jews," *Jewish Quarterly Review*, XIX (O. S.), 751 ff.

———, Jews and English Law, London, 1910.

HERSCHELL, RIDLEY H., A Brief Sketch of the State and Expectations of the Jews, London, 1834.

HERTZ, GERALD BERKELEY, British Imperialism in the Eighteenth Century, Chapter III, "No Jews, no wooden Shoes," London, 1908.

HEWLETT, REV. JOHN, Concise History of the Jews, London, 1813.

HINE, JAMES A., History of the Jews from Titus to the Present Time, London, 1841.

HOLINSHED, RALPH, Chronicles of England, London, 1587, II, 253.

HOSMER, JAMES K., Story of the Jews, London, 1886, Chapter XVI, "The Money Kings;" Chapter XVII, "Sir Moses Montifiore."

Hughson, David, London, a Description from an Actual Perambulation; six volumes, London, 1809, VI, 581 ff.

Hunterberg, Max, The Jew and the Anti-Semite; History and Causes, London, 1913.

Huskisson, William, Speeches, three volumes, London, 1831, "Speech on the Jews Relief Bill," III, 565 ff.

Hyamson, Albert M., A History of the Jews in England, London, 1908.

———, "The Jew Bill of 1753," *Journal of the Jewish Historical Society of England*, VI (1910), 156–189.

Inge, William R., The Jews, London, 1923.

———, The Victorian Age, Cambridge, 1922.

Irving, Joseph, Annals of Our Times, to 1871, London, 1871.

Jackson, F. J. Foakes, Josephus and the Jews, London, 1930.

Jacobs, Joseph, Studies in Jewish Statistics, London, 1890.

———, Jews of Angevin England, London, 1893.

———, "Aaron of Lincoln;" *Journal of the Jewish Historical Society of England*, III (1896), 157 ff.

———, "Little Hugh of Lincoln;" *Journal of the Jewish Historical Society of England*, I (1893–4), 89–173.

———, Jewish Contributions to Civilization, Jewish Publication Society, Philadelphia, 1919.

Jacobs, Joseph, and Wolf, Lucien, Bibliotheca Anglo-Judaica, London, 1888.

Jewish Encyclopedia, The, V (1903), 170 ff.

Joseph, H. D., Reasons for Renouncing Judaism and Embracing Christianity, by H. S. Joseph, late Rabbi of Bedford, now teacher of the Hebrew language, Norwich, 1830.

Kingston, Alfred, The Romance of a Hundred Years, London, 1901.

Karpeles, Gustav, Sketch of Jewish History, Philadelphia, 1897.

———, Jews and Judaism in the Nineteenth Century, translated from the German, Jewish Publication Society, Philadelphia, 1905.

Kastein, Josef, History and Destiny of the Jews, translated from the German by Huntley Paterson, New York, 1933.

KIRSCHSTEIN, ARTHUR J., The Jew; his Contribution to Modern Civilization, Denver, 1930.

LAZARE, BERNARD, Anti-Semitism, its History and Causes, London, 1903.

LAZARUS, M., The Ethics of Judaism, London, 1901.

LECKY, W. E. H., History of England in the Eighteenth Century, London, 1878–1890.

LEE, SIR SIDNEY, Queen Victoria, a Biography, London, 1902.

LE ROY-BEAULIEU, ANATOLE, Israel Among the Nations, translated from the French by Frances Hellman, London, 1895.

LEVY, MARK, As Englishmen, Jew and Christian, London, 1898.

LEVY, MATTHIAS, The Western Synagogue; Some Materials for its History, London, 1897.

LEWINSOHN, LEWIS, The Eternal People, their Sufferings and Accomplishments, Chicago, 1914.

LEWIS, DAVID, Address to the Jews, London, 1800.

LEWISOHN, LUDWIG, Israel, New York, 1926.

LISSACK, MORRIS, Jewish Perseverance; or the Jew at Home and Abroad, An Autobiography with Moral Reflections, London, 1851.

LOEWE, DR. L., Diaries of Sir Moses and Lady Montefiore, two volumes, London, 1890.

London Society for Promoting Christianity among the Jews; Reports, London, 1867.

LONDRES, ALBERT, The Jew has Come Back; study of the Ghetto Jew on the Continent; New York, 1830.

LORNE, THE MARQUIS OF, Queen Victoria, her Life and Empire, London, 1901.

LOW, SIDNEY, History of England, 1837–1901, London, 1907.

LOWENTHAL, MARVIN, A World Passed By, New York, 1933, Chapter XII, 210–230.

———, The Jews of Germany: A Story of Sixteen Centuries, Philadelphia, 1935.

LYNDHURST, LORD, Life, by Sir Theodore Martin, London, 1883.

———, The Victorian Chancellors, by J. B. Atlay, London, 1906.

MACAULAY, LORD, Life and Letters, by Sir G. O. Trevelyan, 2 volumes, London, 1876.

————, Speech on the Civil Disabilities of the Jews, published in *Edinburgh Review*, LII (1831), 363 ff.

MACKENZIE, ROBERT, The Nineteenth Century, London, 1880.

MADOX, THOMAS, History and Antiquities of the Exchequers of the Kings of England, London, 1711, volume I, History of the Jewish Exchequer.

MAGNUS, LADY KATIE, Outlines of Jewish History, Jewish Publication Society, Philadelphia, 1890, 1929.

————, Jewish Portraits, London, 1888.

MAIMON, SOLOMON, An Autobiography, London, 1888.

MALMESBURY, EARL OF, Memoirs of an Ex-Minister, third edition, London, 1884.

MANDELSTAMM, MAX, How Jews Live; a Sidelight on Alien Migration, London, 1890.

MANNING, HENRY EDWARD, CARDINAL, Persecution of the Jews; Speech delivered at the Mansion House, London, February 1, 1882; published in *Modern Eloquence*, IX, 854–860.

MATHIESON, WILLIAM LAW, England in Transition, 1789–1832, London, 1920.

MARGOLIOUTH, REV. MOSES, The Jews in Great Britain, three volumes, London, 1845.

MARTIN, C. TRICE, "The Domus Conversorum," *Journal of the Jewish Historical Society of England*, I (1893), 15–24.

MARVIN, F. S., The Century of Hope, Oxford, 1919.

MAXWELL, SIR HERBERT, A Century of Empire, three volumes, London, 1909.

McCARTHY, JUSTIN, History of Our Own Times, to 1880, two volumes, London, 1880.

————, History of Our Own Times, from 1880 to the Diamond Jubilee, London, 1897.

MENDOZA, DANIEL, Memoirs, printed and published for the author by G. Hayden, Brydges St., Covent Garden, no date.

MILLS, REV. JOHN, The British Jews, London, 1853.

Milman, Dean Henry Hart, History of the Jews, two volumes, London, 1829.

Mitchell, C. S., Record of Events Connected with the History of the Jews, London, 1849.

Montagu, Basil, A Letter to Henry Warburton, M. P., Upon the Emancipation of the Jews, London, 1833.

Monypenny and Buckle, Life of Benjamin Disraeli, four volumes, London, 1910–1916.

Montefiore, C. G., Liberal Judaism, London, 1903.

Morais, Henry Samuel, Eminent Israelites of the Nineteenth Century, Philadelphia, 1880.

Müller, Professor F. Max, "Are there Jews in Cornwall", in *Chips From a German Workshop*, volume III, 299–329.

Murray, Alexander, History of the Jews, London, 1875.

Myers, Jack M., The Story of the Jewish People, three volumes, New York, 1919–1925.

Neubauer, Adolf, Notes on the Jews in Oxford, Oxford, 1890.

Newman, H. (Editor), The Real Jew, some aspects of the Jewish contribution to civilization, with Preface by Chief Rabbi Hertz, and an Introduction by Israel Zangwill, London, 1925.

Nicholas, Thomas, Pedigree of the English People, fifth edition, London, 1878.

Norgate, Kate, John Lackland, London, 1902.

Oman, Sir Charles, England in the Nineteenth Century, New revised edition, London, 1921.

Parkes, James W., The Jew and his Neighbor; a study of the causes of anti-Semitism, London, 1931.

Paul, Herbert, History of Modern England, five volumes, New York and London, 1904–1906.

Pedersen, Johannes, Israel; its Life and Culture, London, 1926.

Peel, Sir Robert, Memoir, by Guizot, London, 1857.

———, Sir Robert Peel from his Private Papers, edited by Charles Stuart Parker, three volumes, London, 1891–1899.

———, Private Letters of Sir Robert Peel, edited by George Peel, London, 1920.

PELLATT, ASPLEY, Brief Memoir of the Jews, in Relation to their Civil and Municipal Disabilities, London, 1829.

PETERS, MADISON CLINTON, Justice to the Jew; what he has done for the world, London, 1900.

PHILIPSON, RABBI DAVID, Old European Jewries, Cincinnati, 1894.

———, The Reform Movement in Judaism, new and revised edition, New York, 1931.

PICCIOTTO, JAMES, Sketches of Anglo-Jewish History, London, 1875.

RAISIN, MAX, History of the Jews in Modern Times, New York, 1919.

RAYMOND, E. T., Disraeli, New York, 1925.

REMY, NAHIDA, Jewish Women, translated by Louise Mannheimer, New York, 1916.

RENAN, ERNEST, History of the People of Israel, five volumes, Boston, 1888.

RICH, EMIL, "Jew Baiting on the Continent," *Nineteenth Century*, XL (1896), 422 ff.

RITTER, I. H., Geschichte der Jüdischen Reformation, Berlin, 1858.

ROBACK, A. A., Jewish Influences in Modern Thought, Cambridge, Mass., 1929.

ROBERT, SAMUEL, The Jews, the English Poor, and the Gypsies, London, 1848.

ROGERS, JAMES E. THOROD, The British Citizen, his Rights and Privileges, London, 1885.

ROSE, J. HOLLAND, The Rise and Growth of Democracy in Great Britain, London, 1898.

ROTH, CECIL, Venice: containing a chapter on Ghetto life, Philadelphia, 1930.

———, A History of the Marranos, Philadelphia, 1932.

———, Magna Bibliotheca Anglo-Judaica, London, 1937.

ROUTH, H. V., England under Victoria, London, 1930.

ROWDEN, ALDRED W., The Primates of the Four Georges, London, 1916.

RUDING, REV. ROGERS, Annals of the Coinage, third edition, three volumes, London, 1840; I, 197 ff.

RUMYANACK, J., "Anglo-Jewry in the Early Nineteenth Century," *Jewish Chronicle Supplement*, December, 1930, ii–iii.

RUPPIN, ARTHUR, The Jews in the Modern World, London, 1934.

RUSSELL, LORD JOHN, Jewish Disabilities, speech delivered in the House of Commons, December, 1847; London, 1848.

SACHAR, A. L., "The Jew Enters Parliament," *Menorah Journal*, X (1924), 333 ff.

———, "The Romance of the Rothschilds," *Menorah Journal*, XI (1925), 347 ff.

———, "Moses Mendelssohn," *B'nai B'rith Magazine*, XLIII (1929), 291 ff.

SALAMAN, C. K., Jews as They Are, London, 1882.

SALZMANN, L. F., English Life in the Middle Ages, Oxford, 1927.

SAMUEL, REV. JACOB, The Remnant Found, London, 1841.

SCHAIBLE, K. H., Die Juden in England, Karlsruhe, 1890.

SEELEY, JOHN ROBERT, Ecce Homo, London, 1865; a consideration of Jesus as a human being. The author makes several astute observations with reference to the source of the Jewish antagonism to Jesus.

SHARP, S., History of the Jewish Nation and its Literature, London, 1869.

SHOHET, DAVID M., The Jewish Court in the Middle Ages, New York, 1931.

SIDNEY, WILLIAM CONNOR, Early Days of the Nineteenth Century, two volumes, London, 1898.

SIMEON, CHARLES, Discourses on Behalf of Jews; published in Simeon's Select Works, II, London, 1854.

SLATER, GILBERT, Making of Modern England, London and New York, 1913.

SOLOMONS, ISRAEL, "Lord George Gordon and Judaism," *Journal of the Jewish Historical Society of England*, VII (1911), 222–271.

———, "Satirical and Political Prints on the Jews' Naturalization Bill, 1753," *Journal of the Jewish Historical Society of England*, VI (1910), 205–233.

SOMBART, WERNER, The Jews and Modern Capitalism, translated by M. Epstein, New York, 1913.

SOMERVELL, D. C., English Thought in the Nineteenth Century, London, 1929.

SPEED, JOHN, History of Great Britain, London, 1650.

STALLARD, J. H., M.D., London Pauperism amongst Jews and Christians, London, 1867.

STANLEY, DEAN ARTHUR PENRHYN, Sinai and Palestine in Connection with their History, London, 1856.

STERLING, ADA, The Jew and Civilization, New York, 1924.

STOKES, CANON H. P., A Short History of the Jews in England, London, 1921.

————, Studies in Anglo-Jewish History, Edinburgh, 1913.

STRACHEY, LYTTON, Queen Victoria, New York, 1921.

STRATFORD, ESME WINGFORD, The History of English Patriotism, New York, 1913.

TAYLOR, G. R. STERLING, Modern English Statesmen, New York, 1921.

————, English Political Portraits of the Nineteenth Century, Boston, 1929.

THARAUD, JEAN and JEROME, The Chosen People, translated from the French by Frances Wilson Huard, London, 1926.

TITCOMB, REV. J. H., The Anglo-Israel Post Bag, London, 1876.

TONYBEE, WILLIAM, Glimpses of the "Twenties," London, 1909.

TOVEY, D'BLOISIER, Anglia Judaica, or History and Antiquities of the Jews in England, London, 1738.

TRAILL, H. D., and MANN, J. S. (Editors), Social England, six volumes, London, 1893–1897.

TREVELYAN, G. M., History of England, London, 1929.

————, British History in the Nineteenth Century, 1782–1901, fifth edition, London and New York, 1922.

VAN OWEN, DR. BARNARD, Ought Baron Rothschild to Sit in Parliament? London, 1847.

————, An Appeal to the British Nation on Behalf of the Jews, London, 1829.

VICKERS, KENNETH H., England in the Late Middle Ages, London, 1913.

Victoria, Queen, Training of a Sovereign, Letters and Diaries edited by Viscount Esher, published by authority of the King, London, 1914.

———, Letters: a selection from Her Majesty's correspondence between 1827 and 1861, edited by A. C. Benson and Viscount Esher, three volumes, London, 1907.

Von Raumer, Frederick, England in 1835, letters written to friends in Germany, translated by Sarah Austin and H. E. Lloyd, Philadelphia, 1836.

Waldstein, Charles, The Jewish Question and the Mission to the Jews, London, 1894, second revised edition, 1899.

Walpole, Sir Spencer, History of England after 1815, four volumes, London, 1885, New Impression, 1912.

Warner, George H., The Jewish Spectre, New York, 1905.

Warner, Susan, The House of Israel, with Preface, notes and colored plates, London, 1867.

Webb, Beatrice, "The Jews of London," in Life and Labor of the People of London, edited by Charles Booth, London, 1892.

Webb, P. C., The Question whether a Jew born within the British Dominions was, before the making of the late Act of Parliament, a person capable by Law to purchase and hold lands, etc., London, 1853.

Wendeborn, Fred Aug., LL.D., A View of England towards the Close of the Eighteenth Century, translated from the original German by the author, London, 1791.

White, Arnold, The Modern Jew, London, 1899.

Wiener, A., "Jewish Doctors in England," Jewish Quarterly Review, October 1905.

Wild, Laura Hulda, The Evolution of the Hebrew People and Their Influence on Civilization, New York, 1917.

Willet, Herbert, The Jew Through the Centuries, London, 1932.

Wirth, Louis, The Ghetto, Chicago, 1928.

Witherby, T. A., A Vindication of the Jews, London, 1804.

———, An Attempt to Remove Prejudices Against the Hebrew Nation, London, 1804.

WITHERBY, T. A., An Attempt to Remove Prejudices against the Jews, London, 1804.

WOLF, LUCIEN, "The Middle Age of Anglo-Jewish History, 1290–1656," *Jewish Historical Exhibition*, 1888.

——, "Notes on Modern Jews," *Leisure Hour* (1882), 372 ff., 440 ff.

——, "The Disraeli Family," *Journal of the Jewish Historical Society of England*, V (1905), 202–218.

——, Sir Moses Montefiore, A Centennial Biography, London, 1884.

——, "The Jewry of the Restoration," *Journal of the Jewish Historical Society of England*, V (1908), 5–33.

——, The Myth of the Jewish Menace in World Affairs; the truth about the Forged Protocols of the Elders of Zion, London, 1921.

——, Menasseh ben Israel's Mission to Cromwell, London, 1901.

——, "Crypto-Jews under the Commonwealth," *Journal of the Jewish Historical Society of England*, I (1893), 55–88.

——, "The First English Jew," *Journal of the Jewish Historical Society of England*, II (1894), 14–23.

——, "Anglo-Jewish Coats of Arms," *Journal of the Jewish Historical Society of England*, II (1894), 153 ff.

ZANGWILL, ISRAEL, The Principle of Nationalities, New York, 1917.

ZUNZ, LEOPOLD, The Sufferings of the Jews during the Middle Ages, New York, 1907.

II. GENERAL LITERARY BACKGROUND

ABRAHAM, PHILIP, Autobiography of a Jewish Gentleman, London, 1860.

——, Curiosities of Judaism, facts, opinions, and remarks relative to the Hebrew Nation, London, 1879.

ABRAHAMS, ISRAEL, The Book of Delight and Other Papers, Jewish Publication Society, Philadelphia, 1912.

——, By-Paths of Hebraic Bookland, Jewish Publication Society, Philadelphia, 1920.

ACKLAN, F. ELVA, Jewish Life in Modern Literature, a bibliography, University of Wisconsin, 1930.

ADDISON, JOSEPH, Spectator Essays; Nos. 149, 213, 531, 496.

——, "Addison and the Jews," by Max J. Kohler, *Menorah Journal*, XXIV (1898), 15–17.

——, "The Spectator's Notable Jew," by John J. Walker, *Studies in Philology*, XXVIII (1931), 519–521.

ADDISON, LANCELOT (father of the essayist), The Present State of the Jews, wherein is contained an account of their customs, secular and religious; London, 1675.

——, "Lancelot Addison on the Barbary Jews," by Israel Abrahams, in *By-Paths of Hebraic Bookland*, Philadelphia, 1920, 153 ff.

AGUILAR, GRACE, Essays and Miscellanies, choice cullings selected by her mother, Sarah Aguilar, London, 1851.

——, "Notes on Grace Aguilar," *Jewish Chronicle Supplement*, June 1930, vii–viii.

——, "Biographical Sketch of Grace Aguilar," by Camilla Toulmin, *Lady's Newspaper*, II (1847), 495–496.

——, The Young Champion, one year in Grace Aguilar's girlhood, by Abraham Isaacs, Philadelphia, 1913.

ALTMAN, REBECCA, "Development of Jewish Fiction," *Maccabaean*, III (1902), 14–19.

——, "Some Jewish Writers of Fiction," *Jewish Comment*, XIX (1904), 1–12.

ARNOLD, MATTHEW, "Heinrich Heine," *Cornhill Magazine*, VIII (1863), 233–249.

———, "Jewish Interest in Matthew Arnold," by L. I. Newman and R. B. Morris, *American Hebrew*, CXII (1922), 185, 189, 191.

BACON, SIR FRANCIS, New Atlantis, reference to Solomon's House and to Joabin, the learned Jewish merchant.

BALDWIN, STANLEY E., "Charles Kingsley," *Cornell Studies in English*, XXV, Ithaca, 1934.

BARING-GOULD, S., Early Reminiscences, London, 1923.

BATES, K. L., English Religious Drama, 1893.

Blackwood's Magazine, (1817–) "Hebraistics," L (1841), 609–617.

———, "The Jew," a tale from the Russian, LXVI (1854), 691–696.

BLAKE, WILLIAM, "William Blake and the Cabala," by Phylis Abrahams, *Jewish Guardian*, II (1929), 25 ff.

BLUM, SAMUEL, "As Great Christian Writers saw the Jews," *Jewish Tribune*, XCIV (1929), 16, 46, 48.

BORROW, GEORGE, Letters to the British and Foreign Bible Society, edited by T. H. Darlow, London, 1911.

———, "Borrow and the Jews," by E. David Goitein, *Jewish Chronicle Supplement*, Numbers 47, 48, 49 (1924–1925).

Boston Public Library, Judaica, a selected reading list of books of Jewish interest, compiled by Fanny Goldstein, 1913: second and enlarged edition, 1934.

BROWNING, ROBERT, "Browning and the Jews," by Michael Adler, *Jewish Chronicle*, April 25, 1890, 14 ff.

———, "Browning's Hebrew Sympathies," by Mary M. Cohen, *Poet Lore*, III (1891), 250–254.

———, "Browning the Hebrew," by John Kelman, in *Prophets of Yesterday*, Cambridge, 1924.

———, "Browning's supposed Jewish Ancestry," *Jewish Chronicle*, August 22, 1890, 12 ff.

———, Other references to Browning's interest in the Jews, *Jewish Chronicle*, April 18, 1890, 7 ff.; *Jewish Chronicle Supplement*, 44 (1924), ii–iii.

———, "Browning's Jewish Studies," *Jewish Tribune*, XLV (1926), 46 ff.

BULLOCH, J. M., "Influence of Jews in Recent English Literature," *Lamp*, V (1904), 473–476.

BURTON, SIR RICHARD F., The Jew, the Gypsy, and El Islam, London, 1898.

BURTON, ROBERT, Anatomy of Melancholy, 1621.

BYRON, LORD, Political Works, edited by Thomas Moore, 17 volumes, London, 1835; X, 75–98; XIV, 293.

———, "Heine and Byron," by Maurice Myers, *Jewish Chronicle Supplement*, XX, October 1923, iii–iv.

CAINE, SIR HALL, "The Jew in English Literature;" address delivered before the Maccabeans, published in *Jewish Chronicle*, May 13, 1892; reprinted in *Literary World*, XLV (1892), 482–484.

CALISCH, EDWARD N., The Jew in English Literature, Richmond, Va., 1909.

CARDOZO, J. L., The Contemporary Jew in the Elizabethan Drama, Amsterdam, 1925.

CARLYLE, THOMAS, History of his Life in London, by J. A. Froude, 2 volumes, London, 1884.

———, Oliver Cromwell's Letters and Speeches, London, 1845.

——— "Carlyle's Attitude towards Jewish Emancipation in England," *Jewish Chronicle Supplement*, December 1930, iv; *Jewish Chronicle*, January 16, 1885, 5.

CASSEL, D., Lehrbuch der Jüdischen Geschichte und Literatur, Leipzig, 1879.

CATTANI, GEORGES, "Some Jewish Influences in Contemporary Literature," *Jewish Chronicle*, London, February 24, 1933, 28.

CHAMBERS, E. K., The Elizabethan Stage, four volumes, Oxford, 1923.

CHAUCER, GEOFFREY, Canterbury Tales: "The Prioress' Tale," edited by W. W. Skeat, Oxford Press, 1880.

———, "The Prioress' Tale and its Analogues," by Carleton Brown, *P. M. L. A.*, XXI (1906), 486.

———, "The Wandering Jew and the Pardoner's Tale," by N. S. Bushnell, *Studies in Philology*, XXVIII (1930), 450–460.

CHESTERTON, G. K., The Victorian Age in Literature, New York, 1913.

CHESTERTON, G. K., The New Jerusalem, New York, 1921.

CHEVALLEY, ABEL, The Modern English Novel (translated), New York, 1925.

COBBETT, WILLIAM, Rural Rides, reprinted from Cobbett's Register, 1830; edited by Pitt Cobbett (Everyman's Library), 2 volumes, New York and London, 1906.

COHEN, A., "English Letter-Writers and the Jews," *Jewish Chronicle Supplement*, 1923, July, vi; August, vi–vii; September, iii–iv; October, i–iii; December, v–vi.

——, "English Writers and Jewish Customs," *Jewish Chronicle Supplement*, March 1929, iv–vi.

——, "The Jewish Garb," *Jewish Chronicle Supplement*, November 1929, iv–v.

COHEN, ISRAEL, A Ghetto Gallery, London, 1931.

COLEMAN, EDWARD DAVIDSON, The Bible in English Drama, New York Public Library Bulletin, 1931.

COLERIDGE, S. T., Table Talk and Omniana (Oxford Standard Authors edition), 1917.

CONANT, MARTHA, The Oriental Tale in England, New York, 1908.

CORYAT, THOMAS, *Crudities* (1611), revised edition, Glasgow, 1905.

COURNOS, JOHN, "The Jewess in Fiction," *Jewish Exponent*, XXXV (1902), 2.

CRABBE, GEORGE, The Borough (1810), edited by H. Williams, London, 1903.

CROSS, WILBUR L., Development of the English Novel, New York, 1899; revised edition, 1926.

CRUSE, AMY, The Englishman and his Books in the Early Nineteenth Century, London, 1930.

CUMBERLAND, RICHARD, The Jew, a play, London, 1794.

——, The Observer, No. 38, 1785.

——, "Richard Cumberland," by Louis Zangwill, *Jewish Historical Society of England*, VII (1911), 147–180.

——, Richard Cumberland, by Louis I. Newman, New York, 1919.

DE QUINCEY, THOMAS, "Toilette of the Hebrew Lady," *Blackwood's Magazine*, XXIII (1828), 295–308.

DE QUINCEY, THOMAS, "The Jewish Confession of De Quincey," by M. J. Landa, *Jewish Chronicle Supplement* (1930), v–vi.

DICKENS, CHARLES, Life, by John Forster, edited by J. W. T. Ley, London, 1928.

——, Charles Dickens, Novelist, by O. Ellison, London, 1908.

——, Charles Dickens, by G. R. Gissing, 1898, new edition, New York, 1925.

——, "Dickens und die Juden," by Philip Aronstein, *Anglia*, XVIII (1896), 246–247.

——, The Philosophy of Charles Dickens, by the Hon. A. S. G. Canning, London, 1880.

——, The Dickens School of Sensational Novelists, W. C. Phillips, New York, 1919.

——, Charles Dickens and his Jewish Characters, by Clark Cumberland, London, 1918.

——, Jenny Wren and Riah the Jew, by Samuel McChord Crothers, Boston, 1910.

——, Appreciations and Criticisms of Charles Dickens, by G. K. Chesterton, London, 1911.

——, "Dickens and the Jews," by M. M. Eichler, *Jewish Exponent*, LIV (1912), 9 ff.

——, Charles Dickens and the Jews, by George Alexander Kohut, Philadelphia, 1912.

——, "As to the Origin of Fagin," *P. M. L. A.*, XL (1925), 892–897.

——, Charles Dickens and other Victorians, by Sir A. T. Quiller-Couch, New York, 1925.

DISRAELI, BENJAMIN, Biography of Lord George Bentinck, fifth edition, London, 1852; chapter XXIV refers to the Jews.

——, Novels and Tales of Benjamin Disraeli, (Hughenden edition), 11 volumes, London, 1881.

——, Life, by Monypenny and Buckle, four volumes, London, 1910–1916.

——, Beaconsfield, ein Charakterbild, by Georg Brandes, Berlin, 1879; translated by Mrs. George Sturge as Lord Beaconsfield, a Study, London, 1880.

DISRAELI, BENJAMIN, "The Novels of Disraeli," by R. E. Gordon, *Nineteenth Century Magazine*, XCVI (1924), 668–676.

———, "Disraeli and his Race," by Herbert Arnstein, *Yale Literary Magazine*, LXX (1905), 212–215.

———, "Disraeli: Legend, Oriental Jew," by Jacob De Haas, *Jewish Comment*, XIX (Baltimore, 1904), 9–10.

———, "Jewish Interest in 'Endymion'," *Jewish Chronicle*, November 26, 1880, 7.

———, "The Genius of Disraeli," by A. H. T. Clarke, *Fortnightly Review*, CXXXI (1929), 98–111.

———, The Earl of Beaconsfield, by J. A. Froude, fifth edition, London, 1891.

———, "An Accidental Victorian," by Wilbur C. Abbott, *Yale Review*, IX (1919), 600 ff.

DOBSEVAGE, I. GEORGE, A Classified List of Standard Books in English on Jewish Subjects, *American Jewish Year Book*, Philadelphia, 1923.

———, A List of Available Stories of Jewish Interest in English, *American Jewish Year Book*, Philadelphia, 1906.

DRUMMOND, ROBERT J., "Three Authors and the Jew," *British Weekly* (London, January 3, 1929), 327.

DUNLOP, J. C., History of Prose Fiction, revised by H. Wilson, New York, 1906.

EDGEWORTH, MARIA, "Maria Edgeworth and the Jews," *Portfolio* (Philadelphia, 1818), 57 ff.

———, "Maria Edgeworth," in *Relics of Literature*, by Thomas Byerley, London, 1823, 171–173.

———, Study of Maria Edgeworth, by Grace Oliver, Boston, 1882.

———, Life of Maria Edgeworth, by Helen Zimmern, Boston, 1883.

———, Maria Edgeworth, Life and Letters, by Augustus J. C. Hare, London, 1894.

ELIOT, GEORGE, Impressions of Theophrastus Such; Essay XVIII, "The Modern Hep! Hep! Hep!"

———, The Spanish Gypsy, a Poem.

ELIOT, GEORGE, "George Eliot and Solomon Maimon," in *Book of Delight and Other Papers*, by Israel Abrahams, Philadelphia, 1912.

——, "Marian Evans on the Jews," by Rebecca Altman, *Maccabaean*, IV (1903), 241–245.

——, "George Eliot's 'Daniel Deronda'," by Joseph Jacobs, *Young Israel*, II (1899), 236 ff., 250 ff., III, 2.

——, George Eliot und das Judenthum, by David Kaufmann, translated from the German by J. W. Ferrier, London, 1877.

——, "George Eliot and Judaism," by Samuel Schulman, *Jewish Exponent*, XXXII (1900), 2.

——, "James Darmesteter et George Eliot," by André Spire (*Quelques Juifs et demi-Juifs*), Paris, 1928, II, 263–265.

——, 'Daniel Deronda' from a Jewish Point of View, by Henry Solomon, London, 1877.

——, "Jewish Interest in 'Daniel Deronda'," by Maurice Wollman, *Jewish Chronicle Supplement*, December, 1926, ii–iv.

——, "George Eliot's Jewish Chracters," *Jewish Forum*, V (1922), 368–369, 374 ff.

——, "Deronda the Jew," by James Picciotto, *Gentleman's Magazine*, XVII (1876), 597 ff.

——, Reviews of "Daniel Deronda:" *Edinburgh Review*, CXXXXIV (1876), 442–470; *Fortnightly Review*, XX (1876), 601–616 (Sidney Colvin); *British Quarterly Review*, LXIV (1876), 472–492; *Gentleman's Magazine*, XVII (1876), 410–427, 593–603; *Atlantic Monthly*, XXXVIII (1876), 684–694; *North American Review*, CXXIV (1877), 31–52; *Nation*, XXIII (1876), 230, 231, 245, 246; *Saturday Review*, XLII (1876), 356–358; *Temple Bar*, XLIX (1877), 542–545; *Macmillan. Magazine*, XXXVI (1877), 101–111; *Jewish Chronicle*, July 21, 1876, 252; September 30, 1892, 14; August 25, 1893, 5; *Supplement*, July 1923, iii–iv.

ELLINGER, M., "The Wandering Jew," *Menorah*, XVI (1894), 97 ff.

ELTON, OLIVER, A Survey of English Literature, 1780–1830, two volumes, London, 1912.

ELTON, OLIVER, A Survey of English Literature, 1830–1880, two volumes, London, 1920.

FRANK, MAUDE, "The Jew in English Fiction," *Critic*, XXXIX (1901), 79–81.

FREEMAN, EDWARD, A Life and Letters, edited by W. R. W. Stephens, Dean of Winchester, two volumes, London, 1895.

———, "Mr. Freeman, the Historian, and the Jews," *Jewish Chronicle*, August 24, 1877, 9 ff.

FRERE, JOHN HOOKHAM, Frere and his Friends, by Gabrielle Festing, London, 1899; Chapter XIV, "An Apostle to the Jews," deals with English interest in the Jews.

FRIEDENBERG, ALBERT, "German Ghetto Tales in England," *American Hebrew*, LXXXI (1907), 545 ff.

FRITZGERALD, PERCY H., The Romance of the English Stage, two volumes, London, 1874.

FROMENSON, ABRAHAM H., "Literary Exploitation of the Ghetto," *Jewish Comment*, XIV (1902), 1–2.

GASTER, REV. MOSES, Jewish Folklore in the Middle Ages, London, 1887.

GEIGER, LUDWIG, Die deutsche Literatur und die Juden, Berlin, 1910.

GERSONI, LEON, "A Summary of English Jewish Fiction," *Maccabaean*, XX (1911), 171–173.

GOLDSMITH, OLIVER, Works, edited by Peter Cunningham, London, 1854; "The Haunch of Venison," I, 57–61.

GOLDSTEIN, FANNY, "The Jew in Modern Literature," *Boston Evening Transcript*, May 2, 1931.

GROSSMAN, RUDOLPH, "The Jew in Novels," *American Hebrew*, L (1892), 122–123.

HAPGOOD, HUTCHINS, "The Picturesque Ghetto," *Century Magazine*, XCIV (1917), 469 ff.

HARRISON, FREDERICK, Studies in Early Victorian Literature, London and New York, 1895.

HAZLITT, WILLIAM, "Emancipation of the Jews," *The Tatler*, II (March 28, 1831), 701–702.

———, "Hazlitt's defense of the Jews," by M. J. Landa, *Jewish Chronicle Supplement*, September, 1930, ii–iii.

HIRSCH, S., "Some Literary Types," *Jewish Quarterly Review*, XIII (1901), 595–619.

HOFFMAN, DAVID, Cartaphilus the Wandering Jew, chronicles embracing a period of nearly nineteen centuries, three volumes, London, 1853.

HOLLANDER, JACOB H., "The Novel Jew," *Jewish Exponent*, LXV (1917), 1–8.

HOOD, THOMAS, Up the Rhine, London, 1939.

HURWITZ, SOLOMON T. H., "Jews and Jewesses in English Literature," *Jewish Forum*, V (1922), 198–203, 243–246, 368–369, 374 ff.

HYAMSON, ALBERT M., "Bibliography of English Books and Articles of Jewish Interest," *Jewish Literary Annual*, London, 1904, 109–110.

Illinois University, Books of Jewish Interest in the University of Illinois Library, Bulletin, 1913

Imperial Magazine (London), "Essays to the Jews," VII (1825), 146, 239, 331, 425, 509, 634, 701, 795.

IRVING, WILLIAM HENRY, John Gay's London, Harvard U. Press, 1928.

ISAACS, MYER SAMUEL, "An Ancient Grudge;" the Jews as portrayed in English Literature, *The Old Guard and Other Addresses*, New York, 1906.

JACOBS, JOSEPH, Jewish Ideals and other Essays, London, 1896.

JACOBS, JOSEPH, and WOLF, LUCIEN, Bibliotheca Anglo-Judaica, London, 1882.

JAPP, ALEXANDER H., "The Present Condition of Judaism in England," *London Quarterly Review*, XCVII (1902), 280–305.

JANSONIUS, HERMAN, Some Aspects of Business Life in Early Victorian Novels, Purmerend, 1926.

JERROLD, DOUGLAS, The Barber's Chair and Hedgehog Letters, edited by his son, Blanchard Jerrold, London, 1874.

KARPELES, GUSTAV, Jewish Life and Other Essays, Philadelphia, 1911.

———, Geschichte der Jüdischen Literatur, Berlin, 1886.

KINGSLEY, CHARLES, Charles Kingsley, Christian Socialist and Social Reformer, by Mr. Kaufmann, London, 1892.

———, Charles Kingsley, Novelist, by J. A. R. Marriott, London, 1892.

KOHUT, ADOLPH, "The Ghetto Novel and its Representatives," Menorah, IV (1888), 351 ff.

KUNITZ, JOSHUA, Russian Literature and the Jew, New York, 1929.

LANGLAND, WILLIAM, Vision of Piers Plowman, edited by W. W. Skeats, Oxford, 1886.

———, Social Life in the Days of Piers Plowman, by D. Chadwick, Cambridge, 1922.

———, Piers Plowman, by J. J. Jusserand, translated from the French by M. E. R., London, 1894.

LAMB, CHARLES, "Imperfect Sympathies," first published in London Magazine, August 1821; in Essays of Elia, Oxford Edition, 1908.

LANDA, M. J., The Jew in Drama, New York, 1927.

———, "Jews in the Distorting Mirror," Jewish Chronicle, London, March 1932, 14.

———, "Slaves are we — to Fiction," Jewish Chronicle, May 6, 1932, 13 ff.

LATHROP, H. B., The Art of the Novelist, New York, 1921.

LEBOWICH, JOSEPH, "Contemporary Anglo-Jewish Writers," American Hebrew, LXXV (1904), 632–634.

LEDERER, EPHRAIM, "The Jew in Fiction," Jewish Exponent, II (1888), 3–4.

LEE, SIR SIDNEY, "Elizabethan England and the Jew," Transactions of the New Shakespearean Society, 1888.

LESSING, GOTTHOLD, Nathan the Wise (1778), edited with English notes, by C. A. Buchheim, Oxford, 1888.

LEVI, HARRY, Jewish Characters in Fiction, second edition, Philadelphia, 1911.

LOCKE, JOHN, A Letter Concerning Toleration, 1689.

LODGE, THOMAS, "An Alarm against Usurers," Shakespeare Society, No. 48 (1853).

LOVETT, ROBERT MORSS, and HUGHES, HELEN S., The History of the Novel in England, Boston, 1932.

MABON, DORIS, "The Jew in Fiction," *Jewish Chronicle Supplement*, June 1929, ii–iii.

MARLOWE, CHRISTOPHER, The Jew of Malta, 1588.

———, "Die Quelle von Marlowe's Jew of Malta," von L. Kellner, *Englische Studien*, X (1887), 80–111.

———, "Analytical Essay on 'The Jew of Malta'," by H. M., *Blackwood's Magazine*, II (1817), 260–266.

MEYER, ANNE NATHAN, and ELLIS, MARTIN B., "The Ghetto in Literature," *Bookman*, X (1900), 532–535.

MICHELSON, HIJMAN, The Jew in Early English Literature, Amsterdam, 1926.

MONCURE, DANIEL CONWAY, The Wandering Jew, London, 1881.

NICOLL, ALLARDYCE, A History of Early Nineteenth Century Drama, 1800–1850, two volumes, Cambridge, 1930.

PARIS, MATTHEW, Chronica Major, edited by Wats, Paris, 1644, 613; edited by Luard (Roll Series), V, 516, 546, 552.

———, "Extracts from *Historia Majora*, by Matthew Paris, Monk of St. Albans; Legend of the Wandering Jew," *Blackwood's Magazine*, VII (1820), 608–609.

PEPYS, SAMUEL, Diary, Entries of October 13, 1663, and February 19, 1666.

PERCY, BISHOP, Reliques of English Poetry, Edited by J. W. Hales and F. J. Furnivall, 2 volumes, London, 1868.

PHILIPSON, DAVID, The Jew in English Fiction, Cincinnati, 1889.

———, Letters of Rebecca Gratz, Jewish Publication Society, Philadelphia, 1929, XXIV, 454.

PIGGOTT, PERCY I., "The Jew in Literature subsequent to Scott," A Prize Essay, *British Weekly*, LXXXI (1927), 633.

PRY, PAUL (pseudonym), Oddities of Life, London, 1838.

PRYNNE, WILLIAM, Short Demurrer to the Jews long discontinued Remitter into England, first published 1655; second part printed 1656; reprinted 1656.

Punch, or the London Charvaria (1841–), "Blood vs. Bullion" C (1891), 234–235; "An Autocrat in Odd Company," CL (1891), 62–63.

QUAYLE, WILLIAM A., Poet's Poet and Other Essays, "The Jew in Fiction," Cincinnati, 1897.

QUILTER, HARRY, Preferences, "Amy Levy," London, 1892.

RAILO, EINO, Haunted Castle, "The Wandering Jew and the Problem of the Never Ending Life," London, 1927.

RALEIGH, SIR WALTER, The English Novel, New York, 1930.

READER, BERNARD G., "The Attitude of the Jews towards Jewish Fiction," *Reader*, I (1902), 43–45.

REEVE, CLARA, The Progress of Romance, London, 1785.

RICHARDS, MARIA T., Life in Israel, or Portraiture of Hebrew Character, London, 1857.

REIDER, JOSEPH, Negative Tendencies in Modern Hebrew Literature, Cincinnati, 1925.

RICHMAN, JACOB, Laughs from Jewish Lore, New York, 1926.

ROBACK, ABRAHAM AARON, Curiosities of Yiddish Literature, Cambridge, Mass., 1933.

RODENBERG, JULIUS, England, Literary and Social; "The Jews in English Literature," London, 1875.

ROSENFELD, MAURICE, "I Sing for Old England" (poem), *Jewish Chronicle*, June 1, 1900, 17.

————, Songs from the Ghetto, translated by Leo Wiener, Boston, 1900.

RUSSELL, FRANCES THERESA, Satire in the Victorian Novel, New York, 1920.

SAMUEL, HORACE, "Israel in Fiction." *Academy*, LXVII (1904), 423–424.

SCOTT, SIR WALTER, Ivanhoe, 1819; Everyman Edition, London, 1906.

————, "Rebecca of Ivanhoe," *Jewish Chronicle*, September 22, 1876, 390; September 30, 1892, 14 ff.

————, "Scott's Rebecca and Isaac," *Jewish Guardian*, October 2, 1891, 8.

————, *Edinburgh Review*, XXXIII (1820), 1–54.

————, *Blackwood's Magazine*, VI (1819), 262–272.

————, *Quarterly Review*, XXVI (1822), 127 ff.

————, "Scott and Shakespeare," *Times Literary Supplement*, XX (1921), 425–426.

SCOTT, SIR WALTER, Journal of Sir Walter Scott, edited by David Douglas, London, 1890.

————, The Private Letter Books of Sir Walter Scott, edited by Wilfred Partington, New York, 1930.

————, Religious Creeds and Philosophies as represented by Characters in Sir Walter Scott's Works and Biography, by K. Bos, 1932.

SEGAL, M. H., Aspects of Hebrew Genius, "Jewish Learning in the Nineteenth Century," London, 1910.

SHAKESPEARE, WILLIAM, Merchant of Venice (c. 1594) edited by H. H. Furness, New Variorum Edition, 1916.

————, Merchant of Venice, edited by F. J. Furnivall, London, 1887.

————, Merchant of Venice, edited by Francis B. Gummere, New York, 1896.

————, Merchant of Venice, edited by Thomas Marc Parrott, New York, 1903.

————, Merchant of Venice, edited by W. G. and W. A. Wright, Oxford, Clarendon Press, 1923.

————, "The Original Shylock," by Sir Sidney Lee, *Gentleman's Magazine*, CCXLVI (1880), 185–200.

————, Shakespeare and his Predecessors, by F. S. Boas, London, 1902.

————, Shakespeare and the Jew, by Gerald Friedlander, New York, 1921.

————, Shaking the Dust from Shakespeare, by Harris Jay Griston, New York, 1924.

————, The Shakespeare Book of Homage, by Israel Gollancz, London, 1916.

————, Shylock in der Sage, im Drama und in der Geschichte, by H. Graetz, Krotoschin, 1880.

————, "Shylock and Nathan the Wise," by Rudolph Grossman, *Menorah*, XVI (1894), 168 ff.

————, "The So-called Conspiracy of Dr. Ruy Lopez," by Major Martin Hume, *Journal of Jewish Historical Society of England*, VI (1908), 32–52.

SHAKESPEARE, WILLIAM, "Shakespearean Character Interpretation: The Merchant of Venice," by Samuel Asa Small, *Hesperia*, X (Göttingen, 1927), 18–52, 67–106.

———, "Shylock", by E. E. Stoll, *Journal of English and Germanic Philology*, X, 241–243.

SHELLEY, PERCY BYSCHE, Poetical Works, edited by H. Buxton Forman, Aldine edition, four volumes, 1892, I, 108 ff.

———, The Real Shelley, "Origin of Shelley's Wandering Jew," London, 1885, I, 125–133.

———, "Shelley's Undying Jew," *Jewish Guardian*, VIII (1927), 5–7.

SHILLMAN, BERNARD, "Legends of the Jew in English Literature," *Reflex*, IV (1929), 17–24.

SHIPLEY, JOSEPH T., "The Pot of Gold; or the Miser in Literature," *Poet Lore*, XXXIV (1923), 111–126.

SOUTHEY, ROBERT, Letters from England, by Don Manuel Alvarez Espriella, three volumes, London, 1807.

———, Selections from Letters, edited by J. W. Warter, four volumes, London, 1856.

SPEARE, MORRIS EDMUND, The Political Novel, Tübingen, 1924.

STANLEY, ARTHUR PENRHYN, Life and Correspondence of Dr. Thomas Arnold, London, 1844.

STEIN, LEO, "The Jew in Fiction," *Jewish Comment*, XI (1900), 6 ff.

SUE, EUGENE, The Wandering Jew (Le Juif Errant), 1845.

———, "Eugene Sue and the Wandering Jew Legend," by R. G. Moulton, *Poet Lore*, III (1891), 322–335.

SWINBURNE, A. C., On Russian Persecution of the Jews (poem), 1882.

———, "Jewish Wailing Place, Jerusalem" (poem), *Cornhill Magazine*, XIII (1866), 210–212.

THACKERAY, W. M., The Kickleburys on the Rhine, by M. A. Titmarsh, 1851.

———, "Thackeray and the Jews," *Jewish Chronicle*, January 4, 1889, 8 ff.

VAN DER VEEN, Jewish Characters in Eighteenth Century English Fiction and Drama, Batavia, 1935.

WALKER, HUGH, Literature of the Victorian Era, Cambridge, 1910.

WALLERSTEIN, DAVID, "The Jew in Fiction," *Jewish Exponent*, I (1887), 4–5.

WARD, A. W., English Dramatic Literature, 1899.

WARD, NED, The London Spy (1698–1703), edited by Ralph Straus, London, 1929.

WIENER, LEO, The History of Yiddish Literature in the Nineteenth Century, New York, 1899.

WORDSWORTH, WILLIAM, Poetical Works, edited by Edward Dowden, London, 1892, II, 41–42, 209–210.

———, "Wordsworth's New Volume", with comments on "A Jewish Family," *Blackwood's Magazine*, XXXVII (1835), 700–722.

ZANGWILL, ISRAEL, The Voice of Jerusalem, New York, 1921.

———, Without Prejudice, New York, 1902.

———, "Zionist Zangwillism," by Frederick Harrison, *Fortnightly Review*, CXIV (1920), 176 ff.

———, "A Dreamer of the Ghetto," by Samuel Roth, *Menorah Journal*, IX (1923), 273–283.

———, "The Jewish Oscar Wilde," by Samuel Schmelhausen, *Modern Quarterly*, III (1926), 285–286.

III. Nineteenth Century Fiction of Jewish Interest

Aguilar, Grace (1816–1847), Home Scenes and Heart Studies, 1843, short stories depicting Jewish life in England and Spain.

——, Vale of Cedars, or the Martyr, 1850, a tale of Jewish experience in Spain of the fifteenth century. New edition with introduction by Walter Jerrold and illustrations by T. H. Robinson, Jewish Publication Society, Philadelphia, 1902.

Ainsworth, William Harrison (1805–1882), Jack Shephard, 1840, a disreputable Jew called Abraham Mendez appears in the "Prison Breaker" scene (Chapter III).

Allen, F. M. (pseudonym of Edmund Downey), The Voyage of the Ark, 1888, from British Museum Catalogue.

Andersen, Hans Christian (1805–1875), Only a Fiddler, a Danish romance, translated into English, 1871. Several Jewish characters appear in the tale.

Anderson, Mary, In the Promised Land, 1898, story of the times of Joshua and Rachel.

Anley, Charlotte, Miriam, or the Power of Truth, 1829, third edition, 1836. A Jewish tale.

Auerbach, Berthold (1812–1882), Poet and Merchant, translated into English by Charles T. Brooks, 1877. A picture of life from the times of Moses Mendelssohn.

——, Spinoza, a novel translated from the German by E. Nicholson, London, 1882.

Balaam, Peter (pseudonym), The Doings of Yakob Baer, story, published in *Young Israel*, III, London, 1899, 139–142.

——, Isaac Tanner's Will, story, published in *Young Israel*, II (London, 1898), 53–55.

——, Maurice Nathan's Change, story, published in *Young Israel*, II (London, 1899), 238–240.

Baring-Gould, Sabine (1834–1924), The Silver Store, 1868, tales collected from Medieval Christian and Jewish sources.

BARING-GOULD, SABINE, Count Royal, 1886, a novel of cross-currents, depicting the career of a poor girl pawned to a Jew who holds mortgages and uses them as instruments of revenge for a personal outrage.

———, Noemi, 1895, a story of Rock Dwellers. The heroine is an Amazonian Jewess.

BARRETT, A. WILSON (1846–1904), and HICHENS, ROBERT, The Daughters of Babylon, 1899, biblical story dealing with the captivity of the children of Israel in Babylon.

BEN AVROM (pseudonym), The Coming of the Messiah, short story, published in *Young Israel*, III (London, 1899), 48–50.

BEN LEVY, G., The Lost Child, a tale, translated from the *Archives Israélites*; published in *Jewish Chronicle*, VI (London, 1850), 100–101.

———, Moral and Religious Tales, adapted from the French of *Les Matinées du Samedi* and rewritten for the Young of the Hebrew Faith, London, 1846.

BESANT, SIR WALTER (1836–1901), The Rebel Queen, 1893, the Queen is a rich and lovely Jewess, a rebel against her husband, and a champion of her sex. A vivid story of cosmopolitan Jewry.

BINGEN, MRS. MAX, Miriam's Triumph, a short story, published in *Young Israel*, I (London, 1897), 75–77, 157–158.

———, Ruth's Sacrifice, a short story, published in *Young Israel*, I (London, 1897), 49–50.

BLANKKENSEE, JULIA, Reuben's Probation, published in *Young Israel*, I (London, 1897), 181–182.

BLESSINGTON, MARGUERITE, COUNTESS OF (1789–1849), The Jew's Daughter, a story of the Golden Time, published in *The Keepsake*, London, 1847, 249–269.

BORROW, GEORGE (1803–1881), Lavengro, 1851.

BRADSHAW, JOHN, Raphael ben Isaac, a tale of 20 C. E., two volumes, London, 1887, from British Museum Catalogue.

BRENDLAH, MADAM, Tales of a Jewess, illustrating the domestic Manners and Customs of the Jews; first series, London, 1838. No doubt a well-intentioned volume. The execution is both weak and egotistical.

BRISTOW, AMELIA, Sophia de Lissau, second edition, 1828, fifth
edition, London, 1840. A portraiture of the Jews of the 19th
Century, being an outline of their religious and domestic
habits, with explanatory notes.

——, Emma de Lissau, third edition, 2 volumes, 1830, a narrative, with notes, illustrative of the manners and customs
of the Jews.

——, Rosette and Meriam, or the Twin Sisters, 1837, a Jewish
narrative of the 18th Century.

——, The Orphans of Lissau, 1845, and other narratives immediately connected with Jewish customs, domestic and
religious, with explanatory notes.

BULWER, SIR EDWARD, LORD LYTTON (1803–1873), My Novel,
1853, in which there is Baron Levy, a Jewish money-lender.

——, Leila, 1882, a Spanish and Moorish romance during the
period of the conquest of Granada. The heroine is a Moorish
Jewess.

BURRY, B. PULLEN, Nobly Won, 1888, a novel concerning the
prophet Jeremiah and his times. British Museum Catalogue.

CAINE, HALL (1853–1931), The Scapegoat, 1891, a romance of
Jewish life in Morocco.

CAREY, CHARLES STOKES, Strength of Judah, and the Vengeance
of Asshur, 1862, tale of the times of Isaiah. Title from the
British Museum Catalogue.

CHURCH, ALFRED JOHN (1829–1912), A Young Macedonian in the
Army of Alexander the Great, 1891, incidental reference to
Jewish life.

——, The Hammer, historical novel of the Maccabean Revolt.

CLIFFORD, LUCY KANE, Mrs. Keith's Crime, 1888.

COHEN, ALFRED ("Alan Dale"), Jonathan's Home, 1885.

COHEN, ISRAEL, On Strike, a story by "Enoch Scribe" (pseudonym), published in *Young Israel*, III (London, 1899),
116–118.

——, The Savant, a Ghetto Sketch.

——, Sense and Sentiment, published in *Young Israel*, III
(London, 1899), 18–19.

CORELLI, MARIE (1864–1924), Barabbas, a Dream of the World's Tragedy (1893). Melodramatic novel founded on the story of the Crucifixion. The crimes of Barabbas are instigated by the wiles of Judith Iscariot, a beautiful Jewess, who also prompts her brother to the betrayal of his Lord. Judas is described as a weak-willed Jew, a willing tool in the hands of his scheming sister. The story shows a certain interest in Jewish manners and customs.

——, Temporal Power, a Study of Supremacy, 1902. A powerful Jewish plutocrat plays an important part in the politics and social life of the late nineteenth century.

CRAIGIE, MRS. ("John Oliver Hobbes", 1867–1906), The School for Saints, 1897, Benjamin Disraeli appears in this portrayal of the political world.

——, Robert Orange, 1898, sequel to the above.

CROLY, REV. GEORGE (1780–1860), Salathiel, a story of the Past, Present and Future, two volumes, 1828. Republished under the title of Tarry Till I Come, two volumes, dedicated to His Grace the Duke of Newcastle, K. G., 1828. Deals with the imaginary figure of the Wandering Jew.

DE HAAS, JACOB, A Mere Story, published in *Young Israel*, II (London, 1899), 254–256.

——, Private Jacob Moses, a story, published in *Young Israel*, III (London, 1900), 219–220.

DE QUINCEY, THOMAS (1785–1859), The Avenger, a long short story, published in *Blackwood's Magazine*, XLIV (August, 1838), 208–233. A tale of 1816 told by the son of a Jewess.

DICKENS, CHARLES (1812–1870), Oliver Twist, or the Parish Boy's Progress, by Boz, three volumes, London, 1838; with Fagin as one of the most repulsive "Jew" characters in English fiction. Indictment of the penal system and the slums. First published in *Bentley's Miscellany*, 1837–1838.

——, Our Mutual Friend, first published in 20 parts, London, 1864–1865. In this novel, the Jewish character, Mr. Riah, is a marked contrast to Fagin.

DISRAELI, BENJAMIN (1804–1881), Contarini Flemming, 1832, if autobiographical, it contains the author's personal experiences in the humiliations accorded to an alien.

———, David Alroy, 1833, exalting David Alroy, the pseudo-Messiah of the twelfth century, an impostor, into the hero of a beautiful oriental romance.

———, Coningsby, 1844, a novel dealing with political conditions in England in 1832–1834. Sidonia, an idealized portrait of Lionel de Rothschild, appears as a philosopher, financier, diplomat.

———, Tancred, 1847, or the New Crusade, relates how the heir to a dukedom, after sundry adventures in high society, goes in quest of light to the Holy Land, where in a trance it is revealed to him that the regeneration of Christendom must come from a new Anglican Christianity refined by Judaism.

———, Endymion, 1880.

DU MAURIER, GEORGE (1834–1896), Trilby, 1894, a novel of artistic and bohemian life in Paris, with a Jewish character, Svengali, who holds the stage as a master-musician and hypnotist.

———, The Martian, 1897; Leah Gibson, the heroine, has the admirable qualities and beauty of the Hebraic race.

EASTLAKE, ELIZABETH (RIGBY) LADY (1809–1893), The Jewess, 1849, a tale from the shores of the Baltic.

———, Livonian Tales, 1861.

EDGEWORTH, MARIA (1767–1849), Castle Rackrent, 1800, Sir Kit's lady was, according to Honest Thady, "a Jewish" whom Sir Kit imprisons in her room for seven years because she refuses to give up her diamonds.

———, Moral Tales, 1801. In "The Prussian Vase," "The Good Aunt" and "Murad the Unlucky", there are three Jewish characters of questionable reputation.

———, Belinda, 1801, presents the Jewish money-lender of the old order.

———, Harrington, 1817, written as an apology to the Jewish people, attempts to make amends for misrepresentation of the Jewish character, and portrays several admirable Jewish men and women in English life.

ELIOT, GEORGE (1819–1880), Daniel Deronda, four volumes, 1876, the novel gives full expression to George Eliot's visions concerning the Jewish people, and of the mighty moulding influence of heredity.

ENOCH, F., The Jewess of Pisa, a story, published in *The Family Herald*, IV (London, 1847), 753–755.

FARJEON, BENJAMIN L. (1833–1903), Solomon Isaacs, 1877, a novel of Jewish life in contemporary England.

———, A Fair Jewess, 1894.

———, Aaron the Jew, 1894–1895, a roseate delineation of the English Jews. The hero may be described as a Hebrew Aristides of the most pronounced type.

———, Miriam Rozella, 1897, presenting Jewish characters and scenes, often touched with a charming sentiment.

———, The Pride of Race, 1900, story of an illiterate Jew who became a millionaire and married his son to one of the nobility. The narrative is filled with dramatic incident.

FIELD, JULIAN, The Limb, 1896, an episode of adventure by "XL". The story deals preëminently with Jewish characters, and the plot tells of the experiences of a Christian brought up as a Jew. Religious persecution is accentuated.

FLORIAN, JEAN PIERRE C. DE (1755–1794), Eleazer and Naphtali, translated from the French by J. J. (ones), published in *European Magazine*, LXVI (London, 1814), 205–206, 301–307, 493–497; translated by R. L. Whitehead, London, 1817.

FRANKAU, MRS. JULIA ("FRANK DANBY"), Dr. Phillips; A Maida Vale Idyl, 1887, a novel with vivid pictures of the life of Orthodox Jewry of the middle class. The book was suppressed in England and in America on account of its realistic treatment of Jewish life.

———, A Babe in Bohemia, 1889, with one Jewish character, Antonelli, a singer, who is described as "an Italian from Whitechapel."

FRANZOS, KARL EMIL (1848–1904), The Jews of Barnow, 1883, eight stories presenting a picture of the havoc that Orthodox Judaism plays in the lives of Ghetto Jews.

GALT, JOHN (1779–1839), The Story of the Wandering Jew, 1818, a new romantic version of the ancient legend.

————, The Ayrshire Legatees, or the Pringle Family, 1821, a passing reference to Mr. Braham, the Jewish proselyte and well-known singer.

————, Sir Andrew Wylie, 1822, Jewish money-lenders make their appearance at intervals.

————, The Steam-Boat, 1822, the clotheshop of one Mr. Solomon, "a Jew man," is frequented by all who desire to be dressed for the fashionable occasions of the day.

GERARD, DOROTHEA (LONGARD DE LONGARDE, DOROTHEA, 1855–1915), Orthodox, 1888, the love story of a Polish Jewess and an Austrian lieutenant.

————, Recha, 1890, a story, published in *Blackwood's*, revealing the ugly side of Jewish life in a miserable Galician town, where Recha's father, a stern orthodox Jew, employs his daughter as an instrument for fleecing foolish young Austrians. In these novels, the unhappy affairs of Jewish women and Austrian officers are depicted.

GOLDSCHMIDT, MEIR AARON (1819–1887), Jacob Bendixen the Jew, three volumes, 1852, adapted from the Danish of Goldschmidt, by Mary Howett, London, 1852. Reviewed in the form of a conversation between two young ladies, *Ladies Companion*, I (London, 1852), 106–109.

GONZALES, EMANUEL, Rachel and Axia, or The Hebrew and the Moorish Maidens, an interesting historical tale, published in *The Family Herald*, VIII (London, May to September, 1850).

GORDON, SAMUEL (1871–), A Handful of Exotics, 1897, short stories of Russo-Jewish life.

————, Daughters of Shem, 1898, fourteen stories of Jewish life, mostly in the western part of Russia, depicting the oppression and suffering of Jewish communities.

————, Lesser Destinies, 1899, more stories of Jewish life.

————, Sons of the Covenant, 1900, a study of the Jews in East and West London, telling of the useful lives of two Jewish youths who do work for the less fortunate of their people.

HAGGARD, H. RIDER (1856–1924), and LANG, ANDREW, (1844–1912). The World's Desire 1891, a romance of ancient Egypt that brings in the exodus of the Israelites.

HARRIS, EMILY MARION, Estelle, 1878, two volumes, deals with a theme unfamiliar to the ordinary reader, the inner life of a cultured middle-class Jewish family, whose members are habitually brought into friendly contact with gentiles.

HART, JAMES W. T., The Autobiography of Judas Iscariot, 1884, a character study.

HATTON, JOSEPH (1841–1907), By Order of the Czar, 1890, the tragic story of Anna Klopstock, the queen of the Ghetto.

HAWKINS, ANTHONY HOPE, Quisante, 1900.

HEIGHWAY, OSBORN W. TRENERY, Adeline, 1854, two volumes; depicting the "mysteries, romance and realities of Jewish life."

————, Leila Ada, or the Jewish Convert, 1853, an "authentic memoir" of a Jewess by birth who was converted to Christianity.

————, The Morning Land, 1854, a family and Jewish history.

————, The Relatives of Leila Ada, 1856, some account of the persecutions of the Jews.

HENTY, G. A. (1832–1902), For the Temple, 1888, tale of the fall of Jerusalem; illustrated by the Jewish artist, Solomon J. Solomon.

————, The Cat of Burbastes, 1888, a tale of Ancient Egypt, with reference to the Israelites in exile.

HERBERT, MRS. MARK, Mrs. Danby Kaufman of Bayswater, 1890, a novel depicting Jewish life. British Museum Catalogue.

HERTZ, BEN PINCHAS (pseudonym), Baron Rothschild and the Phantom, a story, published in *Jewish Chronicle*, VI (London, 1850), 97–98.

HODDER, EDWIN (1837–1904), Ephraim and Elah, 1878, a story of the Exodus.

HOWITT, MARY (1799–1888), The Little Jew Merchant, 1830, published in *The New Year's Gift Book and Juvenile Souvenir*, 1830.

Howitt, William (1792–1879), The German Jew, 1832, published in *The Winter's Wreath*, 1832, 55 ff.

Hurwitz, Hyman (1770–1844), Hebrew Tales, 1826, selected and translated from the writings of the ancient Hebrew sages. Prefixed, an essay on the uninspired literature of the Hebrews.

Jew, The, A Tale from the Russian, published in *Blackwood's*, LXXVI (December, 1854), 691–696.

Jewish Gil Blas, The, Edited and Annotated by an Unprejudiced Person (Der Jüdische Gil Blas), London, 1834.

Kingsley, Charles (1819–1875), Alton Locke, 1850.

———, Hypatia, or New Foes with an Old Face, two volumes, London, 1853; first published in *Fraser's Magazine*, 1852–1853, a story of the fifteenth century, in which several Jewish characters play an important part. *Vide: National Review*, I (London, 1853), 124 ff.

Kingston, William H. G., Zeky Naashon, the Jew of Portsmouth, a yachtman's tale, published in *Ainsworth's Magazine*, XII (London, 1847), 74–83.

Kompert, Leopold, Scenes from the Ghetto, 1882, studies of Jewish life, translated from the German, and giving the story of Schlemiel (1–46), Old Babele (47–76), The Randar's Children (77–280).

Kraszewski, Joseph Ignacy, The Jew, translated from the Polish by Linda Da Kowalewska, 1890; reviewed in *Jewish Chronicle* (London, August 11, 1893), 7.

Lee, Mary E., Aaron's Rod, or the Young Jewess, a story translated from the German, and published in *The Family Herald*, V (London, 1847), 65–68.

Lever, Charles James (1806–1872), That Boy of Norcott's, 1869, a lively and romantic story, full of striking characters of theatrical type, including old Ignaz Oppovich, a Jewish man of business. The hero enters the business house of the Jew, and loves his master's daughter.

Levetus, Celia Moss (1819–1873), Tales of Jewish History, 1843.

———, The King's Physician, 1873.

LEVY, AMY (1861–1889), Reuben Sachs, 1889, a sad, and not very sympathetic, portrayal of Jewish family life in England. The character, religious feelings, and peculiarities of thought are closely analyzed by one who has had an intimate relationship with middle-class Jewish life.

LEWIS, MATTHEW GREGORY (1775–1818), The Monk, 1795, in which the Wandering Jew appears.

MALLOCK, WILLIAM HURRELL (died, 1923), Tristram Lacy, or the Individualist, 1899, contains some references to Jewish character, especially in the person of Mr. Halbeckstein.

MARKS, MRS. MARY, Masters of the World, 1888, story of Domitian's reign, with Jews and Christians appearing among the characters.

MARRYAT, CAPTAIN FREDERICK (1792–1848), Peter Simple, 1834, chapter XI describes Jews who come aboard His Majesty's ships and sell clothes and trinkets to sailors.

———, Japhet in Search of a Father, 1836, chapters XXIX, XXXII, XXXIII, describe Jewish money-lenders who play an important part in the life of the British sailor.

———, Snarley You, or the Dog Field, 1836, chapter XXIII, Jewish money-lenders.

MELVILLE, G. J. W., The Gladiators, 1863, a tale of Rome and Judea.

MEREDITH, GEORGE (1828–1909), The Tragic Comedians, 1880, a love romance based on the life of Ferdinand Lassalle, the Jewish leader of socialism.

———, Athenaeum, London, January 8, 1888, 49–50.

MOSS, CELIA, Neela, a Tale of the Jews of England; published in *Friendship's Offering and Winter's Wreath* for 1842, 217 ff.

———, Jacob, a Tale of Jews in Germany; *Friendship's Offering and Winter's Wreath* for 1843, 257 ff.

MUDDOCK, J. E., For God and the Csar, 1892, an attempt, under the guise of fiction, to lay bare the corruption of Russian officialdom, and to protest against senseless cruelty and oppression of the Jews.

NIEMCEWICZ, HULIUS URSINIUS, Levi and Sarah, 1830, a Polish tale, translated from the German edition, with preface and notes, by the editor of the *Asiatic Journal* II (London, 1830), 273 ff.

PAYN, JAMES (1830–1898), The Burnt Million, 1890, a novel; published by World's Best Library Pub. Co. Reviewed in *Jewish Chronicle*, May 23, 1890.

PEPLOE, ANNIE (MRS. J. B. PEPLOE), Benariah, a tale of the Captivity, by Mrs. J. B. Webb. (n. d.)

———, Julamerk, or the Converted Jewess.

———, Naomi, or the Last days of Jerusalem, reviewed in *The Spectator*, XIII (1840), 1238.

PICKERING, ELLEN (died 1843), The Jew and the Foundling, 1847, a romance by the author of The Merchant's Daughter.

PLATT, JAMES, Tales of the Supernatural, 1894, six romantic stories, of which one concerns the Rabbi Lion (122 ff.).

PORTER, ANNA MARIA (1780–1832), The Village of Mariendorpt, 1821, four volumes. This novel is the basis of Sheridan Knowles's play, the *Maid of Mariendorpt*, produced in 1838.

RADCLIFFE, ANN (1764–1823), Gaston de Blondeville, 1823, in which Aaron, the Jewish money-lender of Henry III's reign, appears at Court.

READE, CHARLES (1814–1884), It is Never Too Late to Mend, A Matter-of-Fact Romance, two volumes, 1856.

RICHARDSON, BENJAMIN WARD, The Son of a Star, 1889, a romance of the second century.

ROMERO, DON EUGENIO MARIA, The Jewish Heroine, 1852, a true story of a Jewish heroine, Phoebe Hachnel; almost a literal translation from the Spanish, by L. Thompson, (1839), published in *Bentley's Miscellany*, XXXI (1852), 89–100, 140–147.

RUSSELL, WILLIAM, The Three Jews of Aldgate, 1859, a story published in the author's *Traditions of London, historical and legendary, by "Waters"* (pseudonym), 153–176.

Sadoc and Mirian, a Jewish Tale, 1833, published under the
direction of the Society for promoting Christian Knowledge;
written largely in dialogue form, the chief object being "to
exhibit the evidences of Christianity as they must have
appeared to a Jew in our Saviour's time."

SCHREINER, OLIVE (1859–1922), Trooper Peter Halkett of Mashonaland, 1897.

SCOTT, MRS., Joseph the Jew, 1857, a tale "founded on fact."

SCOTT, SIR WALTER (1771–1832), Ivanhoe, 1819, a historical
romance presenting two interesting Jewish characters, Isaac
of York and his daughter, Rebecca, the beautiful and beloved
Jewess.

SIDGWICK, CECILY (ULLMAN), "MRS. ALFRED SIDGWICK," The
Grasshoppers, by Mrs. Andrew Dean (pseudonym), 1895,
the villain of the piece is a sort of half-Jew.

———, Isaac Eller's Money, 1899, intimate portraiture of the
community of Frankfort Jews settled in London —"a squalid
race of money-grubbers."

———, Lesser's Daughter, 1894, by Mrs. Andrew Dean (pseudonym), deals with London Jews of the better class.

SIMON, OSWALD JOHN, The World and the Cloister, 1890, a novel,
reviewed in *Menorah* VIII (N. Y. 1890), 233–236.

SMITH, HORACE (1779–1849), Zillah, a tale of the Holy City,
four volumes (1828), presents a cultured Jewish household.

SMITH, J. F., A Tale of the Temple, 1849, published in *The London
Journal*, IX (London, May, 1849), 150–152. Copy in Library
of Congress.

SPINDLER, CARL, The Jew, 1845, a romance of the early fifteenth
century; translated from the German, 1845.

STANFORD, JANE KINDERLY, Anah the Jewess, 1830, a narrative
sketched from a "rector's notebook."

STERN, CHARLOTTE ELIZABETH, Esther, 1880, a tale of modern
Jewish burgher life, by the author of Eliezer. In British
Museum Catalogue.

STIFTER, ADALBERT, Abdias the Jew, 1851, a tale of Hungary and
Hochwald, during the Thirty Years War.

THACKERAY, WILLIAM MAKEPEACE (1811–1863), Rebecca and Rowena, by Mr. M. A. Titmarsh, 1850, a romance upon a romance; a parody of Ivanhoe. The purpose of the extravaganza is to show what an ill-assorted marriage was that of the hero of the romance Ivanhoe.

——, Codlingsby, by D. Shrewsberry Esq., a parody on Disraeli's Coningsby, first published in *Punch's Prize Novelists*, 1853.

——, "Thackeray and the Jews," *Jewish Chronicle* (London, January 4, 1889), 8.

THOMAS, MRS. EDWARD, The Unrevealed Secret of Titus, 1851, published in *Ainsworth's Magazine*, XIX (London, 1851), 162–168.

THOMPSON, LOUISA, Ivan Graham, 1896, a story of the medical mission to the Jews in Russia.

THOMSON, JAMES (1834–1882) "B. V.," The Story of a Famous Old Jewish Firm, 1883, a satirical narrative of the development of Judaism through the ages.

THURSTON, KATHERINE CECIL (died 1911), The Circle, 1903, a novel describing the sordid external conditions to which the Jews are condemned by Governments.

TONNA, MRS. "CHARLOTTE ELIZABETH" (1790–1846), Judah's Lion, c. 1843, a Jewish tale of conversion. The scenes shift between England and Palestine.

TROLLOPE, ANTHONY (1815–1882), Nina Balatka, 1867, a story of a maiden of Prague. The hero is a Jew, around whose marriage to Nina Balatka, the Christian maiden, the plot revolves. First published in *Blackwood's Magazine*, C (1866–1867), in serial form.

——, The Way We Live Now, 1875, a story of English social life in the early part of the nineteenth century, showing the general attitude toward the Jewish man of business.

TROLLOPE, MRS. FRANCES (1780–1863), A Romance of Vienna, 1838, three volumes, glimpses of the Jewish community in Vienna.

TUCKER, CHARLOTTE (1821–1893), Exiles in Babylon, or The Children of Light, 1867.

TUCKER, CHARLOTTE, Rescued from Egypt, by A. L. O. E., 1883.

TURGENEV, IVAN SERGEYEVICH, The Jew, and Other Stories, 1899, translated from the Russian by Constance Garnett.

———, "Turgenev and Dickens and their relation to the Jews," in *Jewish Chronicle* (London, October 19, 1883), 3.

WALKER, A. D., The Jew and his Tenants, 1880, a tale, published by the Wesleyan Conference Office, London, 1880. In British Museum Catalogue.

WALKER, GEORGE (1772–1847), Theodore Cyphon, or the Benevolent Jew, title from British Museum Catalogue; second edition, three volumes, 1823; new edition, three volumes, London, 1847.

———, *Vide* Israel Abrahams' Bypaths in Hebraic Bookland, Philadelphia, 1920, 191–198.

WARD, ELIZABETH STUART (PHELPS), "MRS. H. D. WARD" (1844–1911), Come Forth, 1890.

———, The Master of the Magicians, 1890, a story of Babylon and Daniel.

WARD, MARY AUGUSTA (ARNOLD), "MRS. HUMPHRY WARD" (1851–1920), Sir George Tressady, 1896, a novel with glimpses of Jewish conditions in East-end London.

WESTBURY, HUGH, Acte, 1898, a novel of the time of Nero, with Judith "the Jew maiden," who refused to marry Titus, as one of the characters.

WHEELER, ELIZABETH, From Petticoat Lane to Rotten Row (n. d.), the experiences of a child of the ghetto.

WHEELER, J. T., The Burning of Baal, 1843, a Jewish romance.

WHITE, WILLIAM HALE, "MARK RUTHERFORD" (1829–1913), Clara Hopgood, 1896.

WILSON, MRS. AUGUSTA EVANS, At the Mercy of Tiberius, with erroneous references to Jewish customs.

YONGE, CHARLOTTE M. (1823–1901), Pilgrimage of the Ben Beriah, 1897, exodus of Israel from Egypt; the wanderings in the desert and the death of Moses.

ZANGWILL, ISRAEL (1864–1926), Children of the Ghetto, 1892, "a study, through typical figures, of a race whose persistence is the most remarkable fact in the history of the world, the faith and morals of which it has so largely moulded." The book describes life in the London ghetto.

————, Ghetto Tragedies, 1893, further studies of London ghetto types and adventures.

————, The King of Schnorrers, 1894, grotesques and fantasies. The Jewish *schnorrer* or beggar is as unique among beggars of Israel as Israel is among the nations.

————, Dreamers of the Ghetto, 1898, studies of Hebrew leaders and leadership.

————, The Mantle of Elijah, 1900, stories of Jewish experience.

GLOSSARY

Ashkenazim, German or Polish Jews, as contrasted with Spanish Jews.

Cabala, the Jewish system and literature of occult mysticism, often verging on magic.

Galut, "exile," the diaspora.

Goy, gentile; idiomatically, a Jew estranged from his religion. *Goyim* (goim), plural of *goy* (goi); gentiles.

Haham, title for rabbi of a Sephardic congregation.

Hasidim, "pious ones;" followers of Israel Ba-ʻal Shem Tob (fl. 1750) who opposed the sophisticated intellectualism of the Talmudists and laid stress on emotionalism in prayer and in the performance of religious ceremonies.

Hekdesh, poor house, alms house, free hospital.

Kahal, congregation; especially the organized Jewish community in Poland and Russia.

Karaites, members of a Jewish sect that does not recognize the authority of the Talmud.

Kosher, (Hebrew, meaning *fit*) ritually permissible according to Jewish law; used most frequently of food.

Maggid, a wandering preacher of eastern Europe, a type popular among the Jewish masses because he put ethical lessons into story-telling.

Marranos, Spanish and Portuguese Jews who as a matter of form or necessity became converted to Christianity and continued to observe Judaism in secret.

Melamed, teacher.

Meshummad, an apostate Jew.

Mishna, legal code of Judaism, complied by the Patriarch Judah c. 200.

Mitzvah, divine commandment; plural, *Mitzvot*.

Mohel, one who performs the rite of circumcision (*Berit Mila*).

PoGROM, Russian for devastation due to mob violence; applied to organized attacks on Jews.

PURIM, the Feast of Lots, an historical holiday.

RAB, master.

ROSH HASHANAH, Jewish New Year.

SCHÄCHTER, Yiddish-German from the Hebrew *Shohet*, a slaughterer of *kosher* animals.

SCHNORRER, professional beggar.

SEDER, home service on Passover Eve.

SEPHARDIM, Spanish and Portuguese Jews, as contrasted with German Jews.

SHADCHAN, marriage broker.

SHEMA', Jewish declaration of faith; first word of the Hebrew "Hear, O Israel . . ."

SHEMAD, renunciation of the Jewish faith.

TALIT, a praying shawl worn over the shoulders by male worshippers in the synagogue.

TALMUD, a study, or compilation consisting of the *Mishna* and the *Gemara*.

TALMID, a student, pupil.

TEREFAH, opposite of *kosher*; food forbidden to the Jews.

TORAH, teaching, the scroll of the Law; the Jewish Law in general.

YOM KIPPUR, Day of Atonement; the solemn day of pardon and confession.

ZOHAR, the great book of mystic lore, or *Cabala*, ascribed to Simon ben Johai of the second century.

INDEX